A History of Economic Science in Japan

Japanese economists began publishing scientific papers in renowned journals including *Econometrica* in the 1950s and made significant contributions to the sophistication of general equilibrium analysis by an intensive use of a variety of mathematical instruments. They contributed significantly to the transformation of neoclassical economics. This book examines how it became possible for Japanese economists to do so by shedding light on the "professional" discussion of the international gold standard and parity policies in the early twentieth century, the acceptance of "mathematical economics" in the following period, the impact of the establishment of the Econometric Society (1930) and the swift distribution of theory-oriented economics journals since 1930.

This book also includes topics on the historical research of the Japanese foundations of modern economics, the transformation of the economics of Keynes into Keynesian economics, Japanese developments in econometrics and Martin Bronfenbrenner's visit to Japan in the post-World War II period.

This book provides insight into the economic research done by Japanese scholars in the international context. It traces how, during the period 1900–60, economics was harmonized with mathematics and a standard economics was reshaped on the basis of mathematics thanks to economists' appetite for rigor; and it will help to contribute to existing literature.

Aiko Ikeo is a historian of Japanese economics and economic thought. She has been working on the history of economic science and the internationalization of economics in the twentieth century with a focus on the Japanese contributions to the international community for two decades. Recently she has become interested in the economics of Tameyuki Amano (1861–1938) and the scientific thinking of Sontoku Ninomiya (1787–1856). She has published Japanese books including *Akamatsu Kaname* (Nihonkeizaihyoronsha, 2008), *A History of Economics in Japan* (Nagoya University Press, 2006) and *The Network of Economists in the Twentieth Century* (Yuhikaku, 1994). She has edited *Economic Development in Twentieth Century East Asia* (Routledge, 1997) and *Japanese Economics and Economists since 1945* (Routledge, 1999).

Routledge studies in the history of economics

1 **Economics as Literature**
Willie Henderson

2 **Socialism and Marginalism in Economics 1870–1930**
Edited by Ian Steedman

3 **Hayek's Political Economy**
The socio-economics of order
Steve Fleetwood

4 **On the Origins of Classical Economics**
Distribution and value from William Petty to Adam Smith
Tony Aspromourgos

5 **The Economics of Joan Robinson**
Edited by Maria Cristina Marcuzzo, Luigi Pasinetti and Alesandro Roncaglia

6 **The Evolutionist Economics of Léon Walras**
Albert Jolink

7 **Keynes and the 'Classics'**
A study in language, epistemology and mistaken identities
Michel Verdon

8 **The History of Game Theory, Vol 1**
From the beginnings to 1945
Robert W. Dimand and Mary Ann Dimand

9 **The Economics of W. S. Jevons**
Sandra Peart

10 **Gandhi's Economic Thought**
Ajit K. Dasgupta

11 **Equilibrium and Economic Theory**
Edited by Giovanni Caravale

12 **Austrian Economics in Debate**
Edited by Willem Keizer, Bert Tieben and Rudy van Zijp

13 **Ancient Economic Thought**
Edited by B. B. Price

14 **The Political Economy of Social Credit and Guild Socialism**
Frances Hutchinson and Brian Burkitt

15 **Economic Careers**
Economics and economists in Britain 1930–1970
Keith Tribe

16 **Understanding 'Classical' Economics**
Studies in the long-period theory
Heinz Kurz and Neri Salvadori

17 **History of Environmental Economic Thought**
E. Kula

18 **Economic Thought in Communist and Post-Communist Europe**
Edited by Hans-Jürgen Wagener

19 **Studies in the History of French Political Economy**
From Bodin to Walras
Edited by Gilbert Faccarello

20 **The Economics of John Rae**
Edited by O. F. Hamouda, C. Lee and D. Mair

21 **Keynes and the Neoclassical Synthesis**
Einsteinian versus Newtonian macroeconomics
Teodoro Dario Togati

22 **Historical Perspectives on Macroeconomics**
Sixty years after the 'General Theory'
Edited by Philippe Fontaine and Albert Jolink

23 **The Founding of Institutional Economics**
The leisure class and sovereignty
Edited by Warren J. Samuels

24 **Evolution of Austrian Economics**
From Menger to Lachmann
Sandye Gloria

25 **Marx's Concept of Money**
The God of Commodities
Anitra Nelson

26 **The Economics of James Steuart**
Edited by Ramón Tortajada

27 **The Development of Economics in Europe since 1945**
Edited by A. W. Bob Coats

28 **The Canon in the History of Economics**
Critical essays
Edited by Michalis Psalidopoulos

29 **Money and Growth**
Selected papers of Allyn Abbott Young
Edited by Perry G. Mehrling and Roger J. Sandilands

30 **The Social Economics of Jean-Baptiste Say**
Markets and virtue
Evelyn L. Forget

31 **The Foundations of Laissez-Faire**
The economics of Pierre de Boisguilbert
Gilbert Faccarello

32 **John Ruskin's Political Economy**
Willie Henderson

33 **Contributions to the History of Economic Thought**
Essays in honour of R. D. C. Black
Edited by Antoin E. Murphy and Renee Prendergast

34 **Towards an Unknown Marx**
A commentary on the manuscripts of 1861–63
Enrique Dussel

35 **Economics and Interdisciplinary Exchange**
Edited by Guido Erreygers

36 **Economics as the Art of Thought**
Essays in memory of G. L. S. Shackle
Edited by Stephen F. Frowen and Peter Earl

37 **The Decline of Ricardian Economics**
Politics and economics in post-Ricardian theory
Susan Pashkoff

38 **Piero Sraffa**
His life, thought and cultural heritage
Alessandro Roncaglia

39 **Equilibrium and Disequilibrium in Economic Theory**
The Marshall–Walras divide
Michel de Vroey

40 **The German Historical School**
The historical and ethical approach to economics
Edited by Yuichi Shionoya

41 **Reflections on the Classical Canon in Economics**
Essays in honour of Samuel Hollander
Edited by Sandra Peart and Evelyn Forget

42 **Piero Sraffa's Political Economy**
A centenary estimate
Edited by Terenzio Cozzi and Roberto Marchionatti

43 **The Contribution of Joseph Schumpeter to Economics**
Economic development and institutional change
Richard Arena and Cecile Dangel

44 **On the Development of Long-run Neo-Classical Theory**
Tom Kompas

45 **F. A. Hayek as a Political Economist**
Economic analysis and values
Edited by Jack Birner, Pierre Garrouste and Thierry Aimar

46 **Pareto, Economics and Society**
The mechanical analogy
Michael McLure

47 **The Cambridge Controversies in Capital Theory**
A study in the logic of theory development
Jack Birner

48 **Economics Broadly Considered**
Essays in honour of Warren J. Samuels
Edited by Steven G. Medema, Jeff Biddle and John B. Davis

49 **Physicians and Political Economy**
Six studies of the work of doctor-economists
Edited by Peter Groenewegen

50 **The Spread of Political Economy and the Professionalisation of Economists**
Economic societies in Europe, America and Japan in the nineteenth century
Massimo Augello and Marco Guidi

51 **Historians of Economics and Economic Thought**
The construction of disciplinary memory
Steven G. Medema and Warren J. Samuels

52 **Competing Economic Theories**
Essays in memory of Giovanni Caravale
Sergio Nisticò and Domenico Tosato

53 **Economic Thought and Policy in Less Developed Europe**
The nineteenth century
Edited by Michalis Psalidopoulos and Maria-Eugenia Almedia Mata

54 **Family Fictions and Family Facts**
Harriet Martineau, Adolphe Quetelet and the population question in England 1798–1859
Brian Cooper

55 **Eighteenth-Century Economics**
Peter Groenewegen

56 **The Rise of Political Economy in the Scottish Enlightenment**
Edited by Tatsuya Sakamoto and Hideo Tanaka

57 **Classics and Moderns in Economics, Volume I**
Essays on nineteenth and twentieth century economic thought
Peter Groenewegen

58 **Classics and Moderns in Economics, Volume II**
Essays on nineteenth and twentieth century economic thought
Peter Groenewegen

59 **Marshall's Evolutionary Economics**
Tiziano Raffaelli

60 **Money, Time and Rationality in Max Weber**
Austrian connections
Stephen D. Parsons

61 **Classical Macroeconomics**
Some modern variations and distortions
James C. W. Ahiakpor

62 **The Historical School of Economics in England and Japan**
Tamotsu Nishizawa

63 **Classical Economics and Modern Theory**
Studies in long-period analysis
Heinz D. Kurz and Neri Salvadori

64 **A Bibliography of Female Economic Thought to 1940**
Kirsten K. Madden, Janet A. Sietz and Michele Pujol

65 **Economics, Economists and Expectations**
From microfoundations to macroeconomics
Warren Young, Robert Leeson and William Darity Jnr.

66 **The Political Economy of Public Finance in Britain, 1767–1873**
Takuo Dome

67 **Essays in the History of Economics**
Warren J. Samuels, Willie Henderson, Kirk D. Johnson and Marianne Johnson

68 **History and Political Economy**
Essays in honour of P. D. Groenewegen
Edited by Tony Aspromourgos and John Lodewijks

69 **The Tradition of Free Trade**
Lars Magnusson

70 **Evolution of the Market Process**
Austrian and Swedish economics
Edited by Michel Bellet, Sandye Gloria-Palermo and Abdallah Zouache

71 **Consumption as an Investment**
The fear of goods from Hesiod to Adam Smith
Cosimo Perrotta

72 **Jean-Baptiste Say and the Classical Canon in Economics**
The British connection in French classicism
Samuel Hollander

73 **Knut Wicksell on Poverty**
No place is too exalted
Knut Wicksell

74 **Economists in Cambridge**
A study through their correspondence 1907–1946
Edited by M. C. Marcuzzo and A. Rosselli

75 **The Experiment in the History of Economics**
Edited by Philippe Fontaine and Robert Leonard

76 **At the Origins of Mathematical Economics**
The economics of A. N. Isnard (1748–1803)
Richard van den Berg

77 **Money and Exchange**
Folktales and reality
Sasan Fayazmanesh

78 **Economic Development and Social Change**
Historical roots and modern perspectives
George Stathakis and Gianni Vaggi

79 **Ethical Codes and Income Distribution**
A study of John Bates Clark and Thorstein Veblen
Guglielmo Forges Davanzati

80 **Evaluating Adam Smith**
Creating the wealth of nations
Willie Henderson

81 **Civil Happiness**
Economics and human flourishing in historical perspective
Luigino Bruni

82 **New Voices on Adam Smith**
Edited by Leonidas Montes and Eric Schliesser

83 **Making Chicago Price Theory**
Milton Friedman–George Stigler correspondence, 1945–1957
Edited by J. Daniel Hammond and Claire H. Hammond

84 **William Stanley Jevons and the Cutting Edge of Economics**
Bert Mosselmans

85 **A History of Econometrics in France**
From nature to models
Philippe Le Gall

86 **Money and Markets**
A doctrinal approach
Edited by Alberto Giacomin and Maria Cristina Marcuzzo

87 **Considerations on the Fundamental Principles of Pure Political Economy**
Vilfredo Pareto (Edited by Roberto Marchionatti and Fiorenzo Mornati)

88 **The Years of High Econometrics**
A short history of the generation that reinvented economics
Francisco Louçã

89 **David Hume's Political Economy**
Edited by Carl Wennerlind and Margaret Schabas

90 **Interpreting Classical Economics**
Studies in long-period analysis
Heinz D. Kurz and Neri Salvadori

91 **Keynes's Vision**
Why the great depression did not return
John Philip Jones

92 **Monetary Theory in Retrospect**
The selected essays of Filippo Cesarano
Filippo Cesarano

93 **Keynes's Theoretical Development**
From the tract to the general theory
Toshiaki Hirai

94 **Leading Contemporary Economists**
Economics at the cutting edge
Edited by Steven Pressman

95 **The Science of Wealth**
Adam Smith and the framing of political economy
Tony Aspromourgos

96 **Capital, Time and Transitional Dynamics**
Edited by Harald Hagemann and Roberto Scazzieri

97 **New Essays on Pareto's Economic Theory**
Edited by Luigino Bruni and Aldo Montesano

98 **Frank Knight and the Chicago School in American Economics**
Ross B. Emmett

99 **A History of Economic Theory**
Essays in honour of Takashi Negishi
Edited by Aiko Ikeo and Heinz D. Kurz

100 **Open Economics**
Economics in relation to other disciplines
Edited by Richard Arena, Sheila Dow and Matthias Klaes

101 **Rosa Luxemburg and the Critique of Political Economy**
Edited by Riccardo Bellofiore

102 **Problems and Methods of Econometrics**
The Poincaré lectures of Ragnar Frisch 1933
Edited by Olav Bjerkholt and Ariane Dupont-Keiffer

103 **Criticisms of Classical Political Economy**
Menger, Austrian economics and the German historical school
Gilles Campagnolo

104 **A History of Entrepreneurship**
Robert F. Hébert and Albert N. Link

105 **Keynes on Monetary Policy, Finance and Uncertainty**
Liquidity preference theory and the global financial crisis
Jorg Bibow

106 **Kalecki's Principle of Increasing Risk and Keynesian Economics**
Tracy Mott

107 **Economic Theory and Economic Thought**
Essays in honour of Ian Steedman
John Vint, J. Stanley Metcalfe, Heinz D. Kurz, Neri Salvadori and Paul Samuelson

108 **Political Economy, Public Policy and Monetary Economics**
Ludwig von Mises and the Austrian tradition
Richard M. Ebeling

109 **Keynes and the British Humanist Tradition**
The moral purpose of the market
David R. Andrews

110 **Political Economy and Industrialism**
Banks in Saint-Simonian economic thought
Gilles Jacoud

111 **Studies in Social Economics**
By Leon Walras
Translated by Jan van Daal and Donald Walker

112 **The Making of the Classical Theory of Economic Growth**
By Anthony Brewer

113 **The Origins of David Hume's Economics**
By Willie Henderson

114 **Production, Distribution and Trade**
Edited by Adriano Birolo, Duncan Foley, Heinz D. Kurz, Bertram Schefold and Ian Steedman

115 **The Essential Writings of Thorstein Veblen**
Edited by Charles Camic and Geoffrey Hodgson

116 **Adam Smith and the Economy of the Passions**
By Jan Horst Keppler

117 **The Analysis of Linear Economic Systems**
Father Maurice Potron's pioneering works
Translated by Christian Bidard and Guido Erreygers

118 **A Dynamic Approach to Economic Theory: Frisch**
Edited by Olav Bjerkholt and Duo Qin

119 **Henry A. Abbati: Keynes' Forgotten Precursor**
Selected writings
Edited by Serena Di Gaspare

120 **Generations of Economists**
David Collard

121 **Hayek, Mill and the Liberal Tradition**
Edited by Andrew Farrant

122 **Marshall, Marshallians and Industrial Economics**
Edited by Tiziano Raffaelli

123 **Austrian and German Economic Thought**
Kiichiro Yagi

124 **The Evolution of Economic Theory**
Edited by Volker Caspari

125 **Thomas Tooke and the Monetary Thought of Classical Economics**
Matthew Smith

126 **Political Economy and Liberalism in France**
The contributions of Frédéric Bastiat
Robert Leroux

127 **Stalin's Economist**
The economic contributions of Jenö Varga
André Mommen

128 **E.E. Slutsky as Economist and Mathematician**
Crossing the limits of knowledge
Vincent Barnett

129 **Keynes, Sraffa, and the Criticism of Neoclassical Theory**
Essays in honour of Heinz Kurz
Neri Salvadori and Christian Gehrke

130 **Crises and Cycles in Economic Dictionaries and Encyclopaedias**
Edited by Daniele Bensomi

131 **General Equilibrium Analysis**
A century after Walras
Edited by Pascal Bridel

132 **Sraffa and Modern Economics, Volume I**
Edited by Roberto Ciccone, Christian Gehrke and Gary Mongiovi

133 **Sraffa and Modern Economics, Volume II**
Edited by Roberto Ciccone, Christian Gehrke and Gary Mongiovi

134 **The Minor Marshallians and Alfred Marshall**
An evaluation
Peter Groenewegen

135 **Fighting Market Failure**
Collected essays in the Cambridge tradition of economics
Maria Cristina Marcuzzo

136 **The Economic Reader**
Edited by Massimo M. Augello and Marco E. L. Guido

137 **Classical Political Economy and Modern Theory**
Essays in honour of Heinz Kurz
Neri Salvadori and Christian Gehrke

138 **The Ideas of Ronald H. Coase**
Lawrence W. C. Lai

139 **Anticipating the Wealth of Nations**
Edited by Maren Jonasson and Petri Hyttinen, with an Introduction by Lars Magnusson

140 **Innovation, Knowledge and Growth**
Edited by Heinz D. Kurz

141 **A History of *Homo Economicus***
The nature of the moral in economic theory
William Dixon and David Wilson

142 **The Division of Labour in Economics**
A history
Guang-Zhen Sun

143 **Keynes and Modern Economics**
Edited by Ryuzo Kuroki

144 **Macroeconomics and the History of Economic Thought**
Festschrift in honour of Harald Hagemann
Edited by Hagen M. Krämer, Heinz D. Kurz and Hans-Michael Trautwein

145 **French Liberalism in the Nineteenth Century**
An anthology
Edited by Robert Leroux

146 **Subjectivisim and Objectivism in the History of Economic Thought**
Edited by Yukihiro Ikeda and Kiichiro Yagi

147 **The Rhetoric of the Right**
Language change and the spread of the market
David George

148 **The Theory of Value and Distribution in Economics**
Discussions between Pierangelo Garegnani and Paul Samuelson
Edited by Heinz Kurz

149 **An Economic History of Ireland Since Independence**
Andy Bielenberg

150 **Reinterpreting the Keynesian Revolution**
Robert Cord

151 **Money and Banking in Jean-Baptiste Say's Economic Thought**
Gilles Jacoud

152 **Jean-Baptiste Say**
Revolutionary, entrepreneur, economist
Evert Schoorl

153 **Essays on Classical and Marxian Political Economy**
Samuel Hollander

154 **Marxist Political Economy**
Essays in retrieval: selected works of Geoff Pilling
Edited by Doria Pilling

155 **Interdisciplinary Economics**
Kenneth E. Boulding's engagement in the sciences
Edited by Wilfred Dolfsma and Stefan Kesting

156 **Keynes and Friedman on Laissez-Faire and Planning**
'Where to draw the line?'
Sylvie Rivot

157 **Economic Justice and Liberty**
The social philosophy in John Stuart Mill's utilitarianism
Huei-chun Su

158 **German Utility Theory**
Analysis and translations
John Chipman

159 **A Re-Assessment of Aristotle's Economic Thought**
Ricardo Crespo

160 **The Varieties of Economic Rationality**
From Adam Smith to contemporary behavioural and evolutionary economics
Michel S. Zouboulakis

161 **Economic Development and Global Crisis**
The Latin American economy in historical perspective
Edited by José Luís Cardoso, Maria Cristina Marcuzzo and María Eugenia Romero

162 **The History of Ancient Chinese Economic Thought**
Edited by Cheng Lin, Terry Peach and Wang Fang

163 **A History of Economic Science in Japan**
The internationalization of economics in the twentieth century
Aiko Ikeo

164 **The Paretian Tradition during the Interwar Period**
From dynamics to growth
Mario Pomini

165 **Keynes and his Contemporaries**
Tradition and enterprise in the Cambridge School of Economics
Atsushi Komine

166 **Utilitarianism and Malthus' Virtue Ethics**
Respectable, virtuous and happy
Sergio Cremaschi

167 **Revisiting Classical Economics**
Studies in long-period analysis
Heinz Kurz and Neri Salvadori

168 **The Development of Economics in Japan**
From the inter-war period to the 2000s
Edited by Toichiro Asada

169 **Real Business Cycle Models in Economics**
Warren Young

A History of Economic Science in Japan

The internationalization of economics in the twentieth century

Aiko Ikeo

Routledge
Taylor & Francis Group
LONDON AND NEW YORK

First published 2014
by Routledge
2 Park Square, Milton Park, Abingdon, Oxon OX14 4RN

and by Routledge
711 Third Avenue, New York, NY 10017

Routledge is an imprint of the Taylor & Francis Group, an informa business

British Library Cataloguing in Publication Data
A catalogue record for this book is available from the British Library

Library of Congress Cataloging in Publication Data
Ikeo, Aiko
A history of economic science in Japan: the internationalization of economics in the twentieth century/Aiko Ikeo.
pages cm. – (Routledge studies in the history of economics; 164)
Includes bibliographical references and index.
1. Economics–Japan–History. I. Title.
HB126.J2I35 2014
330.0952–dc23

2013039633

ISBN: 978-0-415-63427-4 (hbk)
ISBN: 978-1-315-79543-0 (ebk)

Typeset in Times New Roman
by Wearset Ltd, Boldon, Tyne and Wear

Printed and bound in the United States of America by Publishers Graphics, LLC on sustainably sourced paper.

Contents

Illustrations

Figures

Tables

Preface

This book is the result of two decades of research which started with my question about how we should write and teach the history of twentieth-century economics in Japan, and others' questions about why many Japanese economists could contribute to international economics journals like *Econometrica* a few years after the conclusion of World War II. It focuses on Japanese economics in the international context mostly from around 1900 till around 1960 (except for Japanese developments in econometrics). It focuses on the Japanese contributions to "mathematical economics" like general equilibrium analysis, which has been familiar to non-Japanese economists, and the establishment and swift circulation of internationally oriented economics journals since around 1930, which has received less attention compared with "mathematical economics." It was the time that economics was harmonized with mathematics.

This book also includes Japanese research of neoclassical economics and monetary economics, and their discussion of the economics of Keynes and Keynesian economics in Japan. I also discuss the relationship of the extremely famous thinker and reformer Sontoku Ninomiya's teachings and the forgotten economist Tameyuki Amano's macroeconomics. It could be said that the Western and Eastern cultures were harmonized in Amano's economics. We pay attention to the important role of Martin Bronfenbrenner in inviting Japanese economists to the international community of economists after the conclusion of World War II.

I interviewed several economists, wrote and presented papers which developed into the chapters of this book, and revised them on the basis of comments and additional information I received. I was inspired with courage to continue my research by the discussion of related themes by participants in conferences and seminars. I used the manuscript of the book in the graduate course in comparative economic thought in the spring semester of 2013 and received comments from the students. I would like to thank all of them for their information, comments and encouragement. I include detailed information of my research process in the introductory chapter and the first note of each chapter. I also thank Kazuhito, my husband, for encouraging me to continue my research leading to publishing it as a book form.

I acknowledge the editors and the publishers of the journals who gave me permission to include revised English versions of my previous articles in this volume. They are *Hotoku Studies* (International Ninomiya Sontoku Association), *History of Japanese Economic Thought* (Society for the History of Japanese Economic Thought), *History of Political Economy* (Duke University Press), *European Journal of the History of Economic Thought* (Taylor & Francis Group), *Research in the History of Economic Thought and Methodology* (Emerald Group Publishing Limited), *Nihon Bunka Kenkyujo Kiyo* (Institute of Japanese Culture and Classics, Kokugakuin University) and Nagoya University Press.

Abbreviations

ACC	American Culture Center
ADB	Asian Development Bank
AEA	American Economic Association
BIS	Bank for International Settlements
BOJ	Bank of Japan
CCE	(International Financial Conference, 1920) Commission on Currency and Exchange
CIC	(International Financial Conference, 1920) Commission on International Credit
ECAFE	Economic Commission for Asia and the Far East (now ESCAP)
EPA	Economic Planning Agency (Japan)
ES	Econometric Society
ESAF (IMF)	Enhanced Structural Adjustment Facility
ESB	Economic Stabilization Board (Japan)
ESCAP	Economic and Social Commission for Asia and the Pacific
ESRI	Economic and Social Research Institute
ESS (SCAP)	Economic and Scientific Section
FPF (SCAP)	Finance and Public Finance
FMC	Fujisawa Memorial Committee
GARIOA	Government Appropriations for Relief in Occupied Areas
IBRD	International Bank for Reconstruction and Development
IDE	Institute of Developing Economies (Japan)
IEA	International Economic Association
IMF	International Monetary Fund
INSA	International Ninomiya Sontoku Association
ISI	International Statistical Institute
JEA	Japanese Economic Association
JES	Japanese Econometric Society (now JEA)
JSHET	Japanese Society for the History of Economic Thought
JSPS	Japan Society for the Promotion of Science
MAC	Ministry of Agriculture and Commerce (Japan)
MAF	Ministry of Agriculture and Forestry (Japan)
MAFF	Ministry of Agriculture, Forestry and Fisheries (Japan)

METI	Ministry of Economy, Trade and Industry (Japan)
MITI	Ministry of International Trade and Industry (Japan, now METI)
MOF	Ministry of Finance (Japan)
MSJ	Mathematical Society of Japan, Editorial Committee of A Hundred Year History of Mathematics in Japan
NSF	National Science Foundation (United States)
OECD	Organization for Economic Co-operation and Development
ONR	Office of Naval Research (United States)
OPA	Office of Price Administration (United States)
PSJ	Physical Society of Japan
SAF (IMF)	Structural Adjustment Facility
SCAP or GHQ	Supreme Commander for the Allied Powers
SHJET	Society for the History of Japanese Economic Thought
TCER	Tokyo Center for Economic Research
UN	United Nations

Note on Japanese names

Japanese names are formally written with *Kanji* characters. Many of them have a couple of pronunciations. Therefore, some Japanese names expressed with *Kanji* characters have two ways of Romanization. For example, the (family) names of Tedzuka and Tezuka may be written with the same *Kanji* characters. Sumio and Juro, Hukukane and Fukukane, Kanbe and Kambe, and Uyeda and Ueda are other examples. I have used the Romanization of a name which the scholar has used him-/herself in his/her journal articles or letters. Moreover, there are many homonyms among *Kanji* characters. Therefore, the same Romanization of names can be expressed with different *Kanji* characters.

1 Introduction

1 Harmonization of economics and mathematics

The project, which has resulted in the publication of this book, started with the limited aim of exploring how the Japanese "mathematical economists" began to publish scientific papers one after another in renowned economics journals like *Econometrica* in the 1950s. Why could they write scientific papers in economics just a few years after the conclusion of the Pacific Campaign? It is because they read every issue of internationally oriented economics journals from around 1930 on and they published journal articles in Japanese which should have received attention if they had been written in English or German. They were naturally using mathematics when they consider questions of capital interest, imputation, and the estimation of demand curves for rice. In the early 1940s, their independent research was halted when Japan was losing the war. After the ceasefire of August 1945, surviving students and professors returned to schools and soon resumed education and research in the remaining buildings, looking for a brighter future for Japan.

In the late 1940s, a number of economists were working on general equilibrium approach, especially on the rigorous conditions for a competitive economy reaching an equilibrium in every market. Thinking of "equilibrium" sounded like a path leading to a harmonious state rather than "staying in destruction." They were using various types of mathematics when they made rigorous examinations of stability conditions and economic dynamics by constructing economic models. Some of them started to write scientific papers in English after thinking over these economic questions in Japanese. Their way of thinking economic issues was changed by building a model rather than analyzing economic issues just by referring to economic data. Thanks to the use of mathematics in economics, for those who speak non-European languages like Japanese, the linguistic and cultural differences became less serious in economic analysis. When economics was harmonized with mathematics, the language used in economics began to change and introduced more scientific terminology. In the context of the English-speaking world, E. Roy Weintraub discussed *Stabilizing Dynamics: Constructing Economic Knowledge* (1991a) and *How Economics Became a Mathematical Science* (2002). I learned many facts and ideas from his works and got hints on how to write the history of economic science in Japan. Around the time, I completed my doctoral thesis *Japanese Economics in the International Context: The Internationalization of Economics in the Twentieth Century* (Ikeo 2002a) and decided to make further elaboration of this topic.

This project also needs to cover the history of mathematics, especially relating to tools used in general equilibrium approach such as the systems of ordinary differential equations, the Liapunov theory, and topology, and to clarify at least the differences between their developments in France, the US, Germany and Japan. It is noteworthy that the style of writing a paper in mathematics for journals changed in the 1920s, from a prosaic expression to a formal presentation including a proof process, although its contents are always formal. Some Japanese mathematicians worked as a sideline on the making of the table of average life expectancy for the basis of actuary calculation, the discussion of foreign exchange rates relating to different international monetary standard systems, and the publication of books on mathematics for economists.

In Tokyo, Takashi Negishi gave me oral information most frequently after I started the research project of writing the history of modern economics. He repeatedly tried to persuade me of the importance of Takuma Yasui's article "Equilibrium analysis and process analysis" (1940a, in Japanese) although he didn't refer to it in his influential survey article of stability analysis (Negishi 1962). Indeed he strongly persuaded Yasui to include Yasui (1940a) in Yasui's *Collected Writings* (three volumes, 1970–1) because it was a very good article for young economists to start to read in their theoretical research. I gradually realized that Yasui (1940a) might be more important for many Japanese economists than Hicks's *Value and Capital* (1939). Probably all the Japanese who worked on economic theory read Yasui (1940a, 1970–1) and followed Yasui's language and style in discussing theoretical issues. When the Japanese started publishing their articles in economics journals outside Japan, they still followed the terms introduced into economics literature first by Yasui, such as *tâtonnement* (groping) process, in stability analysis.

It is also noteworthy that Yasui (1940a) included a survey of the literature discussing the so-called cobweb theorem. I imagine that every economist must have an experience of drawing a decreasing demand curve and increasing supply curve on paper and then describing an adjustment process of the decisions of production made at the observed, lagged market price and the actual market prices determined when their products were supplied to the market. Depending on the relationship of slopes, there are three cases that the adjustment process would converge to the equilibrium determined by the intersection of the two curves, to diverge from it, or to oscillate around it. Yasui (1940a) referred to Schultz (1930), J. Tinbergen (1930), and U. Ricci (1930), all of which were written in German, for the first diagramed explanation of hog cycle. N. Kaldor (1934) named it the cobweb theorem. P. Samuelson and Yasui launched out on stability analysis of general competitive economy. We wonder why Mary Morgan didn't mention this diagramed discussion in her *The World in the Model: How Economists Work and Think* (2012). It might be because Hicks (1939) did not include this type of discussion.

I got hints for my research on the history of monetary economics in Japan first from my participation in A. W. Coats's project, which produced the volume *The Post-1945 Internationalization of Economics* (1996). Coats decided to pay attention to the role of international economic institutions such as the International Monetary Fund and the World Bank for the project. Participants like J. J. Polak and B. A. de Vries maintained that economic and financial conferences held in the 1920s were important for the internationalization of economics prior to the establishment of Bretton-Woods institutions. Richard Webb of the World Bank suggested I include Saburo Okita, who had participated in many international conferences by representing Japan, in my contribution. I took note of it. Retuning to Japan, I found that *Ginko Tsushinroku*, the Journal of the Bankers' Association which was started in December 1885, carried the information of such conferences reported by Japanese participants. And mathematician Rikitaro Fujisawa occasionally gave a talk on the issues of exchange rates and international monetary systems.

Martin Bronfenbrenner was a referee to read my paper on Japan's case for Coats's 1995 conference and gave comments for me to include Japanese economic research activities in the 1930s. Therefore, he suggested that the internationalization of economics started in the 1930s, namely prior to 1945. Later I learned that he was a graduate student at the University of Chicago and he wrote his thesis under Henry Schultz's supervision in the 1930s. But hearing his comments on my conference paper, some historians of economics, including American and Japanese, were surprised to say that Bronfenbrenner had not mentioned his own activities in Japan in the period immediately after September 1945.

I was unable to see Bronfenbrenner at Coats's 1995 conference held at Duke University because he didn't show up. In September 1996, however, I had a chance to talk to Bronfenbrenner at Duke. I made a short list of queries and sent it to E. Roy Weintraub by email just before my departure from Tokyo. Bronfenbrenner responded easily to my queries. Then he wondered if that was all. Thirteen years later, in March 2009, receiving his wife Teruko's permission, I read his unpublished autobiography (Bronfenbrenner 1997) in the manuscript library of Duke University and I thought that he had written the part of his experiences in Japan for my research. It was impossible for me to conceive a query to retrieve what was written in his unpublished autobiography from his memory about his experiences in Japan. I doubt if he read G. C. Allen's autobiography *Appointment in Japan* (1983). Allen stayed in Nagoya in the early 1920s and visited Japan several times. Both autobiographies tell us that their experiences in Japan were invaluable, especially before 1952, when Japan came back to the international community after the end of the Occupation period. Based on this consideration, I feel it necessary to include a chapter on Bronfenbrenner in this book to discuss his role in Japan effectively.

I joined Philip Mirowski's project "Marginalism at the Margins" and wrote a paper on how neoclassical economics, marginal analysis and general equilibrium theory were discussed in Japan. Several mathematicians, not physicists, were interested in mathematical economics and gave advice for economists to use mathematics successfully in their analysis. Some Japanese economists began to examine mathematics for physics after reading Paul Samuelson's series of papers on dynamics and stability analysis. In the 1940s, mathematician Masazo Sono gave lectures to the students in economics, including Michio Morishima, at Kyoto University, and mathematicians at Tohoku University answered questions asked by Takuma Yasui. I needed to revise my contribution by attaching emphasis to the importance of Ichiro Nakayama's *Pure Economics* (1933), which was the first textbook in Japanese on microeconomics and general equilibrium theory by integrating Schumpeter (1908, 1912), Cournot (1838), Schultz (1927), Gossen (1854) and Walras (1874–7) with efficient use of his mathematical ability. He often used the type of mathematical analysis developed by Henry Schultz. I thank Takuma Yasui for pointing it out in his postcard to me of 1994, and I confirmed it recently by using JSTOR (www.jstor.org). It would not have been possible for me to finalize this research without e-databases. We have to emphasize that there were histories on "mathematical economics" in the world especially prior to around 1930 although their histories shared more parts than any other fields of economics.

2 Harmonization of Western and Eastern cultures

I became a member of the Society for the History of Japanese Economic Thought (SHJET) around 1991. I learned many facts and ideas cultivated by Japanese thinkers in the early modern period, especially the time of National Seclusion, by attending its nationwide and local meetings. According to *The Encyclopedia of Japan* (Kodansha International), "National Seclusion" was:

> Policy (1639–1854) adopted by the Tokugawa shogunate (1603–1867) in an effort to legitimize and strengthen its authority, both domestically and in East Asia. The main elements of the policy were the exclusion of Roman Catholic missionaries and traders, the proscription of Christianity in Japan, and the prohibition of foreign travel by Japanese. The seclusion was not total, because Dutch, Chinese, and Koreans were permitted access to Japan. Moreover, designated officials and traders from the domains of Satsuma [now Kagoshima Prefecture] and Tsushima [now part of Nagasaki Prefecture] were allowed to go to the Ryukyus and to Korea, respectively. The Korean trade in Japan, however, was confined to Tsushima, and the only Japanese port open to the Dutch and Chinese was Nagasaki.
>
> (Accessed via the e-database *Knowledge Japan Plus* on September 4, 2013)

During the period, it is not surprising that only a very limited knowledge of and information about Western culture was brought to Japan by the Dutch East Indies. Although there were few cultural or intellectual exchanges with foreigners in the Tokugawa era, Japan had many thinkers, some of whom we list in Chapter 8. Many members of the SHJET maintain that Japanese economic thinkers always looked at the economic data and the record of domestic trading, fees and tax. They doubt if scholars could analyze an economy without using data or a list of numbers. After the end of National Seclusion and the opening of the door to the rest of the world, the new government had to look at the budgetary data all the time.

I joined the International Ninomiya Sontoku Association (INSA) around 2006 because I was interested in how Sontoku Ninomiya was discussed by contemporary international scholars, and I had referred to *Sage Ninomiya's Evening Talks* (Fukuzumi 1884–7) in my contribution to *Money and Affluence* (1988), edited by the Research Center for Savings and Economy. My Chapter 2 "Savings in Japan, a history from an economic theoretical perspective" managed to connect Chapter 1 on the lives and activities in early modern Japan and Chapters 3–8 on modern Japan by shedding light on Ninomiya's teachings. We learned that Ninomiya's teachings were more than morality and virtues, and included the rational thinking leading to the establishment of economic science and management science in the modern period. Actually a few members of INSA and a professor of Kokugakuin University, where I taught from 1985 to 2000, suggested I look up Tameyuki Amano because Amano was one of those responsible for diffusing early modern Japanese thought a few years after he had studied political economy in English at Tokyo University. A number of Japanese scholars, especially professors of Waseda University, were doing research under the slogans of "Harmonization of Western and Eastern Cultures" and "Practical Use of Knowledge."

I knew that Amano played an important part in establishing the Department of Commerce at university level for the purposes of promoting international and domestic trade and establishing modern economic institutions like the international payment system after the end of isolationist policy. He happened to be the first chair for the School of Commerce at Waseda University, where I have been teaching from 2000 on. He was forgotten for many years mainly because his house (built in April 1922) and his valuable documents were burned down by the fire caused by the Great Kanto earthquakes of September 1, 1923. I started to work on Amano in March 2011 because I could learn important points for consideration from one of the speakers, Masanori Yokoyama, in the talk session on Amano held in the city of Karatsu, Saga Prefecture, on March 19. Amano spent his youth in Karatsu and received English lessons from Korekiyo Takahashi. I gave my first paper on Amano to the 2011 SHJET meeting which was held in the city of Saga, Saga Prefecture, on June 4–5.

My participation in the project on the history of econometrics, organized by Marcel Boumans, Arian Dupont-Kieffer and Duo Qin, was also very useful for me to really become involved in the history of econometrics. I confirmed that the establishment of the Econometric Society (1930) was the landmark event in the history of econometrics, and that economists doing econometrics in the world share an increasing part of their history after 1930. Harro Maas and Mary S. Morgan's edited volume *Observing the Economy: Historical Perspectives* (2012) gave me many suggestions of how I could write the history of economic science in Japan before 1930. Judy L. Klein and Mary S. Morgan's edited volume

The Age of Economic Measurement (2001) also suggested to me that I should think over the Japanese tradition of economic measurement. This kind of tradition was found in the economic magazine, *Toyo Keizai Shinpo*, for which Amano frequently wrote editorials; and Tanzan Ishibashi, who began to study economics by reading Amano's writings, established its English edition, *The Oriental Economist*, in 1934 (see Ishibashi 1942). The Americans related to the Occupation, including Martin Bronfenbrenner and Jerome Cohen (Carl Shoup's Tax Reform Mission member), who regarded it as an important source of information about Japan's politics and economy.

A number of economists were engaged in empirical studies by using Japanese economic data and made comparative studies with American and European cases. The results of Japanese empirical studies encouraged the Japanese economists to develop theoretical research by reading and interpreting Western economic literature. It is noteworthy, however, that the quality of Japanese economic data was undermined by the chaotic situation caused by losing position in World War II. By using mathematics and Japanese economic data, Japanese economists managed to overcome the "linguistic barrier" in writing scientific papers.

3 Overview

This book has two parts and ten chapters. In Part I, we will start to discuss indispensable elements for the internationalization of economics in Japan. We cannot overemphasize the conscious formation of the international community of economists, which was witnessed by Japanese economists in the early 1930s, as well as the importance of the international discussion of monetary economics and policy, which ran in parallel with economic globalization. Then we will show a Japanese discussion of neoclassical economics, which was called "mathematical economics" at the time, the research of stability analysis, and the question of the existence of general equilibrium in a general competitive economy. Part II carries a variation of themes. We will consider the Japanese discussion of John Maynard Keynes during the time when Keynes was actively contributing to monetary economics and economic theories, and eventually show how the economics of Keynes shifted to Keynesian economics after the establishment of the international forum of economists on the evidence of the literature written by Japanese economists. Then we will discuss a history of Japanese developments in econometrics; shed light on Tameyuki Amano's macroeconomics and the teachings of Sontoku Ninomiya; and Martin Bronfenbrenner's activities and discussion of the reconstruction of Japan's economy in the period immediately after the conclusion of World War II. In each chapter we will clarify the international context and explain the historical background and domestic argument when they are necessary to understand Japanese contributions to economics.

Chapter 2 looks at the formation of the international community of economists based on the experience of Japanese economists. Around 1930, the internationally oriented economists were eager to form an international community.

They desired to make their works more easily and quickly available to other economists. Moreover, the migration of economists westward from Central Europe to North America fostered the exchange of economic ideas and the creation of new insights. After World War II, the local journals of economics, which were first written in their own native languages, tended to adopt English and became more open to all economists as well as adopting a referee system. This chapter also shows the distance of Japanese economics from the international community. It briefly covers roles of *The Oriental Economist* and Martin Bronfenbrenner to give the background information for Chapter 10.

Chapter 3 shows how Japanese scholars became interested in monetary economics and policy in the international context prior to the conscious formation of the international forum of economists. It explores the process in which Japan became part of the expanding network of global capital markets from around 1890 through the 1910s, and made an effort at creating a stable world monetary system in the 1920s and the early 1930s. Japanese scholars, bankers and officials collected reports on monetary experiences and financial systems in Europe, America and Asia, and studied the finance literature published by monetary experts and economists.

The mathematician Rikitaro Fujisawa contributed several papers to the field of monetary economics from the 1900s till the 1920s. In the 1910s, monetary economists, who were differentiated from monetary experts affiliated with banks and the Ministry of Finance, appeared in Japan. They read the latest issues of economics journals mostly written in English and German, and discussed international monetary problems including the characteristics of the gold standard. In the 1920s, Japanese monetary experts were active participants in international economic conferences. A Swedish ball-bearing company donated Gustav Cassel's research paper on the Japanese currency to the Japanese government in 1926, and the research stimulated the discussion of whether the gold embargo should be lifted with the old rate or a new, lower rate. Korekiyo Takahashi, "the Japanese Keynes", not only conducted deficit financing to rescue impoverished villages during the depression but also abandoned the gold standard completely.

Chapter 4 examines how Japanese scholars began to discuss variations of neoclassical economics and how they began to write scientific papers. The contents of this chapter were originally written for Philip Mirowski's international project entitled "Marginalism at the Margins" with attention to the characteristics of Japan compared to countries such as Brazil, Denmark, Finland, the Netherlands and South Korea. I revised the paper and put emphasis on the important role of Ichiro Nakayama and the publication of his *Pure Economics* (1933, in Japanese) in popularizing microeconomics and general equilibrium theory.

Several versions of neoclassical economics were discussed in Japan through the voluntary efforts of various types of economists and mathematicians. Neoclassical economics was first known with A. Marshall's supply and demand curves. Then, the basic concepts of marginal utility and marginal analysis were discussed in Japan by a few groups, that is, (1) Tokuzo Fukuda and his seminar students, (2) agricultural and applied economists, and (3) mathematicians and mathematical economists. The study of national income became important in the 1930s to measure both the economic welfare and the economic power of Japan in preparing for war.

As noted, it is well known that several Japanese mathematical economists made significant contributions to the study of the general equilibrium approach question in the 1950s. In contrast, it is less known how they embarked on this study, while making cutting-edge contributions. The proofs of existence, stability and uniqueness are important topics for the study of general equilibrium theory. The research of stability analysis was promoted by a different group of scholars prior to the study of the so-called existence question. In the 1940s, several Japanese economists made important contributions to stability analysis, most of them written in Japanese but comparable to the studies which were developed in North America and Europe in the 1950s.

Chapter 5 explores that during the 1930s and 1940s Japanese economists studied the mathematical tools necessary for stability analysis and economic dynamics by reading the mathematical literature mainly written in Japanese or German with the help of Japanese mathematicians. Several Japanese scholars tackled the problem of the stability of a general equilibrium model and produced the research results in Japanese before Western economists published similar results in English in the 1950s. These economists, both Western and Japanese, who were studying the stability problem, mainly borrowed results which had already been published elsewhere in the mathematical literature. The Japanese scholars we take up in this chapter are the theoretical economists such as Takuma Yasui, Hideo Aoyama and Michio Morishima, and the mathematicians such as Masazo Sono, Matsusaburo Fujiwara, Teiji Takagi and Rikitaro Fujiwara. Their research activity gives us an interesting example of a whole process of shift in the economic conceptualization of the economy as well as in the mathematical tools and the specification of the problem. This chapter will show the process of organizing economic knowledge through the introduction of more mathematics into the economics literature.

Chapter 6 aims to investigate how Japanese mathematical economists and mathematicians researched the so-called existence questions with the use of set theory and the convex set method. We trace the research line that includes Kazuo Midutani, Shizuo Kakutani, Hukukane Nikaido, Hirofumi Uzawa and Takashi Negishi, and focus on Japan's direct connection with Karl Menger, John von Neumann, Oskar Morgenstern, Emmy Nöther and Kenneth J. Arrow. We also argue on newly found evidence that Nikaido's submission of his existence paper was treated unfairly by *Econometrica* in the sense that a normal refereeing procedure did not take place.

Japanese scholars studied mathematics in a tradition different from those who had studied mathematics mainly in France and North America, where the structural trend in mathematics was identified with the name of Nicolas Bourbaki in the 1940s and 1950s. Therefore, until the early 1950s, Japanese scholars took a separate course from American and French mathematical economists of the day, such as K. J. Arrow, G. Debreu and L. Mackenzie, to the study of the existence question. However, through the 1950s, mathematical economists, including those in Japan, took a similar procedure for proving the existence of an equilibrium in a competitive economy by borrowing tools from topology and game theory. The mathematical economists of the day clarified the mathematical structure of a competitive economy and the appropriate conditions which were required to claim the existence of equilibrium in a competitive economy. It was necessary to construct an abstract economy by using knowledge of topology in order to maintain that the system had a meaningful solution and to discuss the welfare aspect. In this way, the cannon of modern neoclassical economics, namely Walrasian general equilibrium theory based on set theory and the convex set method, was established.

Chapter 7 discusses Japanese developments in econometrics focusing on research activities mainly from around 1930 to around 1980, about the time when dramatic changes occurred in econometric research thanks to significant improvement in computers, software and databases. The contents of this chapter were written for Marcel Boumans, Arian Dupont-Kieffer and Duo Qin's project "Histories on Econometrics." I made a minor revision and added a few figures in this chapter. Japan has a long history of collecting and processing statistical data, starting in the sixteenth century. Yet external impacts such as direct communications with active statisticians and econometricians at meetings and universities were important, especially in learning the definition of economic concepts for statistical studies and in practicing applied econometrics with economic data and a computer. The Japanese economists were interested in contributing their research results to policymaking and to building econometric models linked with input-output tables. The making of rice policy called for early econometric works in the 1930s, and the making of economic projections and macroeconomic policies needed the building of macroeconometric models in the 1960s. After the end of a rapid growth period in the early 1970s, the Japanese gradually became interested in time series analysis mainly because "trend" became less important than before.

Chapter 8 discusses the first Japanese modern economist Tameyuki Amano (1861–1938). Amano at Tokyo University took the course in Political Economy given in English by Ernest Fenollosa (1853–1908), who graduated from Harvard College and later became famous by introducing Japanese arts to the West. Upon graduation in 1882, Amano started to teach economics in Japanese at Tokyo Senmon Gakko (Tokyo Special School, Waseda University from 1902) and made a big success by publishing his lecture notes as *Theory of Political Economy* (Amano 1886a, in Japanese).

Amano was one of the first scholars since the Meiji Restoration of 1868 to pay attention to Sontoku Ninomiya (1787–1856) and he established "macroeconomics" by shedding light on the balance of savings and the increment of capital (investment) brought by the banking system in an expanding national economy in his *Outline of Economics* (1902a). Amano came to understand the important role of savings for increasing national wealth directly from his reading of Sontoku's teachings (*suijo* and *shiho*) and that he harmonized them with

American political economy (Amano 1902a). Amano had a close relationship with Korekiyo Takahashi (1854–1936) and Tanzan Ishibashi (1884–1973), who would later become known as "the Japanese Keynes" because as early as 1929 they both used "Keynesian" analytical concepts like "multiplier analysis" or "paradox of savings." The two learned economics by reading Amano's writings before the publication of Keynes's revolutionary book *General Theory* (1936).

Moreover, Sontoku's teachings included the "practical knowledge" consisting of the observational records and reform plans derived from his extensive fact-finding surveys which were conducted in troubled villages and domains. They conveyed the importance of thinking and understanding by oneself, the courageous implementation of innovative measures in application of expertise for solving agricultural questions, and the case studies of proper personnel management by the use of incentive mechanism and good sense of morality, which would later become the basis of the so-called Japanese management. They guided Amano to engage in journalistic campaigns for the establishment of business and economic education at the university level.

Chapter 9 discusses the study of John Maynard Keynes (1883–1946) and Keynesian Economics in Japan prior to 1941. It mainly aims at sorting out some confusing facts in the historical course of the study of Keynes and the practice of "Keynesian economics" in Japan. It is true that Keynesian economics is usually regarded as being developed from Keynes's revolutionary book *The General Theory of Employment, Interest and Money* (1936). However, fragmental ideas and theories which are important parts of Keynesian economics were found in Keynes's pamphlets and speeches on current topics published prior to 1936. These fragments were picked up by those Japanese who constantly looked for the latest works published by Keynes, the world-famous economist-journalist of the 1920s and 1930s. In other words, this chapter traces how the Japanese became interested in Keynes, and how they elaborated Keynesian arguments prior to World War II. It eventually looks for the shift from the economics of Keynes to Keynesian economics.

Chapter 10 discusses the activities of Martin Bronfenbrenner (1914–97) in Japan during 1945–52. He was an American economist who was conversant with Japanese counterparts and well informed in Japan's economics and economy. This chapter aims to examine how he managed to communicate with Japanese economists when he visited Japan (three times) during the period immediately after the conclusion of the Pacific Campaign. It also discusses his caustic criticism of the monetary expansion policy started by Japanese Finance Minister Tanzan Ishibashi to bolster up the national reconstruction strategy. It also sheds light on his other activities in Japan and East Asia as a liaison to the Shoup Tax Reform Mission (1949–50) and a consultant to a UN organization in Bangkok (1951–2). It will conclude that one of Bronfenbrenner's first and most important missions in post-World War II Japan was to meet several Japanese modern economists and try to communicate with them on economic issues based on a common knowledge of economics. By sharing his experience in Japan, many economists received new insights into economic knowledge and actual policy implementation by conducting their missions for the recovery and reconstruction of a national economy.

This book aims to discuss the economic research done by Japanese scholars in the international context. It traces how, during the period 1900–60, economics was harmonized with mathematics and a standard economics was re-shaped on the basis of mathematics thanks to economists' appetite for rigor. Standard economics has three pillars. One pillar is neoclassical microeconomics or Walrasian general equilibrium theory; the second is macroeconomics, which had been transformed from early monetary economics via Kenynes's *General Theory* (1936) and Tameyuki Amano's *Outline of Economics* (1902a); and the third is econometrics. They are constructed on the basis of mathematical reasoning and use of economic data. This is why economists with various cultural backgrounds could contribute to the development of standard economics in the twentieth century.

Part I

2 The formation of the international forum for economists[1]

1 The exchange of economic research tradition

In the late 1920s an intensive exchange of scientific research results started among internationally oriented economists. The year 1930 was especially important for the conscious internationalization of the economics profession not only in Japan but also in Europe and North America. As discussed in Ikeo (1993a, 1996c), economists swiftly laid a foundation for the formation of their world community after 1930. We can list three elements that go to make up the new phenomenon.

First of all, for economists in Japan and throughout the world, periodicals and journals became more important than published books as a means of communicating with each other and exchanging new ideas. They were especially important for Japanese economists wanting to learn about the latest economic research appearing in far-off Europe and North America.

Ichiro Nakayama (1898–1980), who later became one of the leading economists in Japan, gave us his reminiscences of the 1930s. He emphasized the impact of the three economics journals as follows:

> Generally speaking, mathematical or theoretical economics rose up on a tidal wave around 1930, I think. One thing was the organization of the Econometric Society in 1930 and the establishment of their *Econometrica* in 1933. Speaking of journals, *Review of Economic Studies* was established in 1933, the same year as *Econometrica*. Four [Three] years before that, *Zeitschrift für Nationalökonomie* was started in Germany [Austria] in 1929 [1930]. These journals for promoting theoretical economics were issued quarterly. Studies by up-and-coming young economists flowed rapidly into Japan, too.
>
> (Nakayama 1979, in Japanese: 61–3, my translation)

Takuma Yasui (1909–95), who from 1933 published numerous journal articles on theoretical economics making use of advanced mathematics, declared in 1990 that he had read every issue of these three journals and that it was incumbent upon professional economists to read journal articles as well as books.[2]

These journals provided Japanese economists with fresh economic insights from Europe and North America and informed them of the current nature of economic research. Under their influence, several young Japanese economists were encouraged to become involved in mathematical economics and empirical studies rather than the alternatives of the German historical school or Marxian economics, which were claiming increased attention in Japan during the Great Depression and the build-up to World War II. The tendency was not particular to the Japanese economists but also true for the internationally oriented economists of the world. They apparently proffered to examine economic data, to draw graphs on paper, and to theorize and model economic ideas rather than take a descriptive, historical approach to economics.

It cannot be emphasized too much that *Zeitschrift für Nationalökonomie* was regarded as the first truly international journal of economics in the world, especially by the Japanese leading economists. This journal was established by professors of the University of Vienna in 1930. It sought to supplant the remaining local, Austrian flavor of its predecessor *Zeitschrift für Volkswirtschaft, Sozialpolitik und Verwaltung* (see section 2). One of the three editors, Hans Mayer, issued a manifesto in the introduction to the very first issue (Mayer 1930, in German: 1):

> *Zeitschrift für Nationalökonomie* will devote itself to advancement in the understanding of economic life; therefore, in the first place, it will serve to promote strict, theoretical research.... The attainment of the above goal may be facilitated if the intellectual community created by scientific journals, in contrast to individual books, becomes an international one by securing the cooperation of leading economists of all cultural backgrounds.
>
> (My translation from German)

Richard Reisch, Richard Schuller, Paul N. Rosenstein-Rodan and Oskar Morgenstern were on the editorial board.

The *Zeitschrift für Nationalökonomie* really provided an international forum for theoretical economists until Hitler's *Anschluss* in 1938 resulted in the fall of Austria. It had extended its information network to Asia through the prompt distribution of each issue. Rather than limit itself to a single point of view, the *Zeitschrift* worked as a receptor for a variety of research traditions then coexisting in Europe and North America. The Lausanne School was represented by L. Walras and V. Pareto, the Austrian School by C. Menger, Böhm-Bawerk and F. von Wieser, the Cambridge School by A. Marshall, and the Stockholm or Swedish School by K. Wicksell and G. Cassel. The journal thereby helped unite economists in a common quest for economic knowledge transcending cultural background. Although published by the University of Vienna, contributors to the journal included many leading economists outside Austria and Germany such as Y. Takata in Japan, A. Amonn in the Czech Republic, the Italian U. Ricci in Cairo, A. Aftalion in France, J. Tinbergen in Holland, B. Ohlin, G. Myrdal and G. Åkerman in Sweden, R. Frisch in Norway, F. H. Knight, I. Fisher and

H. Schultz in the United States, A. J. R. Hicks and R. G. D. Allen in Britain, O. Lange in Poland, and the Russian W. Leontief in the United States. The *Zeitschrift* also carried papers written in English, for example, by J. Robinson and R. Harrod in the UK.

In addition to the *Zeitschrift für Nationalökonomie*, the *Review of Economic Studies* and *Econometrica* were a very important pipeline of information for Japanese as well as European and American economists. As Philip Mirowski argues in his "Physics and the 'marginalist revolution'" (1991), the intellectual center of gravity in economics had shifted in the 1930s from the book or essay to the journal article constructed around a mathematical "model." Gerard Debreu in his "The mathematization of economic theory" (1991) makes a brief assessment of the mathematization of economic theory from 1933, the date when two of the three journals, *Econometrica* and *Review of Economic Studies*, were started. He dates the "takeoff" stage of mathematical economic theory from 1933. Yet both Mirowski and Debreu forgot the *Zeitschrift für Nationalökonomie* as discussed in Ikeo's "Japanese modern economics, 1930–1945" (1993a).

There are two additional points relating to the two journals which demonstrate the Japanese linkage to mainstream economics. The first is that J. A. Schumpeter, the most familiar European economist to the Japanese economists of the day, authored a paper on Léon Walras and Alfred Marshall entitled "The common sense of econometrics" for the first issue of *Econometrica* (1933). Walras was the symbol of economics both on the European continent and in Japan, and Marshall was Walras's counterpart in the English-speaking world. The second is that the 1935 issue of the *Review of Economic Studies* carried O. Lange's "Marxian economics and modern economic theory" in which he referred to Kei Shibata's "Marx's analysis of capitalism and the general equilibrium theory of the Lausanne School" which appeared in *Kyoto University Economic Review* in 1933.[3] Although Lange dissented from Shibata's view of the prospects for Marxian economics, his 1935 paper made Lange familiar to the Japanese economists who were regular readers of the journal. These incidents confirmed to Japanese economists that they had been on the right track of world economics and thus stimulated them to continue their study of neoclassical economics such as "the economics of Walras" or the tradition of general equilibrium theory.[4]

Second, the Econometric Society was established as the first international society for economists on December 29, 1930. It was epoch-making in the process of internationalization and mathematization of economics for the physical sense of communication among the leading economists in the world. Ragner Frisch, a young Norwegian economist, created the word "econometrics," intended for a science devoted to the advancement of economic theory in relation to statistics and mathematics. Frisch met Charles F. Roos, a young mathematician-economist who was secretary of Section K (economics, sociology and statistics) of the American Association for the Advancement of Science. They solicited the aid of Irving Fisher, the father of American neoclassical economics and the solitary user of general equilibrium approach in the United States. Fisher had a bitter experience in failing to organize a similar international society in

1912. In 1929 and 1930, the ambitious three could compile a list of about 160 prospective founding members of the new society. Their bold plan came to fruition in the United States because it was funded by an American named Alfred Cowles. Cowles was discouraged by the poor performance of stock-market and business forecasters (Cowles 1960).

Although no Japanese attended the inaugural meeting, the internationally oriented economists were very familiar with the following part of the Constitution of the Econometric Society:

> The Econometric Society is an international society for the advancement of economic theory in the relation to statistics and mathematics.... Its main object shall be to promote studies that aim at a unification of the theoretical-quantitative and the empirical-quantitative approach to economic problems and that are penetrated by constructive and rigorous thinking similar to that which has come to dominate in the natural sciences.

The organizing group of the Econometric Society consisted of 12 Americans and 4 Europeans: R. Frisch, H. Hotelling, K. Menger, F. C. Mills, W. F. Ogburn, O. Ore, J. H. Rogers, C. F. Roos, M. C. Rorty, J. A. Schumpeter, H. Schultz, W. A. Shewhart, C. Snyder, I. Wedervang, N. Wiener and E. B. Wilson. Fisher was unanimously elected the first president of the society. The following were elected to the Council with a view to representing the various geographic areas in which the Society had members:

L. Amoroso, University of Rome, Italy
L. v. Bortkiewicz, University of Berlin, Germany
A. L. Bowley, London School of Economics, Britain
F. Divisia, Ecole Nationale des Ponts et Chaussees, Paris, France
R. Frisch, University of Oslo, Norway
C. F. Roos, Smithsonian Institution Building, Washington, DC, the United States
J. A. Schumpeter, University of Bonn, Germany
E. B. Wilson, Harvard University, the United States
Wl. Zawadzki, University of Wilno, Poland

It is noteworthy that many of them were trained as mathematicians or statisticians, whereas they were very interested in economics. Moreover, E. B. Wilson was a mathematical physicist and mathematical economist who later taught Paul A. Samuelson at Harvard University (Fischer 1987: 234).[5] The internationally oriented Japanese economists were excited to learn of the establishment of this society with more use of mathematics and statistics in economic research, probably because they felt that this trend would make the linguistic and cultural differences less important than before by formalizing economic knowledge and analysis.

The Econometric Society started an international journal entitled *Econometrica* in January 1933. Frisch became the first editor and held the position of editor-in-chief for 22 years until 1954. He took the initiative in organizing and establishing the broadly international character of the Econometric Society and its journal. Economics was becoming more international and less diverted into "sects" or "schools," as Schumpeter had hoped.

In September 1933 they held the first regular meeting at Lausanne, Switzerland, where two eminent mathematical economists, L. Walras and V. Pareto, were first accepted and had secured their positions. As mentioned, J. A. Schumpeter (1933) praised the economic achievement of L. Walras and A. Marshall in the opening article for *Econometrica* of 1933. Moreover, J. R. Hicks compared L. Walras with A. Marshall in his article entitled "Léon Walras" (1934) which appeared in *Econometrica*. We can see the measure of respect European economists accorded to Walras.

Third, in the 1930s, a considerable number of gifted Central European economists fled from Nazism and fascism, sought refuge in the United States, and started their academic careers there. The Japanese learned of this westward migration from the first or last pages of the journal articles as well as the reports (printed or oral) by Japanese scholars who had visited Europe and North America at the time. The affiliations of the authors switched from European universities to American universities and institutes. The emigration of the intelligentsia for political reasons formed a sharp contrast with the one prior to World War I, which was motivated for the most part by a search for a better economic environment.

There are already several excellent studies of the migration of economists from Central Europe to the United States. Earlene Craver (1986) was part of the result of her collection of oral histories provided by the émigré economists, and Craver and Axel Leijonhufvud (1987) discussed the influence of migrated economists from the European continent in "Economics in America." Harald Hagemann and Claus-Dieter Krohn spent several years in collecting the record of emigration of German-speaking economists and made the results available in a private edition entitled *The Emigration of German-speaking Economists after 1933* (1992, in German). This edition covered 314 émigrés and carried a page-long biographical entry for each economist. Hagemann and Krohn made further collections and gave us a picture of the migration of economists from the German-speaking world to Britain and the United States (Hagemann and Krohn 1999).

Hagemann (2000: 111–12) wrote that the current situation of German economics has resulted from these political events:

> The events in Germany in 1933 marked a significant turning point for the economics profession as well. The Nazi-induced intellectual emigration from Germany and Austria ... had long-term consequences from which German universities never fully recovered.
>
> In East Germany the period from 1945 to 1989, with the worst combination of the old German "mandarin" university with Stalinism, where economics basically was reduced to orthodox Marxism-Leninism and a

> narrowly defined socialist business administration, dealt a further blow to economics as a science. East Germany never produced economists of a similar stature as, for example, Kalecki, Lange and some of their students in Poland or Kornai in Hungary.

F. M. Scherer's "The Emigration of German-speaking Economists after 1933" (2000) reviewed a series of research papers by Hagemann and Krohn and gave supplementary information backed by some statistical evidence. Scherer (2000: 625) pointed out that their study covered only a subset of those who were displaced by World War II and the totalitarian regimes that preceded it. However, on the same page he went on to say, "But even that subset made intellectual contributions, measured by election to honorific positions and citations to their published work equivalent to the output of several top-ranked U.S. economics departments."

Therefore, it is useful for our study to examine the migration of economists in chronological order starting with the first to arrive in the United States and their Japanese connections.

Wassily Leontief (1906–99) was born in Russia and trained at the University of Leningrad (St. Petersburg after 1992) and the University of Berlin. He was surrounded by excellent mathematicians in Berlin.[6] It was there that Leontief met Eiichi Sugimoto (1901–52, Tokyo University of Commerce, now Hitotsubashi University) and established a friendship with him. Seeing the rise of the Nazis, Leontief soon left Berlin for the United States, while Sugimoto transferred to the University of Frankfurt in 1931 to see with his own eyes what would happen in Italy and Germany (Tanese 1953). Leontief joined the staff of the National Bureau of Economic Research in 1931 and after a few months accepted an appointment at Harvard University. Traveling westward from Frankfurt, Sugimoto visited the United States and saw Leontief in April 1932 before returning to Japan. Leontief became the founding father of interindustry analysis, which was regarded as an empirical application of general equilibrium theory. After 1950, his lectures at Harvard fascinated several Japanese students such as Shin-ichi Ichimura (b. 1925), who mastered the technique of carrying out econometric analysis with the use of economic data and computers. After returning to Japan, Ichimura engaged enthusiastically in econometric research (Ichimura 1957, in Japanese).

Joseph Alois Schumpeter (1883–1950) left Europe for personal, rather than political, reasons and accepted an appointment at Harvard University in 1932. Schumpeter was the first Viennese-trained economist to migrate to the United States. Shigeto Tsuru (1912–2006) was a student at Harvard in the 1930s and we will quote his pleasant recollections later. In the mid 1930s, Kei Shibata (1902–86) spent his sabbatical years with Schumpeter at Harvard. Before migration, Seiichi Tobata (1899–1983) met Schumpeter, who was a visiting professor at Harvard in 1927, and studied economics under him in Bonn from 1927. In the same year, Ichiro Nakayama spent six months in Berlin, moved to Bonn, and met Schumpeter and Tobata (more discussion on Nakayama in Chapter 4).

Schumpeter advised Tobata, the agricultural economist, to read Henry Schultz's (1925) statistical study of supply and demand of sugar and H. L. Moore's (1914, 1917) study of business cycles (University of Tokyo, Department of Economics ed. 1976: 578–82). Nakayama realized that Schultz was making a parallel advance with him in "mathematical economics" by using calculus in Schultz (1927). Tobata and Nakayama stayed in Bonn until 1929. In January 1931, Schumpeter visited Japan for a couple of weeks after his second visiting professorship at Harvard.[7] He met his former students Tobata and Nakayama, and delivered lectures at the Imperial University of Tokyo, Kobe University of Commerce, Tokyo University of Commerce and the Industry Club of Japan. After the lecture at the Imperial University of Tokyo, Takuma Yasui asked Schumpeter how best to start a postgraduate study of economics, to which Schumpeter replied, "Begin with Walras if you plan to study economic theories" (Yasui 1988, in Japanese: 5).[8] Yet Yasui became interested in Schumpeter's equilibrium economic theory and published the Japanese version of *Das Wesen und der Hauptinhalt der theoretischen Nationalökonomie* (The Essence and Main Content of Economics, Schumpeter 1908) with Takeyasu Kimura. Tobata and Nakayama devoted themselves to Schumpeter, translated many of his works into Japanese and formed a close relationship with their mentor. In fact, Elizabeth Boody Schumpeter, who edited *The Industrialization of Japan and Machukuo, 1930–1940* (1940), presented the drafts of her husband's *Capitalism, Socialism and Democracy* (1942) to Tobata in 1951 after Tobata and Hiroshi Furuya visited her in a hospital in Boston. These manuscripts are now available in the Mie Prefectural Library in Tobata's birthplace.[9]

Emil Lederer (1882–1939), a Marxian economist, was born in Austria. From 1923 through 1925, he delivered a series of lectures in English on non-Marxian economics by using Cassel (1923) as the textbook at the Imperial University of Tokyo. He returned to Europe and published a book coauthored with his wife Emy Lederer-Seidler, entitled *Japan-Europa: Wandlungen im Fernen Osten* (Japan-Europe: Traveling in the Far East) in 1929. In 1933, however, Lederer moved to the New School for Social Research in New York, where many refugees stayed from 1933 onward. In 1938, the revised English edition of their 1929 book on Japan was published in New Haven and London under the new title of *Japan in Transition.*

John von Neumann (1903–57) was born in Budapest, studied mathematics under David Hilbert and others, and lectured in Central Europe. Around 1930, Yukio Mimura (1904–84), mathematician, attended von Neumann's lecture on operators in Hilbertian space at the University of Berlin. In 1933, von Neumann was appointed to an academic position at the Institute for Advanced Study in Princeton University. In the 1930s, he proved the minimax theorem and constructed a model of balanced economic growth, and in the 1940s he cleared the field of game theory with Oskar Morgenstern (1902–77). At Princeton, in 1940 he also met Shizuo Kakutani, whose fixed-point theorem was to give an important insight to mathematical economists working on general equilibrium analysis and game theory in the 1950s (Chapter 6). Von Neumann was respected by his contemporary mathematicians and regarded as the god of mathematics (personal communication with Shizuo Kakutani and Hukukane Nikaido).

Fritz Machlup (1902–83) studied at the University of Vienna under Ludwig von Mises (1881–1973) and received an appointment at the University of Buffalo in 1935. Nicholas Georgescu-Roegen (1906–94), born in Romania, studied closely with Schumpeter at Harvard from 1934–6 and was appointed professor at Vanderbilt University in 1948 after studying in Romania. In the 1950s and 1960s, he actively served as an assistant editor for *Econometrica* and corresponded with several Japanese economists including Hukukane Nikaido (1923–2001) and Michio Hatanaka (b. 1926). Their correspondences were kept in the Georgescu-Roegen Papers (1944–94) at Duke University. Gottfried Haberler (1900–95), born near Vienna, studied and lectured at the University of Vienna, and was appointed professor at Harvard in 1936. Abba P. Lerner (1905–82), born in Romania and trained at the London School of Economics, was brought to the United States by a Rockefeller fellowship in 1937 and remained there. Georgescu-Roegen, Haberler and Lerner met Shigeto Tsuru at Harvard.

In March 1938, Vienna was occupied by German Nazis. Things came to a serious pass.

Karl Menger (1902–85) was the son of Carl Menger and was an active mathematician at the University of Vienna. He visited Japan in 1931 and delivered a talk on the incompleteness theorem demonstrated by his student Kurt Gödel. He organized an informal mathematical colloquium for mathematicians and economists and published the proceedings as *Ergebnisse eines Mathematischen Kolloquiums* during the period 1931–7. Kazuo Midutani (1897–1981), Yuzo Yamada (1902–95), and Yukio Mimura (1904–84) attended the Kolloquium during their stay in Vienna. After returning to Japan, Midutani and Mimura reported in Japanese on the fervent discussion at the Kolloquium. K. Menger was one of the organizing members of the Econometric Society in 1930. As the path-breaking papers in general equilibrium theory by Abraham Wald and John von Neumann appeared in the *Ergebnisse* (see Chapter 6), Menger received complaints from colleagues about the number of "Jewish" papers in the proceedings (Craver 1986: 28). In 1938, Menger, teaching at Notre Dame, immediately resigned from his professorship at Vienna, accepted a permanent position at the University of Notre Dame and later became professor at the Illinois Institute of Technology (Schwödiauer 1987). Shizuo Kakutani met Menger at a mathematical conference in the United States after World War II.

Oskar Morgenstern, who had been on a lecture tour in the United States since January of that year, learned that he had been blacklisted as "politically unbearable" due to his opposition to the Nazis. He remained in the United States and accepted an offer from Princeton University in 1938. As mentioned, he met Shizuo Kakutani at Princeton during the period 1940–1. Abraham Wald (1902–50), who had studied the so-called existence question in general equilibrium analysis, managed to escape from Vienna to the United States and finally accepted a fellowship at the Cowles Commission in 1938. Yet he lost all of his immediate family except one brother in the Holocaust.[10]

Jacob Marschak (1898–1977), born in Russia, emigrated to Germany during the Russian Revolution in which he participated as a Menshevik (socialist), and, with the rise of Hitler, migrated first to Britain and then to the United States in 1939. Marschak was ubiquitous in seminars held at American universities and impressed Japanese economists like Shigeto Tsuru (Tsuru 1964a, in Japanese).

The socialist calculation debate, which started on the European continent around 1920, arrived in the English-speaking world around 1930. Oskar Lange (1904–65), born in Tomaszow Mazowiecki, was trained in London and at Harvard and Berkeley. Lange and Abba Lerner were on the side of planner in the debate. From 1938–45, Lange lectured in Chicago and took a Walrasian general equilibrium approach to examining market mechanism and researched the question of stability analysis.[11] Lange and Lerner had a similar inclination to a socialist economy with Shigeto Tsuru at Harvard. Lange suggested Martin Bronfenbrenner (1914–97), a graduate student who worked in the similar line under the supervision of Schultz at Chicago, should look up Kei Shibata's scientific articles in *Kyoto University Economic Review*. Bronfenbrenner made his first visit to Japan in September 1945 and occasionally published informative papers on Japan's economic and industrial conditions in American economics journals (see Chapter 10).

Ludwig von Mises, who would receive an offer from the University of Tokyo in the mid 1920s, was born in Austria and studied in Vienna. He began to teach as a professor at the Graduate Institute of International Studies in Geneva in 1934 and immigrated to New York in 1940. The group he formed had credentials of unshakeable liberalism and was called the "Austrian School" in the United States. Mises denied the feasibility of calculation for a planned economy and pointed out the difficulty in information processing of individual activity. He fought with Friedrich von Hayek (1899–1992) against collectivists Lange and Lerner.

At the end of this section, young Shigeto Tsuru's pleasant memories of the 1930s at Harvard are worth quoting at length:

> [T]he presence of Schumpeter and others attracted visiting scholars from abroad on their Rockefeller fellowship to Harvard. And among them were Oscar [*sic*] Lange, Abba Lerner, Nicholas Kaldor, Paul Baran, Eric Roll, Fritz Machlup, Nicholas Georgescu-Roegen, Oscar [*sic*] Morgenstern, and Jacob Marschak. Almost every day, either at lunch, cocktail hour, or late at night, we found an occasion for heated discussions on the state of economic science. It may be said, too, that probably nowhere in the world at the time could one witness a freer and more productive confrontation between front-line modern economics and Marxian orthodoxy.
>
> (Tsuru 1992: 287)

Tsuru studied economics at Harvard from 1933 and received his Ph.D. in 1940. Japan initiated the war against Britain and the United States in December 1941.

Tsuru returned from the United States by exchange ship in 1942.[12] Tsuru and Shizuo Kakutani happened to be on the same ship. After the end of the Pacific Campaign of World War II, Tsuru joined the Economic Stabilization Board, which was organized on the basis of instructions given by the Allied Occupation Force for the purposes of allowing the war-torn economy to become stabilized. He brought back to the community of Japanese economists not only a cosmopolitan attitude in societal activities but also the American economic language, and changed the style of discussing economic policies by editing the first *White Paper on the Japanese Economy* (Ikeo 1996c, Ikeo ed. 2000).

2 Scientific journals of economics and the adoption of the English language

As early as the 1870s and the 1880s, a few of the journals which are still important today were established in Europe and North America. The number of scientific journals, which are open to every economist in the world and usually adopt a referee system, has been increasing since around 1930. Throughout the twentieth century there has been a constant tendency for many journals to adopt English as the official language. From the 1990s on, this tendency has been further invigorated by the explosive growth of the Internet.

For the purpose of the examination of the internationalization of economics in the twentieth century, we should recall the wave of scientific journals which were established in Europe and North America in the nineteenth century or the first half of the twentieth century. We focus on the journals which were readily available to Japanese economists and quoted in their papers from around 1900 till around 1960. As noted, the Econometric Society was established as an international society for the advancement of economic theory in its relation to statistics and mathematics in 1930, and launched its journal *Econometrica* in 1933. The rest of this section gives an overview of scientific journals, which are issued outside of Europe and North America, namely in India and Japan.

In Austria in 1892, *Zeitschrift für Volkswirtschaft, Sozialpolitik und Verwaltung* (Journal of Political Economy, Social Policy and Administration) was started by E. v. Böhm-Bawerk and the economists of the University of Vienna. In 1921, they changed its name to *Zeitschrift für Volkswirtschaft und Sozialpolitik* by dropping the word "*Verwaltung*" (administration or management) and then in 1930, as noted before, to *Zeitschrift für Nationalökonomie*. Japanese economists regarded this journal as the first international journal in theoretical economics because many international economists contributed to it and it carried papers written in a non-German language, English. During the German occupation, the *Zeitschrift für Nationalökonomie* was issued in 1938, 1939 and 1944 with the help of German and Italian economists such as Walter Eucken, Heinrich von Stackelberg, Guglielmo Masci and Eraldo Fossati. After 1948, it resumed under prewar conditions. Since then, the journal gradually carried an increasing number of papers written in English. Finally in 1986, the title was changed to an English one, namely *Journal of Economics*.

In Germany in 1876, the German historical school contributed to the establishment of an academic society and their journals. *Jahrbuch für Gesetzgebung, Verwaltung und Volkswirtschaft in Deutschen Reich* (Yearbook of Legislation, Administration and Political Economy in the German Empire) was born out of *Jahrbuch für Gesetzgebung, Verwaltung und Rechtspflege des Deutschen Reichs* (1871–6), with the inclusion of economic discussion instead of the administration of justice. In 1881, the journal came to be known as *Schmollers Jahrbuch* after the leader of the German historical school Gustav Schmoller (1838–1917) became editor. Schmoller established the Verein für Sozialpolitik in 1872 and was its chairman for a long time. In 1913, it formally changed its name to *Schmollers Jahrbuch für Gesetzgebung, Verwaltung und Volkswirtschaft in Deutschen Reich* and in 1949 dropped "in Deutschen Reich." It has since changed its name to *Zeitschrift für Wirtschafts- und Sozialwissenschaften* (Journal of Economic and Social Sciences) by dropping the name of Schmoller in 1972.

In Italy in 1875, *Giornale degli economisti* was started. It has changed its subtitle twice, and has been *Giornale degli economisti e annali di economia* since 1939. In 1933, *Giornale degli economisti e rivista di statistica* carried Miyoji Hayakawa's "Sulla distribuzione dei terreni agrai Giappone del 1908 al 1930" (On the distribution of agricultural land in Japan from 1908 till 1930). The majority of the papers in recent issues of the journal are written in English.

In France, *Revue d'économie politique* was founded by the influential economist Charles Gide and has been circulated since 1887, although papers written in English are found only occasionally in the recent issues. Nonetheless, this is still regarded as one of the main journals in economics (Schmidt 2000: 130).

In the United States as early as 1886, Harvard University started the *Quarterly Journal of Economics*. The journal has the longest tradition among the English journals. In 1919, Harvard University started *Review of Economic Statistics* including the Supplement of Statistical Data. The purpose of the Review was defined by Charles J. Bullock (1919: 3) in the prefatory statement in the first issue.

> The purpose of the Review is to promote the collection, criticism, and interpretation of economic statistics, with a view to making them more accurate and valuable than they are at present for business and scientific purposes. It will seek to do by investigation of the sources and probable accuracy of existing statistical data, by the collection of additional data in cases where this may prove desirable and practicable, and by developing the application to economic statistics of modern methods of statistical analysis which have hitherto been utilized more extensively in other sciences than in economics.

The name of the Review was changed to *Review of Economics and Statistics* in 1948. In 1893, the University of Chicago established the *Journal of Political Economy*.

The American Economic Association, which was established under the influence of the German historical school in 1885, began to issue *American Economic Review* (AER) as its journal in 1911 after several failed attempts. In 1963 it began to issue the *Journal of Economic Literature* (JEL), which is full of book reviews and article summaries, and in 1987 the *Journal of Economic Perspectives* (JEP), which is intended not for specialists in subdivided fields of economics but for economists in general. From the issue of December 1994 the JEL became available on CD-ROM and in December 2000 the JSTOR (Journal Storage) began to provide electronic copies of back issues of the AER, JEL and JEP up until 36 months prior to the current issue (www.jstor.org/). *American Economic Review: Microeconomics* and *American Economic Review: Macroeconomics* started in 2009.

In Britain, the Royal Economic Society continues to issue its *Economic Journal*, which was started in 1890. An economist needs, however, to join the society in order to submit a paper to the journal. It is noteworthy that special journals of economics were established later in Britain than in France, Germany, Italy and the United States. In 1920, the London School of Economics started *Economica*. As noted before, *Review of Economic Studies* was started in 1933 by a group of young British and American economists, who were associated with the school. The first three editors were Abba P. Lerner, Paul M. Sweezy and Ursula K. Webb (later Ursula K. Hicks). This journal was headquartered in the London School of Economics and Political Science.

In Sweden in 1899, *Ekonomisk Tidskrift* (Journal of Economics) was started by David Davidson. In 1965, its name was changed to *Swedish Journal of Economics* and issued by the Department of Economics of the University of Stockholm. In 1976, the journal grew into *Scandinavian Journal of Economics*. It still features the name of Davidson on the opening page of each issue.

Japanese universities received issues of a scientific journal from India, too. India in 1917, the *Indian Journal of Economics* was started by the Department of Economics of the University of Allahabad, although the editorial foreword was dated January 1916. The editor H. Stanley Jevons, professor of the University of Allahabad, explained the threefold purpose of the journal as follows:

> The Journal is intended in the first place to supply a longfelt need by providing a medium for the publication of articles on Indian Economics by authors of academic standing or authoritative position. In the second place it is designed to furnish a convenient and compact vehicle of publication for the original investigations made by the staff of the Economics Department of the Allahabad University, and for the more important researches of students of the Seminar class in Economics, so as to avoid having such papers scattered throughout various Indian and English periodicals.
>
> The third object of issuing this Journal is to proffer one kind of public service which can be undertaken better by a University department than any other agency: namely the dissemination of information about the economic activities of other countries. National progress can be made swiftly and surely only by utilizing the experience of other territories, and in legislation of an economic character, are being made in all parts of the world. In many lands the economic conditions are similar in some respects to Indian

> conditions; and if knowledge of the effects of economic measures undertaken in these countries can be made public in India, development and reforms are likely to proceed in India more safely and rapidly.
>
> (H. S. Jevons 1917: 1–2)

In Japan in 1926, Kyoto Imperial University (now Kyoto University) began to circulate a journal written in Western languages, including English and German, and thus founded the international forum for Japanese economists. *Kyoto University Economic Review* (*Kyoto Economic Review* since 2004) has the longest tradition of any economics journal written in Western languages and published in Japan. Its publication was an epoch-making event demonstrating that some Japanese economists had embarked on making their own economic research after the period of translating Western economics since Japan's opening the door to the rest of the world in 1854. The editorial foreword of the very first issue of *Kyoto University Economic Review* reflected their firm determination and strong hope for intellectual cooperation with Western economists.

> Many of the studies in the natural and social sciences already published in our country have had far-reaching effects in the advancement of science and the enhancement of human happiness, but as the majority of them were written in the Japanese language they have not been accessible to Western scholars. Although studies in the natural sciences have been published by our scholars through books, university memoirs, reports of various associations and others all of which were written in Western languages, no similar attempt has, so far, been made as regards the studies in the social sciences, the results being that the real condition in the field of our economic science has been almost unknown to the Western countries. Realizing that such a condition is truly regrettable from the standpoint of intellectual cooperation which should be established by the scholars of all nations, the Economic Department of the Imperial University of Kyoto has decided to undertake the work of publishing a series of memoirs.
>
> (*Kyoto University Economic Review*, Editorial Committee 1926: 2, originally written in English)

The phrase "the Japanese Economic School" may sound strange today because economics has been physically internationalized and formalized since around 1930 and there is a mainstream economics with some heretical schools rather than several major schools. What the editors of the journal had in mind were the Lausanne, Stockholm and Cambridge schools which were associated with the locations of the then leading economists. It is now meaningless to identify economists with labels of schools based on their location. Contemporary economists are always communicating, moving and traveling around the globe.

At any rate, they soon appreciated the power of the English language when an article in the journal was cited by a Polish economist. As mentioned before, Shibata (1933) made Kei Shibata known to the rest of the world. Oskar Lange

(1935) referred to Shibata (1933). This event encouraged leading Japanese economists to make efforts to contribute the international community of economists. *Kyoto University Economic Review* was the first economics journal to adopt the English language (as one of the Western languages) among those published in non-English speaking countries outside the British Commonwealth. The *Review* was very good and open in the sense that economists or mathematicians of other departments or universities could contribute excellent papers to it. Throughout the 1930s, Shibata regularly contributed papers on theoretical topics to the *Review*. This led Alfred Cowles to invite Shibata to the Annual Research Conference of the Cowles Commission for Research in Economics, which was to be held in Colorado Springs from July 1 to 26, 1940.[13] However, Japan found this channel to the international community of economists completely closed from 1941 until 1945.

3 Roles of *The Oriental Economist* and Martin Bronfenbrenner for intellectual exchange

Outside of Japan, there have been a number of specialists in "Japanese studies," who have mastered the language first and taken a specific field such as culture, tradition, history, art and politics for their research. When they look up contemporary economic and political issues, they examine related articles in newspapers and magazines in Japanese. *The Oriental Economist*, a monthly, became the most important source written in English for the information of Japan's economy and policies when it was established in May 1934.[14] It was the English edition of the Japanese economic weekly *Toyo Keizai Shinpo* (established in 1895) and sold at the price of 50 *sen* (a half yen) or 25 cents for each issue or charged at a regular subscription fee. It was issued weekly by request of the Supreme Commander for the Allied Powers (SCAP)[15] from January 1946 till August 1952. Then it became a monthly again and continued until 1986.

Tanzan Ishibashi (1884–1973) gradually became known as the President and Editor of *The Oriental Economist* outside of Japan.[16] In 1911, he began to work for the publisher Toyo Keizai Shinposha and then became involved in the editorial of *Toyo Keizai Shinpo* (*The Oriental Economist*). He began to study economics by reading T. Amano's *Outline of Economics* (1902a, in Japanese), Edwin Seligman's *Principles of Economics* (1905), John Stuart Mill, Arnold Toynbee, Tokuzo Fukuda and many other books (see Chapters 7 and 9). Amano was one of the leading writers in *Toyo Keizai Shinpo* and assumed the roles of editor and manager of the company from 1897 until around 1910. The magazine kept carrying various economic data related to international and domestic trade and business as well as economic data of East Asia. The foreword to the inaugural issue of the English edition began with the following statement:

> The Oriental Economist has been lucky.
>
> The gigantic catastrophe of September 1, 1923, which destroyed all other accumulated economic data in Tokyo, left its own files untouched. These

> cover Japan and the rest of the Far East for the last forty years, and are therefore unique.
>
> During these same forty years a staff of seasoned investigators have grown up with Economist, who are now familiar with this unique mass of data, and famed for the accuracy and dependability of their work.
>
> The plant is a six-story … structure with 15,000 square feet of floor space, within a stone's throw of the Bank of Japan, in the very heart of Tokyo's financial district.

The first few issues aimed at refuting the criticism of "social dumping" or "exchange dumping" against the (temporary) increase of Japan's exports to the rest of the world by showing their analysis based on plenty of accurate economic data. After Finance Minister Korekiyo Takahashi decided to leave the gold standard system by the re-embargo of gold in December 1931, the Japanese yen depreciated until December 1932 and then turned around to an upward tendency to December 1933. Japan's exports were decreasing at the time. Each issue carried "Review of the Month" (mostly written by Ishibashi), "Leading Articles" and abundant economic data (stocks and bonds, the commodity market, note circulation and gold reserve, various interest rates and yields, exchange rates, several price indexes, the unemployment index, exports and imports, etc.). In addition, every issue carried the advertisement: "Oriental Economist Intelligence Department is best equipped to furnish the reader with economic, statistical and other information, authentic and exhaustive, at charges proportionate to the work involved." *The Oriental Economist* was proud of the high quality of its economic data, probably supplied originally by the BOJ and the government. It aimed "to give a fair and impartial view of economic conditions in the Orient, free from nationality, race or creed" (foreword to the inaugural issue). The quality of massive data should be able to make foreign readers evaluate Japan's actual economic conditions and difficulties.

It is noteworthy that *The Small Industries of Japan: Their Growth and Development* (1938) edited by Teijiro Uyeda (Tokyo University of Commerce) also carried a number of tables, diagrams, charts and facts related to the title topic. It consisted of papers which were submitted to the Sixth Conference of the Institute of Pacific Relations held in 1936. Thanks to the rapid spread and increase of electric power supply in remote cities and colonies, small Japanese factories usually run by families (ten workers or fewer) could equip themselves with new machines of the latest technology and became competitive enough to produce exportable goods. Trading companies and *nakagainin* (middlemen or brokers) collected their products from their workshops and exported them to the rest of the world. The size of their factories was so small that the official surveys usually did not cover their activities. It is true that they might be working for too many hours but they would suffer from more serious poverty if they had suspended their production operation. Uyeda (1938) supplied the economic data and facts which *The Oriental Economist* could not cover by mainly using official data.

In the spring of 1935, Romaine Elizabeth Boody, the third future wife of Joseph Alois Schumpeter, came into contact with Ishibashi (Ishibashi 1941: 82). She wrote her dissertation on English foreign trade under the supervision of co-directors Abbott Payton Usher and Schumpeter and received her Ph.D. from Radcliffe College in 1934. From 1934 to 1937, she worked as a research associate at Radcliffe and for Harvard's Bureau of International Research (McCraw 2007: 237). She became responsible for organizing a research project which led to the publication of *The Industrialization of Japan and Machukuo, 1930–1940: Population, Raw Material and Industry* (1940) with financial support from the two institutions. Ishibashi supplied her with the detailed results of the investigation of Japanese affairs upon her request and plenty of economic data (except one related to counterintelligence), which deeply impressed her. He also gave her his advice on the points of importance to keep in mind in research of the Japanese economy.

Although she could not come to Japan as she had planned, G. C. Allen, one of her project members and Brunner Professor of Economic Science at the University of Liverpool, managed to visit Japan for the observation of recent economic development on the spot in the summer and autumn of 1936 (Allen 1983: 129). It was his second visit to Japan as he taught at Nagoya Higher Commercial School (now Nagoya University) in the early 1920s (see Chapter 4). He detected the tension and uneasiness regarding Japan's continental policy (in North China) beneath the façade of good manners compared with his previous experience of staying there. Without referring to Elizabeth's project, Allen (1983: 130) wrote his memories of his second visit before his passing.

> In these circumstances it was surprising that so much help was extended to me in my own enquiries. It is true that I had friends in the Japanese Foreign Office who could vouch for me, while Mr. Tanzan Ishibashi of the *Toyo Keizai Shinpo* (*The Oriental Economist*) and his colleagues cooperated whole-heartedly in the research. I also had connections with my former colleagues and students at Nagoya. Nevertheless, the extent of the help I received shows that the suspicions raised by the militants were not shared by the whole country. Many Japanese were still well disposed towards Britain and America and welcomed disinterested enquiries into their affairs.... I remember a leading cotton-spinner who, on hearing that I had a Chair at Liverpool University, wondered if I were not an agent of the Lancashire cotton industry. He nevertheless dismissed his fears and spent some hours answering my detailed enquiries about his industry.

This project needed several years until its completion. Another contributor was E. F. Penrose, Associate Professor of Economics at the University of California and Economic Adviser to the International Labor Office, who had also taught at Nagoya in the late 1920s. In due course, the research emphasis in their research (and in *The Oriental Economist*) shifted from "the depreciation of the yen and its influence on Japanese trade and prices" to the current conditions of "population, raw materials and industrial development with special reference to the strategic possibilities of the Yen Bloc."

When E. B. Schumpeter (1940) was published, Ishibashi was pleased to read the volume and their conclusions.[17] Ishibashi (1941: 85) said:

> The project has turned out unexpectedly to Japan's advantage whose case is presented eloquently and convincingly. The generous supply of materials was by no means to the disadvantage of Japan and was conducive to the creation of understanding friends and well-wishers. The work is an unexpected windfall for Japan. It will be an eye-opener to foreigners who are prepared to look at things judiciously when proper opportunity is given.

Ishibashi kept paying attention to E. B. Schumpeter's article appearing in journals like *Pacific Affairs* (see also McCraw 2007: Chapter 19).

In August 1945, the nature of articles in *The Oriental Economist* changed again. The double issue of July and August carried articles that would convey accurate information about the Japanese domestic situation on the ceasefire of August 15 and would be necessary for the incoming SCAP members. Ishibashi hoped to see a general election of the members of the House of Representatives take place early the following year as announced by the Prime Minister Higashikuni. As he intended, SCAP requested him to submit a report on Japanese affairs every week. Accepting it, he decided to switch *The Oriental Economist* from a monthly to a weekly from January 1946 to make the report public without delay.

In the September issue of *The Oriental Economist*, Ishibashi wrote the article entitled "No Inflation will Arise." This article didn't have a byline but the second half expressed the author's firm resolution to enter the national political arena and caught the eyes of members of the Shoup Tax Reform Mission including Jerome B. Cohen and Martin Bronfenbrenner. It was easy to guess that the article had been written by the Editor and President, Ishibashi himself. Although he lost the general election, Ishibashi was appointed the Finance Minister by the Prime Minister Shigeru Yoshida in May 1946 and a year later he was purged by SCAP in May 1947 (see Chapter 10).

Martin Bronfenbrenner, having made his first visit to Japan in September 1945, tried to find an opportunity to revisit Japan and he came into contact with Carl Shoup at the 1947 meeting of the American Economic Association (AEA) when he heard about a plan to send a Tax Reform Mission led by Shoup to Japan. Shoup and Harold Moss, a SCAP official, decided to assign him as a tax economist of SCAP as well as a liaison to the Shoup Mission and Japan's Ministry of Finance (MOF) (see Chapter 10). Bronfenbrenner himself did his best to keep up with the development of economic science in addition to technical tax work and made a plan to visit a Japanese university. He came into contact with Shigeto Tsuru, "who was at that time the Japanese economist best known in America" (Bronfenbrenner 1997: 15–5).[18] He had heard Tsuru praised by their mutual friends such as Oskar Lange and Abba Lerner when he was a graduate student at the University of Chicago. Tsuru offered him the opportunity to join a graduate seminar on Western macroeconomics at Hitotsubashi University. Bronfenbrenner (1997, 15–16) recalled that he enjoyed driving from the metropolitan area to the Kunitachi campus of Hitotsubashi University in the western suburb of Tokyo once a week.

> I came to look forward to those Wednesday afternoons on the Hitotsubashi campus … especially after buying a little British Austin, which I named *Akaji-Zaisei* or "Deficit Finance" and drove merrily back and forth between Kunitachi and downtown Tokyo. In addition to Tsuru, who was then working on a Marx–Keynes synthesis, the seminar included several young Hitotsubashi professors and students who would later achieve prominence in Japanese economic circles.

The seminar was formally arranged by President Ichiro Nakayama of Hitotsubashi University. The teachers whom Bronfenbrenner recalled best from Hitotsubashi were, apart from Tsuru, Kiyoshi Kojima (international economist, specializing in the Asia-Pacific economy), Miyohei Shinohara (a development economist, who published many books and papers on the Japanese economy and industries, and its policies), Isamu Yamada (an econometrician, who later became the first Japanese person to really communicate with active economists in the US). The Hitotsubashi seminars on Wednesday afternoon attracted those economists who lived out of Tokyo, like Takuma Yasui, as well. A number of Japanese economists visited Kunitachi or Tokyo to meet Bronfenbrenner for their research or to discuss travel plans to the US. Yet on August 12, 1950, for some reason, he left Japan from Haneda Airport.

Bronfenbrenner arranged to spend the summer of 1952 in Japan after leaving Bangkok when his term in the Economic Commission for Asia and the Far East (ECAFE, later the United Nations Economic and Social Commission for Asia and the Pacific, ESCAP) expired. He planned to stay at Doshisha University in Kyoto, one of the former capitals of Japan. The city is famous for its important, traditional Shinto shrines, solemn Buddhist temples and many other historic, fine-looking buildings and houses. This was why it had escaped bombing during the Pacific Campaign and attracted Bronfenbrenner in 1952. His Doshisha connection was a labor economist, Shichiro Matsui, who was a prewar Wisconsin Ph.D., a labor adviser to SCAP, and had visited Madison in 1948. Matsui arranged for Bronfenbrenner to give a series of lectures on various economic-theoretical topics for economists at Doshisha University and Kyoto University. Bronfenbrenner (1981) wrote on the Doshisha seminar and his first meeting with Yasuma Takata, and called him the Japanese Marshall. He also met young Michio Morishima, whose questions and comments impressed him most.

The intellectual connections with Bronfenbrenner continued afterwards. For example, in 1952, he and Robert H. Strotz, the organizer, helped Takuma Yasui participate in the Chicago meeting of the Econometric Society, which was to be held from December 27–29, and Strotz encouraged him to present a paper. Their correspondence remains in the Yasui Library of Saitama University near Tokyo

(Ikeo 2006). Yasui was sent there by the Science Council of Japan (*Nihon Gakujutsu Kaigi*) and gave his "Nonlinear self-exited oscillations and business cycles" in the session "Macro-dynamic Models of Economic Fluctuations" on the twenty-seventh. Yasui became the first Japanese economist to present a paper at a meeting of the Econometric Society (Ikeo 2009).

4 Narrowing the distance of Japanese economics from the international community

In 1951, the Treaty of Peace with Japan was signed in San Francisco to bring Japan formally back into the international community during a time of crisis between the East and the West, namely the Korean War (1950–3). A year before, in October 1950, the first Japanese meeting of the Econometric Society was held in Tokyo. After Ichiro Nakayama made the opening address, Masao Hisatake, Yukichi Kurimura, Kazuo Midutani, Michio Morishima, Seiichi Nakamura, Eiichi Sugimoto, Isamu Yamada and Takuma Yasui presented their papers. The report on the Tokyo meeting (Japanese Econometric Society 1951) and the first article authored by Japanese economist, Miyoji Hayakawa's "The application of Pareto's law of income to Japanese data" (1951) appeared in *Econometrica.*

The generous fund for the Government Appropriations for Relief in Occupied Areas (GARIOA), and later, the Fulbright Scholar Program, brought young Japanese scholars to the United States and other countries to engage in advanced studies. Shin-ichi Ichimura, Tsunehiko Watababe, Tadao Uchida and Ryutaro Komiya were fascinated by "American empirical studies," such as the interindustry analysis originated by W. Leontief, and econometric modeling advanced by Lawrence Klein and Hollis B. Chenery. Returning to Japan, they not only taught neoclassical economics but also embarked on important econometric works in making "economic plans" and predictions in the 1960s. Hiroshi Furuya, who had been trained at Harvard University from 1952–4, not only strongly advised economics students to study advanced mathematics, but also invited mathematics students such as Hirofumi Uzawa and Ken-ichi Inada to study economics. In addition, as a Rockefeller Foundation Fellow Michio Morishima spent two years at Oxford University and Yale University. In the UK, he enjoyed attending the meetings organized by John Richard Hicks around 1956. Mark Blaug (1998: 205) states, "Michio Morishima is a Japanese mathematical economist who has successfully bridged the communications gap between Japanese-speaking and English-speaking economists."

In the 1950s, Japanese mathematical economists such as Hukukane Nikaido, Hirofumi Uzawa, Ken-ichi Inada, Hajime Oniki and Takashi Negishi joined Kenneth J. Arrow's project at Stanford University backed by the Office of Naval Research (ONR).[19] They played active roles in the research of general equilibrium approach including the question of existence and stability of a general equilibrium in a competitive economy, two sector growth models, and welfare economics. In the mid 1950s, the mathematical economist David Gale visited Japan, stayed at Osaka University, and collaborated with Nikaido, Ichimura and

Morishima. The Japanese dream of intellectual collaboration with Western economists finally turned into reality.

Moreover, after 1951, Japanese economists began to contribute scientific papers to internationally oriented journals written in English, including the ones graded highly by econometricians and neoclassical economists such as *Econometrica*, *Review of Economic Studies* and the *Journal of Economic Theory*. Masahiro Kawamata, historian of economics, took a quantitative approach to the scientific contributions made by Japanese economists in the joint project "Statistical Study of Japanese Economics since 1945." Kawamata (2000) used Heck's Economic Literature Database from 1951 through 1968 and EconLit, the database of the American Economic Association, from 1969 through 1995 in order to examine the characteristics of economic research in general that appeared in prestigious journals written in English after 1945. He then extracted data on the contributions of Japanese economists to the similar journals. Kawamata (2000: 100) observed the active Japanese economists and the core journal which they have contributed to as follows:

> The oldest generation of Japanese economists who constantly contribute to the international economics journals consists of the economists Michio Hatanaka, Ken-ichi Inada, Takashi Negishi, Hukukane Nikaido, Miyohei Shinohara, and Hirofumi Uzawa, who are the members of the honorary board of *Japanese Economic Review*, and other several economists including Shigeto Tsuru, Michio Morishima, Shin-ichi Ichimura. They have published papers since the 1950s. Therefore, the core journals that we take up already have to be publishing in 1950. *American Economic Review* was published in 1911, *Econometrica* in 1933, *Economic Journal* in 1891, *Journal of Political Economy* in 1892, *Quarterly Journal of Economics* in 1891, *Review of Economic Studies* in 1933, *Review of Economics and Statistics* [then *Review of Economic Statistics*] in 1920 [1919].

Then Kawamata carefully began to research the 27 journals in order to investigate the Japanese contributions to the field of applied economics (see Appendix). Based on the extensive quantitative analysis, Kawamata (2000: 120) concluded as follows:

> Japanese economists contribute to the international journals in the fields of theoretical, mathematical, and statistical analysis, but not in the fields of practical, institutional, and policy-making analysis. The former fields are abstract and formalized, and the latter concrete and difficult to be formalized. It should be natural that the abstract and formalized fields are easier to be internationalized than the practical fields difficult to be formalized.

In other words, Kawamata confirmed that Japanese economists had kept pace with the development of economic theories and contributed a great deal to the advancement of economics and econometrics.[20]

In this way, many economics journals are open to every economist in the world and usually adopt the referee system. That is to say, economic papers written not only by economists but also by mathematicians can be submitted to a journal with a referee system. The editor of the journal decides whether to accept or reject a submitted paper on the basis of comments provided by one or two referees. The spread of open journals using the referee system has promoted a further division of labor within the economics profession and a specialization in subdivided divisions in economics. It has provided good opportunities for young economists to publish their papers.

In contrast to these international ventures, in Japan each university or department has its own closed research journal mostly written in Japanese, either without the use of anonymous referees or with the referee process being a mere formality. This kind of journal is called *Kiyo*, and is regarded as an "in-house organ" in Bronfenbrenner (1956). Faculty members can freely contribute to their journal whenever they wish, although the door is usually closed to outside economists. Reprints of the papers in *Kiyo* journals are sent to those who might be interested in the topic. In addition to such journals, handwritten papers were circulated among a small group of economists before the rapid spread of Japanese word processors. Some neoclassical or Keynesian economists regard *Kiyo* journals as being close to a discussion paper series, with the difference that a paper in *Kiyo* is a publication which is evaluated for promotion whereas a discussion paper is not. In fact, the spread of discussion paper series occurred only in the early and mid 1990s in Japan. Along with the spread of the Internet, however, the distribution of discussion papers by normal mail dwindled, as it did in the rest of the world.

It is also noteworthy that until the mid 1980s Japan did not have many nationwide academic journals of economics, mainly because it lacked a Japanese typewriter inexpensive enough for each economist to own. Existing Japanese typewriters were also very difficult to operate. The Japanese language uses *Kanji*, *Hiragana* and *Katakana* characters which are totally different from Western alphabets. About 3,000 Japanese (complicated) *Kanji* characters are used in everyday life and more are needed in writing an academic paper. This number is far larger than the 26 characters of the Western alphabet. This fact may contribute to the distance between Japanese culture and the West.[21]

In Japan, therefore, there are two kinds of academic journals published in the field of social sciences, those with the referee system and those without it. There are also some international journals on economics with the referee system which are headquartered in Japan, or edited by Japanese economists (Ikeo 2000a).

Kikan Riron Keizaigaku (Economic Studies Quarterly) was started in 1950 by the leading economists of the day such as Ichiro Nakayama and Seiichi Tobata. It became the journal of the Japan Association of Economics and Econometrics in 1959, and a referee system was introduced in 1960. Even prior to the name change to the *Economic Studies Quarterly* in 1986, it started to carry many papers written in English. It was decided at the 1993 annual meeting that the journal would adopt English, change its title to the Japanese Economic Review, and be published by Basil Blackwell starting in 1995. The Association also issues a book in Japanese called *Gendai Keizaigaiu no Choryu* (Trends in Contemporary Economics) for surveys and business communication because the use of the Japanese language facilitates communication among Japanese-speaking members. English does not convey all the information needed for Japanese members. Translation always loses something from the original.

Keizai Kenkyu is a semi-open journal, whose English title is the *Economic Review*. It has been published by the Economic Research Institute of Hitotsubashi University since 1950. Shigeto Tsuru, who studied at Harvard University in the 1930s, played an important role in starting the *Review*. He believed that economists should be policy oriented and analyze the Japanese economy which was then in the process of recovering from devastating defeat in World War II. He also brought the cosmopolitan attitude and intellectual milieu of Harvard back to Tokyo. Thanks to his "American" connection, Paul M. Sweezy, Paul A. Samuelson, Martin Bronfenbrenner and Maurice Dobb contributed in English to the journal in its first year. Yet in the 1950s the journal was not open to outside economists in general.

The *International Economic Review* was first published by the Kansai Economic Federation in 1960. Their business offices are located in the University of Pennsylvania, US, and in the Osaka University Institute of Social and Economic Research Association, Japan. The first chief editor was Laurence K. Klein of the University of Pennsylvania. The coeditor was Michio Morishima of Osaka University. Their three major objectives in starting the journal were:

> (1) to provide a new truly international forum, (2) to facilitate, through such an international medium, the introduction of new national schools of thought (e.g., the newly developing Japanese school) to the world community of economists, and (3) to foster the development of quantitative economics.
>
> (Klein and Morishima 1960: 1)

This editorial note encouraged many Japanese economists to submit their papers to internationally oriented journals.

Two competing journals on the Japanese economy were established one after another by two groups of Japanese economists. The *Journal of the Japanese and International Economies* was founded in 1987 by M. Aoki, M. Ohyama, K. Hamada and M. Okuno-Fujiwara, in cooperation with the Tokyo Center for Economic Research. The next year, Ryuzo Sato started *Japan and the World Economy*, an international journal of theory and policy. They aim in their journals to promote intensive discussion of the Japanese economy and to help many economists around the world to understand it.

It is also noteworthy that there have been *Kiyo* journals or department memoirs written in Western languages published in Japan. Economists at various departments tended to compete with each other to contribute good articles to their own university journals. In fact, Paul Oslington (2000) found many Japanese contributions to the study of international trade theory in journals of this kind such as *Keio Economic Studies*, *Hitotsubashi Journal of Economics*, *Kobe University Economic Review*, and *Kyoto University Economic Review* (*Kyoto Economic Review* since 2004). Some of these contributions should have been accepted by international, open economics journals if they had been submitted to them.

There is another example of around 1960 which demonstrates Japan's distance from the rest of the world. Young Takashi Negishi (b. 1933) had a chance to write a survey article on stability analysis when he was making a special study of general equilibrium approach at Stanford University. The atmosphere of 1960 in the United States led Takashi Negishi to refrain from referring to articles written in Japanese in his survey article (Negishi 1962) for *Econometrica* on the stability of a competitive economy. For example, he did not include precedent works written in Japanese such as Yasui's "Antei no ippan riron" (A general theory of stability, 1950) or Morishima's "Dogakuteki Keizai Riron" (Dynamic Economic Theory, 1950c) in the references. It is very hard to specify the reasons why Negishi did not refer to papers written in Japanese that would have been referred to in his 1962 survey article if they had been written in English. There are several possible reasons which Negishi himself listed in 1990:[22]

(a) Negishi (1962) was a survey article of the works on the topic published around 1960. He did not intend to list all the papers published before that period except for the well-known works written by L. Walras, J. R. Hicks and P. A. Samuelson and the greatly influential contribution made by M. Allais.
(b) He had made a value judgment (or had a prejudice) that he should not stress the rediscovery of mathematical theorems in economics. Rather he would emphasize the specification of the problems and the economic implication of the solutions.
(c) Japanese mathematical economists had already begun to publish their early works in English. He did not believe that he needed to refer to their papers which had not been published in English.
(d) Few papers published in Japan were available to him when he wrote the survey article in the United States around 1960. This had something to do with the limited international traffic and communication system of the day. For example, most communication between California and Japan was through surface mail and it was too expensive for him (as a Japanese scholar) to make an overseas call at that time. It is also related to his lack of experience as an economist in Japan. He was not familiar with the early works on the topic in Japan.
(e) He was not a historian but a theorist. He aimed in that article to discuss the contemporary research on the topic and only made a rough sketch on the history of the study on the stability of a competitive economy. He was reluctant to refer to papers which were not available at libraries in the United States or in Europe.

(Negishi 1990, my translation)

Until around 1960 "The Japanese school of economics" had not yet been introduced into the world community of economists because they kept writing economic papers in Japanese. This is still true today, even though the spread of the Internet has facilitated communication among economists throughout the world.

Nonetheless, Japanese economists also use the Japanese language in writing scientific papers, in discussing economic policy matters and in publishing textbooks. The works in Japanese are targeted at the Japanese audience, but they are sometimes read by Korean and Chinese economists while they are usually neglected by those economists who have other cultural backgrounds. Nonetheless, Japanese economists continue to produce many works in Japanese, set up a supporting system for economic studies, and create convenient classification codes for Japanese-speaking economists seeking the latest research. Part of the reason might exist in the fact that European languages are based on an alphabet, and in analyzing Japanese matters, a paper written in a European language without ideographs has less content than a paper of the same length written in Japanese (Ikeo 2000: 1–2). The discussion of economic policy issues by Japanese economists, which had often been neglected by non-Japanese scholars, was taken up by T. Minoguchi *et al.* (2000) and A. Noguchi (2000).

Appendix

The criteria that Masahiro Kawamata (2000: 117–18) used as a basis for the selection of the journals for his statistical analysis of Japanese contributions to applied economics were the following:

(1) The journal was already published in 1975, and therefore they had two opportunities to be ranked in the economics journal ranking of D. N. Laband and M. J. Piette's "The relative impacts of economics journals: 1970–1990" (1994).
(2) At each opportunity, the journal was ranked according to the "top-50" economics ranking of Laband and Piette (1994). The relatively low ranking journals which were needed to complete the list of *Journal of Economic Literature*'s Alphabetical Numeric Classification System in the fields of applied economics.

The 27 journals in English in the field of applied economics which Kawamata (2000) chose were:

> C: *Journal of Econometrics*, *Journal of Mathematical Economics*, *Journal of the American Statistical Association*, E: *Journal of Monetary Economics*, *Journal of Money, Credit, and Banking*, F: *Journal of International Economics*, G: *Journal of Finance*, *Journal of Financial and Quantitative Analysis*, *Journal of Financial Economics*, H: *Journal of Public Economics*, *Public Choice*, *Public Finance*, I: *Journal of Economic Education*, J: *Industrial and Labor Relations Review*, *Industrial Relations*, *Journal of Human*

Resources, K: *Journal of Law and Economics*, L: *Journal of Industrial Economics*, M: *Journal of Accounting Research*, *Journal of Business*, N: *Explorations in Economic History*, *Journal of Economic History*, O: *Journal of Development Economics*, Q: *American Journal of Agricultural Economics*, *Journal of Environmental Economics and Management*, R: *Journal of Regional Sciences*, *Journal of Urban Economics*.

Notes

1 This chapter is based on Ikeo (1990, 1991, 1993a, 1994a, 1996c, 2000a, 2006).

2 My personal communication with Takuma Yasui at the annual meeting of Japan Association of Economics and Econometrics (Japanese Economic Association since 1997) in Kwansei Gakuin University on October 13, 1990.

3 *Kyoto University Economic Review* is the first journal of economics written in Western languages in Japan and was established in 1926. See section 4.

4 We can find an example of Walrasian general equilibrium theory as the tradition of neoclassical economics in Jürg Niehans (1990: 313):

> In the early 1920s the progress of economic theory seemed to have slowed almost to a standstill. Hardly any original contributions were made between 1920 and 1925. The academic establishment was dominated by historicism, institutionalism, and pragmatism. The collection of facts had precedence over the collection of theories. Yet within twenty years economists saw their own science in a completely different light. The star of Léon Walras rose and that of Gustav Schmoller sank below the horizon.

I would not say that it is not important for historians of economics to pay attention to the German historical school anymore. See Yuichi Shionoya (2001) and Ikeo (2001, 2002b). We take note that Tokuzo Fukuda, who had studied in Germany, advised his students to make a special study of current economics other than the German historical school probably because he believed that students should get a wide knowledge of economic science rather than German, English or French economics which were attached with national adjectives.

5 It is noteworthy that, being an undergraduate student at the University of Chicago, Samuelson attended the graduate course in mathematical economics by Henry Schultz (1893–1938) around 1934. Schultz was probably the leading mathematical economist in the world. His extraordinary performance overwhelmed graduate students like Martin Bronfenbrenner (1997: Chapter 7).

6 See Kurz and Salvadori (1993).

7 Schumpeter could have got a chance to teach in Japan if he had wished. The Imperial University of Tokyo invited German-speaking economists for a two- or three-year term to promote the understanding of Western economics among their students and themselves. Emil Lederer taught there from 1923 through 1925. There was an interesting episode relating to the hunt for a German-speaking economist as a visiting professor after E. Lederer at the University of Tokyo. This short story appeared in the diary of Eijiro Kawai (1969, in Japanese: 167–74), who was the hunter traveling the German-speaking area in 1924 after he had spent about two years in England. Kawai's three targets were J. A. Schumpeter, L. von Mises and A. Amonn. In December 1924, Kawai met Amonn in Prague and von Mises and Schumpeter in Vienna to recruit one of them as a successor to Lederer. He received the sharpest impression from Schumpeter who looked to him like a samurai, a warrior in early modern Japan. All of the three candidates welcomed Kawai and enjoyed talking with him. But they needed time to make the final decision whether to accept or reject the unexpected offer from a

Japanese university. According to Kawai's diary, although von Mises sent him a very polite letter rejecting the offer, Schumpeter accepted the offer in a letter which Kawai received on December 27. However, this did not come to pass. Schumpeter became a professor at the University of Bonn and returned to European academism after being the Minister of Finance for Imperial Germany. This incident might have lead Schumpeter to visit Japan in 1931. Instead, Amonn arrived in Japan as a visiting professor in 1926. The process of negotiation showed a cosmopolitan spirit of the economists in Central Europe who had some interest in teaching in an Asian country and another root for Schumpeter's connection to Japan.

8 The transcript of Schumpeter's lectures appeared in university memoirs –Schumpeter (1931a, 1931b, 1931c, 1932) and the remaining part was published later (1982, 1991a, 1991b). Robert Loring Allen (1991, vol. 1: 270–3) summarized Schumpeter's visit to Japan. Yuichi Shionoya (1995) reflected the Japanese economists' reading of Schumpeter starting with his *Das Wesen und der Hauptinhalt der theoretischen Nationalökonomie* (1908), whose English version became available only in 2009 (Kanazashi 1991; Shionoya 1990). Arnold Heertje (1987), the entry on Schumpeter to the influential dictionary of economics *New Palgrave* (Eatwell *et al.* 1987), did not include Schumpeter (1908) in the list of selected works. The list started with Schumpeter (1912), whose English version (1934) made Schumpeter known widely in the English-speaking world.

9 Accessed on the website of the Mie Prefectural Library on April 29, 2013 (www.library.pref.mie.lg.jp/list/touhata/tokubetu/Schumpeter.htm).

10 Craver (1986: 28–30) and Weintraub (1987a).

11 Lange arrived at Chicago to teach mathematical economics because Henry Schultz planned to leave Chicago for California to establish a new graduate school of economics. However, he and his family died in an accident on their way to the new location of his place of assignment (personal communication with Teruko Bronfenbrenner in 2009).

12 A few months after Japan opened the war against the United States in December 1941, both governments agreed that they would exchange the Americans who stayed in Japan and preferred to return home and their Japanese counterparts by ship. The people exchanged were mainly diplomats, businessmen, scholars and students. The ships used for this purpose were commonly called *Kokansen*, which meant exchange ships.

13 A. Cowles's letter to K. Shibata of October 14, 1939 (Shibata 1934–79). According to the draft of his letter to Cowles dated December 9, 1939, Shibata could not accept the invitation because the Japanese government would not fund his travel expenses (Shibata 1934–79). In contrast, Shizuo Kakutani was lucky because he had an uncle who was the captain of a freight ship when he was invited from Princeton University (Chapter 6).

14 Several Japanese economic magazines, such as *Tokyo Keizai Zasshi* (*Tokyo Economist*), *Toyo Keizai Shinpo* (*The Oriental Economist*) and *Ekonomisuto*, modeled after the London *Economist* (established in 1843).

15 SCAP stood for the Supreme Commander for the Allied Powers and referred to General MacArthur himself and to the staff of his Tokyo headquarters. Japanese usually referred to SCAP as GHQ.

16 In 1884, Tanzan Ishibashi was born to a son of a Buddhist priest of the Nichiren sect. He studied mainly Oriental Philosophy at the School of Letters, Waseda University. He spent a year in the Army during the period with no combat before he secured the position of the editor of a periodical (which ended soon) in Toyo Keizai Shinposha in 1911.

17 E. B. Schumpeter (1940) found important economic facts relating to Japan. It depended on external areas for certain raw materials, including iron ore and scrap iron. It showed a marked increase in per capita production thanks to technical

improvements in spite of an increase of population. An Asiatic economic bloc under Japanese leadership was a possible development as long as Japan could conclude a satisfactory peace with China. Yet such a bloc would still need to have some trade relations with outside countries. It might be able to bargain for the strategic materials which it lacked with the raw materials which it would control. However, they did not maintain that it was a desirable development. Schumpeter (1940: 474) stated:

> The drive toward autarchy and a regional economic bloc is partly the consequence of insecurity and of the illiberal trade practices of the Western democracies in the past. How far it will go will depend on the outcome of the present war and on political developments in the future.

G. C. Allen suggested that the rise of discriminatory tariffs and quotas in foreign markets had influences on Japan's policies of industrial expansion and territorial enlargement (Schumpeter 1940: 785–6).

18 Bronfenbrenner's autobiography (1997) was paginated chapter by chapter. Therefore (15–5) means Chapter 15 and its page 5.

19 The ONR was essentially acting as the office of *national* research from the postwar period until around 1957, the year in which the Soviet Union launched Sputnik, the first unmanned space satellite (Sapolsky 1990: 38). Kenneth J. Arrow recalled his project at Stanford as follows:

> The title of the project was something like the Project on the Efficiency of Decision Making in the Economic System. It started in 1951 and continued through the 1960s. Scientific research in general has been promoted for defense purposes since the Second World War. It did not matter whether a project was directly related to defense or not. The role of promoting scientific research was gradually taken over by the National Science Foundation in the 1960s.
>
> (Personal communication with Kenneth J. Arrow in Tokyo on September 12, 1994)

The Arrow Paper at Duke University includes the document for the renewal of his project. The title of the project was "Project on the Efficiency of Decision Making in Economic Systems."

20 As shown in Ikeo (ed.) (2000), the practical field of economics, such as applied economics and economic policy studies, were published in Japanese to facilitate the understanding among the Japanese.

21 No one doubts that the linguistic barriers between Western languages and Japanese are more serious than that between German and English. P. R. Senn argued in his "What has happened to Gustav von Schmoller in English?" (1987) that it is most likely that it will take a long time before the English-only reader will get a satisfactory exposition of Schmoller's methods due to his language, German and the lack of translation. This may be one of the reasons why the German historical school declined after 1930, as suggested in Niehans (1990: 313).

22 The letter from Takashi Negishi to me on June 29, 1990 (Negishi 1990b, in Japanese). The recorded message from Negishi to Ikeo of September 12, 1990 (Negishi 1990c, in Japanese). See also Ikeo (1990: 122–3) and Negishi (2012, in Japanese).

3 Monetary economics and policy, 1868–1936[1]

1 Introduction

This chapter aims to clarify how the research of international monetary conditions promoted the internationalization of economics with focus on the Japanese case. By the end of the nineteenth century, the capital market was highly globalized and Japanese bankers, officials and business people conducted their business while closely observing international financial conditions. Financial expertise was gradually called for and scholars who were specialized in finance began to appear in Japan. Japanese scholars and bankers always paid attention to problems of monetary policy and changing monetary systems. They examined financial reports published throughout the world and absorbed monetary theories by reading the finance literature. In Japan, the first academic discussion that appeared in university journals was about the characteristics of the international gold standard and its relations with the domestic financial system, namely the infrastructure for transnational economic activities by Japanese. These discussions and researches promoted the internationalization of economics in Japan as well as in many other countries (De Vries 1996; Polak 1996).[2]

In the period between the two world wars, Japan always researched the individual conditions under which other developing countries borrowed money from Europe, especially Britain and France, where some financiers were eager to trade and invest in Japan. Japan was especially sensitive to the level of interest rates it paid for borrowing money from Europe for the construction of railroad lines and national defense. It can be said that Japanese bankers, officials and scholars were objective watchers of monetary events in the world. Therefore, it is useful to analyze the development of the international monetary policy discussion from the point of view of Japanese experts.[3] This will help us understand how the worldwide network of the economics profession, including the Japanese, was formed as Japan began to prepare for the adoption of the international gold standard. It is worth noting that the world monetary situation prior to World War II was different from that after the war since there was neither a World Bank nor an International Monetary Fund (IMF).

We start with Japan's adoption of the gold standard and the mathematician Rikitaro Fujisawa's proposal for "joint-metallism" in section 2. Fujisawa believed that international cooperation among Europe, North and South America, and Asia was needed for the stability of the international monetary standard in 1903. Section 3 shows that after major financial panics occurred in Germany and the United States in 1907, international economic experts paid serious attention to the two countries' domestic monetary systems and closely watched the reform of their respective systems. It reviews Kakujiro Yamazaki's findings in the early 1910s that few countries with a gold standard had gold currencies circulating in their countries. Other Japanese monetary economists began to discuss the characteristics of various types of the gold standard including the gold exchange standard. They became interested in Irving Fisher's monetary theory and his policy proposals as well as John Maynard Keynes's first book *Indian Currency and Finance* (1913).

Section 4 traces the international economic conferences regarding the postwar economic settlement and the relevant international monetary standard after World War I. Japanese economic experts including officials from the Bank of Japan (BOJ), the Ministry of Finance (MOF) and the Yokohama Specie Bank (the government-sponsored bank specialized in foreign exchange business, now Tokyo Mitsubishi Bank UFJ Group) actively participated in these conferences. They paid attention to Gustav Cassel and John Maynard Keynes, who appeared on the world stage with their objections to the return to the gold standard. Section 5 discusses Cassel's assessment (1926) of the Japanese currency and argues that it made Cassel well known in Japan. Sections 6 and 7 trace a part of the controversy over the return to the gold standard, and the upshot of the lifting of the gold embargo for the period of 23 months from January 1930 to December 1931. They show why Seibi Hijikata (the Imperial University of Tokyo) supported Japan's policy of returning to the gold standard at the old parity. From December 1931 to February 1936, Finance Minister Korekiyo Takahashi and an able central banker Eigo Fukai played a major role in deciding Japan's economic and monetary policies, including deficit financing and market operations. Section 7 draws some conclusions.

2 The question of two monetary standards: the proposal of "joint-metallism"

In 1854, the feudal government called the Tokugawa shogunate gave up its isolationist policy which had lasted for 215 years, and in 1868 it formally returned political power to the Japanese emperor. The newly established government took strong leadership to start the rapid modernization of the Japanese economy. It is noteworthy that Japanese merchants had already developed a nationwide clearing network by the use of bills for the trade of rice in the eighteenth century. It is also important that Japanese people were accustomed to using local paper money and small coins in their daily lives. Therefore, a large amount of money, in the form of gold, silver and copper coins, was usually kept in storehouses of merchants and did not move very much except for use in criminal activities. This kind of "modern" custom was relevant for a great transformation from a closed and self-sufficient economy to an open economy based on the division of labor and international trade and investment, which required a modern financial system including commercial banks, clearing houses, stock exchanges and foreign exchange.

The Japanese government adopted the system of the domestic gold standard with the yen as the basic monetary unit for domestic trade in 1871. It set 1,500 milligrams of gold to be equivalent to 1 yen. In 1878, Japan allowed trade-silver to circulate inside Japan and shifted to bimetallism, because Japan's neighboring countries such as China and Indo-China adopted the silver standard. The Yokohama Specie Bank started business as the foreign exchange bank in 1880 and managed to open a London branch in 1884. The Bank of Japan was established as the central bank in 1882. From around 1890 on, Japan began preparations for the adoption of the international gold standard, because the value of silver was rapidly decreasing and it was becoming a policy nightmare to constantly reset the appropriate exchange rate between gold and silver. It is not surprising that there was a strong trend toward gold from silver or bimetallism throughout the world. In 1893, India, which was a rich country in Asia until the 1950s, adopted the international gold standard without a gold currency in domestic circulation, namely with the circulation of silver currencies.

From August 1894 till March 1895, Japan fought and defeated China. The peace treaty resulted in the "independence" of Korea, the cession of Liaotong Peninsula, Taiwan Island and its neighboring islands, and the reparation of 200 million *liang* (or tael, the Chinese currency unit of the day) of gold from China.[4] However, their agreement prompted intervention by three countries, namely Russia, France and Germany. Russia, which had been making serious investment in China, voiced the strongest opposition among the three. France, which was allied with Russia, naturally took its side, while Germany, which was in control of Shandong, followed the lead of the other two. As a result, Japan did not get the Liaotong Peninsula, which was part of Manchuria (the northeast region of China) and was regarded as a first foothold for Japan on the Chinese continent. Japan was unhappy with the intervention, but it did not have enough economic and military power to resist it. On the other hand, the Japanese government and the Yokohama Specie Bank managed to persuade the Bank of England to open an account for the Yokohama Specie Bank to receive the huge reparation from China, which was estimated at about 14 million pounds sterling in February 1896 (Tamaki 1995: 84).

In 1896, the Japanese government passed a law for issuing bonds in order to expand its Army and Navy, to construct railroad lines and to encourage steel making. Also in 1896, Japanese national bonds, which were issued for the renovation of the government system after the Meiji Restoration in 1868, were for the first time listed on the London Stock Exchange. It was a necessary step towards the adoption of the international gold standard. In 1897, the Japanese government moved to the international gold standard and decided that 750 milligrams of gold would be equivalent to 1 yen. This represented a devaluation of the yen by half in terms of gold compared with the 1871 level. Thanks to its positive access to the financial network in the rest of the world, Japan was incorporated into the world capital market.

Since 1896, international monetary questions including the gold and silver standard had been big issues in Japan as in other countries around the world. Most countries were shifting from bimetallism toward the monometallic gold standard. Asia, China and French Indo-China stayed with the silver standard until the 1930s, whereas India, Korea and Japan moved toward adoption of the international gold standard in the 1890s. In China, one of the two important trade partners for Japan before World War II, no gold coins circulated except during the modest and futile attempt to circulate gold, made by Yunnan Province in 1918 (Soong 1937: 368). Silver had served as currency throughout China for centuries, at least since the T'ang Dynasty (AD *c.*825). In addition, the export of gold was also allowed in China until May 1930. In 1933, the Nationalist government undertook a major reform of the Chinese monetary system to facilitate the establishment of a modern, capitalist economy. In October 1934, it banned the export of silver and suspended its international silver standard. It seems that there was little support in the Chinese government for the adoption of the international gold standard (without a gold currency) as was done by India.[5]

Japan had to handle both standards in some way in order to engage in international trade not only with countries in Europe and America but also its neighbors in Asia. Rikitaro Fujisawa (1861–1933), mathematician at the Imperial University of Tokyo, discussed the international monetary issues on several occasions. In 1903, he proposed a new monetary system called joint-metallism, the mixture of gold and silver standard, instead of adopting the monometallic gold standard. His idea resembled Alfred Marshall's proposal of the so-called fixed-ratio-mintage proposed in 1886–7.[6]

Without knowing Marshall's idea, Fujisawa circulated a paper handwritten in English on this subject not only in Japan but also abroad. He had an idea of a managed currency system based on international cooperation and the exchange of statistical information through the establishment of an international monetary bureau, which was vaguely similar to the International Bureau of Weights and Measures or the International Postal Bureau. The task of the bureau was supposed to be confined within the limits of scientific investigation and executive function. Fujisawa (1903; FMC 1935, vol. 3: 203–4) wrote as follows:

> The work of the International Monetary Bureau is to be strictly limited to gathering by various means trustworthy statistical facts, investigating various aspects of monetary problems and supplying necessary data to the international monetary conference.… Even if joint-metallism should fail to prove itself to be worthy of being actually adopted, the erection of such a bureau is extremely desirable and will surely prove to be the first step towards a satisfactory solution of the silver question.
>
> Any agreement of an international character, if it be at all possible, is to be arrived at an international monetary conference. Such conferences may be held … at a regular interval and also whenever there occurs necessity.

> Some of the more important works of the first conference, on the eve of the adoption of joint-metallism, will be the fixing of the ratio and the jointage ratio together with the allowance which defines the lower limit of the issue of full-value silver coins by the mint of an individual country. The later conferences will have chiefly to deal with alteration, respectively, non-alteration of the jointage ratio.
>
> (Originally written in English)

Fujisawa recognized the importance of international cooperation for stable currencies.[7] Moreover, Fujisawa in this paper neither used the word "parity" nor mentioned what kind of statistical data was to be collected for international monetary conferences. Yet it can be said that his proposal of gathering such data for determining the parity of each currency anticipated the theory of purchasing-power parity, which was later developed by the Swedish economist Gustav Cassel just after World War I.

It is also noteworthy that the two high population countries in Asia, namely China and India, took separate courses on the international monetary issue. As mentioned, China retained a silver standard with silver currencies. In contrast, India moved from the silver standard towards a monetary system of "a gold standard without a gold currency." India's monetary policy was one of the hot issues after India announced the adoption of "international gold standard" in 1889, and the situation was investigated by the Royal Commission on the Indian Monetary System. At least for Fujisawa, the case of India's policy was an example of abnormal monetary conditions. Fujisawa (1903; FMC 1935, vol. 3: 207–8) criticized India's situation from an investor's point of view as follows:

> It seems to me that the present is the high time for supplanting the practice of applying hasty and short-sighted remedy to any pressing local evils in monetary affairs, which, in the long run, can not but end in evils of perhaps greater magnitude, and substituting in its place a far-reaching policy based on world-wide considerations. Let us think not only of the depreciation of silver, but also the depreciation of the capital already invested and, above all, those which are destined to be invested on a silver basis. Let us be reminded of the vast resources, in regions which must inevitably remain silver countries for some long time to come, awaiting the capital of the gold countries.
>
> (Originally written in English)

Fujisawa (1903) believed that it was better for many countries to adopt similar domestic monetary institutions in order to gain more benefits from the globalization of the capital market. By considering those countries which had obstacles for adopting the international gold standard, Fujisawa proposed joint-metallism, which was to peg national exchange rates to a certain set of stable rates on the basis of relevant economic data which were to be collected and processed through the collaboration of national monetary authorities. Fujisawa, a Japanese scholar, like Marshal and Cassel, made a proposal for solving a difficulty for smooth international commerce. He "exported" his economic idea, joint-metallism, to the rest of the world by sending a copy.

From the viewpoint of the history of economics in Japan, Fujisawa's first contribution to this field was the publication of his *Life Insurance* (1889, in Japanese). Actually it was the first book on life insurance written in Japanese. Moreover, Fujisawa was the first Japanese person who had mastered Western mathematics, which is, needless to say, consistent with and more efficient than Japanese traditional mathematics called *Wasan* (Chapter 5; Ikeo 1994a). Fujisawa (1889) lucidly explained probable knowledge and the role of life insurance, and then calculated premium and insurance based on the latest data on Japanese life expectancy. Since around the early 1900s, he had occasionally written papers on monetary affairs which were mostly brought by the interdependence of the domestic financial system and the global capital market (Fujisawa 1906, 1925a, 1925b, in Japanese). We will have another chance to focus on Fujisawa's speech and writings.

3 The first Japanese economists and the gold exchange standard

As shown in Table 3.1, the monetary systems of the United States and Germany as well as China became an important issue in 1907 (BOJ 1982–4, in Japanese). On October 17, a severe financial crisis happened in Hamburg and American securities were sold in large amounts by Europeans. During the first three weeks of October exchange rates were in the neighborhood of the export point. On October 19, $1.5 million was for shipment to Germany from the United States (Sprague 1910: 246). On October 17, the third sharp decline of stock prices in New York that year occurred and it led to another financial panic after the suspension of payment by the Knickerbocker Trust Company of October 22, this time in the United States. The Knickerbocker Trust Company was the third largest trust company in New York. It was neither a bank nor a member of the clearing house. Sprague (1910: 319) said:

> It is impossible to escape the depressing conclusion that the banking situation in 1907 was handled less skillfully and boldly than in 1893, and far less so than in 1873.... A situation which was certainly less serious than in 1873 or 1893 and probably less serious than 1884 was allowed to drift into the most complete interruption of its banking facilities that the country has experienced since the civil war.

Americans tried to withdraw their money from French markets in order to settle their domestic troubles. The money which the Americans were withdrawing was potentially destabilizing for the French market. Therefore, France had to take some measures to prevent a derived panic in Paris, and fortunately managed to get help from Britain. Yet this was not the first case of international cooperation

Table 3.1 Financial events in 1907

March 14	The first great crash that year on the New York Stock Exchange
August 7	The second great crash started on the New York Stock Exchange
October 17	A financial crisis in Hamburg
October 17	The third great crash started on the New York Stock Exchange
October 22	The suspension of payment by the Knickerbocker Trust Company triggered a financial crisis in the United States
November	A financial crisis in China due to the instability of silver currency

Source: *Chronological Table of Japanese Finance, 1868–1992*, BOJ 1993, in Japanese.

during a financial panic. The collaboration of Britain, France, Germany, Russia and other countries became important for the defense of the gold standard in Europe already as early as 1890 (Eichengreen 1995: Chapter 2). It seemed that each country must have some confident monetary authority in order to take the effective policy action needed for monetary stability among several countries.

The German and American governments respectively formed commissions to make comparative studies of the financial systems and central banking in Britain, France, Germany, the United States and Japan for the reform of their own financial institutions. Their final reports became available in 1908 and 1911 (Sprague 1910; Tsurumi 1983, in Japanese). The report entitled "The Banking System of Japan" (Katsura *et al.* 1911) was submitted under the name of Marquis Katsura, Baron Sakatani and S. Naruse to the US National Monetary Commission and stated that based on the experience of establishing the Bank of Japan it was essential to establish the central bank in the United States which had no central bank at the time. O. M. W. Sprague responded to the suggestion and stated that such Japanese experience was not useful for the US because Japan adopted the central banking system under the single bank and the Bank of Japan did not take active policy measures for its domestic economy (Katsura *et al.* 1911). Needless to say, the Japanese government, bankers and economists were seriously reading these reports and comments, and examined the discussions of banking and finance and the related economic ideas including the theory of money. They also read the increasing number of articles and reports on monetary issues appearing in the economics journals written in English such as *Quarterly Journal of Economics* (1886–), *Economic Journal* (1890–), *Journal of Political Economy* (1893–), and the newly established *American Economic Review* (1911–).

In the early 1910s, there were a few Japanese monetary experts in academia and Irving Fisher was the economist they cited most.[8] Among them, Kakujiro Yamazaki (1868–1945) was the best informed monetary economist in Japan from around 1910 until the late 1920s. Yamazaki studied in Germany from 1891 until 1895. He worked for the Technical School of the Imperial University of Tokyo (now the University of Tokyo), the Ministry of Agriculture and Commerce, the Tokyo College of Commerce (now Hitotsubashi University),

Kakegawa Bank and others, before he was appointed as associate professor at the Law School of the Imperial University of Tokyo in 1902. Yamazaki started to teach at the Faculty of Economics, which was newly established by separating from the Law School in 1919. He had close contact with the mathematician Rikitaro Fujisawa, Japanese central bankers and commercial bankers, and economic journalists.[9]

Masao Kanbe (1913a, in Japanese), professor at Kyoto Imperial University, picked up Fisher's plan for a compensated dollar, which was later called "a monetary standard based on price index," to solve the problem of rising living costs (Fisher 1913a). Kanbe somewhat confusedly called Fisher's plan "a compensated gold standard" and also called attention to Muleman's plan for expanding gold reserve. As shown in Table 3.2, Kanbe (1913a) initiated intensive discussion over the monetary standard in general among Japanese monetary economists including Kakujiro Yamazaki of Tokyo Imperial University and

Table 3.2 Japanese debate on the gold standard, 1911–14

1911	K. Yamazaki (1911) 'On the countries with the gold standard without gold currencies.' *Hogaku Kyokai Zasshi*, 29(5): 669–82.
1912	K. Yamazaki (1912) *A Consideration of the Problems in Money and Banking*. Tokyo: Yuhikaku Shobo. Fourth edition, 1920.
1913, March	M. Kanbe (1913a) 'On the plan of eliminating the bad effect of the increase in gold production on money.' *Hogaku Shinpo*, 23(3): 23–33.
June	K. Yamazaki (1913a) 'On Professor Fisher's Plan for compensating the Value of Money.' *Kokka Gakkai Zasshi*, 27(6): 817–38.
July	S. Takagi (1913a) 'On Dr. Kanbe and Yamazaki's comments on Mr. Fisher's plan of compensating the level of prices.' *Kokka Gakkai Zasshi*, 27(7): 981–1007.
August	M. Kanbe (1913b) 'Comments on the comments on the comments on Fisher's compensated dollar plan.' *Kokka Gakkai Zasshi*, 27(8): 1189–204. Yamazaki (1913b) 'Answers to Mr. Senjiro Takagi's comments on Professor Fisher's Plan.' *Kokka Gakkai Zasshi*, 27(8): 1205–17.
September	S. Takagi (1913b) 'Answers to Dr. Kanbe on the value of money.' *Kokka Gakkai Zasshi*, 27(9): 1377–97.
October	S. Takagi (1913c) 'Questions to Dr. Yamazaki on the compensation of money, II.' *Kokka Gakkai Zasshi*, 27(10): 1457–90.
1914, January	K. Yamazaki (1914a) 'Answers to Professor Takagi on the value of money, II.' *Kokka Gakkai Zasshi*, 28(1): 55–76.
April	S. Takagi (1914) 'Answers to Dr. Kanbe and Yamazaki on the value of money.' *Kokka Gakkai Zasshi*, 28(4): 537–62. K. Yamazaki (1914b) 'On the countries with the gold standard without gold currencies, reconsidered.' *Hogaku Kyokai Zasshi*, 32: 4, 553–74.
1915	S. Takashima (1915) *Principles of Money and Prices*. Tokyo: Saibunkan.

Senjiro Takagi of Keiogijuku. The three economists also referred to many papers which were published in *American Economic Review* and *Quarterly Journal of Economics*, including those of Fisher (1911, 1912a, 1912b, 1912c, 1912d, 1913a, 1913b). They followed the rule of writing research articles that an author should clarify their own view or opinion distinctly from other professionals' view or opinion in the writing.

Yamazaki (1911, 1914b) surveyed the real situation of those countries which officially adopted the gold standard, and reached the conclusion that almost no gold currencies were circulated inside these countries. Yamazaki (1911) examined the case of Japan and noted that he had never seen any gold currency in circulation in Japan, although the recent report of the Ministry of Finance stated that the supply of gold coins was more than 320 billion yen. He conjectured that a large number of gold coins might be "consumed" as artistic handicrafts and other industrial arts. He argued that Japan was not an exception and listed Austria and the Netherlands as similar cases, referring to L. von Mises (1909), and Ph. Kalkmann (1901). He pointed out that those countries with the gold exchange standard, such as India and the Philippines, did not aim to circulate gold currencies. Yamazaki (1911) discussed the question of whether it was legitimate to state that these countries had adopted the gold standard. He reached the positive answer, which is now common sense. The current system was a gold standard, as long as the government owned a large amount of gold in bars or bricks, large enough to keep the standard unit of currency at the value of a fixed weight of gold, and it was ready to supply gold and allowed free minting, even if no gold currency circulated inside the country. Yamazaki (1912) articulated his points again.

Yamazaki (1914b) added other examples such as the United States (except the state of California), Belgium, Italy, Sweden, Norway, Denmark and Russia. Compared with these countries, Britain, Germany and France, which were richer countries, circulated a little more gold currency. Yamazaki referred to papers written by Irving Fisher, Ernst Wilmersdorffer and J. Plenge as well as statistical books. Yamazaki (1914b: 560–1) maintained that paper money must have the same credibility as gold currency. Otherwise, people would have asked the monetary authority to convert their paper money into gold coins. He pointed out that the function of deposit money was becoming increasingly important for domestic trade. Yamazaki (1914b: 564–5) agreed with Keynes (1913) that gold was an international currency, not a local currency. Yamazaki argued that this differentiation of the function of money corresponded to Plenge's *Weltgeld* (world money) and *Landesgeld* (local money) (Plenge 1913: 119–22). Yamazaki reported that some British monetary experts persistently objected to the gold standard without gold currency. For example, Lord Farrer, Lord Rothschild, Sir John Lubbock, Samuel Montague and Alfred de Rothschild believed that it was imperative to circulate gold currencies under the gold standard.

In this way, by citing related articles and books, Japanese economists debated the gold standard and the quantity theory of money. Saichiro Takashima (1915) surveyed not only the international monetary discussion in Japan but also the extensive literature on money and prices which was available to him. He was reading the increasing number of articles on monetary issues appearing in the economics journals written in English such as *Quarterly Journal of Economics*, *Economic Journal*, *Journal of Political Economy* and *American Economic Review*. Takashima (1915) placed at the center the quantity theory of money presented by Irving Fisher (1911) and in a series of articles published in the journals above. This is not surprising because Fisher was the most cited and prolific economic writer in the world in the 1910s. Takashima wrote in the introduction as follows (Takashima 1915: i–ii):

> Professor Irving Fisher's [*The*] *Purchasing Power of Money* (1911) has been read so widely [and printed so many times] that the price of paper in Luoyang went up [an old Japanese saying indicating praise for an excellent book]. He is the leading American economist who advocates the quantity theory of money and provokes economists both in the East and the West. I have comprehended the book and mainly followed Fisher's monetary theory. I also summarized the views opposed to the quantity theory, which were represented by Professor J. Laurence Laughlin's *The Principles of Money* (1903). I also relied on D. A. Barker's [*The*] *Theory of Money* (1913), which was published in the series of "The Cambridge Manuals of Science and Literature." I traced not only Fisher and Laughlin, but also David Kinley, E. W. Kemmerer, David Ricardo, W. S. Jevons, Sir David Barbour, J. S. Nicholson, L. L. Price, Henry Sidgwick, Carl Menger, F. W. Taussig, Horace White, J. F. Johnson, Charles Conant, and Alexander Del Mar. I place at the center of the book the quantity theory of money, which is true beyond dispute but ever in dispute, as described by Lord Barbour (Introduction to D. M. Barbour's *The Influence of the Gold Supply on Prices and Profits* (1913)).
>
> (My translation with reference to Takashima's list of references)

The contents of Takashima (1915) are as follows:

Chapter 1 – The functions of money, especially the standard of deferred payments
Chapter 2 – The algebraic explanation of the exchange equation
Chapter 3 – The hydraulic explanation of the exchange equation
Chapter 4 – The velocity of money and current account
Chapter 5 – Quantity theory or production cost theory
Chapter 6 – The measurement of price changes
Chapter 7 – The policies for stabilizing the value of money

Appendices The new trend in monetary system of major countries and the European War:

(1) The discussion of the new currency policy in the leading countries, relating to the working of the Indian currency system
(2) Reading the report on Indian finance and currency in relating to the gold exchange standard

(3) New currency policy and the European War
(4) Germany's financial mobilization and its new currency policy

The first half of Takashima (1915) surveyed contemporary theories of money and prices. In Chapter 1, he surveyed the discussion of the function of money by referring to more than 20 authors from Adam Smith to the Japanese Kiichiro Soda. Takashima focused his attention on the standard for deferred payment and quoted from Henry Sidgwick: "Money is that which passes freely from owner to owner throughout the community in final discharge of debts and full payment for commodities" (Takashima 1915: 143). In Chapters 2–5, mainly following Fisher, he gave an algebraic explanation of the exchange equation, a hydraulic explanation of the exchange equation, and a discussion of the velocity of cash and checking accounts. In Chapter 5, he explained the production cost theory of money and compared it with the quantity theory without making any significant comments. In Chapter 6, he discussed how to measure the changes in prices through the method of index numbers. In Chapter 7, he illustrated policies for stabilizing currency and surveyed the discussion of a desirable system for an international monetary standard, that is, gold, silver or bimetallism. He agreed with Fisher in comparing the quantity theory in economics to the Euclidean theorem in geometry. Fisher (1911) restated the quantity theory of money and adopted an algebraic statement of the equation of exchange. $MV=PT$. This formula says that the money stock in circulation M times its velocity V equals the price level P times the volume of trade T. Fisher used various statistical data and deeply impressed Japanese economists.

The second half of Takashima (1915) gave a review of major current monetary topics such as Indian currency and the financial mobilization for World War I or the European War. His appendix 1 made intensive reference to Keynes's *Indian Currency and Finance* (1913) (see Chapter 9). Appendix 2 summarized J. S. Nicholson (1914), which was a critical review of Keynes (1913). India suffered from the depreciating rupee silver coin against the gold exchange rate due to the declining value of silver against gold. The instability of the rupee affected international trade between India and Britain. Appendix 3 and 4 reviewed Charles A. Conant's "Currency policy and the European War" (1914) and Ludwig Bendix's "Germany's financial mobilization" (1915) respectively. Policy-oriented economists were concerned about the monetary measures which were implemented at the very initial stages of the European War.

4 The managed currency and international economic conferences

The war, which was triggered by the assassination of the Austrian Crown Prince in Sarajevo in 1914, involved not only major European countries, such as Germany, Austria-Hungary, France, Italy, Belgium, the United Kingdom and Russia, but also the United States and Japan, and thus became a world war. This abnormal situation of a world war brought many changes and temporary measures in both international and domestic government policies, and gave governments the chance for bold interference in economic processes through mobilization. Both the fighting and neutral countries abandoned the international gold standard and controlled international trade. It is very important to note that until around the mid 1930s the international gold standard was believed to be the keystone of world free trade.

After the ceasefire of World War I in November 1918, people realized the situation of the world economy had dramatically changed from the prewar period. On one hand, the European countries which were the main fields of battle suffered from reduced productivity, especially in consumer goods, the accumulation of internal and external debt, and severe inflation. On the other hand, the neutral countries in Europe, such as Sweden, Denmark, the Netherlands, Switzerland and Spain, but also since they were far from the battlefield, the United States, Argentina and Japan, received large amounts of gold and foreign currencies due to their massive exports during the war. They not only increased their exports to the fighting countries, but also exported the merchandise which the fighting countries had stopped shipping to other regions.

During World War I, Japan was on the side of the Allies and its financial position was changed due to the sharp increase in its exports for the first time in its history. In 1914, Japan promptly took over the German colonies in China in spite of the protest of the Chinese government. It did not send many soldiers to the European military fields but it supplied munitions for the allied countries. Japan's exports of cotton goods and other industrial products to Asian countries were increased because of the cessation of exports from Europe. Japan's exports of silk to the United States also increased because the US economy was on the upswing due to Europe's demand for munitions. As a result of its rising exports, Japan became a creditor country. Its reserve rose from 376 million yen at the end of 1913 to 2,178 million yen at the end of 1920. The reserves of the United States rose from 1,924 million dollars to 2,929 million dollars during the same period, and the United States was the first to lift the embargo on gold exports in June 1919. Other countries including those in Europe and Japan bided their time in returning to the international gold standard.

The Japanese government chose not to return to the international gold standard at this time. They were extremely concerned about the political instability of neighboring countries such as China and Russia. Several officials decided to hold on to the reserve of gold and foreign currencies and not lift the gold embargo for a time in order to look for better opportunities for direct investment, including the construction of railroad lines in China. In China, people were upset when it was decided in Paris that the German colonies in the northeast area of China were to be taken over by Japan and not returned to China. College students in Beijing initiated a major protest movement on May 4, 1919. It was known as the May Fourth Movement (Lie 1997). In addition, Japan was worried about the Russian political situation and its foreign strategy. Responding to the decision by the leaders of the Allies such as Britain and France in late 1917 to prevent the Soviet revolutionary government from expanding throughout Russia,

Japan sent their soldiers to Siberia in August 1918. However, the anti-revolutionary government in west Siberia fell in late 1919, and the United States, Britain and France withdraw their entire forces from Siberia by June 1920. Nonetheless, Japan kept its soldiers there until October 1922.

In 1919, the Principal Allied and Associated States, including Japan, held the peace conference at Versailles, dealt with the reparation problems of Germany, and began to cooperate consciously toward peace-making after the war. Fifty-eight Japanese officers, including the chief delegate Kinmochi Saionji and Korekiyo Takahashi, visited Paris and participated in the Paris Peace Conference. Also in 1919, the League of Nations was established for further cooperation for free trade and peace-making. After the conference, Japan became a member of the League of Nations Council, though not of the inner committee of the participants.

Through the international conferences during and after the war, a few economists, including Gustav Cassel and John Maynard Keynes, appeared prominently in discussions of the international monetary system. In 1918, the Swedish Cassel advocated his new theory of purchasing-power parity as a guide for each government to set its exchange rate. Cassel (1918: 413) maintained:

> [T]he rate of exchange between two countries is primarily determined by the quotient between the internal purchasing power against goods of the money of each country. The general inflation which has taken place during the war has lowered this purchasing power in all countries, though in a very different degree, and the rates of exchanges should accordingly be expected to deviate from their old parity in proportion to the inflation of each country.
>
> At every moment the real parity between two countries is represented by this quotient between the purchasing power of the money in the one country and the other.

Cassel first in his 1918 article called this parity "the theoretical exchange rate," but later proposed to call this parity "the purchasing power parity" (Cassel 1921a: 37).[10] He further developed this way of thinking and clarified the limitation of the gold standard in his *Money and Foreign Exchange after 1914* (1922).[11] He objected to the return to the gold standard for three reasons. First, there was no guarantee that the price of gold relative to the general prices would be stable in the future. Second, the general price level might be unstable due to the instability in the supply of gold in the longer run. Third, the rise of prices in one country might cause the rise of prices in other countries under the system of the international gold standard. Therefore, he argued that without the international gold standard, when the level of prices changed in one country and not in another, the exchange rate between two countries would change so as to absorb the relative differences in changes of the purchasing-power parity. In other words, the inflation in one country would not be transmitted to the other thanks to the changes in the exchange rates.

The postwar difficulties, which had been caused by the inconsistency between the international monetary system and each domestic monetary institution, not only affected each country's domestic economy but also resulted in international economic problems, such as the instability of exchange rates and the impairment of international trade. Therefore, a series of conferences were held in Europe.

In September and October 1920, the International Financial Conference was held in Brussels for a fortnight under the auspices of the League of Nations. There were 86 experts, who were supposed not to commit themselves to making government policies in their own countries, from 39 nations, including Japan, in attendance. They discussed the then current financial crisis, and searched for solutions relating to finance, currency and exchange, trade, and international financial cooperation. They formed four commissions, namely the Commission on Public Finance, the Commission on Currency and Exchange (CCE), the Commission on International Trade, and the Commission on International Credit (CIC). They exchanged personal opinions and adopted unanimously the resolutions proposed by each of the four commissions.

Eigo Fukai, a Japanese central banker and participant in the conference, thought that these resolutions were abstract, mild and mediocre.[12] Fukai (1929) believed that the most important thing was that experts from various countries did reach four sets of unanimous resolutions through the multilateral exchange of opinions at the same table. He summarized the resolutions proposed by the CCE and the CIC as follows:

(1) Each government and municipality should stick to the rule of sound public finance. In other words, it must limit their expenditure to their revenue. (I, II, IV)
(2) The central bank (bank of issuance) should be freed from political pressures. (III)
(3) The bank rate should be raised for the adjustment of credit. (V)
(4) Commerce should be freed from control. (VI)
(5) The return to the viable gold standard is recommended. Each country does not have to return to the old parity. (VII, VIII, IX, X)
(6) In countries where there is no central bank of issue, one should be established. (XIV)
(7) Attempts to limit fluctuations in exchange by imposing artificial control on exchange operations are futile and mischievous. (XV)
(8) An international organization, which facilitates loans for a country to pay for their imports, should be established.
(9) It is desirable to establish an international organization for the settlements of accounts.

Here, the Roman numerals in parentheses correspond to the ones in the resolutions proposed by the CCE, and (8) and (9) are related to the resolutions proposed by the CIC. These resolutions reflected the then consensus reached by economists from the world. However, it did not take long before economists departed from this consensus. John Maynard Keynes would later criticize (1) as the Treasury View during the Great Depression because it would further worsen the economic conditions. With regard to (2), central banks were exposed to political pressure after the spread of Keynesianism. In (3), a kind of austerity policy was necessary to curb the severe postwar inflation. Internationally oriented economists supported and continue to support (4). The promotion of international trade became one of the important measures to growing economies worldwide and keeping peace in the global economy after World War I. In (5), it is implied that Cassel's theory of purchasing-power parity was accepted immediately to consider a relevant parity. Number (6) refers to the idea that a central bank which has the exclusive right to issue notes should be established in each country. Actually central banks are needed to organize international collaboration of monetary policies. It is noted in (7) that without any benefit it is harmful to interfere with the movement of exchange rates. Numbers (8) and (9) were covered to some degree by the Bank for International Settlement, which was established in 1930 for the purpose of allocating the money received as reparation payment from Germany among member countries. We had to wait until the end of World War II for the establishment of the World Bank and the International Monetary Fund (IMF).

In April and May 1922, the International Economic Conference was held for 40 days in Genoa, Italy. The organizing countries were the United Kingdom, France, Italy, Belgium and Japan. Thirty-one countries sent their experts to the conference, including Russia (the Soviet government) and Germany, which did not attend the Brussels conference in 1920. On the other hand, the United States did not attend the Genoa conference, although it was an active participant in Brussels. The United States was ready to give financial support for Europe to make an economic recovery, and held the Washington conference for disarmament in 1921. However, the US government came to look suspiciously on the European countries, which tended to introduce political disputes into the discussion of economic matters. As a result, the United States kept its distance from multilateral "economic" cooperation (K. Mori 1922, in Japanese: 43). The most important and urgent currency issue for the remaining countries was when and how to return to the international gold standard including the gold exchange standard, which was regarded as the most realistic choice. The representatives from Japan at the Genoa conference included Kengo Mori (Ministry of Finance) and Eigo Fukai (Bank of Japan) (Mori 1922, in Japanese; Fukai 1922, in Japanese).

Starting in March 1920, the Japanese economy was hit by a panic which marked the end of the postwar prosperity. The collapse of the stock exchange was followed by a halt in commercial transactions, dwindling international trade and falling prices. Eigo Fukai pointed out that the Japanese government postponed taking necessary measures to cure the economic troubles. Fukai (1937: 381) wrote:

> Despite a heavy decline in profits, the habits of extravagance and high living still remained, and financial reserves accumulated during the boom period were allowed to be dissipated. In the money market, too, the disposition to

> extreme caution was gradually subdued, and currency and credit, which for a time had tended to contract, tended to expand again.... High prices at home impeded the advance of, and actually caused a considerable decline in, the export trade, with the result that the markets for our goods in the East and the South Seas secured during the War were being lost. In contrast, various kinds of commodities were increasingly imported because of the disparity in prices obtaining at home and abroad. The balance of trade continued to be heavily against us and the country's holdings of foreign funds had to be drawn upon steadily for exchange purposes.
>
> (Originally written in English)

On September 1, 1923, the Tokyo Metropolitan Area and Yokohama were hit by major earthquakes. The death toll was 142,807 with 575,394 houses destroyed. The damage in Tokyo was estimated at 5.5 billion yen, which was about 3.8 times larger than the government budget of 1922, 1,470 million yen. The Japanese government was forced to borrow money from abroad. The would-be creditors demanded that seismologists predict the probability that Japan would be hit by another series of major earthquakes in the future. If another major earthquake hit Japan, their investment would be lost. In addition, the bonds which were issued for the economic reconstruction after the Russo-Japanese War (1904–5) at 4 percent interest were scheduled to mature in 1924. The Japanese government had to roll over the debt. The government had no choice but to boldly float a composite loan, namely floating a new loan and rolling over an old debt at the same time. They floated a composite loan of 150 million US dollars at a 6.5 percent interest rate and another of 25 million pounds sterling at a 6 percent interest rate. Japanese officials believed that the interest rate they had come to pay for the 1924 loan was extremely high because Japan had not adopted the international gold standard again as yet. Japan was not at all ready to return to the international gold standard in the aftermath of the earthquake in Tokyo, although it had been anxious to make such a return (Fujimura 1992b, in Japanese).

The mathematician Rikitaro Fujisawa, one of the best informed on international situations at the time, believed that it was too early for Japan to return to the gold standard. He expected the British government to take some measure related to the gold standard in the near future. He gave a talk entitled "On the changes in the value of currency and the payment of a long term loan" at a meeting of the Japan Actuary Society on March 29, 1925. His address went as follows (Fujisawa 1925a; FMC 1934, vol. 1: 365–6):

> In England, their return to the gold bullion standard has become a topic of conversation. Needless to say, the gold bullion standard requires three conditions, namely first the lifting of the gold embargo, second the unlimited minting of gold coins, and third the unconditional conversion of notes into gold. The 1920 law that has banned the export of gold and silver will become invalid at the end of this year. The British government should make

> some decision in the near future, at least by this coming summer. In fact, the related questions were asked to the British government at a gathering of the British House of Commons three days ago (on March 26). The rate of the sterling against the US dollar is rising recently and approaching the parity of $4.86. I assume there is speculation of Britain's return to the gold standard.... About ten days ago (on March 18), Mr. Keynes made an address at the British House of Commons and strongly maintained that it was no good for Britain to return to the gold bullion standard. I do not know the details because the news was sent by cable. I assume that he doubts that economic stability would follow after the return. In other words, he must have the same reason as I have in objecting to Japan's lifting of the gold embargo at this moment.
>
> (My translation)

In spite of Keynes's strong opposition and Fujisawa's negative statement, the British government decided to return to the gold standard at the prewar parity in April 1925.[13] In October, Fujisawa was worried about the speculation against the Japanese yen on Wall Street (Fujisawa 1925b, in Japanese; FMC 1934, vol. 1: 380). Japan had to await a better opportunity to return to gold. Many other countries were returning to the gold standard starting in the mid 1920s. In April 1924, Sweden resumed converting banknotes into gold at the old parity and lifted the embargo on gold exports. In 1925, the Netherlands and South Africa lifted the embargo on gold exports at the prewar parity. In 1926, the Canadian law that had banned the export of gold became invalid. In 1927, Italy adopted the gold exchange standard at a new, lower parity, which was less than a third of the prewar parity. In 1928, France lifted the gold embargo at about a fifth of the prewar parity.

5 The purchasing power of the Japanese yen

After around the mid 1920s, many countries around the world were returning to the international gold standard, in spite of Gustav Cassel and J. M. Keynes's opinions against it. However, Cassel's idea of purchasing-power parity was useful for the discussion about the level of parity that each country should choose through consideration of the difference in the inflation rates among various countries. Cassel's study of the Japanese yen had an influence on the debate about the parity Japan should choose in returning to the gold standard.

Japan was an attractive target for investment by European and American firms in the 1920s. For example, a Swedish ball-bearing company requested that Gustav Cassel perform a study of the Japanese currency and gave the result to the Japanese government as a mark of courtesy. Cassel wrote in his autobiography (Cassel 1941–2, vol. 2: 86) as follows:

> Svenska kullagerfabriken [a Swedish ball-bearing company] wished, in 1925, as a mark of courtesy to give the Japanese Government a study on the

> Japanese currency, and asked me to perform this study. Therefore, I wrote a memorandum on "The Japanese Currency," which was printed in a very nice quarto, and in a fine suede leather binding handed over to the Japanese ambassador in Stockholm, and to the Japanese Government in Tokio.
>
> (Translated from Swedish by Bo Sandelin)

It seems that the Japanese government handed Cassel's "The Japanese Currency" (1926) over to scholars of the Imperial University of Tokyo, R. Fujisawa and K. Yamazaki. The Japanese version of Cassel's paper appeared in a journal of bankers *Ginko Tsushinroku* (Bankers' Correspondence issued by Tokyo Ginko Shukaijo) in 1926. Cassel's findings and discussion went as follows. First, during 1914 and 1923 the international value of the Japanese yen in terms of gold was remarkably stable, in spite of wide variation in the internal purchasing power of the yen as compared with that of gold. Second, Cassel examined the value of the yen against the US dollar in referring to the differences between price indexes of these countries after the start of World War I. The Japanese exchange had been almost unaltered from 1921 to the end of 1923, in spite of the fact that the price level of Japan was much less reduced that of the United States during the same period. Cassel pointed out that an overvaluation of the yen took place and this overvaluation amounted to 17 percent for 1921 and 11 percent for 1922–3. However, after the major earthquakes hit Japan in September 1923, the international value of the Japanese yen was depreciated and the former overvaluation of the yen disappeared, whereas the internal value of the yen was recovered shortly after a slight inflation in the Japanese economy. The average rate of exchange of the Japanese yen against the US dollar in mid 1925 was 18 percent lower than the prewar level. Cassel (1926: 13–14) recommended that Japan should return to the gold standard at the current exchange rate, not the old rate, and gave a serious warning as follows:

> [T]here is a choice only between two alternatives: a stabilization of the currency at its present value or a return to the old gold par. From the point of view of the economic interest of the country, the first alternative is without doubt to be preferred.... A return to the old gold parity ... means a reduction of the present price level by something about 15%. Of course, such a depression of price is possible. It is a painful process, inevitably involving heavy losses to producers.... As soon as people really come to believe in the official aim of the monetary policy of the country, internal prices will begin to fall violently and at the same time speculation will force up the external value of the currency. If, therefore, Japan chooses to restore its currency to the old gold par, the country should be prepared to have a process of deflation carried through during a very short period.

Cassel's 1926 paper contributed to the fervent debate over Japan's return to the gold standard and the parity of the Japanese currency. Rikitaro Fujisawa gave a copy of Cassel's original paper to Tanzan Ishibashi, an influential economic journalist. Ishibashi summarized Cassel's argument in Japanese in a popular weekly *Toyo Keizai Shinpo* in 1926 (Ishibashi 1929, in Japanese: 130–45). Then Ishibashi began to strongly advocate Japan's return to the gold standard at a lower parity than the prewar level. T. Ishibashi's argument was supported by Kamekichi Takahashi, Toshie Obama, Yasuzumi Yamazaki and Senjiro Takagi (Toyo Keizai Shinposha 1996, in Japanese: 498–510).

However, the continual fluctuations and depreciation of the currency value were arousing popular attention, and the issue of the removal of the gold embargo was occasionally raised. During the period from 1921 to 1923, the level of the exchange rate of the Japanese yen against the US dollar was maintained at 47 to 48 dollars for 100 yen even after the great earthquakes. As noted, loans were raised abroad in quick succession by the Japanese government, municipalities and private corporations. By the end of 1924, the rate dropped sharply to 38 dollars for 100 yen, and fluctuated for some time between 38 dollars and 43 dollars for 100 yen.

6 Returning to the gold standard

The majority of Japanese economists believed that the chance for Japan to return to the international gold standard at the prewar parity came when the price level went down due to the 1927 financial panic. There were few economic experts who objected to the return to the gold standard.

In March 1927, a nationwide financial panic was triggered by the financial difficulties of Suzuki Trading Co. (Suzuki Shoten) and its main bank, the Bank of Taiwan. Naokichi Kaneko of the Suzuki Trading Co. made an enormous profit by speculating in internationally traded commodities such as iron, ships, rice, wheat, wood, gum, fertilizer, silk, cotton, oils and fats from World War I until the mid 1920s. The total debt of the Suzuki Trading Co., 450 million yen, was too large for the Bank of Japan to handle easily. The depositors rushed and tried to withdraw their money from their banks. Foreign banks began to stop trading with their Japanese counterparts.[14]

Korekiyo Takahashi, aged 74, was called on to become the Finance Minister to cope with this unprecedented disquiet. The Bank of Japan greatly expanded its advances in order to prevent the breakdown of the whole credit system. In 1927, the outstanding amount of the loans and discounts of the Bank rose to 2,000 million yen, and its note issue rose to 2,600 million yen (Fukai 1937: 383). Takahashi managed to settle this emergency during his 42 days in cabinet and resigned. Fukai analyzed the situation and summarized how these financial disturbances eliminated unsound banks as follows:

> Consolidation and amalgamation among banks for the purpose of enhancing stability were also accelerated. Many of the defaulting banks and others carrying large unliquidated loans were given advances under the government indemnification, which helped them to carry out reorganization, through mergers with other banks, or otherwise. Industrialists, too, who had

> previously been receiving credits from the banks which closed, were obliged to overhaul their businesses. Reductions in invested capital, mergers, dissolutions, curtailment of production were the order of the day. Thus readjustment and rationalization processes made much headway, leading finally to the lifting of the gold embargo.
>
> (Fukai 1937: 383–4, originally written in English)

In October 1928, the bankers who joined the Tokyo and Osaka Bill Exchange made a resolution that Japan should return to the international gold standard. It was believed that their resolution was supported by business people. However, their resolution came to nothing when stock and bond prices fell sharply within a few days.

In July 1929, a new government came into power and serious and concerted efforts were started for the stabilization of the yen without devaluation (Fukai 1937: 386). There was a big debate among both journalists and academics over when to lift the gold embargo and over what parity to choose. Some inconsistent politicians and journalists favored the return to gold at the prewar parity and repudiated the austerity policy at the same time without analyzing the implications of these policies. Only a handful of university economists, bankers and a few journalists made a serious study of the international monetary problem and used statistical figures and numbers to calculate the relevant parity for the Japanese yen in the 1920s.

Several economists analyzed the effect of lifting the gold embargo on the Japanese economy with the use of time series on price indexes and exchange rates. Seibi Hijikata (1890–1975), economist at the Imperial University of Tokyo, in his *The Lifting of the Gold Embargo* (1929, in Japanese) conducted the most extensive analysis of the currency problems in Japan, referring to other cases of lifting of the gold embargo such as the United Kingdom and France. He traced the historical course of the world monetary events after World War I. Because he expected a stable exchange rate, Hijikata argued for Japan's return to gold at the old parity as follows (Hijikata 1929: 80):

> At all events, there is no doubt that the embargo on gold has caused an enormous instability in the exchange rates and therefore hurt the economy. It seems that Japan could not have avoided this instability if it had lifted the gold embargo, as long as the leading countries banned the export of gold. Upon the ceasefire of the Great European War, the United States became the first to lift the gold embargo. Other leading countries followed it one after another.
>
> (My translation)

Hijikata also expected several effects to follow. The first effect came through the trade relations, depending on the timing and method of the lifting the gold embargo. Japan tended to suffer from trade deficit in the first half of a year whereas its export tended to increase in the second half. Therefore, its gold specie would drain quickly in the period of trade deficit whereas its outflow would be moderated in the period of trade surplus. The second effect came through the speculative motive, namely an outflow of Japan's gold specie at the old, appreciated par.

> Those who expect that the gold embargo will be lifted soon or later and that the Japanese yen is relatively low and will gradually rise have bought the Japanese yen for US dollars or the Chinese tael [*liang*, the Chinese currency unit of the day]. They can make a profit by selling the yen which have been hoarded on the speculative motive at depreciated rates for gold, US dollars, and the Chinese tael.... We should expect that two to three hundred million yen of specie would flow out in a short period if the gold embargo is lifted at the par of 46.5 dollars against 100 yen.
>
> (Hijikata 1929, in Japanese: 99–100, my translation)

Upon lifting the gold embargo, central bankers including Eigo Fukai were faced with bunched sales of the assets denominated in Japanese yen, which served as a big pressure to depreciate the value of yen (to be discussed later).

The third question was the ability of the Bank of Japan to control the flow of gold specie. In other words, it was the question of how much power the Bank of Japan had in preventing the outflow of specie by raising its bank rate. Hijikata examined the current amount of the deposit of commercial banks in the Bank of Japan and concluded that it would not be affected very much by the change of the bank rate. We should note that Hijikata did not pay any attention to the adverse effect of raising interest rates on the Japanese economy.

Hijikata also analyzed the relationship between the lifting of the gold embargo and the changes in the price level. If gold specie flows out, the outstanding stock of convertible notes would be shrunken, and the price level would fall. Therefore, Hijikata paid attention to the gold export for the purpose of exchange profit taking and learned from the report of Japan's Ministry of Finance that 932,000 pounds sterling of gold was exported from Britain to Sweden, India, the Netherlands, etc. during the period of two weeks immediately after its return to the international gold standard in 1925, namely from April 30 to May 13. Britain experienced the net export of 8,000,000 pounds sterling of gold during the whole year of 1925, and the decline in the price level by 3.7 percent on average in 1926. Hijikata (1929: 107) expected that a tremendous amount of specie would flow out and that prices would fall precipitously, if Japan lifted the gold embargo at the old parity, which exceeded the current parity by more than 7 percent. Third, interest rates would rise because of the belt-tightening policy after the lifting of the gold embargo and it would cause small banks to be affected by the bad debt of insolvent domestic companies. Fourth, the rising interest rates and the declining prices would affect domestic industries. The appreciated currency would make exports less competitive, but imported intermediates would be cheaper. Hijikata (1929: 120) expected that the lifting of the gold embargo would most affect industries which used domestic materials and exported their merchandises, that is, the silk industry. Theoretically it was expected that the cotton-spinning industry would be less affected because it imported its material mainly from China and exported its final product. Hijikata referred to the investigation of Japan's Industry Club that even a slight rise in export price would weaken the competitive position of the industry in the world market, which was under fierce competition. Moreover, such industries would continue to suffer from instability in the price of silver. Fifth, Hijikata discussed the effect on employment in detail. He admitted that it was hard to estimate by how much wages would go down. He pointed out that a further decline in prices of finished goods might increase demand (although prices had already declined due to the depression), and it was therefore difficult to determine the final effect on employment.

In spite of these difficulties, Hijikata recommended Japan's return to gold at the old par, instead of the new, lower parity. Hijikata (1929: 140) criticized the idea of returning to gold at the lower parity even if Cassel's theory of purchasing-power parity was correct, because there was no reason to expect the new purchasing-power parity, which was calculated to be much lower than the current exchange rate, to be more stable in practice. He strongly argued that the debt in terms of foreign currency could become a serious problem for the mass of people if Japan lifted the ban on gold at a lower parity. S. Hijikata (1929: 141–2) wrote as follows:

> It is apparent that one should pay more yen against the debt in foreign currency if the exchange rate is set below the old parity.... Those who had the heaviest debt in foreign currency were, not the electric power companies, but the government and the local municipalities. Where is their budgetary resource for the payment of the principal and interest? It is mainly from tax. Sixty percent of their tax revenue comes from the consumption tax levied on the mass of the people. Therefore, the devaluation of yen will impose a greater burden on the mass of people. The outstanding stock of bonds in foreign currency amounts to more than 1,453 million yen.... If the austerity policy is designed to decrease the taxation of the masses, we cannot say that the austerity policy always sacrifices the masses.
>
> (My translation)

Hijikata continued to analyze the expected course toward the return to gold at the old par and its effect on the Japanese economy. Actually, Japan was taking a similar course to the one taken by Britain and vehemently criticized by Keynes during 1923–4, and the course warned against by Cassel in his 1926 paper. Keynes's *The General Theory of Employment, Interest and Money* (1936) had not been published as yet but the ideas leading to his systematic analysis of the depressed economy were just underway. With regard to the return to the international gold standard, like many other countries including Britain, Japanese policymakers gave the international economic relations priority over the domestic economic conditions. First, the Japanese officials were heavily concerned about the international debt of 2,344 pounds sterling which would be due for redemption on January 1, 1931. The adoption of the international gold standard was regarded as the basis for the stability of currency and was required for a country to take a vantage point in the negotiation of the rolling over of huge debt. Second, it was proposed at first that only countries with the international gold standard should become members of the newly established International Bank for Settlement. Japan had a bitter experience in demanding a retraction of the requirement. Moreover, it was decided for political reasons, beyond economic reasoning, that Japan should return to the international gold standard with the higher, old parity rather than with a lower, new parity. The ruling party, Minsei-to, was not the majority but the largest minority. It was considered that Prime Minister Hamaguchi, Minsei-to, could not pass the bill to amend the Ordinance on Money of 1897, which stipulated that 750 milligrams of gold should be equivalent to 1 yen, in the parliament where Seiyukai, the opposition party, was the majority (M. Nakamura 1982: 194–5; BOJ 1983 vol. 3: 391). The Hamaguchi Cabinet (Minsei-to) was established after the resignation of the Tanaka Cabinet (Seiyu-kai), which had been established based on the majority of the parliament, due to the bombing of the warlord Chang Tso-lin's train by Japan's Kwantung Army in Mukden (now Shenyang) in June 1928. Sometimes the best policy measures could not be taken because the ruling party did not have enough political power to pass the legislative process in the parliament. Avid economic agents might be moved by speculative motives because they always pay attention to changes in government policies and make a step toward profit taking activities. The policy of lifting the gold embargo at the prewar parity might be the second-best policy but it was feasible for the policymakers whose country was suffering from the heavy international debt and had the minority government.

Moreover, when stock prices fell sharply on Wall Street in October 1929, no Japanese expected that it would lead to a Great Depression throughout the world. Some even continued to believe in "eternal prosperity." Therefore, the Hamaguchi Cabinet and Finance Minister Junnosuke Inoue finally decided to return to the international gold standard and lifted the embargo on gold exports on January 11, 1930. As a result, the Japanese economy was trapped in unprecedented depression and a substantial trade deficit. The prices of securities and commodities dived. The indexes of industrial and agricultural production decreased. Japan's imports dwindled due to the decline in domestic demand. Exports shrank because of the appreciated yen, the decline in demand from abroad, including the United States, and the protective tariffs set by competitors such as China and India. In addition, 303 million yen of gold specie flowed out in 1930. From September 1931, when Britain came off the gold standard, till January 1932, 445 million yen of gold specie flowed out of Japan.

Eigo Fukai made a retrospective statement in 1941. He thought that the lifting of the gold embargo had been along the line of world trends and had followed most of the popular voices in Japan. However, it was a pity for him because Japan lost a tremendous amount of gold specie. Speculation was beyond the expectation of the policymakers.

7 The suspension of the gold standard and deficit financing

In the midst of the unprecedented depression, following the resolution of sound finance stated as the consensus of the Brussels Conference of 1920, the Finance Minister Junnosuke Inoue believed that government expenditures should be cut when its revenue declined, and that therefore the policy of belt-tightening was unavoidable. He took a deflationary policy and rationalized the administrative organization. He cut spending including the military, the salary of officials, subsidies and pensions, although the Japanese Army managed to resist Inoue's measure of raising the age for receiving a pension. Inoue made Yokohama Specie Bank sell foreign exchange as much as possible to those who were willing to purchase it with the aim of maintaining the gold standard. However, it seemed to be becoming beyond control. Finally Inoue and the central bankers such as Hisaakira Hijikata and Eigo Fukai realized that they should again embargo the export of gold. A change of the cabinet became unavoidable. Korekiyo Takahashi was regarded as the top candidate for Finance Minister for the next administration. Central bankers H. Hijikata and Fukai discussed the gold embargo and Fukai alone saw Takahashi because H. Hijikata was sick. Fukai proposed the following two measures:

> (1) The export of gold should be embargoed again as soon as possible, because there is no possibility of maintaining the gold standard. The announcement should be made immediately after the cabinet is reshuffled, even if late at night.
> (2) The conversion of banknotes into gold should be prohibited as soon as possible, because the single measure of the gold embargo does not seem to be effective enough to settle the current troubles.
>
> (Fukai 1941, in Japanese: 259, my translation)

Takahashi agreed to embargo gold exports at once and, after a little hesitation, decided to stop converting notes into gold (Fukai 1941: 260–1). On December 13, 1931, Tsuyoshi Inukai became the Prime Minister and Takahashi the Finance Minister. On the same day, Takahashi issued the ministerial ordinance that everyone needed permission to export gold and indicated that he would never give permission. Thus, Japan abandoned the international gold standard. On December 17, under the name of the emperor, Japan stopped converting notes into gold. On December 18, the government ordered the Bank of Japan to stop selling gold bullion for any foreign currency. Japan left the gold standard completely.

Takahashi undertook an activist policy in fighting against depression, especially in trying to save impoverished farming villages, which were considered to be a hotbed of left-wing activity (Fujimura 1992b, in Japanese: 149). Takahashi cut the bank rate, supplied abundant finance to the industrial sectors and stimulated Japan's heavy industries including its colonial ones. He avoided raising tax revenue, which he hated, and made up the shortage of revenue by deficit financing for the first time in 1932.[15] Later, Takahashi was called "the Japanese Keynes" (Chapter 9; Ikeo 1997). In 1932, Japan did not have a fiscal problem, but a serious trade deficit problem.

Takahashi, the Finance Minister, and Fukai, the deputy governor of the Bank of Japan, maintained close contact with each other after the gold re-embargo (Fukai 1941: 268–9). Takahashi expanded the limit of fiduciary issue of convertible notes and cut the tax rate for note issue above this limit. He then left final "control" of the currency supply to the Bank of Japan's discretion. Fukai thought that in order to stimulate the depressed economy, it was necessary to increase the general purchasing power by releasing funds from the Bank of Japan, as the money supply had declined due to the fall in gold reserve after the lifting of the gold embargo. Fukai came upon the idea that the Bank of Japan should have close contact with the financial markets through open market operations, and should buy national bonds in exchange for their funds to achieve the necessary level of currency supply. The Bank of Japan had previously bought some national bonds under special consideration of the general financial conditions and the circumstances of a particular bank. Takahashi extended this idea of open market operations with negotiable bonds, and decided to issue national bonds directly through the acceptance of the Bank of Japan. Fukai believed that the Bank of Japan's purchase of negotiable bonds and the Bank of Japan's acceptance of new bonds was the same thing with respect to the supply of currency. According to Fukai (1941: 269), the new measure worked in three ways, that is, it facilitated the additional supply of currency, the bond issue financed the Manchurian Incident, and led to a reduction of the level of interest rates.

The Bank of Japan accepted all of the loans to the government of 200 million yen, at a 4.5 percent interest rate and by the end of 1932 sold them to commercial banks. They continued to accept almost all the new government loans for the next dozen years. In addition, thanks to the embargo on gold exports, the rate of exchange went down and Japan's exports increased. However, capital fled from Japan until the government decided to control foreign exchange.

In 1931 Japan became involved in the so-called Manchurian Incident. Manchuria is now mainly the northeast part of China, which includes a vague border with Russia, Mongolia and North Korea. It is full of natural resources like coal, iron and crude oil. Prior to 1904, Russia monopolized the rights and concessions in Manchuria. In 1904–5, Japan fought against Russia over its interests in Manchuria. Toward the end of the 1920s the struggle for power between Communists, nationalists and Chinese warlords had spilled over into Manchuria. In 1927, the Kuomintang (Nationalist Party) lead by Chiang Kai-shek established their capital in Nanking. Their campaign moved further northward and expanded their sphere of influence to Peking (now Beijing). Then, they came into conflict with Chang Tso-lin, whom Japan had been supporting in Manchuria since 1921. In 1931, at the signal of a bomb explosion on the railroad outside Mukden (now Shenyang), troops from the Kwantung Army, a unit of Japan's Army, moved to seize the city and then to occupy the whole of the three Manchurian provinces, without the authority of the Army high command. However, the Tokyo government chose to furnish financial support for them to extend further operations in Manchuria. In January 1932, the Japanese Navy clashed with Chinese troops in Shanghai. In March 1932, Japan declared that the state of Manchukuo was established. The League of Nations responded to China's appeal and sent a commission of enquiry, chaired by Lord Victor Lytton, to East Asia. Lord Lytton reported that they could find little prospect that the League would find against China. The Manchukuo problem was debated at the table of the League of Nations in Geneva in February 1933, when Japan finally decided to leave the League.

Finance Minister Takahashi had to expand government spending not only for fighting against the economic depression but also for increased military spending. This spending was financed by a budget deficit. When the balance of debt was estimated to amount to 9.8 billion yen at the end of 1935, Takahashi planned to cut the military expenses and decided to set the balance under the ceiling of ten billion yen. The Japanese military, especially the Army, vehemently opposed Takahashi's plan and made a vociferous protest in the Prime Minister's office. In the 1936 national budget, the military budget was increased, although the balance of debt was scheduled to decrease. The military budget was 45.8 percent of the government spending and about 16 percent of national income of 1936.

In November 1935, Takahashi explained the budget of 1936 and criticized the never-ending expansion of military expenses.

> National defense is supposed to protect a country from military assault from its enemies. In general, the military has no common sense.... How on earth are they going to commence operations on the two fronts of America and Russia? Do they really think they are able to wage a war against America and occupy New York and Washington? And, do they plan to fight against Russia and move to Moscow? You often tell us how to win. However, we will really win a war only if the enemy gives up. We will gain nothing even if we say we win. We will win only when the enemy admits they are beaten. It is impossible to occupy Washington and Moscow.... It is nonsense to set more local military schools (*chiho yonen gakko*) as demanded by the Army at present. Every worker should learn the common sense necessary for his job at a secondary school. In fact, one who graduated from a secondary school and studied at a military school can become an excellent marine in the Navy, in which more specialized knowledge and technology are needed. The Army plans to recruit elementary graduates into local military schools. However, secondary education should cultivate children's common sense as ordinary people. To give children special training without secondary education leads to the creation of socially disabled people. It is natural that the Army lacks common sense because only those who were trained at local military schools are regarded as legitimate to become the Army's leaders. It is outrageous and a calamity of the nation that military leaders who have no common sense have a say in politics.
>
> (Quoted in Fujimura 1992b: 184, my translation)

Army Minister Kawashima was listening to Takahashi's speech in silence. The content of the speech was released to news reporters and appeared in the morning papers the next day.

Before dawn on February 26, 1936, hundreds of young nationalists, armed with small weapons, attacked important political figures. They slew several ministers, including Finance Minister Takahashi, their bodyguards and related people. The Prime Minister Keisuke Okada managed to escape their assault and his brother-in-law was mistakenly shot to death instead. The Japanese military was unsatisfied with the treaty of demilitarization signed in London. No civilians in Japan could curb the military expansion or turn back the aggressive steps toward the Asia-Pacific War (1937–45).

After World War II started in 1939, little academic literature was brought from Europe to Japan. Few Japanese scholars could make the long trip to Europe or North America because they could not buy passage on ships due to the regulation of foreign currency. After Japan began the war against the United Kingdom and the United States, almost no literature came in.

8 Some conclusions

From the 1900s to the 1920s, the mathematician Rikitaro Fujisawa contributed several excellent papers to the field of monetary economics. In the 1910s, monetary economists, who were differentiated from monetary experts affiliated with banks and the Ministry of Finance, appeared in Japan, read the latest issues of economics journals mostly written in English, and discussed international monetary questions including the characteristics of the gold standard. In the 1920s, Japanese monetary experts were active participants in the international economic conferences. In 1926, a Swedish ball-bearing company donated Gustav Cassel's research paper on the Japanese currency to the Japanese government, and the research stimulated the discussion of whether the gold embargo should be lifted with the old rate or a new, lower rate. Korekiyo Takahashi, the Japanese Keynes, not only conducted deficit financing to rescue impoverished villages during the depression but also abandoned the gold standard completely.

Notes

1 The papers relating to this chapter were presented at the annual meeting of the Japanese Society for the History of Economic Thought (JSHET) in October 1995, and at the annual meeting of the History of Economics Society in Vancouver in June 1996. See Ikeo (1999, 2003a). I thank the participants for their various comments. Moreover, I thank Bo Sandelin, who found the reason why Gustav Cassel wrote "The Japanese currency" (1926) in his autobiography entitled *I Fornuftests Tjanst* (In the Service of Reason, Cassel 1941–2), and Takahiko Hasegawa, who located one of the original, typed copies of Cassel (1926) in the Faculty of Economics Library, University of Tokyo.

2 T. Kato (ed. 1983, in Japanese) made a detailed survey of Japanese discussion of monetary economics, policy and institutions in the domestic context. Mark Metzler (2002) investigates the pressure of J. P. Morgan and Co. upon Japan's restoration of

the international gold standard, 1927–9. This chapter focuses on open Japanese discussion of monetary economics and policy in the international context. Kikuo Iwata (2004) was a comprehensive research project with active economists focused on the fierce economic debate in Japanese over the Show Depression (1930–1). They extensively surveyed the debate among Japanese economists, journalists, business people and policymakers published in books and magazines, and examined the changes in economic conditions by showing the economic data collected later and new econometric research results. Iwata became a vice governor of the Bank of Japan in April 2013. Masato Shizume (2009), a researcher at the BOJ, reviewed Japan's economic policies during the Great Depression and drew the lessons for the contemporary policymakers of a small open economy.

3 It is noteworthy that the Bank of Japan (BOJ) was one of the founding members of the Bank for International Settlement (BIS), which was established in 1930. A staff from the BOJ was permanently stationed in Basel, where the headquarters of BIS was located. Both the Basel staff and the managing staff from the BOJ who were stationed in London attended the regular meetings of the BIS Board of Trustees every month in the 1930s. However, the Japanese members did not play an active role during this period (Trepp 1993, Introduction to the Japanese edition). See also Yago (2013).

4 Japan prevented China from annexing Korea. Then it annexed Korea from 1910 to 1945.

5 See also Shiroyama (2008).

6 Marshall explained "the fixed-ratio-mintage" in 1886, when he replied to the questions of the Subject of Currency and Prices circulated by the Royal Commission on the Depression of Trade and Industry. At first Marshall gave a projection of the future course of the ordinary bimetallic scheme which proposed that the leading governments should agree to give free mintage to gold and silver at a fixed rate as follows:

> [S]o-called bimetallism would, in my opinion, be very likely to degenerate practically into silver monometallism, silver coins being used for small change, and silver paper for the chief work of business. The value of the currency would then fluctuate with every variation in the value of silver. Without the special advantages of our present currency we should have its disadvantage of being practically dependent on one metal only for the steadying of prices.
>
> (Marshall 1926: 13)

Then Marshall gave his alternative scheme which was to be called "the fixed-ratio-mintage" later:

> My alternative scheme is got … by wedding a bar of silver of, say, 2,000 grams to a bar of gold, say, 100 grams; the Government undertaking to be always ready to buy or sell a wedded pair of bars for a fixed amount of currency.… This would be true bimetallism. The value of the currency would be fixed absolutely by means of the values of a gramme of gold and, say, 20 grammes of silver. It would have no chance of deteriorating into a silver monometallism.…
>
> It would not attempt to exercise any influence on the relative values of the metals.
>
> (Marshall 1926: 14)

Marshall named it the fixed-ratio-mintage in 1887, when he made a statement to the Royal Commission on the Values of Gold and Silver (Marshall 1926: 28). Marshall's "fixed-ratio-mintage" became known in Japan after his *Official Papers* was first published by J. M. Keynes in 1926, whereas Fujisawa's "joint-metallism" was buried in oblivion.

7 On a similar note, Barry Eichengreen (1995) discussed that international solidarity has been needed to support the gold standard in times of crisis in Europe since the nineteenth century.

8 It is hard to make a statistical analysis because there was no open, nationwide journal of economics in Japan until 1960.

9 Yamazaki became the first President of the Japanese Society of Monetary Economics, which was established in June 1943 in order to discuss the international monetary system for the postwar period promptly in Japan as well as in the UK and the US (Ikeo ed. 2000: 29).

10 It is noteworthy that Cassel did not refer to Fisher's purchasing power of money anywhere. He also failed to refer to Walras's economic system of simultaneous equations in his discussion of price formation by the use of a system of simultaneous equations in Cassel (1921b).

11 Cassel's new theory mainly derived from the Swedish monetary experiences in the mid 1910s. Sweden's gold reserve was increased from 27.4 million dollars in 1913 to 75.5 million dollars in 1921. In 1916, the Swedish government decided to close the Swedish mint to the minting of gold, and at the same time the Ricksbank, the central bank of Sweden, was released from its duty to buy gold at the mint par. However, in April 1924, Sweden resumed converting banknotes into gold at the old parity and lifted the embargo on gold exports.

12 Eigo Fukai was an able central banker with economic knowledge. In 1931, Fukai gave crucial advice to Korekiyo Takahashi in setting the re-embargo on the gold export. In 1904, Fukai helped Takahashi float a fund during the Russo-Japanese War. He contributed his "The recent monetary policy of Japan" to *The Lessons of Monetary Experience* (1937) edited by A. D. Gayer. See Chapter 9. It is noteworthy that Ikuo Tanaka's studies on Japanese financial history (I. Tanaka 1985 and 1989, in Japanese) include a detailed discussion of Fukai. See also Fujimura (1992a).

13 Japanese scholars paid attention to Keynes's statements on the gold standard. Kanji Okabe and Naoshi Uchiyama published the Japanese version of Keynes's *A Tract on Monetary Reform* (1923) in 1924.

14 The central banker Eigo Fukai (1937: 383) analyzed the causes of the panic (1927) as follows:

> The real cause of the panic ... must be sought, in the first place, in the excessive business expansion during the postwar years; second, in the retardation of necessary economic readjustment and in the deterioration of the condition of the banks due to the panic of 1920; third, in the earthquake of 1923; and fourth, in the intervening period of prosperity alluded to above.
>
> (Originally written in English)

15 Korekiyo Takahashi already explained the essence of "Keynesian economics" in 1929 (Takahashi 1936b, in Japanese: 247–9, frequently quoted; see Chapter 9 and Ikeo 1997).

4 Neoclassical economics in Japan[1]

1 Introduction

In retrospect, Sontoku Ninomiya (1787–1856) had the concept of *bundo*, which meant the attainment of feasible general equilibrium with fiscal balance and positive savings in a state or early modern domain. Yet it is hard to translate *bundo* into the English accord with British classical political economy. Although we notice the similarity between the concept of *bundo* in Ninomiya's teachings and computational general equilibrium in modern economics, the moral aspect of Ninomiya's teachings, *hotoku* thought (returning virtue by virtue, or repayment of blessing), was gradually emphasized in textbooks of morality for elementary students around 1900. Nonetheless, we can regard Ninomiya as an important forerunner of modern economics in the nineteenth century and the books written by his followers Tomita (1883) and Fukuzumi (1893) as important Japanese economic classics. We will discuss Tameyuki Amano's macroeconomics and Ninomiya's teachings in Chapter 8.

Only some private universities had departments of economics or commerce before Japan's government reformed the system of higher education in 1919 and 1920. The department of economics was newly established in the Imperial University of Tokyo and Kyoto, and several other universities and colleges. As discussed in Chapter 2, in the 1920s, the return to the international gold standard and the adjustment of the domestic monetary system were important economic issues. The first nationwide census (1920), which has been carried out and continued every five years since then, not only showed that the population was rapidly growing but also supplied a good database for statistical analysis. Economic experts had to handle an increasing number of numerical figures such as foreign exchange rates, interest rates, price indexes, salaries, wages and demographics.

Tokuzo Fukuda played a very important part in cultivating neoclassical economic analysis such as Marshallian demand and supply analysis, marginal analysis and optimization, and general equilibrium approach and early econometric analysis in Japan. He used A. Marshall (1890) as the textbook for his course on economics. The basic concept of marginal utility and marginal analysis were discussed in Japan roughly in the four groups, that is, (1) Tokuzo Fukuda's advice to seminar students and his turn to "mathematical economics," (2) Ichiro

Nakayama's integration of parts of neoclassical economics with the use of more mathematics, (3) agricultural and applied economists, and (4) mathematicians and mathematical economists. It is noteworthy that the theory of indifference curves which is regarded as one of the bases of contemporary microeconomics was intensively discussed by the mathematicians.

In 1929, Yasuma Takata began to publish his *New Lectures on Economics* (five volumes, 1929–32, in Japanese). This constituted a survey of what was happening to economics on the research frontier in the rest of the world. After that, many good results of economic theoretical research became available in Japanese. If they had been written in German or English, some of them would have caught the eyes of specialists abroad. Three organizations were important for the advancement of early econometric studies in Japan. They were the Agricultural Economic Society (1924–), the Research Bureau of Nagoya College of Commerce (1926–) and the Japan Society for the Promotion of Science (1932–).

It is well known that Ichiro Nakayama's *Pure Economics* (1933) contributed to the popularizing of "mathematical economics" in Japanese. "Mathematical economics" is later called modern economics, and then microeconomics and general equilibrium theory. In the 1930s, the study of national income became important to measure both the economic welfare and the economic power of Japan. As early as 1941, prior to the beginning of the Asia-Pacific War, a couple of copies of W. Leontief's *The Structure of American Economy, 1919–1939* (1941) arrived in Japan. The book was regarded as a direct application of general equilibrium approach to an empirical research of an actual economy. Yet, the first interindustry table of the Japanese economy (of 1951) became available only in 1955.

Several Japanese economists and historians of economics have already discussed in English a few aspects of early neoclassical research made in Japan. Tamotsu Matsuura (1973) picked up some important neoclassical works and translations made in the early twentieth century by the leading economists including Tokuzo Fukuda, Yasuma Takata, Ichiro Nakayama, Kei Shibata, Takuma Yasui and mathematician Masazo Sono. Shigeto Tsuru (1984) includes the summary of the early works of Shibata and Yasui in the 1930s and 1940s and mentions Takata, who was described as "the Japanese Marshall" by Martin Bronfenbrenner (1956), because Tsuru (1964b) did not include these works. Part IV of Ikeo (1991) shows that general equilibrium theory was examined in Japan through the works of Léon Walras, Joseph Alois Schumpeter and Gustav Cassel in the mid 1920s and some Japanese economists started to make theoretical research in the Walrasian or Casselian framework, namely to do "mathematical economics" from 1930 on.[2] Then she realized that it is necessary to put emphasis on the important role played by the three newly established international journals, *Zeitschrift für Nationalökonomie* (1930–), *Econometrica* (1933–) and *Review of Economic Studies* (1933–) in involving the Japanese in the worldwide community of economists (Ikeo 1993b).[3]

Section 2 gives a brief note on the cultural background of Japan, including the activities of Japanese natural scientists, before directly discussing the main subject. Section 3 has four subsections. Sections 3.1 and 3.2 show how "mathematical economics" was discussed in Japan and shed light on the purchase of Carl Menger's collection by the Tokyo University of Commerce (now Hitotsubashi University) in 1923. The early 1920s became the turning point of the important forerunner Tokuzo Fukuda's attitude toward mathematical economics. Section 3.3 summarizes the early statistical work on rice such as Yoshinosuke Yagi (1932, in Japanese) on the price and quantity indexes of rice. It also stresses the interest of agricultural economists in neoclassical economics during the interwar period. Section 3.4 discusses mathematicians' discussions of mathematical neoclassicism in Japan and the conflict of the Japanese scholars' views on the measurability of utility.

Section 4 summarizes the discussion of general equilibrium theory in Japan. Section 5 tries to search for Japanese economists' interest in physics to respond to the suggestion of Philip Mirowski's "Physics and the 'marginalist revolution'" (1984) and *More Heat than Light* (1989). It discusses several economists who produced theoretical works in the post-Samuelson era. Section 6 summarizes a few conclusions.

2 Some cultural and institutional background

In 1854, the Japanese government gave up its isolationist policy which had lasted for 215 years. During the closed-door period, the only exceptions to isolation were transactions with the Dutch and Chinese, and the Japanese received their information about the rest of the world through these two channels alone. Russia, sometimes moving south, threatened the northern coast of Japan and made a few farsighted people worry about their national security and strength.[4] After opening the door to the rest of the world, Japan took a positive attitude towards the introduction of Western goods and ideas into various fields though there were a few xenophobic incidents.[5] Promising young men were sent to European and American universities to learn the language, culture and special subjects of study; they bore the future Japan toward new international relations on their shoulders. Also, foreign specialists were invited to Japan to teach Western languages and cultures to Japanese youth, and to train officials to transform the former closed country into a modern industrial one on the basis of new diplomatic relations as well as an international trade and settlement system.

In Japan, mathematicians were the first intellectual group since 1854 that managed to produce professional works contributing to the development of an academic field in the world context. The Japanese assimilated European and American mathematics based on the inheritance of Japanese traditional mathematics called *Wasan* which was exclusively cultivated in a guild-type group in Japan during the isolationist policy era. It is noteworthy that several *Wasan-ka*, that is, Japanese traditional mathematicians, did play a positive role in introducing and spreading Western mathematics in Japan because they recognized the efficiency of Western mathematics compared to *Wasan*. *Wasan* used many numbers and geometrical patterns but neither symbol nor function as did

Western mathematics. *Wasan* was replaced by Western mathematics in the educational curriculum in 1872.

Japanese mathematicians have impacted neighboring fields in which mathematical knowledge can be applied. For example, Rikitaro Fujisawa, the first Japanese to master Western mathematics, published his *Life Insurance* (1889, in Japanese) and several articles in economics (mostly domestic and international finance). In the late 1920s, he was eager to support the establishment of the Japan Society for the Promotion of Science (Nihon Gakujutsu Shinkokai), which came into being in 1932, in order to promote not only natural science but also economic science. In 1933, 14 economists were called into the Sixth Subcommittee for the theoretical and practical study of rice policy.

It is said that neo-Confucianism (*Shusigaku*) played some part in the assimilating of Western scientific thinking represented by "machines in factories" in Japan.[6] When an iron mill was built for the first time in Japan, a group of Western engineers and accountants were employed to utilize the necessary technology and skill to run the iron-manufacturing "business." Thus the system of Western bookkeeping, which was written horizontally, was practically adopted in the new industry, while during the seventeenth to nineteenth centuries Western bookkeeping was only used to record the trades with the Dutch in Nagasaki (Nishikawa 1979). The Netherlands was the exceptional trade partner for Japan in the period of isolationist policy during 1639–1854. Japanese traditional bookkeeping such as *choai* and *daifukucho*, which were written vertically and had been used by leading merchants during the seventeenth to nineteenth centuries, was gradually replaced with the Western system of bookkeeping by double-entry (Nishikawa 1979: 291–3). Moreover, the engineers found it necessary to use Arabic numerals and to learn Western-style mathematics in order to draw blueprints for steamboats, large bridges and railroads, and to develop modern technology.[7]

The Japanese scholars needed to create Japanese words corresponding to academic terms in mathematics, physics, political economy, political philosophy and social thought when they translated Western textbooks into Japanese, based on their traditional knowledge such as Japanese, Dutch and neo-Confucian learning. There is usually no one-to-one correspondence between two systems of language which reflect different outlooks on the human world and nature. The Japanese usually combined two or more *Kanji* characters, which are ideograms, into one word to express an unfamiliar concept in a way similar to the German language in which two or more nouns are put together to form a new word.

Some important terms have been translated into different Japanese words in each academic field. This made it difficult for Japanese scholars to trace the metaphorical linkages which were supposed to be very much common in some fields. For example, the term "dynamics" has been translated into three different words, that is, *rikigakukei* in physics, *dogaku* in economics and *rikido* in natural philosophy. Two Japanese words correspond to "equilibrium," namely *heiko* in physics, and *kinko* in sociology, psychology and economics. Yet we should note that John Stuart Mill used the term "equilibrium" in the meaning of bilateral trade balance whereas Léon Walras had the concept of equilibrium in a national economy represented by a system of simultaneous equations. Therefore, some Japanese were confused by the two different meanings of the use of the term "equilibrium." The Japanese words for "probability" are quite different in philosophy and statistics, *gaizenchi* relating to probable knowledge and *kakuritsu* referring to the degree of frequency. Early Japanese scholars managed to create new terms in Japanese corresponding to Western scientific ideas, except for "energy," which has been called *enerugi* in Japanese. The concept of energy was so new that it did not have any Japanese counterpart. It could not be allotted any *Kanji* characters and has been regarded as a word of foreign origin.

It may be noteworthy that Marxist economists or Marxians had a strong influence on Japanese social thought especially after 1945. They stressed the class consciousness of scientific activities in both natural and social sciences. In consequence, they disconnected the metaphorical tie of economics with physics and other natural sciences. They left universities during the war with China and World War II. Even prior to 1945, the theoretical Marxians, who were forced to resign from universities, were able to find a position in the Ohara Institute for Social Research as long as they continued a theoretical study of Marx. The institute was established in Osaka in 1919 for the promotion of research on the causes of social ills such as poverty, unemployment, prostitution and orphans in cities (Ohara Institute for Social Research ed. 1971, in Japanese). Until 1949, it was sponsored by Magosaburo Ohara, a successful businessman who made a fortune in spinning. Iwasaburo Takano, the first president of the institute, compared it to The Marx-Engels Institute and The Lenin Institute in Moscow, and The Institute for Social Research in Frankfurt. After 1945, Marxist economists made a vigorous counterattack against those who had criticized Marxism, socialism, or the inconsistency of Marx's theory of value and market price prior to 1945.

3 Early discussion of marginal analysis

3.1 Tokuzo Fukuda's turn

As described in Matsuura (1973), there is no doubt that Tokuzo Fukuda (1874–1930) was the most important forerunner in research of neoclassical approach in Japan.[8] When he entered the Tokyo College of Commerce (now Hitotsubashi University) in 1891, Tameyuki Amano (1886) might have been a textbook in the course on economics.[9] From 1897–1900, Fukuda studied on a graduate course in Germany and obtained his Ph.D. under the supervision of Lujo Brentano (1844–1931), one of the leading economists of the German historical school. In 1900, Fukuda's thesis entitled "Die gesellschaftliche und wirtschaftliche Entwicklung in Japan" (Social and Economic Development in Japan) was included in the series of Münchener Volkswirtschaftliche Studien (Munich Studies of National Economies) edited by Brentano and Walther Lotz. Brentano was Fukuda's lifelong mentor and kept sending copies of his new books to Fukuda in Japan (see Kanazawa 2011; Inoue and Yagi 1998; Nishizawa 2001). After returning to Japan, Fukuda was ubiquitous on the Japanese economic scene and followed Brentano's wide-angled approach to economics, including economic theory, economic history, statistics and government policy. With regard to the question of distribution Brentano favored trade unionism rather than profit-sharing schemes and Fukuda was one of the economists who paid attention to welfare economics in Japan. Brentano wrote the introduction to the German version of A. Marshall's *Principles of Economics* (1890), and Fukuda used Marshall (1890) as a textbook in his teaching at Keio Gijuku (now Keio University) from 1906 through 1919.

Initially, Fukuda praised only the hedonic approach to economics taken by W. S. Jevons and H. H. Gossen, and the non-mathematical approach taken by C. Menger (1871). Fukuda denounced the mathematical approach which he differentiated from the statistical approach. The first full-scale, clear-cut Japanese translation from the neoclassical literature was Jevons's *The Theory of Political Economy* (1871) by Shinzo Koizumi, one of Fukuda's students at Keio Gijuku, in 1913. A slightly updated version was published in 1944 and printed until the late twentieth century. We can see Fukuda's animosity toward mathematical economics in his introduction (1913: viii) to the translation of Jevons (1871):

> *The Theory of Political Economy* has been known as a book which explained economics mathematically and the author believed this to be the merit of the book. However, it does not matter whether there are mathematical expressions or not in *The Theory of Political Economy* because what looks mathematical is just due to appearance while its content is not at all mathematical. In the non-mathematical aspect, Jevons differs from Cournot in France and is closer to Carl Menger who did not use mathematics in the least. That is why Jevons shares the eternal reputation with Menger.... Economics should not be a mathematical science. I believe that no matter how hard a most excellent economist works on mathematical economics in the future, it will end up as a waste of labor. Although I acknowledge the works of Pareto, Fisher, Edgeworth and others, their study includes useless and laborious mathematical exercises and makes more work for already overworked economists.
>
> (My translation)

After his appointment as professor at Tokyo University of Commerce (now Hitotsubashi University) again, Fukuda had one of his students, Kinnosuke Otsuka, publish the Japanese translation of Marshall (1890) in 1922. Brentano taught the subjective theory of value and placed H. H. Gossen as the first marginal utility theorist in the history of economics, as did Fukuda, who had Sumio Tedzuka study Gossen's *Entwicklung der Gesetze des menschlichen Verkehrs und der daraus fliessenden Regeln für menschliches Handeln* (The Laws of Human Relations and Rules of Human Action Derived Therefrom, 1854) in 1920.[10] Both Brentano and Fukuda were interested in the statistical approach to economic history and demography. Fukuda played a role in supporting the first census investigation in 1920 by giving a series of promotion speeches at local gatherings. Fukuda was a giant star in Japanese academia and nurtured many excellent professors who took more specialized courses than he had himself.

Fukuda advised one of his seminar students, Ichiro Nakayama, who was good at mathematics, to make a special study of Gossen (1854), Cournot (1838), and Walras (1874–7). Only a limited number of economists and students in the world were studying these works, which were called "mathematical economics" at the time, later modern economics, and now microeconomics and general equilibrium theory. Tedzuka's undergraduate thesis, more than a translation, was already published as a Japanese research monograph under the title of *A Study of Gossen* (1920). Fukuda suggested that Nakayama present Cournot using only mathematics and deliver a talk on Walras using no mathematics. Fukuda understood the nature of these French works very well.[11]

The turning point for Fukuda seemed to come around 1919 when he suggested that Tedzuka study Gossen. Then Tokyo University of Commerce managed to acquire Carl Menger's collection around 1922, in the midst of the postwar inflation in Austria.[12] C. Menger, known as a non-mathematical economist, owned mathematical economic literature including not only L. Walras's famous *Eléments d'économie politique pure* (1874–77) and A. Cournot's *Recherches sur les principes mathématiques de la théorie des richesses* (1838) but also rare journals such as *Annales des Ponts et Chaussées* carrying J. Dupuit's "De la measure de l'utilité des travaux publics" (On the measurement of the utility of public works, 1844) and "De l'influence des péages sur l'utilité des vois de communication" (On tolls and transport charges, 1849). Menger's collection provided Japanese scholars with a variety of economic literature which was used by them to learn a new type of economic knowledge and to study the economics of Menger. Fukuda had already dropped his previous hostility towards mathematical economics.

Nakayama translated Cournot (1838) as well as Dupuit (1844 and 1849) on public works and demand analysis into Japanese. The Japanese economists had already come to know these French economic engineers by reading Marshall's writings. They learned especially deeply from Dupuit about the mathematical concept of functions, and that demand declines continuously as prices rise in the price and quantity plane. They confirmed that Cournot had fully developed the concept of the elasticity of demand with respect to price, which was considered to be at the core of demand analysis by Marshall. The interest in Cournot was later renewed and increased by the discussion of E. Chamberlin's *Theory of Monopolistic Competition* (1933) and J. Robinson's *The Economics of Imperfect Competition* (1933). Nakayama was completing the translation of Cournot (1838) during his 40 days on board ship to Europe. He was aided by Yoshitomo Okada, a mathematician (specialized in algebra) of Tohoku Imperial University (now Tohoku University) who happened to be on the same ship in 1927. Nakayama was on his way to Bonn, Germany to meet his lifelong mentor J. A. Schumpeter.[13]

Fukuda added his encouragement for advanced students to study mathematical economics in the 1925 edition of his *Lectures on Economics*.[14] Fukuda (1925: 282–3) said as follows:

> Walras is one of the stars of mathematical economics like Cournot and Gossen. It is certain that his works such as *Éléments d'économie politique pure ou théorie de la richesse sociale* (1900) [the fourth edition of Walras (1874–7)], *Études d'économie politique appliquée* (1898), and *Études d'économie sociale* (1896) are not appropriate for beginners. However, one who plans to make an advanced study of economics must read them seriously *even if it contradicts his opinion* [italics added]. Following Sumio Tedzuka's *A Study of Gossen* (1920), Ichiro Nakayama, one of my students, is recently making a special study of Walras, Pareto, etc. I really pray for great success in his study.
>
> (My translation)

Interestingly, Nakayama did not know of these new paragraphs in Fukuda (1925) until Tadashi Hayasaka, historian of economics, pointed them out around 1970. Yet Nakayama quoted Fukuda's phrase of "*even if it contradicts his opinion*" as the evidence for the change in Fukuda's attitude toward mathematical economics when he delivered a presidential lecture "On modern economics" (Nakayama 1970) to the 1970 meeting of the Association of Theoretical Economics and Econometrics (Now the Japanese Economic Association).[15] Economists sometimes use "discoveries" made by historians of economics without referring to the name of the "discoverer."

3.2 Ichiro Nakayama

Nakayama became interested in Schumpeter when he attended Yasuma Takata's (1883–1972) lectures on the history of economics at the Tokyo University of Commerce in the early 1920s. Takata was also one of the most important figures in Japanese neoclassical economics of the late 1920s and 1930s. He introduced many new ideas into his courses in economics, delivered energetic lectures at several universities, fought against Marxist economists, trained brilliant students in his seminars, and published more than 100 books and 500 articles in his life. His *New Lectures on Economics* (1929–32), five volumes, was welcomed by economists who already had some knowledge about what was happening in the economics profession in the rest of the world. Takata clearly differentiated the general equilibrium theory in the manner of Walras from the partial equilibrium theory in the manner of Marshall. He covered such topics as basic economic ideas, the theory of production, the theory of exchange (including the theories of price and money), theories of income distribution (including wages, rent, interest and profit), and the theory of business cycle.

Takata's lectures, which were inspired so much by reading Schumpeter, brought Nakayama to Bonn rather than the big city of Berlin where, in the 1920s, many Japanese economists were pursuing advanced research and/or collecting economic literature. Marxist economists T. Kushida and S. Kuruma were sent there by the Ohara Institute for Social Research (see section 2). Nakayama studied in Bonn under Schumpeter from 1928–9 and came to know the agricultural economist, Seiichi Tobata. As noted in Chapter 2, Schumpeter advised Tobata to read Henry Schultz's (1925) statistical study of the supply and demand of sugar and H. L. Moore's (1914, 1917) study of business cycles (University of Tokyo, Department of Economics ed.1976: 578–82). Nakayama realized that Schultz (1927) was making a parallel advance with him in "mathematical economics."

Returning from Bonn, Nakayama gave lectures on the theory of economic development. He took over Fukuda's position at the Tokyo University of Commerce in 1930. He lectured on the neoclassical version of economic principles and published his *Pure Economics* (1933). It was a concise book including the method of pure economics, consumers' and producers' behavior, market equilibrium, income distribution, and economic development. It was a good textbook in microeconomics. He put Schumpeter, Cournot, Walras, Gossen, and Schultz in order with the use of mathematics. He owed much to Schumpeter (1908, 1912) and borrowed the title from L. Walras's *Eléments d'économie politique pure* (1874–7).[16] Available in a compact and inexpensive edition, Nakayama (1933), 255 pages long, was widely read among Japanese non-Marxian economists, and thereby contributed to popularizing Schumpeterian ideas and the neoclassical ideas, such as marginal utility theory with focus on subjectivity and the general equilibrium approach, in Japan. He connected the decreasing marginal utility of a consumed commodity to the downward slope of its demand curve. Like Marshall, Nakayama placed mathematical formulae in the appendix. He explained the essence of the general equilibrium theory in terms that were readily understood by Japanese students. He repeated the central points and kept saying that all the quantities significant to economics, such as prices and outputs, quantities supplied and demanded, are always moving in association with others.

The consensus reached by these Japanese neoclassical economists can be summarized by Gossen's two laws in the theory of consumer behavior plus Marshallian supply and demand curves. Gossen's first law stated that marginal utility of each commodity declines when it is consumed continuously. This was considered to be a basis for the downward slope of Marshallian demand curve in a price-quantity diagram. Gossen's second law stated that the ratios of marginal utilities divided by their prices in consuming various goods would be equalized as long as the consumer behaved rationally. This was explained in a table in the manner of Menger. The second law was easily connected to the general equilibrium approach in handling many commodities.

3.3 Agricultural economists and applied economists

It is noteworthy that in the 1920s and the 1930s some agricultural scholars took up a neoclassical approach to the study of agribusiness. They read J. H. von Thünen, who was one of the originators of marginal analysis as well as the father of economic geography. Yasuo Kondo (1899–2005) made a special study of von Thünen's *Der isolierte Staat in Beziehung auf Landswirtschaft und Nationalökonomie* (Isolated State with respect to Agriculture and Political Economy, 1842). Kondo (1928) exposited Thünen's theory of rent, space or agricultural organization and wage including the concept of marginal productivity, and he published the Japanese version of Thünen (1842) in 1929. Yuzo Yamada, an economist, made a sophisticated study of von Thünen's theory of distribution (Y. Yamada 1934, in Japanese).[17]

It seems that A. V. Chayanov's *Die Lehre von der bäuerlichen Wirtschaft* (The Principles of Family Business, 1923) was also widely read and frequently quoted by the Japanese agriculturalists. Chayanov (1923) was a mixture of various approaches to the analysis of agribusiness. He showed that there were many farms run by families who did not have enough funds to hire any laborers in Russia and believed that the application of capitalistic production was not appropriate for Russian agriculture. He maintained that the hours a family would work within a year depended on the calculation of the pleasure they gained from what they produced, and the pains they suffered from farming. This was a good example of an application of the neoclassical theory of subjective equilibrium to economic decision-making.

Agricultural economics was a field for Japanese economists and statisticians to undertake intensive statistical studies in the 1930s. The Agricultural Economic Society was established in 1924 for the study of all the problems related to rural districts and agriculture such as agribusiness, agricultural policy, statistics and its history; and in 1925, initiated *Nogyo-keizai Kenkyu* (Journal of Rural Economics), which carried many statistical works, with some based on neoclassical ideas. In the 1930s, many Japanese economists were absorbed by the study of the so-called rice problem. The most urgent economic problem of the day was the instability of the price of rice and its supply.

They tackled the problem using data relating to rice, that is, the price determined every day in the transaction market, the quantities traded in the market, shipped every month from each region and consumed every year in the whole country, the price indexes, the demographic changes, the transportation cost by railroad and the storage cost. Some of them made a statistical study of the trend of the rice price, per capita consumption of rice and use of fertilizer. During the 1930s and 1940s, agrarian and neoclassical economists at times studied the rice problem side by side.

Yoshinosuke Yagi in his *A Study on the Prices of Rice and Their Control* (1932) conducted a full-scale statistical study on rice by surveying current studies. He confirmed that King's law, namely the law of demand, which was established first for wheat, existed also in the case of rice. Engel's law, i.e., the share of food in total expenditure is inversely related to the household's income, was also shown to hold true in Japan. Yagi calculated not only the demand elasticity of rice with respect to the price, as did some other economists, but also constructed the price and quantity indexes following W. M. Persons's method. Yagi paid attention to price seasonality, rice supplies as a whole and the amounts shipped from each rice-producing region to other regions including big cities. In Japan, rice is seeded and germinated in the nursery from winter to spring, transplanted in the paddy field during the rainy season of early summer, and harvested in fall. The earliest new crop appears in the market in September when the price is still higher than the average.

Y. Yagi (1932) and Seiichi Tobata and Kazushi Ohkawa's *Autonomous Sales Organ of Rice* (1938, in Japanese) suggested that local rice merchants were often landlords who were involved in a highly speculative enterprise. Rice has a rich variety of qualities, such as taste, preservation and appearance when steamed. Tobata and Ohkawa (1938) said that the rice market was governed by the monopolistic competition characterized by commodity differentiation and the increasing expense of sales and advertising in the manner of Chamberlin (1933). The local merchant selected the kind of seeds to grow, made the decisions when to ship and sometimes when to purchase back from the markets located in the big cities like Tokyo and Osaka. From around 1900, the railroad network became much more important for rice shipment than marine transportation. Thanks to the railroad, new routes for rice shipment were developed and more rice was brought to cities whose populations were rapidly growing. The price of rice was the lowest from November through January as the supply of new rice arrived on the market. Some merchants in places remote from big cities preserved their rice in the storage houses until the price became higher prior to the next harvest. They took into consideration the costs of storage and interest.

Yagi (1932: 61–2) was optimistic about the market condition for rice:

> There are some reasons why the rice price constantly changes. The regions good for rice production are limited in Japan. But the Japanese people strongly adhere to rice consumption. And bumper crops and poor crops always happen. However, regional difference in the rice price has been diminishing thanks to the development of the railroad network which has made the rice transportation from one area to another very easy and smooth. Local shortage can be compensated by the supply from other areas and foreign countries.
>
> (My translation)

However, the situation was turning out to be less optimistic. The Sixth Subcommittee, which was formed for the theoretical and practical study of rice policy in the Japan Society for the Promotion of Science (JSPS), requested Eiichi Sugimoto make a statistical study of the law of demand for rice by one of the public committees. We will discuss his econometric research and a shifting demand curve for rice depicted in a three dimension space in Chapter 7. With respect to Mirowski's interest, it should be noted that Sugimoto denied the measurability of utility and rejected utility as one of the basic concepts for economic science. He was interested in physics and urged the introduction of more physics into economic theory. He favored the labor theory of value because he thought that human energy could be measured in terms of working hours.

There were other statistical works on rice and other agricultural products as well as on the life of farmers, written in Japanese (also see Chapter 8). Kan Watanabe's "A theory of the business cycle derived from the elasticity of supply and demand" (1932) was the first well-known article to estimate the demand function for hog, beef and horsemeat. It is noteworthy that Takuma Yasui, who could be called the Japanese Samuelson, was encouraged by Watanabe (1932) as well as the discussion of cobweb theorem in Sugimoto (1935), embarked on the analysis of consumer behavior, that is, the theoretical basis for the demand and later on stability analysis in a market economy (see Chapter 5).

From 1924 on, the rice market gradually became controlled and the rice merchants taken out of the market process. Local non-profit organizations called *Sangyo Kumiai* (Industrial Union) took over the job of distribution. The 1924 Rice Act allowed the government to intervene in the market process to adjust the demand and supply of rice. The Act was revised in 1928 and allowed the government to adjust the "market price" of rice as well as the quantity of rice in the market to prevent the volatility of the rice price especially in the preharvest season. The 1933 Rice Control Act stated that the minimum and maximum price of rice should be determined every year with the consideration of the production cost of rice, living expenses and the general price index. The 1939 Rice Distribution Control Act allowed only the Japan Rice Corporation to hold the "rice market" and abolished the Rice Exchange whose function had been shrinking. The 1942 Food Control Act allowed the government to control all food production and distribution and made it easier for the government to wage the Asia-Pacific War.[18]

3.4 Mathematicians and mathematical economists

In the mid 1920s, a group of mathematicians and statisticians such as Magoichiro Watanabe and Seimatsu Narumi promoted mathematical research in economics. Watanabe, who specialized in algebra, was employed by the Tokyo University of Commerce (now Hitotsubashi University) to teach mathematics to economics students. He trained Masao Hisatake and helped other economists study mathematical economics. Narumi, specialized in statistics and probability, taught at Nagoya Commercial College (now Nagoya University). Narumi trained Isamu Yamada, who later became an econometrician at Tokyo University of Commerce, although he himself withdrew from economics after World War II.

Before looking at the mathematicians, we must mention that at Nagoya two economists from Britain made a contribution toward economics teaching and research in Japan. George Cyril Allen (1900–82) was persuaded by W. J. Ashley (University of Birmingham) to go to Nagoya University and taught there for three years from 1922 (Allen 1983: 1–2). He preferred the historical approach to economics rather than applications of neoclassical techniques, and later he became a specialist in the Japanese economy and contributed to E. B. Schumpeter (1940). Ernest Francis Penrose (1895–1984) was attracted by the request of D. H. Robertson and Austin Robinson (Cambridge University) that he fill a position in Japan.[19] It took him 45 days to sail from Birkenhead to Kobe in 1925. He worked in "a large, mainly bare room of the two-storied, wooden structure" which was then called the Industrial Research Bureau of the College of Commerce from 1925–30. He produced a large amount of statistical data such as indexes of agricultural, mineral and industrial production with the electric calculating machine that had been fortuitously brought to Japan from abroad (Germany or the United States) by one of his Japanese colleagues.

Penrose was a full-time professor at Nagoya Commercial College during the period of 1925–30. His salary and travel expenses from England to Nagoya were paid by the Japanese government.[20] His résumé of that time stated as follows:

> In this period he [E. F. Penrose] carried out the first systematic research into the course of population and production in Japan ... and constructed the first indexes of the physical volume of production ever constructed in Japan for agriculture, fisheries and mining. Geometrically weighted averages for each group and for all three combined were constructed for the years 1894–1927. They were first published in a study in English in which they were compared with an index of population increase, showing conclusively that, contrary to widespread opinion at that time, production per head of population substantially increased in a period of rapid population growth.
>
> (Dore and Sinha, 1987: xvii)

Penrose made a great contribution to initiating the making of index numbers and the empirical studies by using them in Nagoya.

Let us turn to the Japanese mathematicians. At first, Watanabe and Narumi took up the economic works done by English-speaking mathematicians such as W. E. Johnson, A. L. Bowley and G. C. Evans. Watanabe (1924) exposited on British mathematician W. E. Johnson's "The pure theory of utility curves" (1913) and A. W. Zotoff's "Notes on the mathematical theory of production" (1923). He later repeated the arguments in a general equilibrium framework in his *Application of Mathematics to Economics* (1933) coauthored by Hisatake which was published in one of the series of books on mathematics. Johnson removed physics-like flavor and hedonic elements from F. Y. Edgeworth's work and developed Pareto-type argument by modifying Edgeworth's "indifference curves" (Edgeworth 1881). Yet Johnson did not mention Pareto at all, whose *Manual of Political Economy*, in which a very similar line of analysis had been developed, was already available in Italian by 1906 and in French by 1909. Johnson (1913) appeared in *Economic Journal* whose editorship was held by J. M. Keynes. This means that Johnson and Keynes ignored the economic literature written in Italian or French.[21] However, Johnson's paper also "anticipated" Slutsky-type arguments of partitioning the effect of a price change on the quantity demanded into the substitution and income effects. Watanabe's exposition of Johnson reduced the entry barrier for Japanese scholars who wished to tackle the mathematical theory of consumer behavior. Watanabe with his student

Masao Hisatake continued to make a theoretical analysis of consumer behavior in the line of Johnson. They studied the effect of income changes on the demand for commodities as well as the effect of the changes in the price of a commodity on the demand for the commodity itself and other commodities. It looked as if their research result *Application of Mathematics to Economics* (1933) would have led to J. R. Hicks and R. G. D. Allen's "A reconsideration of the theory of value" (1934), which is considered to be the classical paper of modern demand analysis. In fact, Hicks and Allen (1934) caught the eyes of Japanese mathematicians soon after its appearance in *Economica.*

Narumi studied statistics in London, the United States, Germany and Sweden from 1921–3. After returning to Japan, he translated "Theory of utility," Chapter 1 of A. L. Bowley's *Mathematical Groundwork of Economics* (1924), into Japanese. He also translated more than 80 percent of G. C. Evans's *Mathematical Introduction to Economics* (1930) into Japanese and published it in 1938 as one of the series of books on applied mathematics. It is hard to tell to what degree Narumi's work had some influence on his colleague-economists at Nagoya as well as a group of mathematicians. However, it can be said that these mathematicians' attitudes toward economics was explained by the words of Zotoff (1923: 115):

> In spite of the maxim, "Il ne s'agit pas de faire lire, mais de faire penser," we think that mathematical problems should not be given to economists to solve, and that mathematical economics should be treated as simply as possible, with all results worked out in detail.

By the time they found Hicks and Allen (1934), the Japanese were joining the world community of internationally oriented economists, who could be called "mathematical economists," thanks to A. Amonn's lectures at the Imperial University of Tokyo, J. A. Schumpeter's visit to Japan in 1931, and the expeditious shipment of three international journals, *Zeitschrift für Nationalökonomie* (1930–), *Econometrica* (1933–) and *Review of Economic Studies* (1933–). Narumi's student Isamu Yamada translated part 2 of the article, the mathematical part, into Japanese as early as 1934 (I. Yamada 1934). Narumi's introduction (1934: 255) to the translation reflected his understanding of the theory of consumer behavior.

> One of the characteristics of the article is the application of the elasticity of income and price as well as that of substitution. The concept of the elasticity of substitution has been becoming more and more important since Hicks and J. Robinson introduced it into theoretical economics, especially in the theory of distribution. We are able to part with not only the measurability of utility which was followed by Gossen, Jevons, Walras and Marshall, but also the indefiniteness of the signs of the coefficients of the second partial differential derived from the so-called utility function index of Edgeworth and Pareto.
>
> (My translation)

Allen (1934) discussed in English Eugen Slutsky's pioneering analysis, "Sulla teoria del bilancio del consumatore" (On the theory of the budget of the consumer, 1915), which was published during World War I. Hicks (1939) named the fundamental equation of consumer behavior theory – the equation which states the changes in demand for good *j* as the function of prices and income following the changes in the price of good *i* by breaking up of the effect of a price change on demand into a substitution effect and an income effect – Slutsky's equation. Around the same time as the British economists' discussions, the American Henry Schultz (1935) rediscovered Slutsky (1915).

Takuma Yasui (1909–95) was the first Japanese mathematical economist who had not studied advanced mathematics in his student life but went on to teach it to himself with the help of the mathematicians around him. He was trained at the Imperial University of Tokyo, read the books and papers written in Japanese by Ichiro Nakayama and Yasuma Takata, and started to publish a series of theoretical research papers in the Walrasian general equilibrium framework in 1933 (see the next section). His papers appeared in *Keizaigaku Ronshu* (Economic Review), published by the economics department of the Imperial University of Tokyo.[22]

Yasui (1940b) developed a sophisticated analysis of consumer behavior generating the law of demand along the lines of Slutsky and Hicks and Allen. He first summarized Slutsky (1915) to make it easier to discuss the law of demand rather than the substitutability or complementarity of commodities. Slutsky (1915) and Hicks and Allen (1934) had already clarified that the demand for a good has to be a monotonic decreasing function of its own price with a negative slope in the price and quantity plane as long as it is not an inferior good. Yasui made a step forward to obtain the universal law of demand and tried to clarify the conditions under which the demand curve is convex or concave.

Masazo Sono (1886–1969), a mathematician from Kyoto Imperial University, discussed the separability of goods as early as 1943. He was specialized in abstract algebra and a friend of the economist Yasuma Takata. Initially Sono had some doubts about Hicks's definitions of substitutability and complementarity among commodities in Hicks's *Théorie mathématique de la value en régime de libre concurrence* (1937) and *Value and Capital* (1939). Nonetheless, Sono came to the conclusion that he had ascertained the suitability of Hicks's definitions of substitutability and complementarity by developing the idea of the separability of commodities in terms of utility in his "The effect of price changes in the demand and supply of separable goods" (1943, in Japanese). The English version (1961) of Sono (1943) appeared in *International Economic Review* because this work anticipated similar studies published later in the English language (Michio Morishima's editorial note to Sono 1961). Yasui in his "The idea of separability and the assumption of homogeneity in Slutsky theory" (1944: 150, in Japanese) clarified Sono's idea and gave it the following definition in the case of three commodities *X*, *Y* and *Z*:

> *X* and *Y* are separable from *Z* if and only if the marginal rate of substitution between *X* and *Y* is independent of the demand for *Z*.
>
> (My translation)

Yasui in his "Slutsky on the idea of separability and homogeneity postulate" (1944, in Japanese) developed Sono's idea and discussed the case where *Z* was a special commodity called money. Morishima's historical note (1961: 273) gave another example: "the marginal rate of substitution between an evening dress and a kimono [Japanese traditional dress] should be independent of the consumption of bread and rice." Morishima (1961: 273) continued to explain the importance of separability:

> If it is sharpened to additive separability or homogeneous separability, it implies that consumers first allocate expenditure among the several budget categories and then decide how best to spend each budget allotment on the commodities within the category, with no further reference to purchase in other categories.
>
> (Originally in English)

Japanese economists were separated into two groups relating to the measurability of utility. Some economists and mathematicians did not think that utility could be measured, as discussed above. However, others believed that they needed to find some way to measure utility for welfare economics. Hisatake's "The theoretical development of how to measure utility" (1942, in Japanese) discussed Irving Fisher's method to measure the marginal utility of money for the average household and Ragner Frisch's isoquant method to measure the elasticity of money using data on household expenditure. Hisatake's "A reconsideration on the concept of utility" (1959) also included the discussion on expected utility made by John von Neumann and Oskar Morgenstern's *Theory of Games and Economic Behavior* (1944).

4 General equilibrium theory and macroeconomics

Japanese economists were engaged in the general equilibrium approach using mathematics with the help of Alfred Amonn and J. A. Schumpeter in the last half of the 1920s. Some Japanese economists had understood the significance of general equilibrium theory by the late 1920s through the works of Schumpeter (1908), L. Walras (1874–7) and G. Cassel (1927). Amonn (1883–1962), a Czech, taught economics at the Imperial University of Tokyo from 1926–9. He was trained at the University of Vienna and was interested in general equilibrium theory including the Casselian simplified system, the history of marginal utility theory starting with H. H. Gossen, and Ricardian economics (Amonn 1932). His long article "Cassel's economic system" (Amonn 1924, in German) and book entitled *Object and Basic Concepts of Economics* (Amonn 1927, in German) had already been published before his coming to Japan. Amonn in his lectures on economic principles made use of Cassel's *The Theory of Social Economy* (1923) to give Japanese students an excellent explanation of Casselian general equilibrium approach. Moreover, W. Leontief's *The Structure of American Economy, 1919–1939* (1941) was regarded as the first empirical application of general equilibrium theory. As mentioned, Tokuzo Fukuda advised Ichiro Nakayama to make a special study of A. Cournot and L. Walras.

Takuma Yasui and Takeyasu Kimura, who later became "mathematical economists," attended Amonn's lectures. Yasui (1980: 48) writes about his impression of the lectures as follows:

> When I was a student, Amonn gave us a detailed and felicitous explanation of the Casselian system of simultaneous equations. But I did not get the full understanding of its content or significance. I did not understand at all that mathematics is a necessary tool for economists.
>
> I came to realize it when I began to read the papers along the lines of the Lausanne School and its related approach. I realized that I had to study mathematics. I had forgotten mathematics.
>
> (My translation)

A few years later, Yasui started to read papers of the Lausanne School and other related works and became interested in Walrasian economics, that is, general equilibrium theory and mathematical economics. He realized that he needed to study mathematics. He taught himself advanced modern economics by posing questions to the mathematicians around him. Yasui had no formal training in advanced mathematics.

Schumpeter had a direct influence on young scholars who later became the leading "mathematical" economists in Japan. In January 1931, Schumpeter visited Japan and delivered lectures in Tokyo and Kobe. In Tokyo, Schumpeter said to young Yasui, "Begin with Walras if you plan to study economic theories" (Yasui 1988, in Japanese: 5). The story of "Begin with Walras" has become a well-known episode in Japan that symbolizes the dawn of Japanese neoclassical economics, which was called modern economics at the time. In fact, Schumpeter's advice became one factor in Yasui's decision to start the study of economics along the Walrasian line, other factors being Amonn's lectures and his habit of reading international journals of economics.

Yasuma Takata used Cassel's *The Theory of Social Economy* (1921b) in his lectures on economic principles at Kyoto Imperial University in 1929. Takata filled the position from which Hajime Kawakami was forced to resign due to a "charge" of being a left-wing sympathizer in 1928. Kei Shibata, Kawakami's student, attended Takata's lectures and was shocked by the mathematical discussion of Cassel's system of simultaneous equations. At the same time, he became interested in the general equilibrium theory.

Shibata in his "An examination of 'the mechanism of price formation' as explained by Mr. Cassel" (1930, in Japanese) discussed one of the formal problems in Cassel's simplified system of general equilibrium, which was pointed out three years later in H. v. Stackelberg's "Two comments on Gustav Cassel's theory of price" (1933, in German) published in *Zeitschrift für Nationalökonomie*. Shibata first summarized Cassel's system which had n consumption goods, r factors of production and $n \times r$ constant technical coefficients, where a_{ij} was the quantity of the factor of production i, which was needed to produce one unit of consumption good j. He argued that the number of production factors could exceed the number of products in Cassel's system and that then the number of equations would exceed the number of unknowns in the set of equations of the supply and demand for productive factors. In that case, the number of unknowns would exceed the number of equations in the whole system (Sugihara 1987a).

As mentioned in the previous section, in 1933 Takuma Yasui began to publish his papers in the line of neoclassical economics. Yasui regarded the Walrasian system of general equilibrium in its mathematical form as an open-ended framework upon which economists could erect theories. He wrote a series of papers in Japanese attempting to update Walrasian economics in light of Viennese contributions. Yasui examined the important economic concepts which appeared in the works of Walras and his followers and discussed the formal structures of the latest economic theories.

One series of Yasui's papers dealt with problems of capital and its role in production. In his "Pure economics and the price theory" (1933, in Japanese), Yasui examined the role of Walrasian "fixed" and "fluid" (circulation) capital under the assumption of constant coefficients of production, made a critical assessment of Cassel's system of simultaneous equations in light of the commentaries of W. Valk (1928), J. Neubauer (1930, in German), Stackelberg (1933, in German), F. Zeuthen (1932, in German) and K. Shibata (1930, in Japanese), and then applied modern production functions to the theory of production. In his "Imputation theory and marginal productivity" (1934, in Japanese), Yasui extended the analysis of two types of production theories: one with variable-coefficient production functions and another with constant coefficients, which could be readily linked to the imputation theory elaborated by Schumpeter (1908). In his "The time element and capital interest" (1936, in Japanese), which was the most appreciated paper among all those published by him in the 1930s, Yasui, on the basis of the Walrasian general equilibrium framework, made a comprehensive study of the production-period concept developed by Böhm-Bawerk and K. Wicksell, as well as the duration-of-capital-period developed by Åkerman and Wicksell, and the forward-looking theory of capital return developed by F. Knight.

In the early 1930s, Japan's government needed to take measures to cope with the chronic depression. The study of national income, both in theory and in practice, was rapidly developed in order to make observations on Japan's macroeconomy. The data of national income became more and more important as the basis for the policy of increasing production and the rational allocation of the national economic power when Japan entered into the war with China in 1937 and then into World War II in 1941 (Japan Statistical Society ed. 1944).

Around February 1940, Jiro Akimaru, the head of the task force on the war economy in the Japanese Army, called about 20 scholars including economists to make a comparative study of the economic and the military power of Britain and America, Germany, the Soviet Union and Japan. They took up W. Leontief's *The Structure of American Economy, 1919–1939* (1941), a couple of copies of which arrived in Japan in 1941. Nakayama, one of the members of the committee, thought that the general equilibrium theory was linked directly with statistical numbers by Leontief's input-output analysis.

There remained only one copy of the report entitled "The Allied Economic Power of the UK and the USA during a War" (Akimaru ed. 1941, in Japanese) which was kept secretly by Hiromi Arisawa, one of the task force members who was a Marxian economist.[23] Arisawa and Minoru Miyagawa investigated the military and economic power of the two countries assuming they would cooperate in a war against Japan. Arisawa and Miyagawa did not construct a matrix, although Arisawa said that Leontief (1941) was useful for their job. They summarized the productive capacity and employment for each industry including the munitions industry, marine transportation capacity and the structure of the gross national expenditure in Britain and America through the use of many tables and charts. The conclusions regarding the allied economic power of the UK and the USA during a war stated as follows:

> (1) If the UK allies itself with the USA and its shortage of the supply is supplemented by the spare capacity of the USA, the UK has enough economic power to fight a war at the supposed level.
> (2) If the UK and the USA ally with each other, they have more than 1.4 billion pounds sterling (seven billion US dollars) of spare munitions supply for a third country.
> (3) Their supply power will need one year or one year and half to reach its maximum.
> (4) The destruction of more than 500,000 tons of British ships on average per month should be enough to make void the aid to the UK from the USA, because it is assumed that the allied shipbuilding power should be around six million tons per year by the year of 1943.
>
> (Akimaru ed. 1941, in Japanese; quoted in Ikeo 1994a, in Japanese: 195, my translation)

These pessimistic results of their studies were presented at a meeting of the Japanese Army in September 1941. However, their laborious studies were completely neglected by the Army (Nakayama 1973 supplement, in Japanese: 62; Ikeo 1994a, in Japanese: 195–6).

5 On physics

To my knowledge, mathematicians, rather than physicists, initiated mathematical neoclassical economics in Japan in the mid 1920s and have helped mathematize economics since. It can be safely said that no Japanese physicist played any part in the process of introducing neoclassical economics into Japan. Presumably, they were too busy trying to assimilate the foreign view of the world and nature, which meant encountering the revolutionary storms in physics, that is, the shift from Newtonian and the so-called classical physics of the nineteenth century toward the new physics of the twentieth century, including general relativity and quantum mechanics.

Mitsutomo Yuasa's *A Hundred-year History of Science and Technology in Japan* (1980, in Japanese: 151) states:

> It is well known that Hantaro Nagaoka was the first Japanese person to publish his original article (on building an atomic model using an experimental method) in a Western science journal in 1903.... Although many Japanese still tend to believe that the job of theoretical physicists is computation with the help of mathematics, the truth is that the essence of theoretical physics is to study the heart of nature by contemplation. A theoretical physicist should be a natural philosopher rather than a mathematician. It can be said that the first Japanese physicist in this sense was Jun Ishihara.
>
> (My translation)

Ishihara started to work at Tohoku Imperial University in 1911. Yoshio Nishina (1890–1951), the second Japanese physicist in the above sense, studied physics in Europe from 1921–8 and worked under Niels Bohr in Copenhagen from 1923–8. After returning to Japan, Nishina nurtured many physicists including two Nobel laureates, Hideki Yukawa (1907–81) and Sin-itiro Tomonaga (1906–79). Yukawa, the first Japanese Nobel Prize winner in 1949, won his prize for meson theory, while Tomonaga won for renormalization theory in 1965.

It seems that Japanese economists began to read physics when they tried to understand Paul Samuelson's papers on mathematical economics and to make economic theories along his lines. Takuma Yasui, who can be called the Japanese Samuelson, studied not only advanced mathematics but also classical physics to write papers on the stability of a competitive economy. Hiroshi Furuya's "Stability analysis of economic equilibrium" (1949) referred to Tomonaga's *Quantum Mechanics* (1949) when he examined the concept of "correspondence principle" in the history of quantum mechanics. Furuya (1949: 183, 187) said:

> Samuelson's "correspondence principle" ... means both that a study of the dynamic stability of an economic system provides many theorems which are useful for comparative statics and that the knowledge about comparative statics can be used in characterizing the dynamic natures of the system. This is a kind of reversible relationship. Although he mentioned nothing about the origin of the concept, it seems to us that it was borrowed from quantum mechanics.
>
> (My translation)

Three social scientists who had studied both Marxian and neoclassical economics and two physicists came together and discussed modern physics and social sciences. Mitsuo Taketani lectured from a methodological standpoint on the historical development of physics from Hamilton through the formation of quantum mechanics, while Ryogo Kubo explained statistical mechanics. The two were asked questions by Eiichi Sugimoto, Shigeto Tsuru and Zenya

Takashima. Their lectures and discussion were published as *Contemporary Communication between Natural and Social Scientists* (Taketani *et al.* 1949). Taketani had read K. Marx's *Das Kapital* (1867–94) and was interested in the labor theory of value and dialectics. Sugimoto criticized Pareto's general equilibrium theory, functionalism that had discarded the theory of value, as a metaphorical application of classical physics of the nineteenth century. He believed that the Marxian labor theory of value was superior to the general equilibrium theory of the Lausanne School but that economists had to learn many things, including its descriptive content from quantum mechanics.

However, the influence of physics on economic thinking is still ambiguous in the case of Japanese mathematical economists who were trained at the graduate level in the 1940s and 1950s. There are two other kinds of examples: the cases of Shinichi Ichimura and Hukukane Nikaido. Ichimura received a Ph.D. in economics from MIT just after the end of the Asia-Pacific War. He attended not only Samuelson's lectures at MIT but also W. Leontief's at Harvard University. His "A critical note on the definition of related goods" (Ichimura 1951) was followed by J. R. Hicks's comments (1951). Ichimura said in his letter to me of November 12, 1991:

> I attended the lectures on physics at MIT and received credit for mathematical physics. However, it has never had any particular connection with my economic study. Yet its methodology gave me some useful suggestions.
>
> (My translation)

After returning to Japan, Ichimura cooperated with the Ministry of International Trade and Industry (now the Ministry of Economy, Trade and Industry) and started to make one of the first input-output tables of Japan's economy (of 1951) in the summer of 1953. Ichimura's *The Structure of the Japanese Economy* (1957, in Japanese) is the record of the making of the first input-output table in Japan. Twenty-five specialists and ten assistants spent about twenty months and completed their task in 1955. In this process, Japan's data were processed, organized and very much improved to a high quality (see Chapter 7).

Nikaido was trained as a mathematician. He contributed to the studies of the proof of the existence of equilibrium in a competitive economy in the 1950s and published his *Convex Structure and Economic Theory* (1968) (see Chapter 6). He wrote to me on November 22, 1991 that:

> I was interested in physics in my youth. But I was just a dilettante. My study of physics has passed from my remembrance. I encountered physics while I was ranging over an extensive literature. I cannot say that I have ever made a serious study of physics.
>
> (My translation)

We cannot draw any general conclusion on the influence of physics on economic works made by Japanese economists. However, we may conclude that some

Japanese economists began to care about the use of mathematics in physics after reading Samuelson's scientific papers published in the 1940s, namely in the post-Samuelson era.

6 A few conclusions

Several versions of neoclassical economics were introduced into Japan through the voluntary efforts of various types of economists and mathematicians. In 1930, Japan had a population of 64,450,000, which was larger than Great Britain's 44,795,000 in 1931 and France's 41,228,000 in 1931, although smaller than Germany's 66,030,000 in 1933 and the United States of America's 122,775,000 in 1930. There were enough people in Japan to enable pursuit of various types of research.

The Japanese government even utilized Marxian economists, who were good at statistical studies and/or at the two-sector growth model called a reproduction scheme. The most drastic measure taken by the Japanese government in the history of Japanese thought was probably the adoption in 1872 of Western mathematics, which was considered more efficient than Japanese traditional mathematics, in the educational curriculum (see also C. Sasaki 1994).

Notes

1 This chapter is based on my contribution (Ikeo 1996a) to the international comparative research project "Marginalism at the Margins" organized by Philip Mirowski around 1993–4 together with my research, such as Ikeo (1991, 1993b).

Ikeo (1991) was presented at the annual meeting of the Japan Association of Economics and Econometrics at Kansei Gakuin University near Kobe in 1990. Ikeo (1993b) was presented at the annual meeting of the History of Economics Society at the University of Maryland, Washington, DC, in 1991. An early version of Ikeo (1996a) was presented at the first meeting of Veblen Society in Chicago and at a regular meeting of Kress Society at Harvard University in August 1994. I thank all the attendees for giving me useful comments and encouragement. I also thank Shinichi Ichimura, Hukukane Nikaido, Yasunori Fukagai, Masao Fukuoka, Hanjiro Haga, Masahiro Kawamata, Yoshio Nagai, Takashi Negishi, Kaoru Sugihara, Fumihide Toyooka, Kiichiro Yagi and Shigekazu Yamashita for their valuable information relating to this study, and Philip Mirowski and Paul Pecorino for their comments on earlier versions of Ikeo (1996a). I express my special thanks to P. Mirowski for giving me the opportunity to contribute to his challenging project "Marginalism at the Margins" by writing Ikeo (1996a).

2 The Japanese economists like T. Yasui preferred very much to use the phrase "economic research in Walrasian or Casselian framework" rather than the phrase "mathematical economics" probably because they wanted to avoid criticism as much as possible in the use of mathematics in economic research by those who felt hostile to mathematical economics.

Moreover, Ikeo (1991) also shows that few English-speaking people, except Irving Fisher (1925), H. L. Moore and J. R. Hicks, were interested in general equilibrium theory before 1930. In Britain, Hicks began with Vilfredo Pareto's work (on general equilibrium theory). In the US, the theory was spread through the arrival and immigration of economists from Central Europe after around 1930 along with the popularity of Pareto's works on sociology. Few leading American economists seriously read Walras's *Eléments* (1874–7) before the publication of the English translation in 1954. See the book reviews such as Milton Friedman (1955) and Robert Solow (1956).

3 Takashi Negishi (1972, in Japanese; 1996) clarified Takuma Yasui's contributions to the development of general equilibrium to Japan. Negishi (1995, 1998) discussed Kei Shibata and Yasuma Takata's contributions to the research of general equilibrium approach and beyond. Negishi (1990a) examined the studies of von Thünen in Japan.

4 See Yajima (1991, 2003).

5 W. G. Beasley's *The Rise of Modern Japan* (1990) includes a detailed report on the violence directed against foreigners in Japan in the first few years after the opening of the ports. Beasley (1990: 39, 43) reported:

> Two Russians were killed in 1859 and a Dutch merchant captain in February 1860. Townsend Harris' secretary was murdered in January 1861. There was an organized night attack on the British legation at Tozenji [a Buddhist temple] in July 1861, followed by another smaller one a year after....
>
> [S]uch attacks ... were also made on Japanese employed by foreigners and on officials who were thought to have contributed to the continued foreign presence in Japan....
>
> In September 1862 a British party from Yokohama, riding through the nearby village of Namamugi, failed to yield the right of way to [a *daimyo*, that is, Japanese feudal lord] Shimazu Hisamitsu's entourage, which was on its way back to Kyoto from Edo [now Tokyo]. The escorting samurai [Japanese feudal warrior] killed Charles Richardson, a visitor from Shanghai, and wounded two of his companions.

6 Tessa Moriss-Suzuki (1989) gives a bird's-eye view of the theme starting with the discussion of Confucianism. However, she mentions only the Confucian elements which still remain in Japanese society. See also Chapter 8.

7 The construction of large bridges over rivers was banned during the Edo era. The use of stone-made bridges was allowed in a few regions.

8 Utilitarian ideas were not positively examined in Japan because they lacked the concept of family (see Chapter 8). I thank Shigekazu Yamashita and Yasunori Fukagai for their information on utilitarianism in Japan. In August 1994 the second world meeting of the International Society for Utilitarian Studies was held in Japan and one of the themes was the spread of utilitarianism across various countries including Japan. We may have to consider the meaning of "spread" seriously. If it means that at least one scholar read a book or paper on the relevant subject seriously, Japanese ideas should be spread with the research results by specialists in Japanese studies.

9 Kanazawa (2011: 14–15) states that at the Tokyo College of Commerce economics was taught by Juichi Soyeda (1864–1929) in 1891 and by Amano (1861–1938) in 1892. Both Amano and Soyeda studied at Tokyo University and took the course on Political Economy by Earnest Fenollosa. From 1884–7 Soyeda studied economics at Cambridge University. Marshall agreed to become his supervisor and Soyeda took courses by H. S. Foxwell, Henry Sidgwick and William Cunningham (Hirowatari 1924: 8–11). Soyeda sent several reports on the Japanese economy to *Economic Journal*.

10 I misspelled Sumio Tedzuka's given name before 2013.

11 See also Jean-Philippe Touffut (ed.) *Augustin Cournot: Modelling Economics* (2007).

12 Menger's collection arrived in Japan in 1923. Hitotsubashi University owns Menger's library collection including the books and journals he had obtained in his life, whereas Duke University owns Menger's papers including his handwritten, unpublished correspondence.

13 Schumpeter was in the US in 1927 and returned to Bonn in 1928.
14 Hayasaka (1971–2) "Various aspects of Japanese economic thought in retrospect" Part 2, March 1972, pp. 115–16.
15 With regard to Nakayama (1970), see also Nakayama's introduction to Volume 2 of his *Collected Works* (1972).
16 In 1930, Kinnosuke Otsuka, the translator of Marshall's *Principles of Economics* (1890), lectured on the Marxian version of the principles of economics at Tokyo University of Commerce because he preferred Marxian to neoclassical economics. This suggests that there was no great antagonism between neoclassical and Marxian economists there. In contrast, Shinzo Koizumi of Keio University and Yasuma Takata of Kyoto Imperial University fought against Marxians, such as Tamizo Kushida of the Ohara Institute for Social Research. Seibi Hijikata of the Imperial University of Tokyo also clashed with Kushida. The so-called parallel lectures on the principles of economics, neoclassical and Marxian versions, were institutionalized in the curriculums of many Japanese universities until the late twentieth century.
17 Both Kondo and Y. Yamada criticized von Thünen's formal treatment of wages and this question was later elaborated by Takashi Negishi (1990a) including the contributions by Paul Samuelson and Robert Dorfman.
18 The 1942 Food Control Act was effective until 1995.
19 E. E. Penrose's "Memoirs of Japan, 1925–30" (1987: 6–7).
20 I thank Fumihide Toyooka of Nagoya University for the information about E. F. Penrose.
21 Schumpeter (1954: 1063) wrote about Johnson (1913) as follows:

> This important paper contains several results that should secure for its author a place in any history of our science. But, having apparently been written in ignorance of Pareto's work, it aroused not unnatural resentment on the part of Italian economists because of its failure to acknowledge Pareto's priority in most essentials.

22 When Yasui (1933) appeared in the university journal, the chairman of the economics department warned Yasui and said, "There are too many mathematical expressions in your paper. It is strange to use mathematical formulae in economics. You should use them as little as possible." Yasui (1988: 4). See also Ikeo (1993a). The chairman was a specialist in insurance who regarded insurance policy as a measure of social policy, that is, the redistribution of income or wealth, and did not use any mathematical expression at all in his writings. It is noteworthy that insurance is the first division of economics to which Japanese mathematicians such as R. Fujisawa made a contribution (Fujisawa 1889, see Chapter 2).
23 According to Hayasaka and Arisawa (1983, in Japanese: 100), the Marxian economist Arisawa was included in the task force because the Army wanted to guarantee the objectivity of the study independent of any speculation and any intention of the Army.

5 General equilibrium theory (1)

Stability analysis[1]

1 Introduction

In Japan, mathematicians played a leading part in assimilating Western scientific approach and providing an internationally oriented attitude from the mid nineteenth century on. From around 1930 on, they spread contemporary mathematical knowledge by publishing many new textbooks in Japanese. As shown in Chapter 4, some were interested in mathematical economics and were unsatisfied with economists' use of mathematics. During the 1945–50 period, when Japan was still occupied by the Allied after the Pacific Campaign of World War II, Japanese theoretical economists were making more intensive research in mathematical economics with the cooperation of Japanese mathematicians than ever before.

During the 1940s, Japanese theoretical economists such as Takuma Yasui, Hideo Aoyama and Michio Morishima, and one mathematician Masazo Sono, intensively worked on the so-called stability analysis, namely the question of market mechanism and economic dynamics, discussing not only mathematical implications of economic models but also economic meanings of mathematical models. As a consequence, they mathematized economics more rapidly and intensively than ever before. In particular, Yasui's contributions to the development of general equilibrium theory were examined by Takashi Negishi (1972, in Japanese) and Yasui and Morishima's stability analysis was discussed in English in E. Roy Weintraub (1987b). Then Weintraub in his *Stabilizing Dynamics* (1991a) clarified that, by 1950, two Japanese economists, Yasui and Morishima, had reached the qualitative theory of stability developed by A. M. Liapunov although their contributions in Japanese were not included in Negishi's influential survey article "The stability of a competitive economy" (Chapter 2; Negishi 1962). Liapunov was gaining popularity outside the Soviet Union (now Russia) but was as yet little known to the Western economists of the day.

It is worth discussing their works in this period not only because they were all published in Japanese and relatively inaccessible to economists outside Japan, but also because their research activity gives us an interesting example of a whole process of shift in the economic conceptualization of the economy as well as in the mathematical tools and the specification of the question. This chapter will show the process of organizing economic knowledge through the introduction of more mathematics into the economics literature.[2]

Section 2 gives a brief history of mathematics in Japan and shows how the mathematics useful for stability analysis became available to economists. Yasui's mathematical study is embedded in this section. Section 3 discusses work by H. Aoyama, Sono, Morishima and Yasui, and focuses on the analytical images of the economy and the ideas of the working of the competitive market which they had in mind. It also pays attention to why several Japanese economists became interested in J. R. Hicks's *Value and Capital* (1939) right after its publication. Section 4 draws some conclusions.

2 The melting pot of various mathematical traditions

We will start with a brief history of mathematics in Japan in order to discuss the history of stability analysis. This analysis is very mathematical in essence as well as in its outward form. Many Japanese scientists tend to organize their scientific knowledge based on and around various types of mathematics and to discuss the interpretative contents of the formulations. The reason this practice has been adopted is probably due to mathematicians having been the leaders in Japan's scientific society and the relatively low linguistic barrier. Mathematicians were the first intellectual group in Japan that managed to produce professional works that contributed to the development of an academic field in the world context after Japan opened its door to the rest of the world in 1854.

The Mathematical Society of Tokyo was established as the first academic society in Japan in 1877, the same year as the establishment of Tokyo University (now the University of Tokyo) as the first (national) university in Japan.[3] Although more than half of the members were *Wasan-ka*, they recognized the importance of Western mathematics and advocated its systematic introduction into the educational curriculum. They realized that Western mathematics was more efficient than *Wasan* when it was shown in a journal that the integral calculations which *Wasan-ka* had obtained with painful effort for many years were simply solved by using functional symbols in Western mathematics (PSJ 1978, vol. 1: 121).

At a meeting in 1884, the name of the society was changed to the Mathematical and Physical Society of Tokyo with the "unanimous" consent given by only 16 attendees to the proposal made by D. Kikuchi (1855–1917). He claimed that both subjects were closely related. Kikuchi studied at University College London and Cambridge from 1870 through 1877, passed the tripos of mathematics with first-class honors in April 1877 and was appointed professor at the University of Tokyo in June. The successful coup by Kikuchi and the mathematicians of the University of Tokyo was followed by the gradual withdrawal of *Wasan-ka*, who were not interested in physics, as well as the naval people and amateur mathematicians who did contribute to the assimilation of Western mathematics in Japan (PSJ 1978, vol. 1: 128). The name of the society was changed again to the Mathematical and Physical Society of Japan in 1919. The society broke into two, the

Mathematical Society of Japan and the Physical Society of Japan, in October 1945, two months after the end of the Pacific Campaign of World War II. Then, both edited their history for the commemoration of their centennial anniversary in 1977 and published *The History of Physics in Japan* (PSJ 1978, in Japanese) and *A Hundred Year History of Mathematics in Japan* (MSJ 1983–4, in Japanese).

A young Japanese person who wanted to become a mathematician in the nineteenth century had to study in Europe or North America because there was no education system in which to study mathematics at an advanced level in Japan but for a few visiting mathematicians from abroad.[4] Rikitaro Fujisawa (1861–1933) was the most important mathematician in this group for the process of introducing Western mathematics into Japan because he was "the first Japanese who had mastered mathematics" (MSJ 1983, vol. 1: 183). Before him, mathematics was not created in Japan; it was just memorized by students. One of his best students, Teiji Takagi (1875–1960), wrote:

> Of course, Western mathematics had been introduced into Japan before Professor Fujisawa. There were British, French and German mathematics.... At best, there was only the notion of calculus in Japan when "this new figure of Fujisawa" came back with Christopher's functional analysis, Reye's projection geometry, Kronecker's algebra and many other souvenirs. Fujisawa brought back "the whole mathematics" of the world which was neither anachronistic nor narrow. It was unduly important for Japan's mathematics and a big turning point in the history of new Japanese mathematics which should be written in the future.[5]
>
> (Takagi 1935b, my translation)

Fujisawa trained several excellent mathematicians who became known to the rest of the world. They included Takagi and M. Fujiwara. Takagi was "one of the half dozen mathematicians who [developed] the ideas of class-fields which Hilbert had sketched out in his paper on algebraic number fields" (Reid 1986: 84). He became famous, especially among German-speaking mathematicians, for his "On a relative Abelian number field" (Takagi 1920, in German). He also published enlightening textbooks in Japanese including his *Lectures on Algebra* (Takagi 1935a, third edn.), which was referred to by T. Yasui in his "The convergency postulate and dynamic stability conditions" (1948a, in Japanese: 123) when he discussed Hicksian stability conditions in quadratic forms.

A Hundred Year History of Mathematics in Japan (MSJ 1983, vol. 1: 183, 280) listed those who studied mathematics in Germany, France, Britain or the United States after 1890 (that is, post-Fujisawa mathematicians).[6] There were apparent changes in the pattern of study abroad before and after Fujisawa. First, more Japanese visited Europe and North America to study mathematics after they had already studied mathematics at an undergraduate level or beyond. Second, Japanese mathematicians tended to choose German universities for their advanced study up to the 1920s. Third, some mathematicians visited several places not only to study but also to make presentations beginning around 1920.

For the economists, Matsusaburo Fujiwara (1881–1946) and a group of mathematicians in Sendai, and Msazo Sono (1886–1969) in Kyoto were particularly important among the above aspiring mathematicians. Sono was taught by J. Kawai, K. Miwa and J. Yoshikawa at Kyoto Imperial University (Kyoto University after 1946), which was established in 1897. Around 1914, he came to know economist-sociologist Y. Takata (1883–1972). In the early 1940s, Sono not only published a few papers on economic theories but also delivered lectures on mathematical economics at the Faculty of Economics, Kyoto Imperial University. His contribution to the so-called stability analysis will be discussed in the next section.

The contribution of M. Fujiwara and the people at Tohoku Imperial University (now Tohoku University) in Sendai, 350 kilometers northeast of Tokyo, to mathematics and mathematical sciences will be examined next. Fujiwara, who was a student of R. Fujisawa at the Imperial University of Tokyo (the University of Tokyo between 1877 and 1886 as well as after 1946), studied in Europe from 1907–11 and was appointed professor of Tohoku Imperial University in 1911. He specialized in analysis and was interested in integer, algebra, geometry, applied mathematics, *Wasan* or Japanese traditional mathematics and Oriental mathematics. Fujiwara made a valuable contribution to the spread of accurate mathematical knowledge among young scholars, including economists after around 1930 on, by publishing excellent books written in Japanese incorporating the latest mathematical achievements. His *Algebra* (two volumes, the first edition, 1928 and 1929) and *Calculus* (two volumes, 1934 and 1939) were widely read. The readers of his books included young mathematically oriented economists such as M. Morishima who found G. Frobenius's "On the matrices with positive elements" (1908, in German) in Fujiwara's *Algebra* (vol. 1, 1929).

From 1911 through 1943, it can be safely said that Tohoku Imperial University was an enclave of the world mathematics community in Asia. Young Chinese scholars including Chen Kien-Kwong (1893–1971) and Su Bun-Chin (1902–) studied mathematics as students in the 1920s and became the leading mathematicians in China after World War II. The Sendai mathematicians kept close contact with European and American mathematicians including the Berlin group. From 1925 through 1930, the mathematicians in Sendai such as Fujiwara, Kubota, Y. Okada (1892–1957) and T. Takasu (1890–1972) contributed their papers to *Mathematische Zeitschrift* edited by Leon Lichtenstein in Berlin with the cooperation of K. Knopp, E. Schmidt and I. Schur.

What was most important is that *Tohoku Mathematical Journal*, the first international journal of mathematics in Japan, was established privately by T. Hayashi (1873–1935) a month before the birth of the mathematics department at Tohoku Imperial University in 1911. The journal accepted good papers by both Japanese and foreigners written in five languages and the instructions of submission were as follows:

> The Editor of this Journal, T. HAYASHI, College of Science, Tohoku Imperial University, Sendai, Japan, accepts contributions from any person.

> Contributions should be written legibly in English, French, German, Italian or Japanese.

Hayashi never traveled abroad but he had contributed his papers to journals published in the United States, England, Germany, France and Italy as well as in Switzerland, Holland, Portugal and India. He also enjoyed corresponding with mathematicians abroad. Establishing an international journal was his long-time dream. This journal, with the cooperation of M. Fujiwara, T. Kubota, K. Ogura and physicist J. Ishihara, was very successful and marked a "striking epoch" in the history of mathematics in Japan.

According to M. Fujiwara, before the establishment of *Tohoku Mathematical Journal*, both the number of papers and that of authors were miserably small. There were three mathematical journals in Japan, namely the journal issued by the Mathematical and Physical Society of Tokyo, the *Kiyo* journal issued by Tokyo Imperial University, and the *Kiyo* journal issued by Kyoto Imperial University. M. Fujiwara in his obituary note of T. Hayashi wrote about the significance of the journal as follows:

> In those days the state of mathematics in Japan was very poor.... The number of papers on mathematics at that time did not exceed one dozen every year. To found a new journal, periodically issued, in such a time, was a very bold enterprise. His foresight and audacity only could do this. The publication of the Tohoku Mathematical Journal marked a striking epoch in the history of mathematics in Japan. The management of the Journal was afterwards transferred to the Mathematical Institute from his own hand, he remained, however, as the Chief-Editor until his last day.
>
> (Fujiwara 1935: 266–7)

Tables 5.1 and 5.2 show the historical changes in the numbers of mathematical papers and their authors. Twelve papers were published in the three existing journals of mathematics in Japan by seven authors in 1908, six papers by four authors in 1909, eight papers by four authors in 1910, nine papers by five authors in 1911 and six papers by five authors in 1912. In contrast, *Tohoku Mathematical Journal* carried 131 papers written by Sendai people, 49 by other Japanese and 45 from abroad from 1911–16; 114, 47 and 72 respectively from 1917–21; 116, 101 and 136 respectively from 1922–9; 76, 106 and 249 respectively from 1929–35; and 101, 81 and 154 respectively from 1935–43 (Ikeo 1994b: 582).[7] The contributors from abroad included G. M. Mittag-Leffler, A. Hurwitz, E. Landau, R. W. Weizenböck, D. E. Smith and K. Menger (MSJ 1983, vol. 1: 247–51).

Several leading Japanese mathematicians including Shizuo Kakutani (1911–2004) were born out of this internationally oriented milieu in Sendai. Kakutani became famous for his fixed-point theorem when he published the paper in *Duke Mathematical Journal* of 1941 during his stay at Princeton University. He extended Brouwer's fixed-point theorem to a formulation which can be applied to the existence of a solution in von Neumann's game theory (see Chapter 6).[8]

Table 5.1 The number of contributors to the three mathematical journals in Japan

	1908	*1909*	*1910*	*1911*	*1912*
Number of articles	12	6	8	9	6
Number of authors	7	4	4	5	5

Source: MSJ 1983, vol. 1: 248.

Table 5.2 The number of contributors to *Tohoku Mathematical Journal*

Volumes (years)	*Number of contributors inside of Tohoku University*	*Number of Japanese contributors outside of Tohoku University*	*Number of international contributors*
1–10 (1911–16)	131	49	45
11–20 (1917–21)	114	47	72
21–30 (1922–29)	116	101	136
31–40 (1929–35)	76	106	249
41–49 (1935–43)	101	81	154

Source: MSJ 1983, vol. 1: 249.

In 1944, economist T. Yasui happened to move to Tohoku Imperial University from the Imperial University of Tokyo. He was very much encouraged by the internationally oriented mathematicians in Sendai and kept up vigorous research in theoretical economics. The intellectual environment surrounding him was hospitable for thinking over the mathematical implications of economic models which were appearing one after another in international journals like *Econometrica*. He could ask questions on mathematics directly of the productive mathematicians around him whenever he searched for mathematical literature for his frontier economic research. For example, T. Tannaka suggested that Yasui should read G. Frobenius's "On the matrices with positive elements" (1908, in German) and "On the matrices with positive elements, II" (1909, in German) when he was investigating the properties of the matrices whose elements were positive or nonnegative for his research on stability, especially the so-called Metzlerian condition (Yasui 1971, in Japanese: 164).

M. Fujiwara's mathematical works invited Japanese economists to discuss the properties of differential/difference equation systems more thoroughly and led Yasui to study classical dynamics presented by E. J. Routh, A. Hurwitz, A. Liénard and Chipart. Yasui's "Dynamic stability conditions for the economic equilibrium" (1948b, in Japanese) referred to Routh (1877, 1907), Hurwitz's "On the conditions that an algebraic equation has only roots with negative real parts" (1895, in German), and Liénard and Chipart's "On the sign of the real part of the roots of an algebraic equation" (1914, in French). Yasui (1948b, in Japanese: 141–2) nicely summarized their contribution as follows:

> Routh in relating to a dynamic problem in 1877 solved the problem of finding necessary and sufficient conditions for all the roots of an algebraic

> equation with real coefficients having negative real parts (E. J. Routh, *A Treatise on the Stability of a Given State of Motion*, 1877; ditto, *Advanced Rigid Dynamics*, sixth edition, 1907, SS. 256–307). Later Hurwitz solved the problem independently of Routh (A. Hurwitz, "Über die Bedingungen, unter welchen eine Gleichung nur Wurzeln mit negative reelen Theilen besitzt," *Mathematische Annalen*, Bd. 46, 1895, SS. 273–84). Therefore, it is known as the Routh-Hurwitz problem, or simply the Hurwitz problem. Then, Liénard and Chipart solved it nicely with the use of Bezout-type quadratic form (Liénard, A. et Chipart, "Sur le signe de la partie réele des racines d'une équation algébrique," *Journal de mathématiques pures et appliquées*, 6e série, tome X, 1914, pp. 291–346).
>
> (My translation)

Yasui's "Dynamic stability conditions for the economic equilibrium" (1948b, in Japanese) referred to J. Schur's "On the potential which is limited in a unit circle" (1918, in German) and A. Cohn's "On the number of roots of an algebraic equation in a domain" (1922, in German). Yasui (1948b: 157) summarized their mathematical contribution as follows:

> The problem of finding necessary and sufficient conditions that all the roots of an algebraic equation with any coefficients … being less than unity in absolute value was solved first functionally by Schur and next algebraically by Cohn. (J. Schur, "Über Potenzreichen, die im Innern des Einheitskreises beschränkt sind," *Journal für die reine und angewandte Mathematik*, 148, 1918, SS. 122–145; A. Cohn, "Über die Anzahl der Wurzeln einer algebraischen Gleichung in einem Kreise," *Mathematische Zeitschrift*, 14, 1922, SS. 110–148.)
>
> (My translation)

In fact, M. Fujiwara discussed the so-called Schur-Cohn problem, the Routh-Hurwitz problem and the Hermit problem in his "On algebraic equations whose root lies in a domain or on half line" (1926, in German), his "On the Bezout-type binomial expression" (1925, in German) and his *Algebra*, volume one (1928, in Japanese). Fujiwara's contribution in these works was summarized by Yasui (1948b, in Japanese: 141–2, 157) as follows:

> Fujiwara for the first time showed how to solve the three problems comprehensively, that is, the Routh-Hurwitz problem, the Schur-Cohn problem, and the so-called Hermit problem of finding necessary and sufficient conditions that all the roots of an algebraic equation have positive imaginary parts. He reduced both the Schur-Cohn problem and the Routh-Hurwitz problem to the Hermit problem by making an appropriate linear transformation of variables and applying the method of Liénard and Chipart both to an algebraic equation with real coefficients and to one with any coefficients. (M. Fujiwara, "Über die algebraischen Gleichungen, deren Wurzeln in einem Kreise oder in einer

Halbebene liegen," *Mathematische Zeitschrift*, Bd. 24, 1926, SS. 161–169; ditto, "Über die Bezoutiante zweier Polynome," *Japanese Journal of Mathematics*, Vol. II, pp. 9–12; *Daisugaku* [Algebra], volume one, p. 595.)

(My translation)

It is also noteworthy that Tohoku Imperial University owned the best collection of mathematical literature in Japan. Fujiwara made great efforts to get back numbers of the mathematical journals and books in mathematics published abroad and collected mathematical models for the establishment of the department of mathematics of 1911 during his stay in Europe. After starting *Tohoku Mathematical Journal*, Sendai mathematicians could get European journals of mathematics in exchange for copies of their own gorgeous journal. Fortunately their library survived the fire caused by the attack of B-29 bombers on July 9, 1945. Fujiwara, Kubota and Tannaka all were hurt, and all the classrooms and offices fell victim to the attack (Tohoku University 1960, vol. 1, in Japanese: 573).

It was in the library of the mathematics department that Yasui finally (he said fortuitously) in the spring of 1949 discovered Liapunov's long article entitled "Problème général de la stabilité du mouvement" (1907) which appeared in volume 9 of the *Annales de la Faculté des Sciences de Toulouse*. The paper was published first in Russian in 1892. Yasui in 1949 had already asked the mathematicians around him, in vain, for any paper on the global or general stability of nonlinear dynamic systems. No mathematician in Sendai was interested in the topic at the time. Yasui claimed that he had spent several hours every day in the library taking a look at some 50 papers (maybe 50 was too many) whose titles contained the words "stabilité," "Stabilität" or "stability."[9] He read not only the classical paper written by Liapunov, taking detailed notes, but also other important papers including contemporary papers. He examined the mathematical literature on stability more thoroughly than did Paul Samuelson. The other articles Yasui found important were written by H. Poincaré, A. Liapounoff [*sic*], P. Bohl, E. Cotton, O. Perron published in *Acta Mathématica*, *Journal de mathématiques pures et appliquées*, *Journal für die reine und angewandte Mathematik*, *Bulletin de la société mathématique de France*, *Annales scientifiques de l'école normale supérieure, Mathematische Zeitschrift*. He considered Chapter 8 of Émile Picard's *Traité d'analyse* (1908) and Chapter 7 of Henri Poincaré's *Les méthodes nouvelles de la mécanique céleste* (1892) important, too. It was not an accident that Yasui dug up Liapunov's important paper. For Yasui to say that he "fortuitously" came across the paper is modesty.

A little later, Yasui learned that many Soviet mathematicians had been working on the topic and that this kind of mathematics had been translated into English and spread in North America by the effort of Solomon Lefschetz. E. Roy Weintraub (1987b, 1991a) discusses in detail Yasui's "rediscovery of this mathematical tool" and Weintraub (1991a: Chapter 4) also investigates the spread of Liapunov theory in the United States. In fact, M. Morishima found Liapunov's work on stability in the English version of A. A. Andronow and C. E. Chaikin's *Theory of Oscillations* (1949) which was edited under the direction of Lefschetz.

3 *Tâtonnement* and dynamic systems

As World War II approached its end, no economic literature was arriving in Japan. The limited paper supply rationed for economics was used for reprints of J. R. Hicks's *Value and Capital* (1939), K. Wicksell's *Lectures on Political Economy* (1934–5) and F. Hayek's *Pure Theory of Capital* (1941). A few years after the war, journals and books published abroad were gradually brought into Japan. Japanese economists longed for foreign journals and books, both new and a few years old, because they had to fill up the blank which the war and the postwar turmoil had left in economic research. Economists like Takuma Yasui, who lived in remote areas and had difficulties obtaining copies, came all the way to Tokyo to make copies of journal articles by hand. Large cities like Tokyo, Osaka and Kyoto had such a severe food problem that those who refused to get food from the black market and relied only on rationed food starved to death. The death toll included mathematician J. Kawai at Kyoto, teacher of M. Sono. It is said that mathematician T. Yoshie at the Imperial University of Tokyo died of a heart attack caused by hunger. Yoshie edited *An Introduction to Ordinary Differential Equations* (seventh edn., 1946, in Japanese), which was welcomed by the economists who were interested in stability analysis.

The problem of finding stability conditions for the market economy or the competitive equilibrium was the first theoretical topic of the postwar period for a group of economists and mathematicians in Japan. They earnestly read O. Lange's *Price Flexibility and Employment* (1944), L. A. Metzler's "Stability of multiple markets" (1945), P. Samuelson's series of papers (1941a, 1941b, 1942, 1944) on the stability of equilibrium and *Foundations of Economic Analysis* (1947) as well as the second edition (1946) of Hicks's *Value and Capital*. A little later, Keynesian literature such as L. R. Klein's *Keynesian Revolution* (1947), D. Dillard's *The Economics of John Maynard Keynes* (1948) and A. H. Hansen's *A Guide to Keynes* (1953) were widely read along with J. M. Keynes's *The General Theory of Employment, Interest and Money* (1936). Stability conditions were discussed not only in the Walrasian general equilibrium line, but also in Keynesian contexts such as the multiplier and the liquidity preference approach.

The rest of this section shows how these works on stability were read and studied in Japan, and the kinds of images of an economy which the Japanese scholars had in mind. They needed to create an analytical image of an economy which was adjusting toward equilibrium and of the stability of equilibrium. They searched for a dynamic image of an economy in motion to provide a basis for further mathematical analysis. They resorted to greater mathematical formalism to organize their thoughts on stability analysis.

3.1 A way around Hicks's Value and Capital *(1939)*

It can be said that in the 1920s and 1930s, J. R. Hicks, together with other economists of the London School of Economics, was among the few British economists who paid serious attention to the works published in non-English languages. Hicks's *Value and Capital* (1939) nicely synthesized several important approaches of economic research developing in the intellectual community of economists.[10] The forum was secured by internationally oriented journals of economics such as *Zeitschrift für Nationalökonomie* (1930–), *Econometrica* (1933–) and *Review of Economic Studies* (1933–) as well as by the Econometric Society established in 1930. The Japanese economists including T. Yasui and H. Aoyama read every issue of these journals and were studying problems similar to the ones which Hicks and other internationally oriented economists were discussing in the 1930s. Aoyama also read Scandinavian journals, copies of which were brought back to Japan by Yuzo Yamada. Y. Yamada was studying under O. Morgenstern in Vienna in the mid 1930s.[11] Therefore, the Japanese economists recognized the significance of Hicks (1939) immediately after it was published. The following four points should be emphasized to understand the current situation of economic studies in the 1930s.

First, Hicks and R. G. D. Allen (1934) and R. G. D. Allen (1936) had already elaborated the theory of consumers' behavior, which was set down by the Italian V. Pareto. Hicks (1939) attributed the priority of the breaking up of the effect of a price change on demand into a substitution effect and an income effect to the Russian statistician E. Slutsky's "On the theory of the budget of the consumer" (1915, in Italian). In the 1920s, a couple of Japanese mathematicians became interested in the theory of indifference curves through the works of English-speaking mathematicians, and M. Watanabe and M. Hisatake in their *Application of Mathematics to Economics* (1933, in Japanese) explained the case of three goods or more. The mathematical part of Hicks and Allen (1934) was translated into Japanese by Isamu Yamada as early as 1934 (Chapter 4; Ikeo 1996a).

Second, Hicks's *Value and Capital* (1939) explicitly introduced the general equilibrium approach, which was cultivated on the European continent, into the English-speaking world. The theory was first established by Frenchman L. Walras in Switzerland, followed by V. Pareto, and Swedes K. Wicksell and G. Cassel. I. Nakayama's *Pure Economics* (1933, in Japanese) explained the methodology of general equilibrium theory and contributed to popularizing a Schumpeterian version of Walrasian economics in Japan. T. Yasui started to publish articles along Walrasian lines written in Japanese in 1933 (Chapter 4; Ikeo 1993a).[12]

Third, Hicks adopted process analysis (or in B. Ohlin's terminology period analysis) to deal with the dynamics of economic changes. This line of study already had a rich history and was intensively discussed in Japanese by H. Aoyama in the 1930s and 1940s (Negishi and Ikeo 1999, in Japanese). Aoyama in his "Myrdal's theory of economic fluctuation" (1938b, in Japanese) started with the cumulative processes of inflation and deflation which were articulated in K. Wicksell's monetary economics. He elaborated the step-by-step analysis which was formulated by Englishman D. H. Robertson in his *Banking Policy and the Price Level* (1932) and followed by Scandinavians in their studies of monetary policy and period analysis such as G. Myrdal's *The Problem of Price Formation and Changeability* (1927, in Swedish) and "On monetary equilibrium" (1931, in Swedish), E. Lindahl's *The Means of Monetary Policy* (1930, in Swedish) and *Studies in the Theory of Money and Capital* (1939), and B. Ohlin's "Some notes on the Stockholm theory of savings and investment" (1937). Aoyama also traced differential/difference models which were set out in R. Frisch's "Propagation problems and impulse problems in dynamic economics" (1933), Frisch and H. Holme's "The characteristic solutions of a mixed difference and differential equation occurring in economic dynamics" (1935), and M. Kalecki's "A macrodynamic theory of business cycles" (1935). Aoyama in his "Robertson on the theory of price changes" (1939, in Japanese) followed Robertson's assumption of a "day," "which is finite but nevertheless so short that the income which a man receives on a given day cannot be allocated during its course to any particular use" (Robertson 1933: 399). Later Aoyama published "A critical note on D. H. Robertson's theory of savings and investment" (Aoyama 1940a) in *Kyoto University Economic Review* and made his research results of the 1930s accessible to Western economists.

Hicks modeled a competitive economy moving over time as a chain of static equilibrium, which he labeled temporary equilibrium. He assumed that the adjustment of the market-clearing processes toward a temporary equilibrium was completed in a short period called a "week," and that his economic system consisted of a series of temporary equilibria by making the "week" short enough to ignore the changes in prices. Aoyama in his "The static theory of general equilibrium and its dynamization" (1938a, in Japanese) picked the concept of momentary dynamic equilibrium in Frisch's "Statics and dynamics" (1929, in Norwegian) and discussed a sequence of momentary equilibrium which was established in a Walrasian exchange economy with multiple commodities. Aoyama in his "On the law of market in the contemporary theories of business cycles" (Aoyama 1942, in Japanese) examined the concept of general dynamic economic equilibrium in G. La Volpe's *Studies on the Theory of General Dynamic Economic Equilibrium* (1936, in Italian) and pointed out that Hicks's "temporary equilibrium" was the same notion as Frisch's "momentary dynamic equilibrium" and La Volpe's "general dynamic economic equilibrium."

Fourth, Hicks's *Value and Capital* (1939) handled the existence and stability of competitive equilibrium mathematically in the appendix, although he did not use mathematical expressions in the text except on the topic of the interest rate. In Japan, the existence of a solution in Cassel's system of general equilibrium was already questioned in K. Shibata (1930, in Japanese). The discussion of the stability of the *tâtonnement* process was located in Walras's *Eléments d'économie politique pure* (1874–7), the first half of which was translated into Japanese by S. Tedzuka in 1933. Hicks's mathematical theory of stability caught the eyes of the Japanese mathematician as well as those of the economists. The earlier version of Hicks's mathematical treatment was given in the form of demand elasticity in his *Théorie mathématique de la value en régime de libre concurrence* (1937). Thus, it is not surprising that Hicks (1939) provided the impetus for much of the literature on stability in the 1940s in Japan as well as in Europe and North America. Yet, Hicks's stability was a static one, not dynamic.

After reading Hicks's *Value and Capital* (1939), T. Yasui, in his "Equilibrium analysis and process analysis" (1940a, in Japanese), made a detailed study of the Walrasian theory of *tâtonnement* or groping, that is, the process in which the equilibrium state would be established in a competitive market starting from a disequilibrium state.[13] Yasui was the first to introduce the word "*tâtonnement*" in the literature of stability analysis.[14] He regarded the Walrasian system of general equilibrium in mathematical formulae as an open-ended framework, on which he had already started to create economic theories. He examined the so-called cobweb theorem, which supposes that producers decide their supply at a certain period based on the equilibrium price determined in the market at a period lag behind rather than at the current period. The theorem states that the course of changes in the price depends on the relations of demand and supply curves in a price-quantity plane. Yasui draws three cases of these relations depending on slopes of two curves in the form of diagrams as shown in Figure 5.1. Graph 1 shows that the movement of the price should be converse to the equilibrium when the slope of supply curve is steeper than the slope of demand curve. Graph 2 shows that the price should oscillate between a higher and lower price depending on the initial market price. Graph 3 shows that the movement of the price should diverge from the equilibrium price when the slope of demand curve is steeper than the slope of supply curve. Graph 4 shows that in each period a market price should be determined at the intersection of the decreasing demand curve and the vertical supply curve, namely the supply of given quantity, which was produced and decided in looking at the price of the previous period. Yasui confirmed that H. Schultz (1930, in German), Tinbergen (1930, in German), and Ricci (1930, in German) used this kind of diagramed explanation for the first time simultaneously in 1930, and that Kaldor (1934, in English) named it as the cobweb theorem. This graphic examination was taken up by many other economists including W. Leontief, O. Lange, R. H. Coase, R. F. Fowler, A. M. McIsaac, J. G. Smith, L. M. Lachmann, E. Lundberg, E. Ezekiel, N. S. Buchanan, M. Abramovitz, and E. Sugimoto (Yasui 1940a). Yasui tried to extend the cobweb theorem of price adjustment in one market to a general equilibrium model accompanying many goods.

While Hicks was gaining popularity in Japan around 1940, M. Sono, a specialist in abstract algebra in Kyoto, was unsatisfied with Hicks's mathematical argument. Sono's treatment of Hicksian stability conditions in his "Stability conditions for market equilibrium" (1944, in Japanese) was thoroughly mathematical. As this work was published in a non-European language in the midst of World War II, his conditions were reproduced in English in his "Positive and negative relations and stability conditions" (Sono 1955). He discussed definitions and conditions for stability and instability by using his knowledge of the properties of vectors and matrices. He claimed that supply and demand were stable when the variation of the excess demand of many commodities with respect to their prices were negative at the given prices. The condition for this

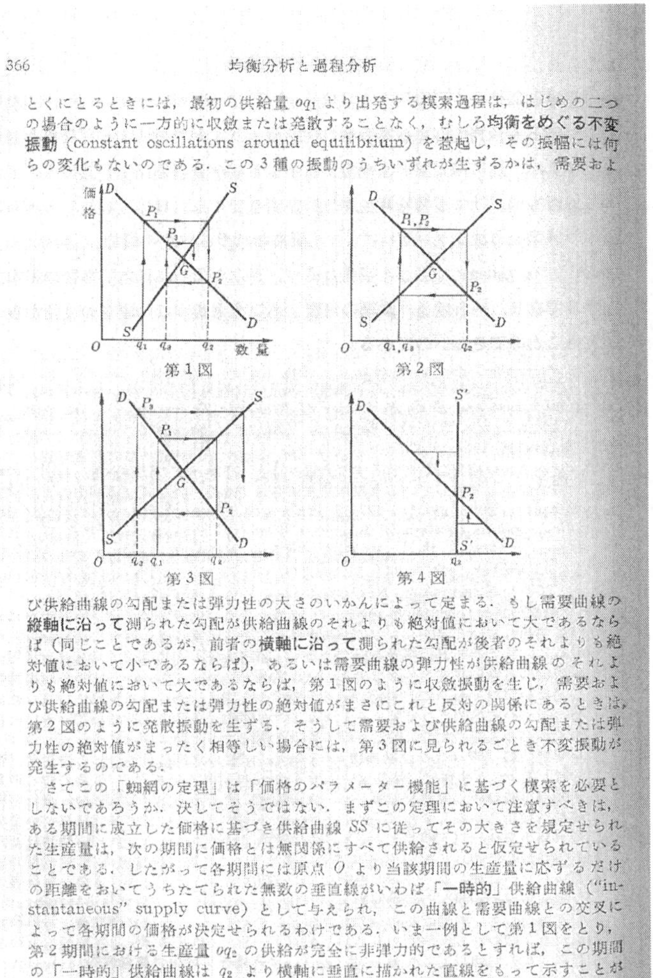

366 均衡分析と過程分析

とくにとるときには，最初の供給量 oq_1 より出発する模索過程は，はじめの二つの場合のように一方的に収斂または発散することなく，むしろ**均衡をめぐる不変振動** (constant oscillations around equilibrium) を惹起し，その振幅には何らの変化もないのである．この 3 種の振動のうちいずれが生ずるかは，需要およ

第 1 図

第 2 図

第 3 図

第 4 図

び供給曲線の勾配または弾力性の大きさのいかんによって定まる．もし需要曲線の**縦軸に沿って**測られた勾配が供給曲線のそれよりも絶対値において大であるならば（同じことであるが，前者の**横軸に沿って**測られた勾配が後者のそれよりも絶対値において小であるならば），あるいは需要曲線の弾力性が供給曲線のそれよりも絶対値において大であるならば，第 1 図のように収斂振動を生じ，需要および供給曲線の勾配または弾力性の絶対値がまさにこれと反対の関係にあるときは，第 2 図のように発散振動を生ずる．そうして需要および供給曲線の勾配または弾力性の絶対値がまったく相等しい場合には，第 3 図に見られるごとき不変振動が発生するのである．

さてこの「蜘網の定理」は「価格のパラメーター機能」に基づく模索を必要としないであろうか．決してそうではない．まずこの定理において注意すべきは，ある期間に成立した価格に基づき供給曲線 SS に従ってその大きさを規定せられた生産量は，次の期間に価格とは無関係にすべて供給されると仮定せられていることである．したがって各期間には原点 O より当該期間の生産量に応ずるだけの距離をおいてうちたてられた無数の垂直線がいわば「**一時的**」供給曲線 ("instantaneous" supply curve) として与えられ，この曲線と需要曲線との交叉によって各期間の価格が決定せられるわけである．いま一例として第 1 図をとり，第 2 期間における生産量 oq_2 の供給が完全に非弾力的であるとすれば，この期間の「一時的」供給曲線は q_2 より横軸に垂直に描かれた直線をもって示すことができるであろう．図形の複雑化を防ぐために，この直線を第 4 図において $S'S'$ とし，需要曲線を第 1 図よりそのまま移して DD としよう．$S'S'$ と DD との交点

Figure 5.1 You can understand what Yasui was discussing on the page even if you do not understand Japanese at all. Graph 1 (upper left) shows that the adjustment process converges to the equilibrium. Graph 2 (upper right) shows that the price oscillates around the equilibrium. Graph 3 (lower left) shows the adjustment process moves away from the equilibrium. Graph 4 (lower right) shows the price adjustment process during a market day when the supply curve is vertical because the production of the goods needs a certain period of time and a given number of products are supplied to the market as the results of the decision made based on the price of the previous period. The equilibrium price should be determined at the intersection of demand and supply curves in each market day (Yasui's 1940a discussion of the cobweb theorem in Yasui 1970: 366).

was that the matrix (a_{ij}) whose elements were the partial differential coefficients of the excess demand of the *i*th commodity with respect to the price of the *j*th commodity evaluated at equilibrium was negative-definite, that is, the sign of the determinants of the principal minors of the matrix was alternately negative and positive.

3.2 Images of the economy

The Keynesian research program had strong and wide influence on postwar economic research from theoretical economics to econometrics to economic policy. O. Lange was no exception. Lange in the text of his *Price Flexibility and Employment* (1944) focused on the role of money as a means of exchange in the monetary economy. However, the Japanese theoretical economists became more interested in the stability analysis discussed in the appendix. They promptly read back to the works discussed by Lange, that is, the appendix to Hicks's *Value and Capital* (1939) and Samuelson's "The stability of equilibrium" (1941a), and soon found Metzler's "Stability of multiple markets" (1945) in *Econometrica* and the second edition (1946) of Hicks's *Value and Capital* (1939). As discussed earlier, Yasui and Sono had already published their papers along Hicksian lines. A group of Japanese scholars then embarked on an intensive study of the stability conditions of a competitive economy.

M. Morishima (1923–2004) has been very good at creating a visual image of the working of the economy, or transaction process. He held fast to the economic conceptualizations such as *tâtonnement* presented by Walras and developed by Hicks and Yasui, though he became interested in the stability problem through Samuelson's "The stability of equilibrium" (1941a).[15] Hicks's *Value and Capital* (1939) had been his "bible" since he became immersed in this insightful book in three different classes given by Y. Takata, M. Sono and H. Aoyama at Kyoto Imperial University in 1942.

Morishima's image of the economy was borrowed from the Japanese rice market which had been well organized prior to 1924.[16] Morishima differentiated two types of transactions in the market, that is, auction and bilateral negotiation. It can be said that Morishima's auction in Japan's rice market was equivalent to Walras's *tâtonnement* based on the stock market in Paris. In fact, Morishima explained his description as the trading at the stock exchange when he published the English version (1996) of his *Dynamic Economic Theory* (1950c). Morishima (1996: 2–3) went as follows:

> When a session of competitive trading starts, officials of the stock exchange, the hammer striker, the recorder, and the watchman, take their respective seats on the stage. The striker tells the opening of the session. Buyers and sellers, by means of calling out and gestures, express what kinds of commodities they want to buy or sell and in what amounts; in other words, they reveal their own demand or supply functions. In this way the hammer striker will get knowledge of the market, on the basis of which he proposes a price which

> he thinks most appropriate. Buyers and sellers will react to the price proposed in this way, and each will search for his opposite number. When they find each other they will shake hands to show that a bargain has been made between them. The watchman tells the recorder of the bargains he observes in the hall and the recorder makes a record of all of them.... If, at the proposed price, all the traders find their opposite numbers, then competitive buying and selling will finish immediately, but, if there remains someone who cannot find a trader, the hammer striker will alter the price and the procedure will be repeated at the new price. Transactions which have been made at the new price are also recorded.... Continuing in this way demand and supply will be exhausted in the market and the price of the commodity will be settled at an appropriate value when no one is left in the market to demand or supply commodities. When the hammer striker finds such a situation he will strike his hammer and say that trading is finished. The price thus obtained is the effective price and is also a temporary equilibrium price.

It was Samuelson (1941a) that first represented the (price) motion of a competitive economy by a system of ordinary differential equations, that is, the movement of the price system depending on the state variables of price. The price of a commodity changes smoothly in accordance with its excess demand function which depends on all the prices. Samuelson maintained that a dynamic adjustment process should be specified when the stability problem is considered. He showed that if excess demands are approximated linearly at equilibrium and the ratios of the rate of the changes of price to the excess demand are set equal to one, the stability condition is that the real part of all the characteristic roots of the matrix (a_{ij}), defined above, be negative. His treatment is called the "true dynamic stability," using his own phrase, in comparison with Hicksian stability (Negishi 1962: 643). Samuelson gave the modern mathematical expression of ordinary differential equation to the discussion on the stability of the competitive economy and thereby accelerated the mathematization of economics.

Yasui felt that he had found the relevant method for dealing with Walrasian *tâtonnement* in a series of Samuelson's papers starting with Samuelson (1941a). Yasui (1971, in Japanese: 283) writes:

> Samuelson's dynamic theory of stability was not only a local theory but also mechanical in the sense that the adjustment speed was constant. Yet it seemed to be a very excellent and novel theory as the first approximation to the *tâtonnement* theory. The reason why I was fascinated by Samuelson was because he presented the **method** I had been looking for, not because he presented the **question** I had never noticed before.
>
> (My translation, gothic in the original)

Thus Yasui introduced the Walrasian *tâtonnement* process in the literature of economic stability for the first time in the world and delved into the mathematics literature (Ikeo 2004b).

3.2 The Japanese Samuelson: Takuma Yasui (1909–1995)[17]

What Yasui was trying to accomplish after reading Samuelson's "The stability of equilibrium" (1941a) was to clarify the "mathematical implications of economic models" which economists began to form by borrowing mathematical tools in a somewhat intuitive and naive way. He could get advice and suggestions directly by speaking with the active mathematicians around him in Sendai. This circumstance made it possible for him to delve deeply into the classical literature presented by G. Frobenius, E. J. Routh, A. Hurwitz, J. Schur, A. Cohn, M. Fujiwara and others. Yasui published a series of papers on stability all in Japanese from 1948–50.

Yasui in his "The convergency postulate and dynamic stability conditions" (1948a, in Japanese) questioned the Metzlerian condition, that is, the largest eigenvalue in absolute value of a matrix whose elements were all real and positive should be real and positive. Later he learned from G. Frobenius's "On the matrices with positive elements" (1908, 1909, in German) that this kind of matrix always has this property (Yasui 1948b, in Japanese: 164).[18]

Yasui in his "Dynamic stability conditions for the economic equilibrium" (1948b, in Japanese) applied Fujiwara's work on differential/difference equations to economics. He discussed Hicksian stability conditions by using the Routh-Hurwitz and Schur-Cohn conditions for stability in quadratic form. He showed that Hicksian stability conditions are neither necessary nor sufficient for the dynamic stability of a differential equation system in the case of three or more commodities. He also showed that Hicksian conditions are neither necessary nor sufficient for the stability of a difference equation system in any case. The conditions for stability were restated in the context of the multi-sector multiplier in J. S. Chipman's "The multi-sector multiplier" (1950) with the assistance of mathematician A. H. Clifford (Chipman 1950: 355).

Yasui always sought the general or mathematical, rather than particular, treatment of market stability to clarify the multiplicity of conditions for stability put forth one after another. He picked up not only E. Picard and H. Poincaré but also the qualitative theory of stability presented by A. M. Liapunov. He read over the Liapunov paper with the help of mathematician S. Izumi. Then he wrote his "The general theory of stability" (Yasui 1950, in Japanese) for those economists who were interested in the conditions of market stability, and made a detailed discussion of two kinds of stability differentiated by Samuelson in a more generalized manner. Samuelson (1947: 262) explained stability of the second kind referring to the oscillation of a frictionless pendulum as follows:

> If one displaces a frictionless pendulum, it will oscillate endlessly around the position of stable equilibrium. Its motion is bounded, however, and it never remains on one side of the equilibrium position for more than a finite time interval. Such behavior may be characterized as *stability of the second kind* or as stability in the second sense.

Yasui (1950, in Japanese: 75) rightly pointed out that this stability should be called Liapunov stability. Samuelson did not go further with his stability of the second kind or Liapunov stability and rather confined himself to stability of the first kind. Samuelson (1947: 261–2) gave this the following definition:

> The equilibrium position possesses *perfect stability of the first kind* if from any initial conditions all the variables approach their equilibrium values in the limit as time becomes infinite.... Alternatively, it is sometimes stated that an equilibrium is stable if a displacement from equilibrium is followed by a return to equilibrium.

Yasui (1950, in Japanese) treated in a more generalized, mathematical manner stability of the second kind, that is, Liapunov stability, which is not restricted to the motion of an oscillating pendulum but for the more general motion of rigid bodies. He discussed in detail what is now called the direct or second method of Liapunov to prove the stability of systems of ordinary differential equations although he did not use it to solve the stability problem in the sense of K. J. Arrow, H. D. Block and L. Hurwicz's "On the stability of the competitive equilibrium, II" (1959).[19]

Yasui started with a system of n ordinary differential equations of first order and used the symbol of state variables x, rather than prices, to study the stability problem in the most generalized manner. He utilized variational equations as a first approximation to the problem. Second, he introduced quadratic forms, in a more familiar phrase a distance measure, and formed a function V that was later to be called a Liapunov function. He discussed both the stability and instability conditions of stationary solutions of the primal system and arranged Liapunov's theorems in a Samuelsonian language.[20] Yasui (1950, in Japanese: 85) presented the following proposition:

> The stationary solution of the system of ordinary differential equations exhibits stability of the first and second kind if the [Liapunov] function V, which is given in a definite, quadratic form and the derivative dV/dt have opposite signs. It is exhibits instability of the first and second kind if V and dV/dt have the same sign.
>
> (My translation)

Thus Yasui introduced Liapunov's general theory of stability into the economic literature directly from the French version of the "original" paper, not from other explanatory books or articles. It was about the same time as Morishima introduced Liapunov's theory into his *Dynamic economic theory* (1950c, in Japanese) through Andronow and Chaikin's *Theory of Oscillations* (1949) with the use of their metaphor of the oscillating pendulum for the image of stability. This was earlier than the general discussion of Liapunov theory in English in Bushaw and Clower's "Price determination in a stock-flow economy" (1954).

It is noteworthy that later economists are exclusively interested in the stability case rather than the general case including instability. They usually state that a measure of the Euclidean distance of the actual price vector (p) from the equilibrium price vector (p^*), such as $V(p)=[1/2](p_i, - p_i^*)^2$, is a Liapunov function if the price of a good moves with excess demand for the good and excess demand is a continuously differentiable function of the prices of all goods. Then the system is stable if the excess-demand functions are homogeneous of degree one and satisfy Walras's law.

4 Conclusions

In 1951, the San Francisco Peace Treaty was signed to bring Japan formally back to the international community during a time of crisis between the East and the West, that is, during the Korean War (1950–3). A year before, in 1950, the first Japanese meeting of the Econometric Society was held in Tokyo. After I. Nakayama made the opening address, M. Hisatake, Y. Kurimura, K. Midutani, M. Morishima, S. Nakamura, E. Sugimoto, I. Yamada and T. Yasui presented their papers. The anonymous report on the Tokyo meeting and M. Hayakawa's article on the income distribution in Hokkaido entitled "The application of Pareto's law of income to Japanese data" appeared in *Econometrica* in 1951 (Japanese Econometric Society 1951; Hayakawa 1951).

Yasui furnished a firm and solid basis for the younger generation of mathematical economists in Japan. H. Furuya, M. Fukuoka and H. Haga followed Yasui's way of making economics. Mathematicians became interested in the dynamics of the market economy. Those who had been trained in departments of mathematics, including H. Nikaido, H. Uzawa, K. Inada and T. Yokoyama, as well as a young graduate from a department of economics, T. Negishi, joined the squad of mathematical economists. Morishima began to publish his papers written in English in journals both in Japan and abroad after 1952. They joined the international community of economists in time to ride on the tidal wave of stability analysis of a competitive economy.

In Japan from the mid 1940s throughout the 1950s, mathematicians, especially those who were specialized in algebra, played an important part in the discussion of stability analysis. Their community was well informed about various types of mathematics. Some mathematicians not only gave help to the economists with the mathematics, but also wrote papers and books in economics on the side. Others entered the field of economics using their advantage of mathematical knowledge. Thus, the participation of mathematicians in economic research accelerated the process of mathematizing economics in Japan.

Personal communications

Michio Morishima at the London School of Economics and Political Science in August 1990.

Notes

1 This chapter is based on Ikeo (1994b). An earlier version of the paper was presented at the tenth world congress of the International Economic Association in Moscow on August 24, 1992. I thank Erich W. Streissler, who was my discussant at the congress, and two anonymous referees of the *European Journal of the History of Economic Thought* for their detailed comments. I also thank Paul Pecorino and the participants in the workshop on the history of economic theory in Tokyo in October 1991 for their comments on the earliest version of the chapter. Finally, I thank Takashi Negishi, E. Roy Weintraub, Takuma Yasui, Philip Mirowski, Masao Fukuoka and Hanjiro Haga for giving me valuable information and suggestions about the title topic of the chapter. Needless to say, all remaining errors are my own.

2 Weintraub (1991a: part one) discusses the changes in the manner of economic theorizing resulting from the use of new mathematical tools in the development of stability analysis. Moreover, French economist Maurice Allais became interested in stability analysis around 1940 and published *Traité d'économie pure* (1943) in Paris in the midst of World War II. See Weintraub (1991b) and Negishi (1962).

3 The name of the University of Tokyo was changed to the Imperial University in 1886, and renamed the Imperial University of Tokyo during 1897–1946.

4 *A Hundred Year History of Mathematics in Japan* (MSJ 1983, vol. 1, in Japanese: 115) listed the following people, excluding Kikuchi, who were sent abroad by the Japanese government before 1889. Some left Japan as teenagers and stayed long enough to learn the language and culture of their place of study as well as mathematics. J. Kitao (1853–1907) studied in Berlin and Göttingen from 1870–83, K. Furuichi (1854–1934) from 1875–80 at Ecole Central and the Sorbonne, Y. Noguchi (1860–1943) in Paris from 1877–83, H. Muraoka (1853–1929) in Strasbourg from 1878–81, H. Terao (1855–1923) in Paris from 1879–83, Rikitaro Fujisawa (1861–1933) in England, Berlin and Strasbourg from 1883–7, and F. Senbon (1854–1918) in Paris and Saint Crue from 1885–7.

5 Takagi (1935b: 1343–4). Quoted in MSJ (1983, vol. 1: 183).

6 S. Kimura (1866–1938) studied at Harvard and Yale from 1893–6, M. Ikoma (1867–1937) in Germany from 1898–1900, T. Takagi (1875–1960) in Berlin and Göttingen from 1898–1901, T. Yoshie (1874–1947) in Göttingen from 1899–1902, J. Kawai (1865–1945) in Berlin from 1901–3, S. Nakagawa (1876–1942) in Berlin from 1901–5, D. Motoda (1867–1948) in Germany and England from 1901–6, K. Miwa (1861–1920) in Germany and France from 1903–5, Matsusaburo Fujiwara (1881–1946) in Germany and France from 1907–11, S. Kaba (1863–1925) in Pennsylvania from 1908–9, S. Mori (1866–1936) in England and Germany from 1909–11, J. Yoshikawa (1878–1915) in England and Göttingen from 1909–11, M. Kuroda (Dateki) (1878–1922) in Berlin and Göttingen from 1910–13, T. Kubota (1885–1952) in England and Germany from 1912–15, S. Kakeya (1886–1947) at Harvard from 1918–19, Msazo Sono (1886–1969) in England, France and Germany from 1919–21, K. Ogura (1885–1962) in France from 1919–22, S. Narumi (1895–1977) in London from 1921–3. Thirteen other mathematicians were listed on page 280. They brought various mathematical traditions back to Japan.

7 Ikeo (1994b: 582) in the second line lacks several words needed for consistency.

8 Kakutani chose to leave the United States and was sent back to Japan by exchange ship after the Pacific War started in December 1941. See Chapter 6 and MSJ (1984, vol. 2: 97).

9 Yasui (1980, in Japanese: 136). Yasui's letter to E. R. Weintraub quoted in Weintraub (1991a: 88).

10 American historian of economics E. R. Weintraub in his *General Equilibrium Analysis* (1985) rightly characterized the publication of Hicks's book as "a signal event for economists" and summarized Hicks's contribution as follows:

> Hicks's book developed the classical general equilibrium theory from the theory of the household and the theory of the firm in modern, neoclassical language. He then provided equilibrium and stability analysis, the former by equation counting, the latter by static characteristics of the equilibrium relationships. The properties of equilibrium were well treated.
>
> (Weintraub 1985: 84)

11 Yuzo Yamada attended Karl Menger's mathematical colloquium (see Chapter 6).

12 From around 1900 till the end of World War II, Sontoku Ninomiya was very popular as a good moral example for the Japanese children and neither regarded as an early economist nor a forerunner of general equilibrium analysis (see Chapter 8). Miyoji Hayakawa was an economic statistician rather than an economic theorist. Later he published his "On the distribution of agricultural land in Japan from 1908 till 1930" (Hayakawa 1933, in Italian) and "The application of Pareto's law of income to Japanese data" (Hayakawa 1951).

13 Negishi (1996: 229) regards Yasui (1940a) as "a very important contribution, which anticipated and greatly influenced the later developments in the stability analysis of an economic equilibrium." He picks up two other points of significance. (1) "Yasui considered properly the relation between the so-called Walrasian process of adjustment and the Marshallian process of adjustment, or that between parametric functions of prices and those of quantities." (2) "Yasui emphasized the importance of the study not of the preliminary *tâtonnement* with no transactions at disequilibria, but of the reformulated tâtonnement through actual transactions" (Negishi 1996: 229). We can see that Negishi deeply owed his stability analysis to Yasui.

14 Yasui delightedly stated in 1990, "It's me that introduced Walrasian tâtonnement into the economics literature for the first time!" (personal communication with Yasui; Ikeo 2004b, 2006). See also Negishi (2003).

15 From my interview with Morishima around August 23, 1990.

16 The rice market gradually became controlled by the central government from 1924 on. In 1939, the Rice Exchange, whose role had already been shrunken by a series of regulatory laws, was finally abolished and the Japan Rice Corporation was exclusively allowed to hold "the rice market." Morishima (1950c) included his own discussion in Morishima (1949, 1950a, 1950b).

17 E. W. Streissler (1992) said, "I think it a little grandiloquent to call Takuma Yasui 'the Japanese Samuelson.'" It might be true. Yet I think that it is an appropriate characterization of Yasui's contributions to theoretical economics in Japan. The appellation makes it easier for the non-Japanese audience who do not know Yasui to understand his position in Japanese economics. See also Negishi (1972, in Japanese; 1996).

18 A number of young Japanese economists including Hanjiro Haga followed Yasui. Haga (1951, in Japanese) discussed a case with a matrix whose elements were all real and nonnegative, with reference to Frobenius's "On the matrices with non-negative elements" (1912, in German).

19 Weintraub (1987b, 1991a: 87–9) and Negishi (1972, in Japanese; 1996) discussed Yasui's contribution to general equilibrium analysis in detail. Randall Bausor's (1995) argument of stability analysis bears a reasonable resemblance to Yasui (1950) with reference to Weintraub (1987b).

20 Samuelson was only interested in the stability of the second kind.

6 General equilibrium theory (2)

The existence question[1]

1 Introduction

The proofs of existence, stability and uniqueness are important topics for the research of general equilibrium theory. In the 1950s, the proof of the existence of a general equilibrium utilized topology and fixed-point theorems or set theory and the convex set method, which were mathematical tools different from those used for the proof of stability (like Liapunov theory).[2] Japanese mathematician Seiji Takizawa gave an intuitive exposition and said:

> Topology is the geometry that studies unchangeable characteristics in one-to-one bicontinuous transformations (both mapping and reverse mapping are continuous). Roughly speaking, it is the geometry on an elastic plane. It considers if two points are connected and does not care about whether the lines are straight or curved, long or short.
>
> (Takizawa 1991, in Japanese: 1067, my translation)

Moreover, the research of stability analysis was promoted by a different group of scholars prior to the study of the so-called existence question. In the 1940s, several Japanese economists made important contributions to stability analysis, most of them written in Japanese but comparable to the studies which were developed in North America and Europe in the 1950s (Chapter 5; Ikeo 1994a). It is well known that several Japanese mathematical economists made significant contributions to the study of the existence question in the 1950s. In contrast, it is less known how they embarked on this study, while making cutting-edge contributions. This chapter uses not only my personal communications with several scholars but also the correspondence among the economists of the day kept in the Special Collection Library of Duke University (see Weintraub *et al.* 1998).

The history of the research of the existence question is so complicated that we also have to pay attention to the equally complicated history of modern algebra. A number of Japanese mathematicians studied in Göttingen, Berlin and Vienna from the 1920s to the 1930s, and therefore Japanese scholars who began to study mathematics prior to 1960 mastered well the mathematics which had been discussed and published in German. In this respect, the Japanese studied mathematics in a tradition different from those who had studied mathematics mainly in

France and North America, where the structural trend in mathematics was identified with the name of Nicolas Bourbaki in the 1940s and 1950s.

This chapter investigates how Japanese mathematical economists as well as mathematicians studied the questions relating to the existence of a general equilibrium and fixed-point theorems, which were keys to the proof, from the late 1920s till the early 1960s. We trace the research line that includes Kazuo Midutani, Shizuo Kakutani, Hukukane Nikaido (1923–2001), Hirofumi Uzawa (b. 1928) and Takashi Negishi, and focus on Japan's direct connection with Karl Menger, John von Neumann, Oskar Morgenstern, Emmy Nöther and Kenneth J. Arrow. Eventually we reconstruct the process through which the cannon of modern neoclassical economics, namely Walrasian general equilibrium theory, was established through the use of set theory and the convex set method in the 1950s. These mathematical tools were rapidly developed by formalist mathematicians including Emmy Nöther from the mid 1920s on, and spread rapidly by a group of mathematicians known collectively as Nicolas Bourbaki.

When we look into the conditions in which Japanese scholars became involved in the study of the existence question, we find that the prompt circulation of scientific journals, most of which were refereed and published in the United States, was crucial for active scholars in Japan as well as in the rest of the world. The Japanese scholars were not exceptions and began to work on similar subjects within a few years of the conclusion of the Asia-Pacific War in August 1945, as did those economists who made it a rule to read every issue of the scientific journals. In contrast, no refereed journal of economics with free submission had existed in Japan prior to 1960, when *Kikan Riron Keizaigaku*, later renamed *Japanese Economic Review*, introduced a referee system for the first time. On the other hand, each university had its own organ, called *Kiyo*, which was usually closed to scholars outside of the university or the department. Therefore, in the 1950s, a mathematical economist like Hukukane Nikaido, who had graduated from the department of mathematics, had no opportunity to publish his papers in any journal of economics in Japan, and had no choice but to submit his papers to scientific journals published abroad. Moreover, it is noteworthy that without such scientific journals with free submission and a referee system the Japanese economists would not have been able to contribute their scientific works to the international forum of economists. Unfortunately there were occasionally unlucky decisions in the refereeing process such as the rejection of Nikaido's existence paper by *Econometrica*, which we will discuss in the penultimate section.

The study which has resulted in this chapter has some other implications as well. It carefully discusses the historical development of the research of existence of general equilibrium, which was complicated by the parallel development of relevant mathematical tools and game theory, and the interactions and communications among migrating and traveling scholars in the 1930s and 1940s. We have discovered that the controversy over the foundation of mathematics, which culminated in 1927 in the clash between the formalist David Hilbert (1862–1943) and the intuitionist Luitzen Egbertus Jan Brouwer (1881–1966), did not matter, at least for the research of the so-called existence question, in the sense that Brouwer's fixed-point theorem was formalized by Hilbert's students and became available for economists as well as mathematicians who used the traditional, non-intuitionist language of mathematics. Later fixed-point theorems became familiar to economists through John von Neumann (1937), Shizuo Kakutani (1941), Samuel Eilenberg and Deane Montgomery (1946), Solomon Lefschetz (1949) and Edward G. Begle (1950). Yet the research line of the existence question was sometimes heavily blurred by the formalist–intuitionist controversy.

By tracing the complicated interaction and debate among economists and mathematicians from the late 1920s to the 1950s, we can reconstruct the process by which the cannon of modern neoclassical economics, that is, Walrasian general equilibrium theory, was established in the 1950s. To be more specific, the structure of the post-World War II general equilibrium theory has been based on set theory and the convex set method or topology and fixed-point theorems, and it is an (important) part of the post-World War II neoclassical economics. We have to be careful about the fact that there are several mathematical structures of neoclassical economics based on different mathematics, such as topology, matrix algebra and ordinary differential equations.

Section 2 summarizes the beginning and the ending point of our history of the proof of the existence of a general competitive equilibrium and the current condition of the historical study of this question and its related subjects. Section 3 observes the development of abstract algebra or modern algebra, including the formalization of Brouwer's fixed-point theorem, from the mid 1920s to the 1930s, and focuses on Karl Menger's connection with Japanese scholars in Vienna. Section 4 takes a look at the connection between John von Neumann and Shizuo Kakutani at Princeton. Section 5 discusses how Japanese scholars found the intensive use of modern algebra in economic studies and the progress of the study of the existence question. It also discusses what they contributed to the study of the proof of the existence of a general equilibrium. Section 6 focuses on H. Nikaido's case in particular and discusses how he initiated the study of the existence question. We argue that the submission of his existence papers was not handled fairly by *Econometrica*, based on the evidence remaining in the Nicholas Georgescu-Roegen Papers at Duke University. Section 7 draws some conclusions.

2 Proof of the existence of general equilibrium through 1962

This section clarifies the beginning and the ending point of our history of the theoretical research of the existence of a general equilibrium in a competitive economy and the current condition of the historical research of the so-called existence question. Our history of the research of the existence question will end around 1962, although the research continued after that year. The reason is because in writing a history of general equilibrium theory it is meaningless to pay attention to only the Japanese and their related internationally oriented economists after the 1960s.

In retrospect, Léon Walras (1834–1910) developed the concept of a price system in the context of interrelated markets within the economy by utilizing a system of simultaneous equations in his *Eléments d'économie politique pure* (1874–7). However, it was neither Walras's book nor Gustav Cassel's early paper "Grundriss einer elementaren Preislehre" (1899) but G. Cassel's simplified system of general equilibrium in the fourth edition of his *Theoretische Sozialökonomie* (1927) that gave an opportunity to seriously investigate the existence of competitive equilibrium.[3] Cassel's 1927 book was first published in German in 1918 instead of his native tongue Swedish, and became one of the most famous (advanced) textbooks in the world after World War I. There are five German editions of the book. It was translated into English as *The Theory of Social Economy* in 1923 with a revised edition appearing in 1932. The Japanese version was published from the third German edition in 1926. French and Swedish editions are also available (Gustafsson 1987). Around 1930, the problems in Cassel's own handling of price determinacy became an issue in both Central Europe and Japan. For example, Kei Shibata in his "An examination of 'the mechanism of price formation' as explained by Mr. Cassel" (1930, in Japanese) explained one of the formal problems in Cassel's simplified system of general equilibrium, which was pointed out three years later in H. v. Stackelberg's "Two comments on Gustav Cassel's theory of price" (1933, in German) published in *Zeitschrift für Nationalökonomie* (Ikeo 1994a, 1994b). Mathematicians, physicists and those economists who were less allergic to mathematical arguments became interested in the research of general equilibrium theory.

Independent economic research was more or less interrupted by World War II in Europe and Japan. After the conclusion of the war, American and European scholars resumed their scientific research, cooperating with each other in the United States through the organization of conferences supported by the US government. The Dutch economist T. C. Koopmans was one of the leaders in the rapid development of activity analysis and mathematical economics in the 1940s and 1950s. In 1951, Koopmans briefly summarized the discussions among European economists in the 1930s on generalizations of the Walrasian general competitive equilibrium analysis as follows:

> Neisser (1932) and von Stackelberg (1933) raised questions of existence and uniqueness of a solution to Cassel's formulation of the Walrasian system, with reference in particular to the requirement that prices and rates of production be represented by nonnegative numbers. In a mathematical seminar conducted in Vienna by Karl Menger, Schlesinger (1933) formulated a suggestion, made also by Zeuthen (1932), that economic theory should explain not only the nonnegative prices and quantities produced of scarce goods but also which goods are scarce and which are free (i.e., have a zero price). Wald (1935, 1936a, b) proved the existence and uniqueness of a solution to an equation system expressing this problem.
>
> (Koopmans ed. 1951: 1)

It can be said that this summary provided the common understanding of the development of general equilibrium theory in the 1930s. A little later, one pair of economists and three individual economists independently proved the existence of a competitive economy with the use of set theory and the convex set method including a particular fixed-point theorem (this is the history of the research of the existence question that Japanese economists understand).

- L. W. McKenzie, "On equilibrium in Graham's model of world trade and other competitive systems," *Econometrica*, April 1954.
  Brouwer's fixed-point theorem for point-to-point continuous transformations (1911).
- K. J. Arrow and G. Debreu, "Existence of an equilibrium for a competitive economy," *Econometrica*, July 1954.
  Eilenberg and Montgomery's fixed-point theorem for set-to-set continuous transformations (1946).
- D. Gale, "The law of supply and demand," *Mathematica Scandinavia*, 1955.
  Kakutani's fixed-point theorem for point-to-set continuous transformations (1941).
- H. Nikaido, "On the classical multilateral exchange problem," *Metroeconomica*, 1956.
  Kakutani's fixed-point theorem for point-to-set continuous transformations (1941).

G. Debreu in his survey article "Existence of competitive equilibrium" (1982) clearly differentiates the two approaches to the question of the existence of a competitive equilibrium for an economy. One was the "Simultaneous Optimization Approach" taken in Arrow and Debreu (1954), in which the existence question was transformed into the question of "existence of an equilibrium for a social system composed of a finite set of agents simultaneously seeking to maximize their utility functions, or, more generally, to optimize with respect to their preference relations" (Debreu 1982: 715). Or, this was called the "Abstract Economy Approach" (Border 1985: 95). Another was the "Excess Demand Approach" focusing on the excess demand correspondence of the economy, taken in Gale (1955) and Nikaido (1956). We will discuss the proving process later in section 7.

Then Hirofumi Uzawa in his "Walras's existence theorem and Brouwer's fixed-point theorem" (1962) proved that the two theorems in the title were equivalent. Although he was at Stanford University, the paper appeared in *Kikan Riron Keizaigaku* (Economic Studies Quarterly), which was the formal journal of the Japanese Association of Theoretical Economics and the Japanese Econometric Society (now *Japanese Economic Review* published by the Japanese Economic Association, see Chapter 2).[4] Uzawa followed the excess demand approach taken in Gale (1955) and Nikaido (1956), but restated Walras's existence theorem and Brouwer's fixed-point theorem more simply. Uzawa's formulation went as follows:

There are n commodities, p is a price vector, and x is a commodity bundle. Price vectors are assumed to be nonzero and nonnegative; commodity bundles are arbitrary n-vectors. P and X are the sets of all price vectors and of all commodities bundles. The excess demand function $x(p)$ is a mapping from P into X. A price vector $\bar{p}$ is called an equilibrium if $x_i(\bar{p}) \leq 0$, with equality unless $\bar{p}_i = 0$.

Walras's existence theorem. Let an excess demand function $x(p)$ satisfy the following conditions:

A $x(p)$ is a continuous mapping from P into X.
B $x(p)$ is homogeneous of order 0; that is, $x(tp)=x(p)$, for all $t>0$ and $p \in P$.
C Walras's law holds: $\sum_{i=1}^{n} p_i x_i(p) = 0$, for all $p \in P$.

Then there exists at least an equilibrium price vector p for $x(p)$.

The fundamental $(n-1)$ -simplex Π is the set of all nonnegative n-vectors whose component sums are one: $\Pi = \left\{ \pi = (\pi_1, \ldots, \pi_n); \pi \geq 0, \sum_{i=1}^{n} \pi_i = 1 \right\}$.

Brouwer's fixed-point theorem. Let $\varphi(\pi)$ be a continuous mapping from Π into itself. Then there is at least a fixed-point π in Π: $\bar{\pi} = \varphi(\bar{\pi})$.

Equivalence theorem. Walras's existence theorem and Brouwer's fixed-point theorem are equivalent.

As Uzawa said, it had already been well established that Brouwer's fixed-point Theorem implies Walras's existence theorem. He constructed an excess demand function which satisfied conditions (A), (B) and (C). With dividing a price by the summation of prices, Uzawa neatly proved that Walras's existence theorem implies Brouwer's fixed-Point theorem (see Appendix to this chapter). Before its publication in *Economic Studies Quarterly* in Japan, Uzawa sent a copy of his equivalence theorem paper to Kenneth Arrow at Stanford University.

Upon reading it, Arrow was so impressed by the sparks of genius and brilliance of the proof of the equivalence theorem that he immediately sent an invitation letter for Uzawa to come and join his own project at Stanford (communication with Arrow in 1994, etc.). Uzawa's result implies that "any algorithm that is guaranteed to compute equilibria of arbitrary economies specified in terms of aggregate excess demand functions must be guaranteed to compute fixed points of arbitrary mapping of the simplex into itself" (Kehoe 1991: 2055–6). Later in the 1960s such an algorithm was developed by H. E. Scarf. Then Scarf's algorithm method was exploited in the proof of the existence of competitive equilibrium in Arrow and Hahn's famous advanced textbook *General Competitive Analysis* (1971).

Prior to the publication of Uzawa's equivalence theorem, young Takashi Negishi (b. 1933) embarked on the research of general equilibrium theory including the existence and stability of a general competitive equilibrium. Negishi in his master thesis "Existence and stability of economic equilibrium" (The Graduate School of Economics, University of Tokyo) discussed the welfare aspects of a competitive equilibrium by relating the existence question to the question of constrained maximization. He applied the approximation approach developed in the method of mathematical planning to the research of general economic equilibrium with reference to equilibrium in an infinite dimensional setting as well as a computable general equilibrium. Negishi sent the English version of the relevant part of his study to Arrow and then he received an invitation letter offering him a post of project researcher at Stanford. Negishi revised the paper by referring to the comments made by Arrow and Uzawa at Stanford, and published it as "Welfare economics and existence of an equilibrium for a competitive economy" (1960) in *Metroeconomica*. Negishi used the method that focuses upon whether a general equilibrium at a macro level could be reached by the optimization activities taken by individuals at the micro level. In the 1970s, the method became well known as the Negishi method or Negishi's approach when it was used for computing general equilibria and then in a variety of ways in both theoretical research and application research. (Mas-Colell and Zame 1991).[5] Adelman and Robinson (1989: 970) nicely states:

> Negishi (1960) proved that a competitive equilibrium can be described as the result of maximizing a "Paretian" social welfare function consisting of the weighted sum of individual utilities. The weights in the "Paretian" social welfare function are determined endogenously and depend on the initial distribution of endowments.

It might be interesting to note that in 2007, when the author told him about these computational applications, Negishi did not know his method was so useful for government policy analysis and development economics. Negishi is such an avid researcher and Negishi (2008) has found that his method was used by von Thünen for the case of equal Negishi weights, namely identical households in a stationary economy with zero net rate of interest.

Back to the 1960s, Negishi (1961) initiated the study of imperfect competition in general equilibrium analysis. He assumed that consumers were price takers while firms were monopolistically competitive. His firms had subjective inverse demand (supply) functions for their outputs (inputs), being consistent with the given information of the present state of the market. He further assumed the convexity of possible production sets of firms. Then he proved the existence of equilibrium in an imperfectly competitive market (see also Young 2008).

It is noteworthy that from 1950 to the 1960s, Nikaido, Uzawa and Negishi all joined Arrow's project on the Efficiency of Decision Making in Economic Systems at Stanford, which was backed by the Office of Naval Research. Other Japanese mathematical economists such as Ken-ichi Inada and Hajime Oniki also joined Arrow's project.[6] Thus Japanese mathematical economists played active roles in the study of the existence and stability of a general equilibrium in a competitive economy, two sector growth models and welfare economics. Our history, shedding special light on the Japanese scholars, will end around this period.

Needless to say, the research of the existence question continued as surveyed in Debreu (1982). Debreu listed 386 references and 88 percent (339 references) were published after 1962. More than 10 percent (40 references) were authored or coauthored by Japanese economists. It is easy to pick up Japanese names because they are unique, whereas there seem to be many non-American names but in the case of Westerners it is hard to tell the nationality of authors accurately only from names. Certainly it is not of great importance to write the history of general equilibrium theory with a focus on the Japanese contribution after 1962. Leading economists of the world worked individually to elaborate the theory, whereas many of them had studied in the US. The chance of studying general equilibrium theory is open to economists of every nationality, although Hukukane Nikaido had difficulty in getting his research results published in the 1950s. In other words, nationality does not matter for the study of economic theory, although the chance of publishing research results was much more limited in Japan than the US.

Several historians of economic thought have been working on the intriguing development of general equilibrium analysis. The intellectual legacy of general equilibrium analysis from the German-speaking world has been often represented by the seminar works of Karl Menger (1902–85), son of the eminent Austrian economist Carl Menger (1840–1921). K. Menger was the key person who connected mathematical reasoning and economic thinking by organizing the informal mathematical colloquium in Vienna and publishing its proceedings as *Ergebnisse eines Mathematischen Kolloquiums* from 1931–7. Menger's colloquium was examined in E. R. Weintraub (1983, 1985), L. Punzo (1989, 1991).[7] We will discuss Menger's role in the study of the existence question in section 4.

The development of the research of the existence question was known and remembered by many general equilibrium theorists of the time, who were the majority of mathematical economists in the 1950s. The topic was first studied historically in E. R. Weintraub's "The existence of a competitive equilibrium: 1930–1954" (1983) and *General Equilibrium Analysis: Studies in Appraisal* (1985: Chapter 6), and he examined the research line of the existence of a competitive equilibrium including the part summarized by Koopmans and leading to K. J. Arrow, G. Debreu and L. McKenzie. Interestingly Weintraub found that Arrow, Debreu and McKenzie proved the existence of general equilibrium independently of Wald (1935, 1936a, 1936b). In reality, Arrow had not been very familiar with Wald's study of general equilibrium analysis until he cooperated with Weintraub's historical research, although he knew that Wald had been conducting interesting research into statistical approaches to economics in the United States. Therefore, it is not surprising that Nikaido read neither Wald's papers nor Kazuo Midutani's "Comments on Wald's proof of the uniqueness of the solution for the Cassel-Schlesinger system of production" (1939, in Japanese; see section 3), when he started working on this question around 1950. Yet later, Nikaido in his *Convex Structure and Economic Theory* (1968: 249) stated, "Naturally, the pioneering work of Wald (1935, 1936a) which proved the existence of equilibrium for a Casselian system, is remarkable." It is common among academicians to accord respect to a precedent contribution when they find it even if they studied the subject independently of it.

B. Ingrao and G. Israel in their *The Invisible Hand* (1990) made a detailed study of G. Debreu's research line to the existence question, including the French mathematical tradition, and regarded Nicholas Bourbaki's works as the important intellectual background of Debreu. Nicholas Bourbaki was the name given to a group of French mathematicians, formed in the mid 1930s, who started to use the axiomatic method consciously in French under the influence of modern algebra intensively discussed and rapidly developed in German. This group was later joined by American mathematicians such as Samuel Eilenberg. Weintraub and P. Mirowski in their "The pure and applied: Bourbakism comes to mathematical economics" (1994) made a thorough study of Debreu's line and discussed the philosophical background of mathematical structurism. They showed that it was Debreu who introduced Bourbakism into the community of mathematical economists in the United States. L. Corry, the Israeli historian of mathematics, endorsed that trend in her *Modern Algebra and the Rise of Mathematical Structure* (1996: 301) and writes, "Bourbaki has directly influenced mainstream trends in mathematical economics since the 1960s [*sic*], through the work of Nobel laureate Gerard Debreu." Based on the Duke collections of twentieth-century economists Weintraub and Ted Gayer (2000, 2001) shed new light on the study of the existence question in a general competitive analysis and show the intensive discussion of the use of mathematics including topology among the economists and mathematicians in the 1950s. Weintraub's *How Economics Became a Mathematical Science* (2002) discussed the mathematization of economics from a perspective of the English-speaking economist (and French economist). P. Nicola's *Mainstream Mathematical Economics in the 20th Century* (2000) also showed a history of mathematical economics and gave an intensive mathematical discussion of theoretical issues such as general equilibrium theory, game theory, linear programming, growth theory, and dynamics. The research tradition shown by Nicola is different from Japanese tradition.

We have to carefully examine the historical development of the research of the existence of general equilibrium, which was complicated by the development of relevant mathematical tools and game theory. It is noteworthy that in the period between the two world wars most French traditional mathematicians were not interested in the rapid development of abstract algebra or modern algebra centered around the German-speaking world. We have to examine the mathematical discussion that took place in German because from the late 1920s to the 1930s the existence of a general equilibrium in a competitive economy was studied in close association with the new trend of abstract algebra. It was around the mid 1930s that the Bourbaki group started to incorporate the new results in whole mathematics and brought revolutionary changes to French traditional mathematics. As mentioned, Corry (1996: 301) recognized that Bourbaki mathematics had *since the 1950s* directly influenced mainstream trends in mathematical economics through the work of Nobel laureate Gerard Debreu.

On the other hand, until around 1939 many Japanese leading mathematicians had studied mathematics in the German-speaking world and therefore the Japanese scholars in general who began to study mathematics prior to 1960 mastered well the mathematics which had been discussed and published in German. In this respect, the Japanese studied mathematics in a tradition different from those who had studied mathematics in other areas such as France and North America. For example, Kazuo Midutani, Shizuo Kakutani and Hukukane Nikaido studied mathematics through reading literature written in German, and in contrast to Debreu none of the three was very much interested in Bourbaki's "new" mathematics.

It is very interesting to compare Corry's history of modern algebra with the *A Hundred Year History of Mathematics in Japan* (MSJ 1983–4, in Japanese) written by the editorial committee for the Mathematical Society of Japan (MSJ). On one hand, Corry (1996: 309–10) states:

> In retrospect, the main thrust of Bourbaki's initial motivation may be seen as an attempt to reorient French mathematics away from its traditionally dominant conceptions and into new perspectives lately developed in Germany. In particular, Bourbaki's treatise, as it gradually came to be conceived and worked out, may actually be seen as an extension of van der Waerden's achievement to the whole of mathematics; that is, much the same as van der Waerden had succeeded in presenting the whole of algebra as a hierarchy of structures, so did Bourbaki present much larger portions of mathematics in a similar way.

Van der Waerden was one of Emmy Nöther's students at Göttingen University. Nöther had a large number of excellent students including the Japanese Kenjiro Shoda in the 1920s (as discussed later). On the other hand, looking at the history of mathematics from a Japanese point of view, MSJ (1984: 59) writes:

> Mathematics made such progress that it had gained the character of twentieth-century mathematics, namely the conscious use of the axiomatic method. This method was strongly promoted from the last half of the 1920s till the 1930s. In Göttingen, E. Nöther was active and van der Waerden's *Moderne Algebra*, I, II (1930, 1931) had a significant influence on the mathematical community.... Alexandroff and Hopf's *Topologie I* (1935) was also written under her influence. Around that time, von Neumann and others were active in Berlin.... Although the classical trend was generally strong in France, Bourbaki's activities were started as late as the mid 1930s.
>
> (My translation)

Thus we can confirm that the Japanese studied mathematics in a tradition different from those who had studied mathematics under the strong influence of Nicolas Bourbaki. We argue that the case of the Japanese scholars expands the variety of routes to the application of a fixed-point theory to the solution of the existence question in a competitive economy, compared with those identified by Weintraub, Mirowski, Ingrao and Israel. This demonstrates that there was not a single path to the goal for the proof of the existence of general competitive equilibrium.

3 Emerging abstract algebra and fixed-point theorems[8]

The mathematical equipment needed for the rigorous proof of the existence of general competitive equilibrium began to become available after Léon Walras, the originator of the general equilibrium theory, died in 1910. Set theory, modern algebra and fixed-point theorems were burgeoning on the European continent. However, the historical course toward the proof of the existence of a general equilibrium was so complicated that newcomers to the field of mathematical economics, including general equilibrium theory and game theory, easily got lost and guessed wrong. Therefore, we should look very carefully at the "division" of the European mathematical community, especially the estrangement between French and German societies, during and after World War I, namely from 1914 to the late 1930s.

Since the beginning of World War I (1914–18), German mathematicians had not been invited to any international meetings. They lacked contact with foreign mathematicians during the war. A few years after the conclusion of the war, many students began to come to Göttingen again from various countries including Japan. However, in the 1920s, European mathematicians were politically divided due to the hostility left by World War I. For example, when they held official meetings, the *Union Mathématique Internationale* formally restricted its invitations to countries belonging to the *Conseil International des Recherches*, which Germany had not joined.

Moreover, they were also philosophically split on the foundations of mathematics, for instance intuitionism and formalism.[9] Formalists led by the German mathematician David Hilbert (1862–1943) were the most vigorous group and were increasing in number (mainly in the German-speaking world). Hilbert set himself the goal of proving that analysis and the fruitful parts of set theory are free from contradiction. For him, the only criterion of acceptability of a mathematical concept or system is its freedom from contradiction. On the other hand, the basic proof on fixed-point theorems was first given by the Dutch mathematician L. E. J. Brouwer (1881–1966), who was the systematic founder of modern intuitionism in the field of mathematics.[10] In the 1920s until the summer of 1928, when the ultimate clash occurred between Brouwer and Hilbert, Brouwer's mathematical achievement and interesting personality attracted several scholars, including the German Hermann Weyl (1885–1955), the Russian Pavel S. Alexandroff (1896–1982), the Austrian L. Wittgenstein, as well as Karl Menger.[11] Menger in his "An intuitionistic-formalistic dictionary of set theory" (1928, in German) established a close connection between Brouwer's definition of set in intuitionism and the concept of analytic set in traditional set theory (Menger 1928: 225, 1979b: 85). It seems that the dictionary helped many mathematicians to overcome the difficulties of Brouwer's phraseology, which was different from the traditional one used by the majority. Therefore, it can be said that thanks to Menger's efforts Brouwer's mathematical achievement became more available to many mathematicians. In fact, without this help, Shizuo Kakutani recalled that, "My colleague and I listed up Brouwer's papers including the ones on fixed point theorems [(Brouwer 1911, 1912)] and tried to read them one by one. Yet we did not understand his concept at all and gave it up" (personal communication with Kakutani). Brouwer, however, seemed to dislike Menger's dictionary (Menger 1979b: 246).

In 1928, the ultimate clash occurred between Brouwer and Hilbert (see Menger 1979b). The editorial board for the *Mathematische Annalen* was drastically reshuffled between volume 100 in 1928 and 101 in 1929. The former main editorial board included Hilbert, Albert Einstein, Otto Blumenthal and Constantin Caratheodory, with the cooperation of coeditors Brouwer, Ludwig Bieberbach, Harald Bohr, Richard Courant, Walther v. Dyck, Otto Holder, Thedor v. Karman and Arnold Sommerfeld. In 1929, Hilbert became the editor, with Blumenthal and Erich Hecke as the only two coeditors. It is worth noting that after 1929 the *Mathematische Annalen* began to carry papers written in English and French and became gradually internationalized.

In September 1928, German mathematicians made a comeback at the eighth International Congress of Mathematicians held in Bologna, thanks to organizer S. Pincherle's bold decision. Although there were still anti-German feelings, the participants numbered over 800 from 36 countries, including more than 70 Germans (MSJ 1984: 55). Eleven Japanese mathematicians attended the congress as well. There were 15 invited lectures such as Hilbert on the foundation of mathematics, H. C. H. Wyle on the representation of Lie group, J. Hadamard on functional analysis, M. Frechet on abstract space, N. N. Luzin on analytical set, and F. Enriques and G. Castelnuovo on algebraic geometry. These lectures reflected the new trend of mathematics. American mathematicians G. D. Birkoff (1884–1944) and Oswald Veblen (1880–1960) of Princeton University also gave invited lectures.

The axiomatic approaches in mathematics became more important in these years and the axiomatization of economics was also initiated in the middle of this intellectual morass. The formalist mathematicians began to use axiomatic methods more consciously than ever before. A. Emmy Nöther, a student of Hilbert's, urged the use of axiomatic methods not only in her subject of algebra but also in mathematics more generally. Through her energetic lectures and discussions Nöther had direct influence on many young mathematicians not only from the German-speaking world but also from Russia and Japan. She gave them her lecture notes in order for them to write books. B. L. van der Waerden published his *Moderne Algebra* volumes I and II (1930–1), which had an immense influence on the community of mathematicians including those from Japan (MSJ 1984: 59). The introduction stated the purpose of the book as follows:

> The "abstract," "formal," or "axiomatic" direction, to which the fresh impetus in algebra is due, has led to a number of new formulations of ideas, insight into new interrelations, and far-reaching results, especially in *group*

> *theory*, *field theory*, *valuation theory*, *ideal theory*, and the *theory of hypercomplex numbers*. The principal objective of this book is to introduce the reader this entire world of concepts.
>
> (van der Waerden 1955: iv, italics in original)

Van der Waerden listed the sources of the book as follows:

> This book has in part grown out of the following courses:
>
> Lectures given by E. Artin on Algebra.
>
> (Hamburg, Summer session 1926)
>
> A seminar on *Theory of Ideals*, conducted by E. Artin, W. Balaschke, O. Schreier, and the author.
>
> (Hamburg, Winter 1926–7)
>
> Lectures by W. Noether [Nöther] on *Group Theory* and *Hypercomplex Numbers*.
>
> (Göttingen, Winter 1924–5 and Winter 1927–8)
>
> New proofs or new arrangements of proofs in this book are in most cases due to the lectures and seminars mentioned, regardless of whether the source is expressly quoted.
>
> (van der Waerden 1955: x, italics in original)

Moreover, Japanese mathematicians Kenjiro Shoda (1902–77), Zyoiti Suetuna (1898–1970), and Shinjiro Mori (1893–1979) studied under Nöther mostly in the last quarter of the 1920s.[12] After returning to Japan, they taught abstract algebra at Osaka, Tokyo and Hiroshima. Shoda published an advanced textbook entitled *Abstract Algebra* (1932, in Japanese), which included chapters on sets, groups, modules, rings, commutative fields, representation theory and hypercomplex system. He explained Ideal theory, Galois theory and even the structure of the hypercomplex system or algebra based on Nöther's lecture notes at Göttingen from 1929–30, which Nöther kindly mailed in order for him to write the textbook. It is amazing from the viewpoint of an economist that a student was allowed to use his/her professor's lecture notes in writing a textbook. MSJ (1984: 142) states, "[This book] modernized the study of algebra thoroughly and had a strong influence especially on young scholars [in Japan] [my translation]." Shoda played an important part in establishing the department of mathematics at Osaka Imperial University, whose graduate school of mathematics Shizuo Kakutani entered after he had graduated from Tohoku Imperial University in Sendai.

The ninth International Congress of Mathematicians was held in Zurich in September 1932. About 700 mathematicians got together from 41 countries. There were 20 invited lectures, which included topics directly related to contemporary mathematics such as hypercomplex numbers presented by Nöther, algebraic geometry by F. Severi, topology by J. W. Alexander (Princeton

University), symmetric Riemannian space by E. Cartan, and set theory by W. Sierpinski (MSJ 1984: 56).

In 1933, Adolf Hitler came to power, and Nöther had to leave Germany for the United States because of her religious and political beliefs. She passed away in 1935. However, under the strong influence of the axiomatic movement and encouragement by Nöther, P. Alexandroff and Heinz Hopf were contributing a series of papers on topology to the *Mathematische Annalen*. They later organized them in book form and published it under the title of *Topologie I* (1935) in German. The book had four parts on set-theoretical topology, topology of complexes, topological invariance and related abstraction, combination in Euclidean space-continuous mapping on polyhedron, including a detailed discussion of Brouwer's fixed-point theorem. Although the authors spent several productive years at Göttingen from 1925 to 1931, they dedicated the book to Brouwer. This was because they were greatly influenced by Brouwer and especially Alexandroff, who spent one year (1925–6) close to Brouwer. Both authors stayed at Princeton in the winter of 1927–8 and soaked up the stimulating milieu of the Princeton school of topology. They thanked Oswald Veblen (1880–1960), J. W. Alexander and especially Solomon Lefschetz (1884–1972).

As first discovered by K. Menger, the concepts in set theory developed by Brouwer could be translated into traditional concepts. In other words, Menger's "An intuitionistic-formalistic dictionary of set theory" (1928, in German) established a close connection between Brouwer's definition of set in intuitionism and the concept of analytic set in traditional set theory. Menger (1927: 225, 1979a: 85) summarized the connection as follows:[13]

Totalities in Brouwer's Terminology:	Subsets of the Plane in Traditional Terminology:
Sets with finite generations	Bounded closed sets
Individualized sets	Borelian sets
Sets	Analytic sets
Species	Sets

It seems that the dictionary helped many mathematicians to overcome the difficulties of Brouwer's phraseology. Therefore, it can be said that thanks to Menger's efforts Brouwer's mathematical achievement became more available to many mathematicians. Yet Brouwer seemed to dislike Menger's dictionary (Menger 1979a: 246). At any rate, the historian of mathematics M. Klein (1972: 1199) maintained that much of Brouwer's mathematical work, notably in topology, was not in accord with his philosophy. Alexandroff and Hopf's *Topologie I* (1935) was widely read and referred to in several important papers relating to the existence of a general equilibrium such as von Neumann (1937) and Uzawa (1962). Kakutani had already read those of their papers which had appeared in journals when he obtained a copy of Alexandroff and Hopf (1935).

Moreover, Kurt Gödel's incompleteness theorem for any formalized system did not have a big influence on the formalization of mathematics, although it applies to the formal system constructed by the logicists Alfred North Whitehead and Bertrand Russell in their *Principia Mathematica* (1927), the Zermelo-Fraenkel system based on set theory, and Hilbert's axiomatization of number theory. It is worth quoting from von Neumann:

> Gödel produced a most remarkable result.... Its essential importance ... was this: If a system of mathematics does not lead into contradiction, then this fact cannot be demonstrated with the procedures of that system. Gödel's proof satisfied the strictest criterion of mathematical rigor – the intuitionistic one. Its influence on Hilbert's program is somewhat controversial.
>
> (von Neumann [1947] 1961: 6)

Von Neumann doubted the influence of Gödel's incompleteness theorem on Hilbert's axiomatic method in mathematics.

4 Karl Menger at the intersection

This section investigates the intellectual network that spread out from Karl Menger in order to clarify the mathematical development for the study of the existence question in general equilibrium theory. This is not only because he was responsible for connecting together mathematical reasoning with economic thinking, but also because he was ubiquitous on the scene of the foundations of logic, mathematics and science. In 1902 he was born to the son of Carl Menger, who was an eminent economist at the University of Vienna and had established the tradition of the Austrian School. K. Menger received his doctoral degree in mathematics from the University of Vienna.

Karl Menger was an active mathematician and traveler. The following five activities were his most important relating to the development of economic research. First, Menger worked with L. E. J. Brouwer (1881–1966), the intuitionist mathematician who proved a fixed-point theorem, at Amsterdam. Second, due to his strong philosophical interests Menger joined the so-called *Wienerkreis*, the Vienna Circle of logical-empiricist philosophers founded by Moritz Schlick and Hans Hahn. Hahn was Menger's teacher. Third, Menger was one of the organizing members of the Econometric Society in the United States near the end of 1930. Fourth, Menger visited Japan in the spring of 1931 and delivered a talk on the incompleteness theorem demonstrated by his student Kurt Gödel. Fifth, Menger organized the mathematical colloquium in Vienna, in which Abraham Wald and John von Neumann participated. However, when Austria became part of Nazi Germany under the *Anschluss* in March 1938, Menger, teaching at Notre Dame, immediately resigned from his professorship in Vienna and stayed in the United States (Craver 1986).

It is well known that Karl Menger informally organized the mathematical colloquium for mathematicians and economists in Vienna from 1928 to 1936 (K. Menger 1973: 47). He published their reports and proceedings as *Ergebnisse eines Mathematischen Kolloquiums* from 1931 to 1937. However, it is relatively unknown that three Japanese scholars, mathematician Yukio Mimura (1904–84, Osaka Imperial University, now Osaka University), and economists Kazuo Midutani (1897–1981, Kobe University of Commerce, now Kobe University) and Yuzo Yamada (1902–95, Tokyo University of Commerce, now Hitotsubashi University), attended Menger's mathematical colloquium in Vienna.[14] Mimura made the report on the colloquium entitled "An impression on the University of Berlin and the University of Vienna" (1933, in Japanese) and Midutani in his "The significance of axiomatic economics and its method" (1935, in Japanese) and "Comments on Wald's proof of the uniqueness of the solution for the Cassel-Schlesinger system of production" (1939, in Japanese) exposed the detailed discussion in the colloquium. Young Shizuo Kakutani, who proved a fixed-point theorem in 1941, met both Mimura and Midutani at local mathematical meetings in the Osaka-Kobe area and often heard Midutani talk about Menger's mathematical colloquium held in Vienna. Kakutani was studying the emerging new algebra. Kakutani was directly advised by Mimura to study the works of von Neumann and he was naturally fascinated by von Neumann, as were many other mathematicians of the day (see section 5).[15]

Menger's informal *Kolloquium* was held usually at night once a week. Mimura presented two mathematical papers ("Über die Stetigkeit des Inhaltes konvexer geschlossener Flächen" and "Über die Bogenlange," namely "On the continuity within closed convex surface" and "On the arc length") in November 1931 and March 1932. American mathematician G. C. Evans, the author of *Mathematical Introduction to Economics* (1930), also gave a talk on the axiom of dimension in September 1931. Mimura (1933, in Japanese: 17–18) made a report to Japan, "Menger holds an informal Kolloquium once a week, usually at night. He forgot the time when the discussion was heated.... Gödel was the most important speaker in the colloquium [my translation]." It is well known that other members of Menger's colloquium included Karl Schlesinger (1889–1938), Abraham Wald (1902–50), and Oskar Morgenstern (1902–77).

It is also well known that at Menger's colloquium Wald presented a groundbreaking paper on the question of the existence of general equilibrium. Wald's two papers "On the unique non-negative solvability of the new production equations, part I" and "On the production equations of economic value theory II" (both in German) appeared in 1935 and 1936. When Wald's papers were published, it reminded von Neumann of equations he had formulated and presented at Princeton in 1932. Von Neumann offered to present the paper to the colloquium (K. Menger 1973: 55). His "Über ein ökonomisches Gleichungssystem und eine Verallgemeinerung des Brouwerschen Fixpunktsätzes" (On a system of economic equilibrium and the generalization of Brouwer's fixed-point theorem) appeared in Menger's *Ergebnisse* in 1937 (The title of the English version became "A model of general equilibrium," 1945–6). This 11-page-long paper has many elements including general equilibrium theory, balanced growth, the minimax theorem and Brouwer's fixed-point theorem. It is noteworthy that the paper attracted mathematicians at first, rather than economists. The achievement of Menger's colloquium and *Ergebnisse*, especially von Neumann's paper, became the basis for the intensive study of linear algebra and mathematical economics starting in the 1940s.

Midutani attended Menger's colloquium during his stay in Vienna in 1932–4. After returning from Vienna, he published a series of papers in Japanese on various mathematical approaches to economics such as "The significance of axiomatic economics and its method" (1935, in Japanese) and "Comments on Wald's proof of the uniqueness of the solution for the Cassel-Schlesinger system of production" (1939, in Japanese). However, economists like Takuma Yasui, who was working on Walrasian general equilibrium theory in the 1930s and stability analysis in the 1940s (Chapter 5; Ikeo 1994b), did not realize the importance of Wald's papers until after World War II. Yasui recalled:

> Midutani gave part of the economics of the *Ergebnisse* to me after he came back to Japan from Vienna. This part included Wald's papers. But I did not realize the importance of the papers until the end of the war.
>
> (Yasui, personal communication, my translation)

Midutani paid attention to the axiomatic method and a system of inequalities described as the price system instead of a system of simultaneous equations used by Cassel and Walras. He was one of the three Japanese scholars who referred to the existence question in publication prior to 1950. In fact, H. Nikaido clearly remembered the research situation of the existence question of the early 1950s in Japan and said, "There were almost no Japanese economists who knew of the existence problem of equilibrium as such" (Nikaido 1996–7, my translation).

5 John von Neumann – Shizuo Kakutani

In the twentieth century, there were numerous mathematicians who were fascinated by John von Neumann's mathematical works and adored him from their heart. Yukio Mimura, Shizuo Kakutani and Hukukane Nikaido were no exceptions. In fact, Kakutani had a delightful time working with von Neumann at Princeton University from October 1940 to June 1942. The study in this section owes greatly to my personal communications with Kakutani.

Von Neumann was born in Budapest in December 1903.[16] He entered the University of Budapest in 1921 to study mathematics. Yet most of the time between 1921 and 1923, he stayed in Berlin and attended Fritz Haber's lectures on chemistry and Albert Einstein's on statistical mechanics. He enrolled at the Eidgenossische Technische Hochschule in Zurich to study chemical engineering in 1923, and had contacts with Hermann Weyl and George Polya (1887–1985), both of whom were in Zurich at the time. He was a Rockefeller Fellow at the University of Göttingen during 1926 and 1927. From 1927 to 1929 he was appointed as Privatdozent at the University of Berlin, the youngest in the university's history. Von Neumann gave lectures on operators in Hilbertian space and the Japanese mathematician Yukio Mimura was among the scholars at the University of Berlin. In his report entitled "An impression on the University of

Berlin and the University of Vienna" (1933), Mimura remembered that he had difficulty understanding the lectures because von Neumann spoke too quickly and with a Hungarian accent but he was fascinated by von Neumann's works of genius. Mimura (1933, in Japanese: 14) said:

> I wonder how I should express what von Neumann has done in the study of operator in Hilbertian space. He has finished a stage of the research program initiated by Hilbert and developed by himself, in other words he completed the theory of finite operator. I cannot tell the whole of his contributions to mathematics or how diverse mathematical works he has done. I think it amazing that he captured large, classical questions and utilizes new mathematics as he pleases.

In 1929, von Neumann was transferred to the University of Hamburg (and left for the United States in 1930). In 1931, Mimura moved to the University of Vienna and attended Karl Menger's lectures and informal colloquium.

Mimura returned from Vienna to Japan and was appointed as an associate professor at the mathematics department of Osaka Imperial University in 1934 (the name was changed to Osaka University in 1947). The university was established in 1931 and classes started in 1933. Kenjiro Shoda, a student of Emmy Nöther's, was appointed professor there in 1933 and taught algebra. About 20 copies of B. L. van der Waerden's *Moderne Algebra* (1930–1) were acquired at the library for the students to check out (MSJ 1984: 34).

In 1934, Shizuo Kakutani graduated from Tohoku Imperial University in Sendai and entered the graduate school in Osaka Imperial University, which was located much nearer to his home town. In 1935 he was appointed as research assistant at Osaka. Mimura advised Kakutani to read von Neumann's papers. Kakutani followed Mimura's advice and started with von Neumann's "Zur Theorie der Gesellschaftsspiele" (1928; "On the theory of games and strategy" in 1959). He found the *Ergebnisse eines Mathematische Kolloquiums* (K. Menger ed. 1931–7) in the library[17] and von Neumann's "Über ein ökonomisches Gleichungssystem und eine Verallgemeinerung des Brouwerschen Fixpunktsatzes" (1937). Kakutani recalled that, "Von Neumann's papers were rather difficult" (personal communication with Kakutani). Therefore, Kakutani in Osaka began to make a step forward to become a mathematician in an intellectual environment similar to that in Germany and Austria. (Kakutani did not meet Karl Menger when Menger visited Japan in 1931, but he did meet Menger in the United States.)

Kakutani got a chance to study at the Institute for Advanced Study in Princeton University in 1940. He was extremely lucky to be invited by his uncle to board a freight ship for the United States as a (free) guest. Japan had already been involved in the war against China since 1937. The Japanese government restricted the outflow of foreign currency so that Kakutani could not buy his travel tickets. Kakutani left Japan in the summer of 1940 and arrived at Princeton in September.

In October 1940, Kakutani started to attend the seminar run by von Neumann and gave a talk on the extension of Brouwer's fixed-point theorem. Brouwer's fixed-point theorem is related to point-to-point mapping, while Kakutani's related to multi-valued or point-to-set mapping. Kakutani's idea was published as "A generalization of Brouwer's fixed point theorem" in the *Duke Mathematical Journal* of 1941. In October 1941, von Neumann and Morgenstern started to run the seminar on the theory of games. Kakutani and A. W. Tucker were the only participants. Tucker was a student of Solomon Lefschetz, naturally specialized in topology and became famous for his articulation of the game theoretic situation called "Priznerz's Dilemma" (Tucker 1950). Kakutani had already read von Neumann's papers before he came to Princeton and therefore he had no problems in attending the seminar.

When Japan began the war against the United States by attacking Pearl Harbor in December 1941, the Institute for Advanced Study allowed Kakutani to stay there and continue his research. However, in the spring of 1942, he received a letter from Japan via the Swiss Red Cross telling him to come back because his mother was ill. He left the United States for Japan by exchange ship in May.[18] At that time, von Neumann and Morgenstern's manuscript for their *Theory of Games and Economic Behavior* (1944) was quite incomplete. Kakutani confirmed that he did not help them produce a clean manuscript.[19] Kakutani was the only Japanese person at Princeton at the time. He recalled that there was a young Japanese-American mathematician in Princeton but, even so, the person was an American. He repeatedly said, "It's strange," when I asked him whether he did the manuscript work in April 1995. Honestly speaking, I asked the question after I had investigated a series of manuscripts for von Neumann and Morgenstern (1944) which remain in the Oskar Morgenstern Papers at Duke University and had convinced myself that something was wrong with the above quotation.

After the conclusion of World War II, Kakutani came back to Princeton in 1948, when the Occupation policy by the Allies became less restricted and allowed Japanese people to leave the country only with the inviting country's entry permission. He found that the mathematics relating to economics had developed during the war. He met young John Nash (b. 1928), who received a Nobel Prize in 1994 for his pioneering analysis of equilibria in the theory of noncooperative games, but he did not have a good opportunity to have any discussion on game theory or other mathematics. As von Neumann was spending increasing time in Washington, DC, Kakutani decided to move to Yale University in 1949. A few years later, Gerard Debreu moved to Yale from Chicago and met Kakutani. Debreu was putting the final touches to his *Theory of Value* (1959).

6 Japanese mathematical economists and the existence question

This section is summarized mostly from the writings of Takuma Yasui (1909–95), who made contributions to the research of stability analysis, rather than my personal communications with him. This section uses my personal communications with Hukukane Nikaido (1923–2001).

Within a few years after the end of World War II, the Japanese were working on similar subjects, in both mathematics and economics, as the mathematicians and economists abroad thanks to the prompt circulation of scientific, refereed journals. Around 1950 in Japan, Hiroshi Furuya (1920–57), a former student of Yasui, noticed the strong trend toward the thorough mathematization of economics. He invited mathematics students such as Tamotsu Yokoyama (1921–96), Kenichi Inada (1925–2002) and Hirofumi Uzawa (b. 1928) to the community of economists on one hand, and strongly advised economics graduates to study mathematics on the other. Another mathematics student, Hukukane Nikaido, realized that John von Neumann's and Kenneth J. Arrow's economic works were different from those of J. R. Hicks and Paul Samuelson, which were based on calculus. In the new approach, the abstract economy was modeled based on the knowledge of set theory and convex set methods to establish the existence of general equilibrium and to clarify the welfare aspects of the competitive economy.

The first conference on mathematical programming had been held at the University of Chicago in 1949. The proceedings entitled *Activity Analysis of Production and Allocation* were published as a Cowles Commission monograph in 1951 and soon copies arrived in Japan. Their themes were, directly or indirectly, related to the best allocation of limited means toward desired ends. The organizer was Tjalling C. Koopmans. Other contributors were Kenneth J. Arrow, Paul A. Samuelson, Robert Dorfman, Nicholas Georgescu-Roegen, Oskar Morgenstern and Herbert A. Simon; mathematicians Albert W. Tucker, Harold W. Kuhn and David Gale; George B. Dantzig, Murray A. Geisler and Marshall K. Wood from the US Department of the Air Force. Francis W. Dresch from the US Naval Proving Ground, Walter H. Keen and Fred D. Rigby from the US Department of the Navy also participated.

Also in 1951, K. J. Arrow's "An extension of the basic theorems of classical welfare economics" appeared in *Proceedings of the Second Berkeley Symposium on Mathematical Statistics and Probability* edited by Jerzy Neyman. Thanks to the Office of Naval Research (ONR) and other institutions, the symposium had been held over a fortnight with the participation of several scholars from abroad. Arrow reviewed Pareto optimality from the viewpoint of convex set theory. Gerard Debreu in his "The coefficient of resource utilization" (1951), independently of Arrow, embarked on the set-theoretic and convex-set method in the study of the optimality of competitive equilibrium. At first, the set-theoretic approach taken by these mathematical economists seemed to refute the differential calculus basis for economics taken by J. R. Hicks and Paul A. Samuelson. Then, mathematically trained scholars increasingly entered the field of mathematical economics on one hand, and theoretical economists found it necessary to study topology themselves on the other.

Those mathematical economists who had recognized the problem of existence of a competitive equilibrium were directly stimulated by John Nash's

"Non-cooperative games" (1951), which appeared in *Annals of Mathematics*. This paper was "a more polished version of his doctoral thesis" (Nash 1996: 32) at Princeton University. Nash called the *n*-person games, which were developed in von Neumann and Morgenstern's *Theory of Games and Economic Behavior* (1944), cooperative. Their theory was based on an analysis of the interrelationships of various coalitions which can be formed by the players of the game. Nash embarked on the theory of non-cooperative games, which was based on the absence of coalitions or on the assumption that each participant acted independently, without collaboration or communication with any of the others (Nash 1996: 286). Nash (1951) proved the existence of equilibrium points by the use of Brouwer's fixed-point theorem for point-to-point transformations, whereas he used Kakutani's theorem for point-to-set transformations in his previous paper "Equilibrium points in n-person games" (1950b). Nash (1951) constructed a continuous transformation *T* of the space of *n*-tuples such that the fixed points of *T* are the equilibrium points of the game.[20]

On the other hand, mathematicians were also working hard on topology, and the treatment of fixed-point theorems had been further improved since Kakutani published his version in 1941. Samuel Eilenberg, an active American member of Nicolas Bourbaki, and Deane Montgomery in their "Fixed point theorems for multi-valued transformations" (1946) extended Solomon Lefschetz's trace formula to set-valued mapping. They proved that if Y is an acyclic absolute neighborhood retract and f is an upper hemi-continuous mapping which assigns to each point y of Y an acyclic subset $f(y)$ of Y, then f has a fixed point, namely there is some y such that $f(y)$ contains y. Here, an acyclic set is one which has the same homology groups as does a set consisting of just one point. Eilenberg and Montgomery's fixed-point theorem is the most general and included Kakutani's. Then Edward G. Begle in his "A fixed point theorem" (1950) gave another proof to the most general fixed-point theorem.

Hukukane Nikaido was following this trend and knew very well what was happening in the forefront of topology. Nikaido in his "Coincidence and some systems of inequalities" (1959) examined the generalization of fixed-point theorem in the study of systems of inequalities originated with von Neumann's works on his minimax theorem, reformulated by Kakutani and developed by Eilenberg, Montgomery and Begle. Nikaido (1959: 354–5) states as follows:

> [S]ince … von Neumann's initial work attention had mainly been confined to some game problems or their variants, and no attack had ever made against relevant conjectures [the existence of a general equilibrium solution] in the orthodox mathematical economics until in recent times Arrow-Debreu [1954], McKenzie [1954], Gale [1955] and this writer [Nikaido 1956] independently and almost simultaneously gave reformulations and proofs to the most basic conjecture in the theory of general equilibrium as founded by L. Walras around the end of the last century [the nineteenth century].… [A]s in the theory of games fixed point theorems or their equivalent propositions proved to be very helpful. It is interesting as well as significant that the

minimax problems and those of economic equilibrium have some intersection in common and reveal a certain similarity between them.

Takuma Yasui, who had studied the conditions for the stability of a competitive equilibrium with the use of a system of ordinary differential equations in Japan in the 1940s (Chapter 5; Ikeo 1994b), sent letters to members of the Econometric Society around the time when the Treaty of Peace with Japan became effective. Receiving warm replies (kept in the Yasui Library at Saitama University), he participated in the American winter meeting of the Econometric Society held in Chicago from December 27–29, 1952. He was sent there by the Science Council of Japan (Nihon Gakujutsu Kaigi) and presented his "Nonlinear self-exited oscillations and business cycles" in the session "Macro-dynamic Models of Economic Fluctuations" on the twenty-seventh. On the same day he attended the session "The Theory of Games," in which K. J. Arrow and G. Debreu presented their "Existence of an equilibrium for a competitive economy," which was discussed by L. J. Savage. On the twenty-ninth, he attended the session of "Selected Papers," in which L. W. McKenzie presented his "The existence and uniqueness of equilibrium in Graham's model of international trade." At this meeting, Yasui for the first time learned the application of fixed-point theorem, which had been used in game theory, to the proof of the existence of a competitive economy (Yasui 1971, in Japanese: 286). Yet Yasui did not report the heated argument between McKenzie and Arrow and Debreu on their formulations of an abstract economy and the priority of the proof (see Weintraub and Gayer 2001; Weintraub 2002). A summary of McKenzie's presentation appeared in *Econometrica* of 1953, while Arrow and Debreu's was not available. Their full papers were both published in *Econometrica* in 1954, with the title of McKenzie's paper changed to "On equilibrium in Graham's model of world trade and other competitive systems."

McKenzie proved the existence and uniqueness of competitive equilibrium in Frank D. Graham's model for world trade by using Kakutani's fixed-point theorem. The production aspect of the model was represented by a linear activity model in which the primary goods are the labor supplies of the several countries. McKenzie frequently emphasized that the method of his proof was sufficiently general that the restrictive assumptions in Graham's model could be considerably relaxed. Thus, his results might be applied to other models of competitive economy. His proof of existence of an equilibrium point was given in section 6, the second to last section, by resorting to the knowledge of topology for the first time. This proof was supplemented by the mathematical appendix in McKenzie (1954). McKenzie did not refer to John Nash's papers on game theory, which were very important for other economists in solving the existence question.

Arrow and Debreu in the published version used set-theoretical techniques to specify the precise assumptions of a competitive economy as the basic starting point. They confined themselves to proving the existence of competitive equilibrium and extended Nash's notion of an equilibrium point for a non-cooperative game to their abstract economy, which was first discussed in Debreu (1951).

They discussed the question of the existence of a competitive equilibrium by constructing an abstract economy through a generalization of the concept of a game. They appealed indirectly to Eilenberg and Montgomery's fixed-point theorem, although they did not refer to Eilenberg and Montgomery (1946) or Begle (1950) (Arrow's letter to Georgescu-Roegen of January 12, 1955, quoted in section 7; Nikaido 1959). Yet later Debreu's *Theory of Value* (1959: 27) referred to these mathematical papers.

Around 1954, Hukukane Nikaido in Tokyo and David Gale in Copenhagen were working on the existence question along a similar line, though independently of each other. Gale's "The law of supply and demand" appeared in *Mathematica Scandinavica* of 1955. Gale obtained a simpler proof of the existence of an equilibrium than Arrow and Debreu (1954) by using a lemma of combinatorial topology and Kakutani's fixed-point theorem instead of Eilenberg and Montgomery's. Nikaido's "On the classical multilateral exchange problem" was published in *Metroeconomica* of 1956. In contrast to Gale, Nikaido elaborated the existence question independently of Arrow and Debreu (see the next section). A footnote in Nikaido's paper stated, "The result of this paper has been obtained independently of the important work carried out by Professors Arrow and Debreu ... and prior to its appearance in *Econometrica*, although it should be expressly acknowledged that there is much intersection" (Nikaido 1956: 135). Nikaido formulated the basic propositions of the existence of general equilibrium as a theorem relating to the excess demand correspondence in the case of multilateral exchange of many commodities. Nikaido resorted to slightly more restricted assumptions than Arrow and Debreu (1954) such as an upper hemicontinuous correspondence. Nikaido adapted the basic mapping formula so as to apply it to a model of world trade as well as to Graham's model treated in McKenzie (1954), and proved the existence of a general equilibrium solution with the direct use of Kakutani's fixed-point theorem.

Then Hirofumi Uzawa (1962) proved that Walras's existence theorem and Brouwer's fixed-point theorem were equivalent as discussed in section 2. Our history ends at 1962 although the study of the existence question continues to the present.

7 Hukukane Nikaido – Kenneth J. Arrow

Hukukane Nikaido's experience of the 1950s is very intriguing and shows how Japanese scholars entered the field of mathematical economics and struggled to publish their scientific papers at a time when Japan had just reopened the academic channel to the international community of economists after World War II. Yet, the reason why Nikaido became interested in mathematical economics and then the question of existence was somewhat accidental.[21]

Nikaido was an undergraduate student in mathematics at the University of Tokyo when he was allowed to attend Shokichi Iyanaga's seminar for graduate students. In 1948, Tsuneyoshi Seki (1924–2013) began to attend Iyanaga's seminar to become a mathematical economist after he graduated from the economics department of Hitotsubashi University. Seki was interested in the question of the existence of general equilibrium which was discussed not only in M. Watanabe and M. Hisatake's *Application of Mathematics to Economics* (1933, in Japanese) but also in K. Menger's *Ergebnisse eines Mathematische Kolloquiums* (Seki 1986, in Japanese: 334). Seki delivered a talk on von Neumann's 1937 paper, which stimulated Nikaido to read von Neumann's "Über ein ökonomisches Gleichungssystem und eine Verallgemeinerung des Brouwerschen Fixpunktsatzes" (1937) in *Ergebnisse*, and von Neumann and Morgenstern's *Theory of Games and Economic Theory* (1944) in a pirated edition. Nikaido recalled,

> Game theory was a new field at the time. Fixed-point theorems were always used in proving existence in game theory, but it was not true of economics. I wondered why. I started to examine Hicks' *Value and Capital* (1939). It was also a pirated edition. An idea came to me from Nash's paper. Interestingly, the mathematical structure of a competitive economy is the same as that of game theory.
>
> (Nikaido, personal communication, my translation)

Nikaido first wrote papers in the mathematical line. He began with P. Alexandroff and H. Hopf's *Topologie I* (1935) and published his first note on fixed-point theorems in German, namely "Zusatz und Berichtigung für meine Mitteilung 'Zum Beweis der Verallgemenerung des Fixpunktsatzes'" (A supplement and correction to my report "Proofs of the generalization of fixed point theorems," 1954a). He also wrote two papers on von Neumann's game theory and general equilibrium theory in 1952. However, he did not know what to do with his papers because it seemed to him that he did not have any opportunity to get his papers published in the mostly closed economics journals of Japanese universities, which carried only staff papers. As mentioned, there were no refereed economics journals with free submission in Japan until 1960. Nikaido sent the papers to von Neumann and Kakutani at Princeton University, and soon received a response from von Neumann. Following von Neumann's comments and advice, Nikaido submitted the papers to two different journals. They were published as "On von Neumann's minimax theorem" (1954b) in *Pacific Journal of Mathematics* and "Note on the general economic equilibrium for nonlinear production functions" (1954c) in *Econometrica*. Nikaido kept von Neumann's letters as his treasure, although he did not make it a custom to keep the other letters he received in the 1950s. He did not keep a copy of his own letter either (personal communication with Nikaido).

Nikaido was in Japan working out the existence question of competitive equilibrium along with the minimax theorem in game theory, the theorem of Nash's equilibrium in non-cooperative games, the von Neumann growth model, and fixed-point theorems given by Brouwer and Kakutani. Nikaido did not know McKenzie or Arrow and Debreu's presentations on the same question at the 1952 Chicago meeting of the Econometric Society (Econometric Society 1953). In Japan, in June or July of 1954, when he came across McKenzie's

"On equilibrium in Graham's model of world trade and other competitive systems" in the April issue of *Econometrica* (which would have been shipped by surface mail), Nikaido immediately submitted his first existence paper to *Econometrica*. Although no copy of the paper is available, we can conjecture that the title of the paper was "Exchange equilibrium and a fixed point theorem." This is because the record of the Japanese Econometric Society (1956) tells us that Hukukane Nikaido presented a paper entitled "Kokan-kinko to fudoten-teiri" at the annual meeting at Osaka University on October 29, 1954. "Kokan-kinko to fudoten-teiri" means "Exchange equilibrium and a fixed-point theorem." Then Nikaido found Arrow and G. Debreu's "Existence of an equilibrium for a competitive economy" in the July issue of *Econometrica*.

The correspondence relating to the existence question, part of which remains in the Georgescu-Roegen Papers at Duke University and Nikaido's home, tells us the treatment of Nikaido's submission to *Econometrica*. The editorial board of *Econometrica* made a typed copy of those letters it received, and made a few carbon copies of the letters it mailed.

Nikaido's first submission was rejected although his mathematical argument seemed to be of a high quality. Nikaido received the rejection letter of October 1, 1954 (sent airmail) from Robert H. Strotz, the managing editor for *Econometrica*.[22] Nikaido accepted the reasons why his paper was rejected and replied in his letter of October 7, a copy of which remains at Duke University, as follows:

> I received yesterday your letter of October 1 ... I think the referee's comment on my manuscript judges appropriately the value of my result and I therefore understand completely your processing of my paper based on this comment. Thus I only hope that I might be able to submit a paper of more economic merit in a future opportunity.
>
> As to Professor McKenzie's article you mentioned I have read it, and thus my manuscript was written with the reference to it, while unfortunately I had no opportunity to read Arrow–Debreu article before having submitted the manuscript to you.

At the same time, Nikaido was asked to make comments on a draft of a "Letter to the Editor" submitted by Cecil Phipps, the mathematician who was one of the two referees for Arrow and Debreu's existence paper submitted to *Econometrica*. Phipps was unsatisfied with the mathematical arguments made by these mathematical economists (E. R. Weintraub and T. Gayer 2000, 2001; Weintraub 2002).[23] Nikaido concluded "this letter has not succeeded in criticizing the essential portions of Arrow–Debreu's article." The letter never appeared in *Econometrica*.

Nikaido submitted his second existence paper entitled "On the classical multilateral exchange problem" to the *Econometrica* in December 1954. Strotz wrote to Nicholas Georgescu-Roegen, one of the assistant editors, on December 24 and asked him to handle the refereeing of the manuscript (Strotz's letter to Georgescu-Roegen of December 24, 1954). In turn, Georgescu-Roegen chose

K. J. Arrow as a referee. However, Arrow promptly wrote back to Georgescu-Roegen and the referee process came to a stop. Arrow's letter to Georgescu-Roegen of January 12, 1955 said as follows (full quotation of the text):

> I have just read carefully the paper of Mr. Nikaido. Although it is an excellently written paper, I cannot recommend its publication because of its extremely close overlap with the paper that Debreu and I have published. The technique of proof is almost identical. Such simplifications as exist are due to his having made stronger hypotheses. It is true that he appeals directly to Kakutani's theorem rather than as we do indirectly to the more general Eilenberg-Montgomery theorem. However, as we note explicitly, it would be quite easy to modify our proof to make use of the Kakutani theorem and we only made use of Debreu's because it is already available in the literature.
>
> As for more detailed comments, I know there will be very little to make since the organization and exposition of the paper are admirable. I have not read every line in detail and there will be minor suggestions, but I do not think it worthwhile going into unless you decide to publish the paper anyway. I will, therefore, hold the manuscript for another week and, if you wish me to, I will be glad to referee it in detail. If not, I will return the manuscript to you. Perhaps it would be better to have some person other than myself or Debreu review the question of publication since it is possible that I am prejudiced. However, in all frankness, I feel quite sure of my position.

Georgescu-Roegen arrived at the same opinion as Arrow without consulting another referee and said in his letter to Arrow of January 17, 1955 as follows:

> Thank you very much indeed for your prompt comments on Nikaido's paper.
>
> After a superficial reading, I arrived exactly at the same opinion as yours, and I am glad to have it now supported by someone else.
>
> I thought that if Nikaido believes that he brings out some additional result, not included in your paper, he might submit it as a note of a length proportionate to his contribution and without re-proving your own results. No matter what one can think about the merits of Nikaido's proof, I feel that Econometrica cannot afford to devote space to mere analytical refinements.
>
> Before making this recommendation to the editor, I would like to know whether you agree with it.

While getting Arrow's agreement (in Arrow's letter to Georgescu-Roegen of January 21), Georgescu-Roegen said in his letter to Strotz of February 4 as follows:

> Nikaido's proof is somewhat neater and simpler than that of Arrow–Debreu, but I feel that this merit alone does not justify its publication. It would be a very poor allocation of our resources. Indeed, his paper brings nothing new.

> I understand that the reason may not be well received by Nikaido and that he might feel particularly dissatisfied after he sees a paper dealing only with a new proof of Arrow–Debreu results by McKenzie published in the forthcoming proceedings of the last conference on Linear programing. Notwithstanding, I do not see what we can do about it.

Nikaido was not aware of the strange refereeing process. Moreover, he barely remembered that he did not receive a rejection letter this time. Instead, he unexpectedly received a letter from Arrow and was advised to resubmit his paper to *Metroeconomica*, a journal which he had never heard of. Fortunately Nikaido's "On the classical multilateral exchange problem" was published in *Metroeconomica* in 1956. A footnote says, "The result of this paper has been obtained independently of the important work carried on by Professors Arrow and Debreu [1954] and prior to its appearance in *Econometrica*, although it should be expressly acknowledged that there is much intersection."

Nikaido and Arrow continued to correspond. At the time, Nikaido was eager to leave Japan for a better place to study and asked Arrow if there was a possibility of his staying in the United States. Arrow's letter to Nikaido of March 1, 1955 remains at Nikaido's house. Arrow wrote as follows:

> Thank you for your letter of February 21. I have been following your work with great interest and I am very impressed with its quality. I would be very happy to see you enter the field of economics and I would like to do everything in my power to help you.
>
> Unfortunately, however, my powers are limited in this regard. I can offer you the position of research associate in a group working here under my direction for the coming year but the salary is only $2,400. I believe it is possible for you to supplement this by a Fulbright Grant for travel expenses. If this arrangement appeals to you, I would feel greatly privileged to have you join us. Please let me know whether you can come beginning this coming September.

Nikaido took a chance and was appointed as Research Associate in the Applied Mathematics and Statistics Laboratory at Stanford University. According to D. Whitaker's letter to Nikaido of April 15, 1955, Nikaido's salary was 275 dollars a month for the period of October 1, 1955 to June 30, 1956. Nikaido arrived at Stanford in the summer of 1955. He was informed by Arrow that research results similar to his rejected paper had been achieved by David Gale (1955).

Later Debreu in his *Theory of Value* (1959: 88) noted that Nikaido independently proved the existence of a competitive equilibrium in his 1956 paper. As mentioned in section 2, Debreu differentiates Nikaido and Gale's approach, calling it the "Excess Demand Approach," from Arrow and Debreu's "Simultaneous Optimization Approach" (Debreu 1982, see also Debreu 1987: 217–18).

Then Arrow in his entry "Economic Equilibrium" (1968: 379–80) for the *International Encyclopedia of the Social Sciences* stated as follows:

> Von Neumann deduced his saddle-point theorem from a generalization of Brouwer's fixed point theorem, a famous proposition in the branch of mathematics known as topology. A simplified version of von Neumann's theorem was presented a few years later by the mathematician Shizuo Kakutani, and Kakutani's theorem has been the basic tool in virtually all subsequent work. With this foundation, and the influence of the rapid development of linear programming on both the mathematical–again closely related to saddle-point theorems–and economic sides (the work of George B. Dantzig, Albert W. Tucker, Harold W. Kuhn, Tjalling C. Koopmans, and others, collected for the most part in an influential volume [Koopmans ed. 1951]) and the work of John Nash, Jr. (1950[b]), it was perceived independently by a number of scholars that existence theorems of greater simplicity and generality than Wald's were possible. The first papers were those of McKenzie (1954) and Arrow and Debreu (1954). Subsequent developments were due to Hukukane Nikaido and Hirofumi Uzawa, Debreu, and McKenzie.

Arrow (1968) clearly stated Nikaido's contribution to the study of the existence question, although it did not include Nikaido (1956) in the references. The material of Arrow (1968) was incorporated into Chapter 1 of Arrow and Hahn's *General Competitive Analysis* (1971: 11), with reference to the particular paper, Nikaido (1956). It is worth quoting from Arrow's Foreword to Shepherd's edited book *Rejected: Leading Economists Ponder the Publication Process* (1995: vii):

> But to suggest that the normal process of scholarship works well on the whole and in the long run is in no way contradictory to the view that the processes of selection and sifting which are essential to the scholarly process are filled with error and sometimes prejudice. George Shepherd has seized on one aspect of the process, publication, and it is a key one in the allocation process by which the existing structure of scholarship controls new entry.

Nikaido showed me the letters he had received in the 1950s and told me with pleasure details about why and how he had come to join Arrow's project at Stanford. However, he did not talk much about the project as a whole and how he had spent his research time at Stanford. I assume there are two reasons. One reason was that he must feel very uncomfortable with the fact that Arrow's project had been financially supported by the ONR, which was part of the Navy. Yet he felt relieved when he learned that the ONR had been essentially acting as the office of national research from 1945 until around 1957, the year in which the former Soviet Union launched Sputnik, the first unmanned space satellite and it had managed to hobble the newly established National Science Foundation (NSF) by sending Navy-related people to the top of the NSF (Sapolsky 1990: 38, 54) by reading the Japanese version (Ikeo ed. 2000 [1999]) of *Japanese Economics and Economists since 1945* (Ikeo ed. 2000). Nonetheless, it seemed to me that Nikaido was hiding something which he was very reluctant to tell me and this suggested to me that something strange had occurred in the referring process of his existence paper (Nikaido 1956) in *Econometrica*.

8 Conclusions

Let us draw five conclusions from the historical study we have presented in this chapter.

First, until the early 1950s Japanese scholars took a separate course from Arrow, Debreu and Mackenzie on the research of the so-called existence question. However, through the 1950s, mathematical economists including those in Japan followed a similar procedure for proving the existence of equilibrium in a competitive economy by borrowing tools from topology and game theory. (We find that the swift circulation of scientific journals, most of which were refereed and published in the United States, was crucial for active scholars in Japan as well as in the rest of the world.) The mathematical economists of the day clarified the mathematical structure of a competitive economy and the rigorous conditions which were required to claim the existence of equilibrium in a competitive economy. It was necessary to construct an abstract economy or excess demand function by using knowledge of topology including closed sets, convexity, compactness and boundedness in order to maintain that the system had a meaningful solution and to discuss the welfare aspect. They "eliminated classical assumptions inessential to the existence problem (differentiability of utility indicators and production functions)" (Nikaido 1970: 271). As shown by Uzawa's equivalence theorem (Uzawa 1962), they were giving economic interpretations to fixed-point theorems, which were being studied by mathematicians around the same time.

Second, the cannon of modern neoclassical economics, namely Walrasian general equilibrium theory based on set theory and the convex set method, was established. Mathematical economists introduced different types of mathematics to handle each theoretical topic of economics, namely matrix algebra and ordinary differential equations into stability analysis, and convex set theory or topology into the study of the existence of general equilibrium. They used several variations of mathematical theorems in writing papers with the focus on some difference in the modeling. Economists now have to follow the mathematicians' way of writing papers, namely to clarify their premises and theorems and to proceed with the proof process. Economic theories are understood and discussed in different ways, depending on the degree of mathematical training and the taste in mathematics.

Third, the controversy over the foundation of mathematics, especially between the formalist David Hilbert and the intuitionist L. E. J. Brouwer in the 1920s, did not matter, at least for the research of the so-called existence question, in the sense that Brouwer's fixed-point theorem has been more formalized by Hilbert's students. Moreover, Kurt Gödel's incompleteness theorem for any formalized system did not have a big influence on the formalization of mathematics.

Fourth, Hukukane Nikaido worked out the proof of the existence of a competitive equilibrium independently of McKenzie (1954) and Arrow and Debreu (1954), both of which appeared in *Econometrica*, the foremost influential journal of mathematical economics in the mid twentieth century. Nikaido (1956) was published in a new journal *Metroeconomica*, after Gale (1955) came out in *Mathematica Scandinavia*. The remaining evidence tells us that Nikaido's submission of his existence paper to *Econometrica* was rejected twice but accepted by a refereed journal a few months after another mathematical economist had published a paper along similar lines. In other words, Nikaido's existence paper was unluckily treated at *Econometrica* in the sense that the editor and the referee, who received his submission, were not willing to read his manuscript seriously enough to find the merits of his contributions. Nikaido's existence paper might have been accepted at *Econometrica* after a normal refereeing process, if Arrow of 1968 or Debreu had refereed it. Yet thanks to Arrow, Nikaido obtained a better research environment in the US than in Japan.

Fifth, finally, certainly encouraged by the research by mathematically trained economists like Nikaido and Uzawa, Negishi utilized the method of mathematical programming to consider the proof of existence and stability of general competitive equilibrium. Unexpectedly it became the seeds for the future application of the Negishi method. Indeed, various types of mathematics have been readily available for economists in Japan.

Mathematical appendix

Hirofumi Uzawa in his "Walras's existence theorem and Brouwer's fixed-point theorem" (1962) proved that the two theorems in the title were equivalent. It had already been well established that Brouwer's fixed-point theorem implies Walras's existence theorem. Uzawa (1962) proved that Walras's existence theorem implies Brouwer's fixed-point theorem. He constructed an excess demand function $x(p)=[x_1(p),\ldots,x_n(p)]$ by

$$x_i(p)=\varphi_i\left(\frac{p}{\lambda(p)}\right)-p_i\mu(p),\ (i=1,\ldots,n,\ p\in P) \tag{1}$$

where

$$\lambda(p)=\sum_{i=1}^{n}p_i$$

$$\mu(p)=\frac{\sum_{i=1}^{n}p_i\varphi_i\left[\frac{p}{\lambda(p)}\right]}{\sum_{i=1}^{n}p_i^2}$$

Uzawa notes that both $\varphi_i(p/\lambda(p))$ and $p_i\mu(p)$ are positively homogeneous of order 0. Therefore, the excess demand function thus defined satisfies conditions (A), (B) and (C). From Walras's theorem, there is an equilibrium price p^*. From (1) we have

$$\varphi_i\left(\frac{\bar{p}}{\lambda(\bar{p})}\right) \leq \bar{p}_i\mu(\bar{p}), \ (i=1,\ldots, n) \tag{2}$$

with equality unless $\bar{p}_i=0$. Uzawa defines $\bar{\pi}$ and β as follows:

$$\bar{\pi} = \frac{\bar{p}}{\lambda(\bar{p})}, \ \beta = \lambda(\bar{p})\mu(\bar{p}).$$

Then the relation (2) is rewritten as follows:

$$\varphi_i(\bar{\pi}) \leq \beta\bar{\pi}_i, \tag{3}$$

with equality unless $\bar{\pi}_i=0$.

By summing (3) over $i=1,\ldots, n$, and considering that $\bar{\pi}$, $\varphi_i(\bar{\pi}) \in \Pi$, we have $\beta=1$; therefore,

$$\varphi_i(\bar{\pi}) \leq \bar{\pi}_i, \tag{4}$$

with equality unless $\bar{\pi}_i=0$.

The relation (4), again together with $\bar{\pi}$, $\varphi_i(\bar{\pi}) \in \Pi$, implies that

$$\varphi_i(\bar{\pi}) = \bar{\pi}_i, \ (i=1,\ldots, n).$$

This means that $\bar{\pi}$ is a fixed-point for the mapping $\varphi_i(\bar{\pi})$. Thus Walras's existence theorem implies Brouwer's fixed-point theorem. QED.

Personal communications

Kenneth J. Arrow in Tokyo on September 12, 1994.

Masao Fukuoka at Keio University in Tokyo on February 1, 1993.

Shizuo Kakutani at Yale University in New Haven on January 5 and April 3–4, 1995.

Hukukane Nikaido on the phone on July 7, 1993, at Tokyo International University on May 6, 1994, and correspondence etc. during September 1996 and January 1997.

Takuma Yasui at Kwansei Gakuin University in Kobe on October 13, 1990.

Notes

1 Variations of this chapter have been presented several times but never before published in a journal but as Chapter 5 in Ikeo (2006). After each presentation I came across other new material to be included in the conference paper. Not surprisingly, this chapter has had the longest gestation period of all the chapters. In the meantime, many scholars patiently gave me information relating to the research presented in this chapter. They are Kenneth J. Arrow, Masao Fukuoka, Ted Gayer, the late Shizuo Kakutani, Manabu Toda, Takashi Negishi, E. Roy Weintraub, the late Hukukane Nikaido and the late Takuma Yasui. Koichi Hamada helped me contact Kakutani. Paul Pecorino gave me comments on an early manuscript.

Fragments of this chapter were given at the microeconomics workshop at the University of Tokyo in May 1994, at the annual meeting of the History of Economics Society in Babson College, Boston, at the economics workshop in Tokyo Keizai University in June 1994, at the tenth World Congress of the International Economic Association in Tunis in December 1995, at the Third European Conference on the History of Economics in Athens in April 1997, at the Duke Workshop on the history of political economy in September 1997, at the Duke Workshop on the history of political economy in March 2009, and at the annual meeting of the History of Economics Society in the University of Colorado at Denver in June 2009. Jan van Daal, Mary Ann Dimand, Takashi Negishi, Robin Neill, Christian Schmidt, Nancy Wulwick, Henk W. Plasmeijer, Akira Yamazaki, Wade Hands and other participants gave me good questions and related information. I thank all of them. Needless to say, the remaining errors are my own.

2 See also T. Hutchison (2000), M. Blaug (2003) and P. Bridel (2011).

3 G. Cassel presented his simplified Walrasian system for the first time in his article "Grundriss einer elementaren Preislehre" (Introduction to the theory of price, 1899). The system is known as the Cassel-Walras System. I thank Henk W. Plasmeijer for bringing Cassel (1899) to my attention.

4 Uzawa's autobiographical article "Born in the shadow of the mountains" (1999) said nothing about Uzawa (1962).

5 W. Young's "Negishi's contributions to the development of economic analysis" (2008) includes later evaluations of the Negishi method by corresponding with V. Ginsburgh, one of the users of the Negishi method. Cunning and Keyzer (1995) discussed the merits of using the Negishi theorem in making computable general equilibrium models. See S. Robinson (1989), Arrow (2001) and Kawamata (2009). Negishi (2008) "discovered" predecessors of the Negishi theorem.

6 There remains a copy of the renewal documents for the continuation of the project in the K. J. Arrow Papers at Duke University.

7 I. Muto in his "Mathematical economics in Vienna and Hilbert's view of mathematics" (1993, in Japanese) made a similar argument.

8 My personal communication with Shizuo Kakutani helped me understand the characteristics of Brouwer's mathematics and write this section. Kakutani did not know the clash between David Hilbert and Brouwer when I interviewed him in 1995.

9 Menger's "On intuitionism" (1930, in German) summarized the points in the discussion between formalism and intuitionism in the 1920s. See also Brouwer (1913) and note 8.

10 Brouwer objected that Hilbert's identification of the consistency with the correctness of a mathematical theorem presupposed the law of the excluded middle: a proposition *p* is true or *p* is false. The intuitionists stated that a consistency proof for mathematics is meaningless, that mathematical theorems derive their validity solely from their intuitive proofs, and that mathematical considerations cannot increase our collection of meaningful theorems in the least (Menger 1979b: 54–5).

11 In the summer of 1928, the ultimate clash occurred. In March 1928, Brouwer

disparaged the international mathematical congress sponsored by the *Union Mathématique Internationale* which was scheduled to meet in Bologna in September. He did not like the Italian organizers inviting individual mathematicians from non-*Conseil International des Recherches* countries without officially retracting the interdiction of the dispatch of invitations to these countries. The *Union* formally restricted its invitations to official meetings to countries belonging to the *Conseil*, which Germany had not joined. In the summer, it became known that David Hilbert, the leader of the German formalist school, had accepted an invitation to deliver a lecture at the Bologna congress. A few weeks before the congress, Brouwer circulated a letter insulting German mathematicians. Menger (1979b [1978]: 249) explains what happened next as follows:

> Hilbert, outraged by Brouwer's circular letter at once reorganized the editorial board of the *Mathematische Annalen* dismissing Brouwer despite his violent protests and despite a flood of letters that he sent to mathematicians and publishers. As common friends wrote me from Amsterdam, Brouwer was so completely beside himself that they feared for his mental stability.

12 Corry (1996: 223, footnote 5) misspelled Kenjiro Shoda's given name.

13 Menger (1927: 225) stated:

Mengenklassen in der Brouwerschen Terminologie:	Teilmengen euklidischer Räume:
die finiten Mengen	die beschrökten abgeschlossenen Mengen
die individualisirten Mengen	die Borelschen Mengen
die Mengen	die analytischen Mengen
die Spenzies	die beliebigen Mengen

14 S. Shiroyama (1996, in Japanese: 72, 79, and 114). Y. Yamada practiced German conversation with the help of Oskar Morgenstern's sister by using a book on ethics written by Karl Menger. Probably this is the reason why some people misunderstood and believed that the third Japanese person who had attended Menger's colloquium was a philosopher. I thank Atsushi Komine for bringing Shiroyama (1996, in Japanese) to my attention. Shiroyama is a novelist and was a student of Y. Yamada's at Hitotsubashi University.

15 Hukukane Nikaido called himself von Neumann's student.

16 I focus on the Japanese connection with von Neumann in this chapter. However, Dore *et al.* (eds) (1989) and Aspray (1990) were useful for me in writing the section related to von Neumann. See also Leonard (2010) on the creation of game theory.

17 Yet a librarian of Kokugakuin University confirmed in 1995 that there was no copy of *Ergebnisse* in any libraries of Osaka University.

18 In early 1942, the American and the Japanese governments reached agreement that they would exchange by ship the Americans in Japan who preferred to return home and their Japanese counterparts. The ships used for this purpose are commonly called exchange ships. The people exchanged were mainly diplomats, businessmen, scholars and students.

19 S. Kakutani had no way to explain the following passage in Morgenstern (1976: 812), a copy of which was sent him by me:

> After the manuscript had been completed … there was the need to produce a clean manuscript; everything had to be retyped and all formulas had to be put into the new copy.… This was done and then a Japanese "enemy alien," a young mathematician, put in all the formulas from the original manuscript. Johnny remarked in his usual manner that it is the fate of enemy aliens who are mathematicians to be punished for being enemies by having to put other people's formulas into manuscripts.

20 John Nash also published "The bargaining problem" (Nash 1950a) and "Two-person cooperative games" (Nash 1953). All of his papers were included in Nash's *Essays on Game Theory* (1996).

21 The research resulting in this section is based on both the Georgescu-Roegen Papers at Duke University and my personal communications with H. Nikaido. I took Nikaido's course on mathematical economics when I was an undergraduate student (of social studies) at Hitotsubashi University in the 1970s. He did not remember me when I began to research the history of mathematical economics resulting in this chapter. Nonetheless, he was so nice that he answered almost all of the questions I asked. He even began to help me *interpret* the historical materials I showed to him. The completion of the research for this chapter was delayed whenever I located new facts, some of which were contradictory to the previous reconstructions including Nikaido's. Moreover, I realized that it was necessary for me to read between the lines and to conjecture the relevant things that Nikaido had decided not to tell me from the things that he did tell me.

22 Strotz's rejection letter remains neither in the Georgescu-Roegen Papers at Duke nor in Nikaido's house. See the Japanese Econometric Society (1956, in Japanese).

23 I thank Ted Gayer for providing me with the information about the refereeing process of Arrow and Debreu's existence paper. E. R. Weintraub and T. Gayer in their "Equilibrium proofmaking" (2001) discussed how the existence of a general competitive equilibrium was proved and established in the 1950s, and why Arrow and Debreu (1954) appeared in *Econometrica* in spite of the negative comments from the mathematician Cecil Phipps, one of the two referees.

7 A history of Japanese developments in econometrics[1]

The belief that the role of the government is to make the world better and save the people has represented the Japanese (indeed, Eastern) tradition of strong government leadership in the economy for many centuries (Ikeo 1997: 39, 53). It is at the root of the Japanese term for "the subject of economic science," namely, *Keizai*. In 1868, the new government began promoting the modernization of Japan and the collection of economic data to measure national power. It realized in the 1910s that the Japanese population was growing rapidly and the Malthusian problem was emerging. The first nationwide census (conducted in 1920) confirmed the fact. By the University Ordinance of 1919–20, economics departments were established in national universities, and the existing private higher schools that had economics departments were upgraded to universities. Thanks to the reform, both the quantity and quality of economic research in Japan were enhanced to cover such wide-ranging fields as the German historical school, neoclassical economics, and mathematical and statistical studies. The government especially needed statistical analyses of the demand for and the supply of rice, Japan's staple food, in order to make a relevant policy for rice (including its importation) and for emigration for the near future.[2]

As shown in section 1, early econometric studies in Japan also received significant momentum from the outside. The Tokyo meeting of the International Statistical Institute (1930), the founding meeting of the Econometric Society (1930), and Joseph A. Schumpeter's visit to Japan (1931) all led to new collaborative arrangements between researchers and statistical experts for collecting economic data and staying abreast of economic studies coming out of Europe and the United States. Section 2 traces Japanese econometric research during the 1920s and 1930s and clarifies its relationship with economic theory-making via the cobweb theorem. Section 3 shows that it was important for young Japanese students to gain experience in econometric practices in the United States in order to learn the trial-and-error process of knowledge creation in this particular field. After returning to Japan, they played an important part in organizing econometric projects and publishing scientific articles in journals. Section 4 summarizes macroeconometric model-building activities since 1945 with reference to my personal communication with Shinichi Ichimura. Section 5 is mainly based on my personal communication with Michio Hatanaka and

Takeshi Amemiya on how they started their careers. Section 6 draws a couple of conclusions.

1 The establishment of academic societies and statistical bureaus: institutional impact

In retrospect, the early 1930s witnessed the internationalization of economics as a result of the spread of the Great Depression worldwide, the collapse of the international gold standard, the establishment of new economic research organizations, and the prompt circulation of every issue of internationally oriented economics journals.

The nineteenth meeting of the International Statistical Institute (ISI, established 1885) was held in Japan's parliament building in Tokyo in September 1930 and involved a limited number of scholars and official statisticians inside and outside Japan. It was organized at the end of Albert Delatour's fourth term as ISI president and included such specialists as Corrado Gini, Arthur Lyon Bowley, Friedrich Zahn, Walter Francis Willcox, Henri Willem Methorst, Hyoye Ouchi, Taijiro Matsuda and Tatsuo Morito (ISI 1933). They discussed the undertaking of a nationwide census and the processing of various statistical data, including data on agricultural and industrial products, stock prices, national wealth and income, and inequality. The intensive discussion was crucial for the Japanese to learn how to define relevant concepts in economic and social studies for the purpose of international comparison. The meeting greatly encouraged empirical research in general in Japan. Japan's government was promoting the use of statistical approaches in both the natural and the social sciences. The Japan Statistical Society was established in 1931 and issued its *Annual Report* with papers on Ragnar Frisch (confluence analysis, price and income elasticity in the price index, and macrodynamic theory; see Aoyama 1937, 1940, and Yamada 1940), the handling of transportation in economic statistics, and the definitions of national income.

The founding meeting of the Econometric Society, which was the first international society for economists, was held in Cleveland in December 1930. Although no Japanese economists attended the meeting, they nevertheless knew about the founding of the society and repeatedly quoted its constitution: "The Econometric Society is an international society for the advancement of economic theory in relation to statistics and mathematics." Japanese economists wished to follow Japanese natural scientists and mathematicians who already had contact with Western counterparts and some of whom were contributing papers to international journals.

In January 1931 Schumpeter, one of the society's founding members, visited Japan for a couple of weeks after his second visiting professorship at Harvard. He met his former "students" Ichiro Nakayama and Seiichi Tobata, who had stayed at the University of Bonn as visiting scholars, and told them about the Econometric Society and his membership on the executive committee. He delivered lectures in Tokyo, Kobe and Kyoto.[3] Karl Menger, another founding member of the Econometric Society, also visited Japan, in the spring of 1931, and gave a talk on the incompleteness theorem demonstrated by his student Kurt Gödel. Menger visited Hitotsubashi University in Tokyo to see his father's library, which had been brought from Vienna in 1923. The Japanese had been impressed by the fact that Carl Menger achieved his brilliant results without the use of mathematics or statistics – even though he had seen examples of economists who had used mathematics and statistics: he owned copies of Cournot 1838 and Dupuit 1844 and 1849.

The Japan Society for the Promotion of Science (JSPS) was established in 1932, thanks to Rikitaro Fujisawa (1861–1933), a mathematician and Member of Parliament. Fujisawa published *Life Insurance* (1889) and several economic articles (mostly on currency and international finance). In 1933, 14 economists were called into the Sixth Subcommittee for the theoretical and practical research of rice policy. The committee asked Eiichi Sugimoto (1901–52) to make a statistical study of the law of demand for rice (discussed below).

In 1934, leading Japanese economists established the Japanese Economic Association (JEA) to promote economic theorizing and its statistical application. They had been encouraged by the ISI Tokyo meeting, the establishment of the Econometric Society and their participation in the JSPS meetings. The leading economists were reading every issue of newly established internationally oriented economics journals such as the *Zeitschrift für Nationalökonomie* (1930–), *Econometrica* (1933–), and the *Review of Economic Studies* (1933–) (Suzumura 1999; Ikeo 1993a, 2006).

Yet internationalization also generated some misunderstandings. In 1950, a few tentative regional meetings were planned by the Econometric Society (ES), and the first one was held in Tokyo in October 1950 (instead of July 1950 as originally planned).[4] The Japanese (mistakenly) regarded it as the first meeting of the Japanese Econometric Society for establishing a branch of the ES (JES 1956). The second meeting of the Japanese Econometric Society was held in Tokyo in November 1951 and was attended by 49 economists. The papers presented included "The Structure of the Japanese Export Industry and the Standard of Living" (Hidetaro Iemoto), "The Marginal Productivity Theory and the Douglas Function" (Kazuo Mizutani or Midutani, the single Japanese ES fellow in the 1930s), and "Note on Consolidation within a Leontief System" (Michio Hatanaka). Hatanaka's note became available in *Econometrica* (April 1952) with the help of Nicholas Georgescu-Roegen, one of the editors, and led Hatanaka to enter the Graduate School of Economics at Vanderbilt University (discussed below). Moreover, Hayakawa 1951, which applied Pareto's law of income to Japanese data (Hokkaido region), was the first article written by a Japanese scholar to be published in *Econometrica*.[5] It encouraged the Japanese to continue their research along the lines of articles published in *Econometrica* and to join the international community of economists.

As reported in *Econometrica*, the Japanese Association of Economics and Econometrics (a temporary name for the JEA) organized biennial Far Eastern meetings in the 1970s and gave its full support to holding the 1995 ES World

Congress in Tokyo (Suzumura 1999; Ikeo 2000, Chapter 1). Japanese econometricians learned new ideas, research skills and approaches to holding international conferences from a wide-ranging collaboration with ES members.

2 Early econometrics and the research tradition before World War II

As discussed in Ikeo 1993b and 1996a, agricultural economics was a field for intensive statistical studies, and the instability of rice prices and rice supplies was an urgent issue in the 1930s. The Japanese tackled the problem using data relating to rice: the price determined every day in the transaction market; the quantities traded in the market, shipped every month from each region, and consumed every year in the whole country; the price indexes; dynamic changes in the population; the transportation cost by railroad; and the storage cost. The Japanese paid attention to the cobweb theorem because they could observe the changes in the prices of domestic animals in Japan. They came to know identification problems in the statistical estimation of demand functions and also became interested in theoretical research on the stability conditions of the market mechanism (Ikeo 1994b).

Yoshinosuke Yagi (1932) provided a comprehensive study of rice production, distribution and policy, and a survey of the recent voluminous literature on rice issues. He confirmed that the law of demand (the reverse relation of price and demand), which had been established first for wheat, also existed in the case of rice. Engel's law (the share of food in total expenditure is inversely related to the household's income) was also shown to hold true in Japan. Yagi and other economists calculated the demand elasticity of rice with respect to the price and constructed the price and quantity indexes following Warren M. Persons's method. Yagi focused on price seasonality, rice supplies as a whole and the amounts shipped from each rice-producing region to large cities.

As mentioned earlier, a JSPS committee asked Eiichi Sugimoto (1901–52) to make a statistical study of the law of demand for rice.[6] He had studied economics and statistics in Berlin and brought back a keen interest in differentiating what was observable and measurable from what was not. He also read the relevant writings such as Schultz 1928 and Moore 1929. After mentioning William Stanley Jevons's hope for statistical representation of the law of demand and the pessimism showed by F. Y. Edgeworth and E. W. Gilboy, Sugimoto ([1935] 1937: 38) claimed:

> A law in theoretical economics should never be a speculative product that has no connection with reality. It should be constructed upon real economic life, which is always changing. On the other hand, statistical figures are numerical representations of real economic life following the law of large numbers. Therefore it was not a satisfactory situation that the theoretical law of demand had no inner structure based on statistical facts.
>
> (My translation)

Sugimoto used the annual data for the period between 1917 and 1933. He regarded per capita consumed rice as the demand for rice, following the cobweb theorem. Referring to Henry L. Moore's extension of Marshallian demand analysis, Sugimoto included the rice price, the prices of all other commodities, and time as variables in the rice demand function. He judged that the effects of the changes in the prices of non-rice commodities on the demand for rice should cancel each other because there were neither close substitutes nor complementary goods for rice. He divided the rice price index by the general price index and got the rice rate to remove the effect of the changes in the other prices on the rice price. He drew shifting rice demand curves in three-dimensional space with the adjusted price, demand and time (Figure 7.1). But the coefficient of correlation between the logarithm of the rice rate and the logarithm of the demand for rice was only −0.28. Therefore Sugimoto calculated the three-year moving average of the demand and that of the rice rates and called them the normal values. The coefficient of correlation between the deviation of the rice rate from its normal rate (P) and the deviation of the per capita rice demand from its normal value (D) was −0.79. Then he estimated the demand functions

$$D = BP^{b} \text{ or } \log D = \log B + b \log P$$

for every seven years using the least squares method. The estimates of b, the elasticity of demand with respect to the price change, fluctuated between −0.2 and −0.4. He did not write any error terms in his equations. Instead he found various causes for the discrepancy of the observed numbers from the estimated functions (see Matsuda 1972).

There were other statistical works on rice and agricultural products as well as on the life of farmers, written in Japanese. Kan Watanabe (1932) produced the first well-known article to estimate the demand function for hog, beef and horsemeat. Keiji Kamiya (1941) estimated the productivity of rice farming using a Cobb-Douglas function. And Takuma Yasui, one of the early Japanese neoclassical economists, encouraged by Watanabe 1932 and Sugimoto [1935] 1937, embarked on an analysis of consumer behavior, that is, the theoretical basis for demand.

Early Japanese econometricians also maintained a close intellectual connection with their European counterparts, some of whom migrated to the United States in the pre-World War II period. Yuzo Yamada (1902–96) stayed in Vienna, kept in close contact with Karl Menger and Oskar Morgenstern, and corresponded with many economists in Europe. These intellectual connections helped Isamu Yamada to communicate with those working in the United States, which he visited in 1951. Yuzo Yamada (1951) compiled national income statistics and correlated them with various statistical data for the first time. Yet his definition of national income was different from James E. Meade and Richard Stone's (Ichimura 2010: 3). Non-Marxian economists like Yamada were not satisfied with the materialistic definition of national products given by Marxist economists and discussed the definition of national income from the viewpoint of welfare economics.

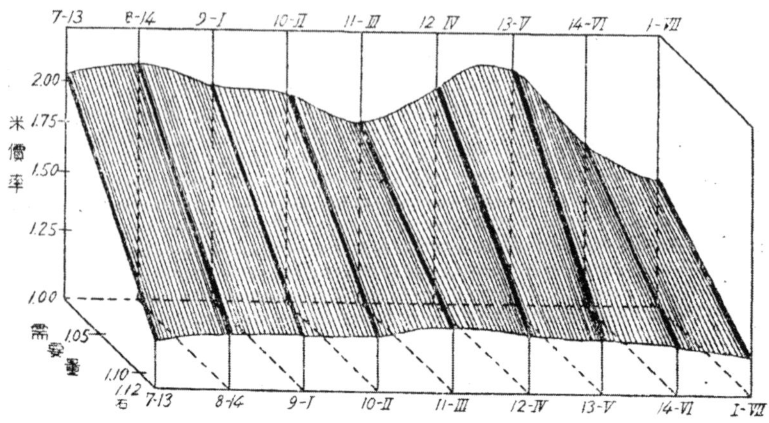

第十三圖 米穀需要曲線の動的變化

第七表 需要函數の七ヶ年移動平均 (絶對額)

大正 大正		
7——13	$\log d = 0.06152 - 0.19815 \log p$	$d = 1.152 \times p^{-0.19815}$ (石)
8——14	$\log d = 0.06354 - 0.19383 \log p$	$d = 1.158 \times p^{-0.19383}$
9——I (昭和)	$\log d = 0.06674 - 0.22613 \log p$	$d = 1.166 \times p^{-0.22613}$
10——II	$\log d = 0.06835 - 0.23440 \log p$	$d = 1.171 \times p^{-0.23440}$
11——III	$\log d = 0.07623 - 0.30215 \log p$	$d = 1.192 \times p^{-0.30215}$
12——IV	$\log d = 0.06904 - 0.22974 \log p$	$d = 1.173 \times p^{-0.22974}$
13——V	$\log d = 0.06382 - 0.19589 \log p$	$d = 1.158 \times p^{-0.19589}$
14——VI	$\log d = 0.07000 - 0.31040 \log p$	$d = 1.175 \times p^{-0.31040}$
昭和 I——VII	$\log d = 0.04377 - 0.40601 \log p$	$d = 1.106 \times p^{-0.40601}$

Figure 7.1 Sugimoto [1935] 1937 contained 19 tables and 18 figures with the help of a technical assistant who used 2 electric calculators. This is a scan of Figure 13 in Sugimoto [1935] 1937. Sugimoto estimated the average logarithms of rice demand and rice rates for every seven years and obtained nine short-run normal demand functions for the period between 1917 and 1933 (dynamic changes in the demand curves for rice (Sugimoto [1935] 1937: 86).

The discussion of national income by Yuzo Yamada (1959: 16) could be summarized as follows. Thanks to Alfred Marshall's and A. C. Pigou's welfare economics, the focal point in economic conceptualization shifted from a trade-centered to a life-centered view. Pigou regarded the increment, equity and stability in national income as objectives of economic policies and pointed out that it is important to observe real income generated from market transactions by way of money and price signals. Yamada (1959: 16) wrote:

> The increment of real national income or its per capita was often called the growth rate rather than the rate of increment. Growth is a biological term and compared with the growth of an organic body such as an animal or plant, national economic development depends on extremely complex factors. It cannot be explained simply in a mechanical manner.
>
> (My translation)

The economy can grow by itself like a living creature, although it occasionally suffers from sickness and needs relevant treatment.[7] Yamada directed his readers' attention to the work of several econometricians such as Yoshimasa Kurabayashi (b. 1926) and Hidekazu Eguchi (b. 1929). Kurabayashi became the Japanese expert of the System of National Account after studying under Simon Kuznets in the United States. Eguchi became the first econometrician at the Bank of Japan (BOJ). Both he and Kurabayashi participated in several related international conferences.[8] Yet it could be said that many Japanese in the public sector were engaged in on-the-job training by building econometric models because Marxist economists, who made up the majority of Japanese academics until around the mid 1960s, did not think that economics departments should be offering courses in econometrics.

3 Experiences of econometric research in the United States and Japan since 1945

As discussed in Ikeo (1996b), World War II brought changes in Japan's international policies and ended close relations with neighboring countries such as China and Korea. The American presence became ubiquitous in Japanese society after the Allied Powers led by the United States began their Occupation of Japan in 1945. During the Occupation, the communists and Marxists enjoyed a favorable reputation because they were the one political group that had opposed the war and were rehabilitated in Japanese society including at the University of Tokyo, where Michio Hatanaka spent his undergraduate student life. The majority of economists in Japan were Marxists from 1945 until the mid 1960s.

The generous fund for GARIOA (Government Appropriations for Relief in Occupied Areas) and, later, the Fulbright Scholar Program was given to Japanese scholars and officials for their "enlightening" trip to the United States.[9] Hitotsubashi University renewed its Institute of Economic Research and appointed Shigeto Tsuru (1912–2006) as its director, who was the best-known Japanese economist to American economists like Martin Bronfenbrenner (1914–97).[10] Working as a tax economist in Tokyo, Bronfenbrenner ran a Wednesday seminar with Tsuru from the fall of 1949 until around June 1950. Thanks to the close tie with Bronfenbrenner, Ichiro Nakayama and Hanya Ito visited the United States for a couple of weeks.[11] Isamu Yamada was invited to the Cowles Commission at Chicago because William B. Simpson, who was on the council, visited Japan in the spring of 1947, and he communicated with economists in the United States from March to June 1951. Returning to Tokyo, Yamada organized research projects with his colleagues and published the Japanese translation of Haavelmo 1944 in 1955 and Leontief 1941 in 1959. Yamada's *Theory and Application of Interindustry Analysis* (1961) was published as part of the Economic Research Series in English organized by the Institute of Economic Research at Hitotsubashi. In reviewing the book, Hatanaka (1963) had to mention the poor quality of current data. Around 1950, the fellowship program brought Japanese students to the United States and even other countries for advanced studies.

Shinichi Ichimura (b. 1925), Tsunehiko Watanabe (1926–76), Tadao Uchida (1923–86), and Ryutaro Komiya (b. 1928) were fascinated by "American empirical studies," such as the interindustry analysis originated by Wassily Leontief, and econometric modeling. Ichimura was a student of Hideo Aoyama at Kyoto, as was Michio Morishima (1923–2004), who was later appointed at universities in the United Kingdom. Ichimura attended Morishima's informal seminar on his expanding interpretation of John R. Hicks ([1939] 1946).[12] Aoyama was a student of Yasuma Takata (1883–1972), who was described as the Japanese Marshall (Bronfenbrenner 1956). Aoyama called attention to the importance of balancing theoretical and empirical studies, and suggested that Ichimura and Noboru Kamakura (1924–69) reorganize Hicks's *The Social Framework of the American Economy* (1945) on the basis of skills in bookkeeping. They were shocked to find that Meade and Stone's *National Income and Expenditure* (1944), copies of which were available in the American Culture Center (ACC) libraries,[13] had been ahead of them by engaging in the project for the League of Nations and the United Nations (personal communication with Ichimura, November 17, 2009). Yet they managed to publish their *National Income and Resources* (Ichimura and Kamakura 1951), which was the research result based on a similar track as Meade and Stone 1944. Securing a GARIOA fellowship, Ichimura first entered the graduate school of Columbia University in 1950. Transferring to MIT, he obtained his Ph.D. under the supervision of Paul Samuelson and Robert Solow in 1953. Ichimura was mesmerized by Leontief's own lectures in input-output analysis at Harvard. Around the same time, Tsunehiko Watanabe was enthralled by the lectures of H. B. Chenery, a student of Leontief's, at Stanford. It was an advantage to learn econometric works from the originator and practitioners. Returning to Japan, Ichimura, Watanabe, Uchida and Komiya taught "American economics" to Japanese students and conducted important econometric works in making economic predictions in the 1960s. The balance of power in Japanese academia subsequently shifted from Marxists to neoclassical and Keynesian economists as Japanese economic life was enhanced by rapid economic growth. Michio Hatanaka recalled that the Japanese economy showed a strong (growth) trend compared with an economy like the United States (personal communication with Hatanaka, September 18, 2009).

Ichimura was appointed at Osaka in 1953. In cooperation with the Ministry of International Trade and Industry (MITI, now the Ministry of Economy, Trade and Industry), he started to make one of the first input-output (IO) tables of Japan's economy (the matrix of 33×33) of 1951 in the summer of 1953. Ichimura 1957 is a detailed record of this endeavor. Twenty-five specialists and ten assistants took about twenty months and completed their task in 1955. Ichimura (2010: 4) says, "The estimation methods followed closely the ones used for the production of the U.S. table for 1947, but with many original devices." The MITI project was larger than those completed by the Ministry of Finance (MOF) and the Ministry of Agriculture and Forestry (MAF). The ministries decided to cooperate with one another to make the 1955 interindustry table. In this process, Japan's data were processed, organized and improved to a high quality. Since then, Ichimura has led many projects to compile input–output tables and build econometric models in Japan and East Asian countries.

According to Ichimura (2010), immediately after the first IO table project was completed, each local government at the prefecture level started to construct IO tables, and soon all 47 prefectural IO tables were available. He described Japan as "a paradise for IO specialists" (Ichimura 2010: 4):

> Some go so far as to produce an interregional table within each prefecture and use it for regional designing for the prefecture. In 1958 the first 1951 interregional IO table for the Kinki region and the rest of Japan was produced by the Kansai Economic Federation's secretariat under the guidance of S. Ichimura, using the data of each prefecture in the Kinki region. Soon it spread to other regions as well as to the central government. They integrated these regional IO tables to produce the interregional IO table, dividing Japan into several regions. Soon the MITI began producing the interregional and interindustrial relations table for nine regions every five years.

News of "paradise" attracted the attention of statisticians in other Asian countries such as the Philippines and Indonesia. Japan's Institute of Developing Economies (IDE) collaborated with Tsunehiko Watanabe to use international IO models for north–south issues. Then the IDE experts collaborated with national statistical offices and research institutes to complete three national IO tables (Indonesia in 1971, Singapore in 1973 and Thailand in 1975) and three bilateral IO tables in 1970 (Korea–Japan, the US–Japan and the Philippines–Japan). This laid the foundation of their subsequent works such as multilateral IO tables among East Asian countries and the United States (Ichimura 2010: 4–5).

Yet Ichimura believed that an IO model should be connected with an econometric simultaneous-equations model to learn the effects in each sector by simulating economic policies. When he was asked about his image of an economy, he unconsciously started constructing a macroeconometric model, with concrete economic issues such as estimating a policy's unbalanced effects on industrial sectors. He did not describe an economy as a living creature but as a mechanical model. During the 1950s and the 1960s, in constituting the tables, the statistical data for national income and wealth were greatly improved in quality. By linking with historical sources, the Hitotsubashi University group produced long-term economic statistics from around 1875 to 1940 in 14 volumes, titled *Estimates of Long-Term Economic Statistics of Japan since 1868* (1965–85) and edited by Kazushi Ohkawa, Miyohei Shinohara and Mataji Umemura.

4 Macroeconometric model-building since 1945

It is unanimously recognized that the most salient characteristics of Japanese econometrics have been the energetic building of macroeconometric models and the processing of statistical data collected for policymaking in the government and the Bank of Japan. The Ministry of Internal Affairs and Communication (*Somusho*) needs collaboration from the private sector to acquire samples of high quality. Therefore academic econometricians rely on the databases processed and supplied by the statistics bureaus. Not surprisingly, some econometricians maintain close relationships with particular public offices by giving advice and, in return, receiving better data. As noted, around 1950 Japan's government and economists started to use the definition of national income from Meade and Stone's *National Income and Expenditure*. Japan has usually shared the definitions of economic data with members of the Organization for Economic Co-operation and Development (OECD) from its establishment in 1961, as Japan was a member of the Development Assistance Group and the Development Assistance Committee before joining the parent organization in 1964. We have already had several surveys of Japanese statistical and econometric practices, which have been presented at related conferences. Each survey introduced some interesting points to promote the understanding of Japanese econometrics.

As stated in Sato 1991, the Economic Planning Agency (EPA, 1955–2000), with the help of the econometric committee under the Economic Council, played an important role in learning, practicing and building the latest econometric models from the post-World War II period until 2000 (Ikeo 2000).[14] The mission has been taken over by the Economic and Social Research Institute (ESRI), within the cabinet office since 2001. Kazuo Sato (1991) covered econometric models built by academic econometricians such as a variation of the Tokyo Center for Economic Research (TCER) models by Tadao Uchida and Tsunehiko Watanabe, the ones by Yoichi Shinkai and colleagues at Osaka, and long-term models by Hiroya Ueno at Nagoya. Sato (1991) counted more than 40 full-fledged macroeconometric models.[15] The rapidly growing economy showed different shapes over time and shifted in industrial structure, such as the major sector shifting from agriculture to manufacturing and then to tertiary industries, as suggested by Colin Clark. Clark visited Japan in the 1960s to help government officials process economic data and prepare statistical data for the analysis of policymaking.

In the 1950s, Osaka University invited a number of active economists from abroad and promoted intellectual exchange between faculty and graduate students. Lawrence Klein stayed at the Institute of Social and Economic Research at Osaka from June to September 1960 (partly because he wished to avoid the backwash of McCarthyism in the United States) and tried historical econometric research with reference to Ohkawa 1957 (Klein 1961). From this intellectual milieu emerged several econometricians such as Mitsuo Saito and Masahiro Amano. It is also noteworthy that both Shinichi Ichimura and Lawrence Klein were students of Paul Samuelson at MIT and that they have been promoting international communication among active econometric practitioners as playing the part of the nexus in building simultaneous-equations models in the world.

Looking back to the late 1950s, those who were trained in the United States began to make econometric models using Japanese data. In 1960, the Ikeda Cabinet decided on the income doubling plan, that is, the doubling of per capita real national income in a decade. Just after 1960, the politicians asked econometricians to prepare a midterm plan because they realized that the planning at the macroeconomic level was not consistent with those at industrial-sector levels. A variety of macroeconometric models of the Japanese economy was constructed with various data (annual or quarterly) for specific purposes, such as long-term economic forecasts, business cycles explained by changes in investment, and the Klein–Goldberger-type model of the Japanese economy. Tadao Uchida, Tsunehiko Watanabe, Masahiro Tatemoto and Kei Mori played leading roles in simulating government policies with the use of the latest computer technology. Through on-the-job-training, Shuntaro Shishido, who had studied statistics in the economics department at the University of Tokyo, became an econometrician in the public sector and received the Leontief Award in 2006.

The calculation of the multiplier effect of a spending policy as well as economic forecasting became important tasks of macroeconometric model-building in the central government. Their models always contain a Keynesian consumption function, whereas over time other equations may change form in accordance with various eclectic models that reflect changes in econometric techniques. As for economic forecasting, they use both econometric models and survey analysis based on the answer-to-questioners data received from a number of think tanks on their forecasting of annual real gross domestic product, consumer price index and unemployment rate. The survey analysis is done by the Economic Planning Association and the result is called ESP forecasting.[16] Although the ESRI working papers, including Komine *et al.* 2009 and Iiduka and Kawagoe 2009, compared the economic forecasting results done by specialists with high-tech equipment and the others by nonspecialists (economists), they felt that more examination was needed to reach a better, decisive conclusion. Something that an econometric model based only on past data does not tell tends to improve general economists' low-tech forecasting results.

5 Advanced econometric analysis

Time-series-based analysis was brought to Japan by those who had not only studied economics and econometrics but also engaged in econometric practice by handling high-quality data in the United States.

Michio Hatanaka (b. 1926) entered the University of Tokyo in April 1945 and remembers that classes resumed in September on the Hongo campus. In 1949, Hatanaka entered the graduate school of Tohoku University in Sendai, where the Japanese Samuelson, Takuma Yasui, was teaching economics (Ikeo 1994b). In 1953, Hatanaka entered Vanderbilt University because he learned that Nicholas Georgescu-Roegen, associate editor of *Econometrica*, rewrote the draft he had submitted to the journal and accepted it. Thus Vanderbilt opened Hatanaka's eyes to empirical studies and econometrics. From 1955 to 1963 he worked as a member of a project run by Oskar Morgenstern at Princeton. For the first time in his life he handled the data, applied the statistical inference techniques, and, with a program he wrote, operated an electronic computer having only 210 bits in its memory, which had been designed by John von Neumann. In 1959, Morgenstern embarked on an applied econometric analysis by using a high-speed computer of the time, which had been suggested by von Neumann.[17]

Clive Granger and Hatanaka had a series of meetings with John Tukey (a mathematician and friend of von Neumann) and then undertook harmonic analysis of economic time series and spectral analysis by computing on an IBM 650.[18] Hatanaka (Hatanaka *et al.* 1990: 390) said:

> Beginning with some time series charts John [Tukey] suggested what to compute; then after gazing at the graphs of the results John suggested what to compute next. Though I did not understand his reasoning well, I was impressed by his pragmatic approach.

Granger and Hatanaka 1964 was released after Granger went back to England. In 1963, Hatanaka moved to Rochester; in 1966, he was appointed research professor at Osaka University, which, unusually for Japan, had no Marxist economists. He tried hard to catch up on the new ideas and approaches appearing one after another in econometrics by using FORTRAN. He became interested in the problem of underidentification presented by Ta-Chun Liu (1960). Hatanaka (1975) discussed the possibility of global identification of the dynamic simultaneous-equations model with stationary disturbances (Sims 1980). He published his research results in *International Economic Review*, which was established in 1960 with the first joint editorship of Lawrence Klein at Pennsylvania and Michio Morishima at Osaka. He was asked to submit his papers to the journal because only a few Japanese contributed to the journal (personal communication with Hatanaka, September 18, 2009). Responding to my query, Hatanaka thought many times and found the image of a living creature the most fitted with his research.

In 1981, Hatanaka, who took part in the panel session "Econometric Analysis versus Time Series Analysis" at the BOJ conference, impressed his Japanese colleagues. Referring to Harvey 1989, Hatanaka (Hatanaka *et al.* 1990: 395) recalls,

> At that time some people, unaware of the general trends of econometrics, contrasted "econometrics" and "time series analysis."... The proper contrast is between (1) modeling least dependent upon information other than the data, and (2) modeling utilizing heavily the assumptions and the constraints on the parameters that cannot be verified by the data alone.

In 1981, the number of Japanese economists who worked on the cutting edge of econometric analysis by using computers was very small, and most had never studied econometrics at all. Things began to change with the rapid spread of inexpensive personal computers and excellent software. It is good for econometricians to have direct talks with experienced experts to clarify anything over their head in practice. Interestingly, Hatanaka did not regard himself as Japanese when he did econometrics.

Takeshi Amemiya (b. 1935), whose father had worked for a major Japanese shipping line, came back from the United States to Japan by exchange ship in 1942. He was on the same ship as Shizuo Kakutani and Shigeto Tsuru. He studied economics at the International Christian University in Tokyo, and then American University and Johns Hopkins University. He became interested in econometrics, especially econometric theory, when estimating the demand for water in Maryland. Advised by Geoff Watson, who was the chair of the statistics department, Amemiya started to publish his scientific papers in 1966. He was appointed assistant professor at Stanford, although interestingly Stanford had not allowed him to enter its graduate school. Collaborating with and talking to active statisticians such as Wayne Fuller (time-series statistician), Herbert Rubin and Ted Anderson, Amemiya completed his thesis at Stanford in 1964. Amemiya was appointed research professor at Hitotsubashi University by Tsuru. Two years later, he was reappointed at Stanford.

In the early 1970s, a Stanford economist, Michael Boskin, posed questions about statistical problems such as how to do inference and how to prove asymptotic properties of the maximum likelihood estimator, questions that made him interested in censored regression models called Tobit models (Tobin 1958; see Amemiya and Powell 2007). Amemiya started to publish many papers on limited dependent variable models including Amemiya 1973. In response to a question about what kind of vision he had for an economy, he said:

> I believe … we should not minimize the importance of pure statistical fit, or the idea of letting data speak for themselves, because economic theory is often too formal to accommodate complex economic phenomena. In this regard I would like to point out that Brown and Deaton (1972), in their authoritative survey of empirical research on demand relationships since World War II, noted that much empirical work on demand had been purely pragmatic and carried out with very little reference to any theory of consumer behavior. Simultaneous-equations models have lost some of their attraction over the years, being replaced by multivariate time-series analysis. You may find useful my recent paper (Amemiya 2009), in which I graphically show recent trends in various areas of econometrics.
>
> I guess what I have written above provides an indirect answer to your question (2). To answer it more specifically, I would pick "a complex living creature" among the choices you have given. I believe the most important way to understand an economy is fact gathering and on the basis of it trying to come up with an overall intuitive comprehension of the economy rather than formulating a complicated mathematical model.
>
> (Personal communication with Amemiya, March 19, 2010)

Amemiya was rather critical of both simultaneous-equations models and economic theory-making without referencing economic data. He emphasized the importance of fact gathering and letting data speak for themselves. Alan Brown and Angus Deaton (1972) surveyed 244 papers and books related to empirical studies of models of consumer behavior including the decision to buy durable goods. This kind of behavior was analyzed using abundant economic data (high quality) with reference to economic theory. It should be mentioned that Hidehiko Ichimura (2010), who had taught in the United States, still complained about the availability of databases in Japan and said that researchers were sometimes declined by the bureau when they asked for the same data set to reuse for revising scientific papers after receiving comments from journal referees.

6 Conclusions

Japan has a long history of collecting and processing statistical data, starting in the sixteenth century. Yet external impacts such as direct communications with active statisticians and econometricians at meetings and universities were important, especially in learning the definition of economic concepts for statistical studies and in practicing applied econometrics with economic data and a computer. Both the quality of economic data and computers improved significantly, and econometrics itself was enhanced by this progress. The Japanese economists were interested in contributing their research results to policymaking and to building econometric models linked with input-output tables. The making of rice policy called for early econometric works in the 1930s, and the making of economic projections and macroeconomic policies needed the building of macroeconometric models in the 1960s. After the end of a rapid growth period in the early 1970s, the Japanese gradually became interested in econometric "modeling least dependent on information other than the data" (Hatanaka *et al.* 1990).

Prior to 1930, Japanese students mostly visited Germany, Austria and the UK to pursue advanced studies of statistics and economics. After 1950, the same generation began to study economics and econometrics at the graduate level in the United States and the UK. Some of them were hired as assistants for econometric works at US universities. They hoped to advance beyond the discussion of the welfare aspects of an economy made by Marshall and John Maynard Keynes. Japanese forerunners such as Hatanaka and Amemiya studied statistics and econometrics in the United States by handling data on a computer under experienced scholars when they began to enter the professional field.

In Japan, Marxist economists were the majority in academia until the mid 1960s and wielded power over university curricula until around 1970. They were interested in collecting statistical data but were left behind by the progress in econometric theories and techniques as well as the improvement of databases (Ikeo 1996b). Japan was required to make an economic plan (as a reimbursement plan) to borrow money from the World Bank in the 1950s. Empirical works and economic forecasting were also necessary for planning and evaluating public policies such as the construction of infrastructure and power-generating facilities.

Government officials took a special intensive course in Keynesian and neoclassical economics a couple of years after they got jobs and were trained on the job, making empirical studies and building econometric models, to become economists until universities had modernized their curricula by increasing the number of courses in non-Marxian economics in the early 1970s. Japanese econometricians collaborated with their counterparts in East Asia as well to improve the quality of economic data and input-output tables in the region.

Notes

1 This chapter is a revised edition of Ikeo (2011b). I would like to give special thanks to Shinichi Ichimura, Michio Hatanaka and Takeshi Amemiya for their personal communications with me, and thanks to Hidekazu Eguchi, Hidehiko Ichimura, Koichi Yano and Koichiro Iwamoto for their information.

2 As noted in Ichimura (2010: 1), the first land survey, including the acreage and productivity of cultivated land, could go back to the so-called Taiko Kenchi (1582–91). The data on rice prices, which were good enough to be used in contemporary econometrics (Wakita 2001), were available from the sixteenth century.

3 In Japan Schumpeter gave lectures on the theoretical apparatus of modern economics; the theory of business cycles; the world depression with special reference to the United States; the present state of international commercial policy; the present state of economics on systems, schools and methods; and the theory of interest (Allen 1991, 270–4; Ikeo 2006).

4 Without the outbreak of the Korean War in June 1950, the meeting would have taken place as originally planned. Martin Bronfenbrenner, who was stationed as a tax economist in Japan between August 1949 and August 1950, missed the commemorative meeting. See JES 1951, 1952; and Ikeo 2009, 2011b.

5 Hayakawa (1933) was an earlier version written in Italian.

6 Sugimoto (at Hitotsubashi University) was sent to Germany by Japan's government to study economics from 1929–30. At the University of Berlin he took such courses as E. F. Wagemann's seminar and lectures on money and banking and on business cycles, and Ladislau von Bortkiewicz on statistics. Sugimoto denied the measurability of utility and rejected utility as one of the basic concepts for economic science. He adopted the labor theory of value because he thought that the energy of human labor could be measured in terms of working hours. He was interested in physics and urged the introduction of more physics, rather than biological metaphors, into economic theory. Moreover, at Berlin Sugimoto met Wassily Leontief and became close friends with him. Seeing the rise of the Nazis, Leontief left Berlin for the United States, and at a port met Sugimoto, who had witnessed the Nazis take power.

7 This is the way I learned how to view "an economy" when I was a student at Hitotsubashi.

8 For example, Eguchi participated in the First Pacific Basin Central Bank Conference on Econometric Modeling in San Francisco in 1976. Eguchi (1976) reported their first quarterly econometric models and the model-building of the monetary sector. Kurabayashi participated in many UN-related conferences such as one on estimating the purchasing-power parity.

9 GARIOA later became a Fulbright fellowship.

10 Bronfenbrenner was trained at the University of Chicago and completed his thesis, "Monetary Theory and General Equilibrium," before the premature death of his supervisor, Henry Schultz (1893–1938), and defended it in 1939. The thesis was a vast survey of his contemporary analytic achievement, and it later helped him share common economic knowledge with young economists in Japan from 1949–50. His

list of references includes books by Léon Walras, Vilfredo Pareto, and Keynes (1936), articles by John R. Hicks, and Kei Shibata's (1937, 1939) critical review article on the *General Theory*, although it was written prior to the publication of Hicks [1939] 1946, which covered similar ground to Bronfenbrenner's thesis. Paul Douglas (1892–1976) hired Bronfenbrenner as one of his assistants in statistical studies of the Douglas function (Biddle 2011; Ikeo 2009, 2011b).

11 I misspelled Hanya Ito's family name in Ikeo (2011b).

12 Ichimura's note (1951) on the definition of related goods was followed by Hicks's (1951) comments.

13 On September 22, 1945 the Civil Information and Education (CIE) Section within the Supreme Commander for the Allied Powers (SCAP) established 22 CIE information centers to make the information written in English available to the general public. In 1952 the US Department of State took over the project and continued a similar service in newly established ACCs. In 1972, the number of ACCs was reduced to 6 from 13 (Ishihara 2008).

14 The Economic Stabilization Board was established in 1946, reorganized into the Economic Deliberation Agency in 1952, and became the EPA in 1955. After Japan lost World War II, Marxist economists joined several governmental committees like the one in economic reconstruction and enjoyed a good relationship with American officials until 1947.

15 K. Sato (1980, 1984, 1999) are edited volumes on Japanese business and economy, and their changes.

16 ESP stands for economy, society and policy.

17 Granger and Hatanaka did choose harmonic analysis by themselves. Shizuo Kakutani (mathematician, 1911–2004) attended the mathematical seminar on game theory run by von Neumann and Morgenstern in the fall of 1941, but he decided to return to Japan by exchange ship in 1942 (Ikeo 2006). No Japanese person was allowed to participate in the project of applied game theory in the United States.

18 Reading Ikeo (2011b), Hatanaka wrote to me and said that Granger and Hatanaka did choose harmonic analysis by themselves.

Part II

8 Tameyuki Amano and the teachings of Sontoku Ninomiya[1]

This chapter aims to link economic ideas between early modern and modern Japan by focusing on Tameyuki Amano (1861–1938), the first Japanese modern economist, and Sontoku Ninomiya (1787–1856). In 1886, by publishing his *Theory of Political Economy* in his own language, Amano established economic science in Japan. Korekiyo Takahashi (1854–1936) and Tanzan Ishibashi (1884–1973) were known as the "Japanese Keynes" because as early as 1929 and 1931 respectively, they both used Keynesian analytical concepts such as "multiplier analysis" and "the paradox of saving." At the end of World War II, Ishibashi's expansionist policy for the reconstruction of Japan's economy, which he considered Keynesian, was vehemently criticized by expert American economists such as Martin Bronfenbrenner and Joseph Dodge.

Our first step is to show that Takahashi and Ishibashi had an intellectual relationship with Amano and learned economics from his writings. The second aim is to clarify that Amano was one of the first scholars since the Meiji Restoration of 1868 to pay attention to Sontoku Ninomiya, a great reader of Japanese and Chinese classics, a thinker and an agricultural reformer in the early modern period. While studying at Tokyo University, Amano enrolled on a course in Political Economy (in English) taught by Ernest Fenollosa (1853–1908). Fenollosa graduated from Harvard College in 1874, took a two-year postgraduate course in Philosophy, and studied at the Divinity School and at the school of the art museum in Boston. He later became famous by introducing Japanese art to the West. Upon graduation in 1882, Amano taught economics (in Japanese) at the Tokyo Senmon Gakko (the Tokyo Special School, called the Waseda University as of 1902). In 1886, subsequent to publishing his lecture notes, he became hugely successful.

Our second step is to prove that Amano's *Outline of Economics* (1902a) shaped modern macroeconomics by merging the teachings of the Japanese Ninomiya with ideas gained from the study of American political economy. During this time, an evolutionary and creative process of "Harmonization of Eastern and Western Cultures" took place. The entire set of Ninomiya's teachings and practical knowledge consisted of observation records and reform plans derived from his extensive fact-finding surveys conducted in troubled villages and domains. His teachings conveyed the importance of one's thinking and understanding toward the courageous implementation of the expertise-driven innovative measures for solving agricultural questions and toward the use of the incentives mechanism and good moral judgment for proper personnel management. These teachings are regarded as the basis of Japanese management. Furthermore, Amano used these teachings to shape his ideas on macroeconomics (including the idea of balancing savings and "the increment of capital," i.e., investment, through the efficient functioning of the banking system) and to engage in a journalistic campaign for the establishment of business education at the university level. He has been praised as a good economic journalist and educator rather than just as an inspired macroeconomist.

1 Reappraisal of Tameyuki Amano

Tameyuki Amano's 1886a publication, *Theory of Political Economy*, was the first best-selling economics textbook written in Japanese prior to the publication of his work, *Outline of Economics* (1902a).[2] But despite the fact that he established economic science in Japan by publishing the content of his Waseda University lectures in his books, Amano is a forgotten economist. There were two main reasons for this. First, in 1917, due to an internal squabble over leadership (the Waseda dispute of 1917), he ended his relationship with executive members of the Waseda University. More than a decade after World War II, in 1957, he was finally reinstated following the inclusion of Hirata's short piece "Tameyuki Amano" in *Social Sciences in Modern Japan and Waseda University*, the memorial volume for the university's seventy-fifth anniversary. In 1961, the memorial event for the celebration of Amano's centennial birthday was held at the university, during which several notable economists were invited to pay tribute to him. J. Okada (1975), a historian of economics, regarded Amano as "the creator of economic science in Japan," an appraisal that was recognized in Miyajima and Hanai (2004).

Second, Amano's writings were not so easily accessible outside of the Waseda University Central Library; this was because the Tokyo Metropolitan area was hit by the Great Kanto earthquakes of 1923, as a result of which many buildings, including libraries and his new house, were burnt to the ground by the subsequent fire. Many books and written documents, prepared in the Meiji and Taisho eras, were reduced to ashes. Amano remained in his workplace for about ten days and then moved into an apartment.

The scarcity of available copies of Amano's writings severely restricted access to his research. The development of electronic technology has seen to the removal of this obstacle. Since 2006, most of his books, translations and textbooks for correspondence courses are now available in the Modern Digital Library, supplied by Japan's National Diet Library (http://kindai.ndl.go.jp). With his critical assessment of the difference in "productive consumption" (hiring workers for his/her company) and "unproductive consumption" (hiring maids or servants for domestic services), Amano made a step toward modern macroeconomics and away from British classical economics. However, we could see that his idea of balancing savings and "the increment of capital," i.e., investment, by means of the effective functioning of the banking system in *Outline of Economics* (1902a, in Chinese 1902b) came from his updated discussion on savings in his *Discourse on Thrift and Savings* (1901), with reference to Sontoku Ninomiya's teachings on *suijo* (concession). Amano's 1902 economic ideas, which were founded on Ninomiya's teachings and on an American version of J. S. Mill's *Principles of Political Economy* (seventh edn., 1871), defines economics as the science of discussing the production, distribution, exchange and consumption of goods. This could be called macroeconomics by including discussions on utility, savings, the increment of capital (investment), trade, currency and banking, commercial policies (the role of government) and public finance.

Both Mill and Amano believed that the social goal of production was the supply of consumables and noticed that at the aggregate level, the savings, which were not spent out of one's income, would serve to increase capital. While capital stocks were fixed in a society, the banking system could provide liquidity or money supply and furthermore attain the optimal allocation of loanable funds. For Amano, the banking system should function for the adjustment of savings and increased capital while the decreasing savings and increasing spending on luxuries should increase the employment in the production of luxuries. Therefore, this short run effect on an economy should be nothing at the aggregate level but should change the allocation of production factors. Moreover, active and professional trading (including short selling and buying on margin) could destabilize stock markets and thus an economy as a whole. As this would resonate with the revolutionary messages of J. M. Keynes, both Takahashi and Ishibashi would be able to include "Keynesian ideas" such as "multiplier analysis" and "the paradox of saving" in their public statements around 1929 against the current austerity policy in the midst of the depression.

In order to apply any theory to a real-world condition, especially to make a policy proposal, we need some reference to economic thought. Amano did not choose Mill's or Benthum's utilitarian thoughts but rather Sontoku Ninomiya's (*hotoku*) thoughts and teachings (*suijo*, *bundo* and *shiho*).[3] Section 2 shows how Amano developed his macroeconomics and discovered Ninomiya's teachings. Section 3 discusses the similarities which could be found in the arguments made by Amano and Ninomiya. Section 4 emphasizes that Ninomiya's *bundo* meant a macroeconomic equilibrium accompanying the fiscal balance and an optimal (positive) ratio of savings by using later terms. *Bundo* could be translated into a computational general equilibrium and sustainable growth.[4] Section 5 carries a postface.

2 Tameyuki Amano and his discovery of Sontoku Ninomiya

In this section, we present an overview of Amano's process of formulating his economic ideas and the period in which he touched on Ninomiya's teachings. Amano and Ninomiya never met, as Ninomiya died in 1856 in Nikko, and Amano was born five years later. Amano came to know Ninomiya's teachings through his followers and through his own contemporary intellectuals (see Table 8.1).

Amano was born in Edo (Tokyo), where his father was a doctor of Chinese medicine serving at the Edo domain residence of the Ogasawara family, which headed the Karatsu domain (Northern Kyushu). Even in this National Seclusion period, doctors of Chinese medicine paid serious attention to the medicines they could import from Dutch merchants operating in Nagasaki. These doctors enjoyed exceptional circumstances, as trade under strict shogunate control meant access to the Dutch merchants was very limited. Naturally, they also had a keen interest in issues related to international trade and open-door policies. In 1867, the Tokugawa shogunate returned political power to the Emperor. In June 1868, after the death of his father, Amano returned to Karatsu (Saga Prefecture after the Abolishment of Domains and Establishment of Prefectures of 1871) with his mother and brother. Around 1871–2, in Karatsu, he had the notable opportunity to attend an English course given by Korekiyo Takahashi (Takahashi would go on to become a governor of the Bank of Japan, Minister of Agriculture and Commerce, the Prime Minister and then later Finance Minister).[5] Takahashi did not use Japanese when teaching English to the boys in his class, including Amano. Impressed by Amano's performance, Takahashi advised him to go to Tokyo for higher education (Takahashi 1936a: 169).

Table 8.1 Sontoku Ninomiya, Tameyuki Amano and their contemporaries

Hakuseki Arai	(1657–1725)
Sorai Ogyu	(1666–1728)
Konyo Aoki	(1698–1769)
Adam Smith	(1723–90)
Sontoku Ninomiya	**(1787–1856)**
Yugaku Ohara	(1797–1858)
John Stuart Mill	(1806–73)
Kokei Tomita	(1814–90)
John Elliott Cairnes	(1823–75)
Masae Fukuzumi	(1824–92)
Charles Franklin Dunbar	(1830–1900)
Yukichi Fukuzawa	(1833–1901)
Léon Walras	(1834–1910)
Masana Maeda	(1850–1921)
James Laurence Laughlin	(1850–1933)
Azusa Ono	(1852–86)
Ernest Francisco Fenollosa	(1853–1908)
Korekiyo Takahashi	(1854–1936)
Ukichi Taguchi	(1855–1905)
Sanae Takata	(1860–1938)
Tameyuki Amano	**(1861–1938)**
Rohan Koda	(1867–1947)
John Maynard Keynes	(1883–1946)
Joseph A. Schumpeter	(1883–1950)
Tanzan Ishibashi	(1884–1973)
Martin Bronfenbrenner	(1914–97)

In 1878, Amano entered Tokyo University's Faculty of Letters.[6] In 1879, he took a course in the History of Philosophy, as well as courses in Political Economy and Political Philosophy during the period 1880–2. Lectures in these courses were conducted in English by Ernest Fenollosa.[7] It seemed that Fenollosa received advice on teaching political economy from Charles Dunbar, who taught the subject at Harvard around 1878.[8] Referring to the 1880 syllabi and course reports for the first-year course in Political Economy, Fenollosa used Mill (1871) as a textbook and Cairnes (1875) as his first choice for recommended reading. We assume he explained the production, distribution, exchange and consumption of goods, and also lectured on macroeconomy as a whole, as well as on economic law, trade and money. In their second year, students studied labor issues, tax law, foreign trade, banking law and money. Each student was also required to write a graduation thesis, for which the topics chosen in 1881 included currency, banking, commerce, and foreign trade.

The Tokyo Senmon Gakko (Waseda University) was established in 1882. Upon graduation from university that year, Amano taught Political Economy in Japanese at the school from the time of its establishment. He published his works *Theory of Political Economy* (1886a) and *The Principles of Commercial Legislation* (1886b) separately. Amano's work (1886a) looked more theoretical and abstract than either of Mill's publications (1871, 1884), because Amano (1886a) had no discussion of policy or legislation. Mill (1884) was a textbook edited for American college students by Laurence Laughlin and translated into Japanese by Amano in 1891. Amano's work (1886a) also looked more American than Mill (1871, 1884) because Amano (1886a) did not include Japanese topics and included few European exemplifications; however, there were some American illustrations in each chapter. In addition, he did not supply a theory applicable to practical purposes, but rather a list of economic terms, economic topics and a theoretical skeleton of macroeconomics. From 1886 to 1903, despite its high price of 1.3 yen, his 1886 publication went through 25 editions and sold 30,000 copies. At that time in Japan, books were the most important media for providing new economic knowledge to intellectuals such as professors of economics, central and private bankers, government officials, business people and students in economics, prior to the establishment in 1895 of the economic periodical *Toyo Keizai Shinpo* (*The Oriental Economist*, in English), for which Amano would become the main contributor of editorial articles.[9] Figure 8.1 shows a picture of Amano around 1886.

Seeing the success of Amano's *Theory of Political Economy*, Fuzanbo, its publisher, planned to publish textbooks for elementary school students and asked Amano to write them. Amano had taken several courses in political economy, in English, at Tokyo University. After his graduation, he pondered over the relevance of Japanese education subsequent to the opening of seaports to the rest of the world and the Meiji Restoration. According to Amano's recollection in a 1932 interview, "In the 1880s, there were few textbooks targeted for elementary school students and even fewer written originally in Japanese" (quote translated, Asakawa and Nishida 1950: 168–9). Now he had to establish a course in political

Figure 8.1 Tameyuki Amano (around 1886) in Waseda University History Center. This picture was taken around the time he published his first book *Theory of Political Economy*, 1886a (Waseda University History Center 1982: 16).

economy and the principles of political economy, in Japanese for Japanese youth.

From around the end of the period of the National Seclusion, the shogunate lifted the ban on international trade and promoted the translation of Western books. In retrospect, it seems that early modern Japanese knowledge had been put aside in schools during the Meiji Restoration of 1868, and that Western knowledge was considered the center of research and education. It wasn't long before the new government decided to search for Japanese knowledge and traditions that should be carried over to the new Meiji era and included in the school curriculum. When Michitane Soma, the former lord of Soma domain, presented

Kokei Tomita's biography entitled *Hotokuki* (The Record of Returning Virtue by Virtue)[10] to the Emperor in 1880, Sontoku Ninomiya finally received nationwide attention beyond the regional praise that had been limited to Fukushima, Shizuoka, Kanagawa and Tochigi Prefectures. In 1883, the Department of the Imperial House made the biography widely available, giving a copy to each prefectural governor and higher-ranking official. By 1885, it had become required reading for officials in the Ministry of Agriculture and Commerce (MAC). In 1890, Dainokai (an agricultural association) published a popular edition. Masae Fukuzumi, who was also well read and had written a transcript of Ninomiya's speeches, edited *Sage Ninomiya's Evening Talks* and Shizuoka Hotokusha published it as five volumes of Japanese binding edition in the period 1884–7. In 1893, Shizuoka Library published a popular edition.

MAC was a gigantic ministry established in 1881 by combining the official agendas of the Ministry of Home Affairs and the Ministry of Finance, which may be comparable to a ministry combining the present Ministry of Economy, Trade and Industry (METI) and the Ministry of Agriculture, Forestry and Fisheries (MAFF). MAC was set to become the center for industrial policy development. In 1880, the Yokohama Specie Bank (the government-sponsored bank specializing in foreign exchange, now the Tokyo Mitsubishi UFJ Bank) began as a bank specializing in foreign exchange settlement and opened its London branch. Without government intervention, it could become the institutional basis for direct trade among private merchants. The Bank of Japan was established in 1882. In 1881, Korekiyo Takahashi, who had returned from the US and given Amano English classes in Karatsu (Saga Prefecture, Kyushu), entered MAC. Around 1883, Arinori Mori set up a meeting between Takahashi and the Chief Secretary of MAC, Masana Maeda. Maeda, having spent several years in France and other European countries, found in Takahashi a like-minded friend. In 1884, Maeda and his 40 officials conducted fact-finding surveys of Japan's economic and industrial conditions and edited *Suggestions for the Promotion of Industrial Enterprises* (30 Japanese binding volumes). They declined a laissez-faire approach and advocated the promotion of industry. Concerned about the lives of ordinary people "with debt and without savings," *Suggestions* listed the enhancement of agriculture, manufacturing and commerce in rural areas and suggested increased savings and capital equipment, bank loans without mortgages for entrepreneurs, construction of a transportation system and storage houses, and expansion of business education. They found cases where those who were trained in mechanical engineering could not operate imported foreign machines, so they decided to promote traditional exportable industries such as silk, tea and ceramics, in the hope that these industries would establish the basis for the development of heavy industries, particularly those related to defense. Volume 11 (entitled *Spirits*) of *Suggestions* hoped to see new entrepreneurs and leaders emerging from each rural area and industry. Maeda's investigations and comprehensive surveys overlapped with Ninomiya's investigations and reform plans. So we could call Maeda the Ninomiya of the Meiji era. Also the emergence of an individual like Ninomiya was hoped for in each rural area and industry.

In 1886, Shigeki Nishimura criticized the excessive Westernization taking place in the country and began to promote "Japanese morals" (Kenjo 2009). Amano and Nishimura together took note of Ninomiya's teachings because they were stimulated by the campaign to return to Japanese traditions promoted by Tomita (1883) and Fukuzumi (1884–7). Moreover, some officials, Takahashi or Maeda in particular, suggested that Amano shed light on Ninomiya. Amano and Nishimura included a section on Ninomiya in their two elementary textbooks on morality. Lesson 26, "Sontoku Ninomiya" of their *Elementary Moral Textbook for Upper Grades* (1894) began as follows:

> The sage was born to a son of a peasant in Sagami. He was brought up in poverty and beset with difficulties. His generous father gradually lost his property including that inherited from his grandfather. A few years later, after their lands were filled with sediment brought by the flooding Sakawa River, he lost his father and then his mother. Living with his uncle, he worked hard while rice farming under the sun and read books after dark. He exchanged the rapeseed he grew on wasteland for rapeseed oil (for light) and obtained money by selling the fagots (firewood) he collected in the commons.[11] Thanks to his thrift and diligence, he managed to restore his lands and house. Moreover, he put in order the financial affairs of others, created jobs for the poor, inaugurated new industrial enterprises, and made countless contributions to the community. He was a great man of the early modern age.
>
> (My translation)

Lesson 26 explored the life and works of the great man, namely his thrift and diligence, his reading habits, self-help (for the capable and for himself), mutual help (for others, especially the weak), the adjustment of domestic finance and reconstruction of the domain's finances. The reader could gain a foundation in public finance and in the techniques for repayment and settlement. Amano and Nishimura's *Elementary Moral Textbook for Lower Grades* (1894) did not include text, but had illustrations of scenes depicting ethical education (see Figure 8.2). Lesson 20 contained an illustration of young Ninomiya reading a book aloud (*Great Learning*, a Chinese classic) and carrying a bundle of fagots on his back as well as a picture of an adult Ninomiya. It seems that Amano and Nishimura followed Rohan Koda's biography for children, *Sage Sontoku Ninomiya* (1891), which included a similar illustration of young Ninomiya. Amano and Nishimura (1894) became one of the first textbooks to include Ninomiya's life and works (Hisaki 1984).

Amano was eager to issue economic periodicals. Amano became a guest writer for *Toyo Keizai Shinpo* (*The Oriental Economist*) when Chuzo Machida established it as an economic magazine issued every ten days.[12] Amano wrote a byline editorial and other anonymous articles in every issue. He also contributed to the diffusion of economic questions and policy discussions among intellectual readers. The magazine aimed to promote international trade and business by

Figure 8.2 Young Sontoku Ninomiya reading a book aloud with fagots on his back, adult Ninomiya in the circle in Amano and Nishimura's *Elementary Moral Textbook for Lower Grades*. A few years after its publication, Ninomiya became a model of diligence for Japanese youth. Japan's government continued to resort to Ninomiya in ethical education for elementary students as well as in the promotion of concession and savings until around 1950 (in Amano and Nishimura 1894).

spreading various economic data and the conditions of financial markets it deemed useful for both domestic and international trade, data probably supplied by the Bank of Japan (BOJ) and MAC. It also guided Japan's adoption of the international gold standard, which was actualized in 1897. After Machida was transferred to the BOJ in 1897, Amano assumed responsibility for running the publishing company.

From April to September 1900, Amano authored a series of strong editorials for the reform of the Tokyo Stock Exchange and against the practice of short selling and buying on margin. Modern economic institutions such as credit, finance and rice exchanges were founded in early modern Japan. Future trading transacted at the Dojima Rice Exchange (Osaka) preceded one already established at the Chicago Mercantile Exchange. The practices of short selling and margin buying at the Dojima in the early modern era were naturally carried over to securities transactions at the Tokyo Stock Exchange during the Meiji era. As will be noted later, Amano hoped to see the development of industrial finance through the smooth intermediation provided by the commercial banks rather than through equity financing. Many novice traders (including Korekiyo Takahashi) lost their savings in the stock exchange, while professional traders became the new rich by quickly making massive gains. Moreover, Amano believed that to promote international trade, not only would Japanese banks have to handle the business of international settlements, but also Japan's government and the Yokohama Specie Bank would have to make deals in the London financial market.

It is noteworthy that Amano should read MAC's *Suggestions for the Promotion of Industrial Enterprises* (1884) and share his concerns about Japan's terrible capital-short position. From September to November 1900, Amano wrote a serial editorial on a new discourse on thrift and savings. It appeared to be an updated discussion of Ninomiya's thrift and savings, which he advocated in the Edo era, although Amano made no reference to him. Criticizing the practices of short selling and margin buying in the securities market, Amano maintained that the practice of thrift and savings (which would increase capital and national wealth) served the public. He argued for business education and the stability of the banking system. Amano collected his arguments and the BOJ governor's related public lectures and published them as a book titled *Discourse on Thrift and Savings* (1901). On the basis of his belief that human resource training, including the development of managers and business leaders with integrity, was needed to promote international trade, Amano campaigned for the establishment of economic education (including moral education) at the university level and for a pursuit of the "Practical Utilization of Knowledge" (Amano 1902c).

3 Amano's macroeconomics and his new discourse on thrift and savings

Despite the fact that Amano and Nishimura (1893, 1894) included a picture and/or story of Sontoku Ninomiya, Amano's economic writings never did refer to Ninomiya or to other Japanese economic literature. Nevertheless, we can find similarities in the arguments made by the two economists only if we read both their writings. This section discusses Amano's economics with reference to Ninomiya.

First, we look at Amano's (1890: 36–7) section on the relationship between economics and other disciplines, which is highly praised by historians of Japanese thought:

> Although economics is different from social morality, the two are closely related under decision-making conditions. In the practical application of economics, social morality should be placed first over economics. The highest moral teachings should not be overlooked merely in the pursuit of economic benefit. Moreover, it is not enough for us to learn a general argument for priorities on decisions based on social morality over decisions based on economic benefit, but to every time refer to moral sentiments when making decisions.
>
> (My translation)

We recall Ninomiya's discourse on truth from "the Sutras of Heaven and Earth" in Fukuzumi (1884–7). Ninomiya said:

> Without either being taught or studying one naturally knows what is the true way. It has neither books nor records to describe nor any teacher to explain. Everybody grasps its meaning by himself and does not forget it. Such is the essential character of the true way.
>
> (Fukuzumi 1970: 19)

Amano's explanation was compatible with Ninomiya's teaching: it is important for one to think for oneself and understand for oneself without memorizing written words or resorting to the authority of expertise.

Second, as shown in the previous section, Amano maintained that thrift and savings have been very important and they supported the increment of capital. He published his *Discourse on Thrift and Savings* (1901), which resonated with Ninomiya's teachings. Amano (1901) argued for the public benefit of thrift and savings, and stated that thrift and savings, which meant "to concede things produced today for tomorrow," would increase national capital. We quote Ninomiya's following teachings on industry, thrift and concession as the basis of Amano's argument.

> My way consists of the three component parts of industry, thrift and concession. Industry means efforts put forth for the production of goods needed for clothing, feeding and sheltering mankind, while thrift is endeavour not to waste such goods and concession is the act of transference by one to others of such goods owned by him. There are various forms of concession. To keep things produced this year for use during the following year is concession. According to one's means and social status, one should concede his

> possessions either to his children, to his relatives and friends, to his native place or to his country. Even a mere employee engaged for half a year should endeavour to practice at least concession of things belonging to his employer, which have been obtained this year, for use during the coming year. He should also yield things possessed by him to his children. These three are like the three legs of a tripod kettle. None should be left unpracticed.
>
> (Fukuzumi 1970: 76–7)

In the Edo era, as reflected in the saying that no Edokko (now Tokyoite) would keep his earnings overnight, many Edokko felt it shameful to save money or accumulate wealth. In the rice-based economy, rice was placed above money in people's minds. Ninomiya had to preach that industry, thrift and concession were important in reconstructing troubled domains and villages and in implementing measures for economic stability against starvation.

In his economic framework, Amano (1902a) repeated the discussion of thrift and savings and managed to include economic theory and policy matters in one book. He resorted to Ninomiya's teachings on the idea of balancing savings and "the increment of capital," i.e., investment, by means of the effective functioning of the banking system from Ninomiya's teachings on *suijo* (concession). We discuss this point in detail.

A contemporary textbook on macroeconomics usually starts with the presentation of a simple model of a national economy with goods circulating from production, distribution and consumption; it then explains the definition of GDP. Amano listed natural resources, labor and capital as three production factors; natural resources consisted of land.

At the time of study, the scarcity of capital was the most serious economic problem in Japan. Amano associated savings with an increase in capital. He defined capital as follows:

> Capital can take various forms such as material goods or money. Capital is the products used for production or the goods saved for this purpose. For example, machines, tools and raw materials in a factory are capital and can be used for production. The money or goods saved for this purpose are also considered capital.
>
> (Amano 1902a: 13, my translation)

He saw the difference between capital such as machines, tools, buildings and factories, and capital in circulation such as fuel, raw materials and wages.

The question then became "What caused the increase in capital?" He listed six causes: first, the acquisition of new land or territory (which might lead to the increase in domestic supply of raw materials); second, the import and export of capital; third, the size of personal income, because savings increase as income rises and so does the size of disposable income. Amano explained the fourth factor as follows:

> The fourth factor related to the increase in capital is "the mind for savings." As the size of capital depends on the size of savings, capital should be small if the mind for savings is weak. (A) Education. The mind for savings depends on the size of economic knowledge. Learned people tend to save more because they make future plans for living. (B) Morality or philanthropy. One should save money if he/she wants to engage in moral activities from the love for family, for country, or for the world. Therefore, the more moral the citizen, the higher the ratio of savings.
>
> (Amano 1902a: 30, my translation)

Amano's factor affecting the mind for savings (B) overlapped with the teachings of Ninomiya as discussed above. In thinking of the motives for savings, we need to set aside the idea of individualism and take the concept of family or country into consideration.

Amano's fifth factor was interest rate. The mind for savings became stronger as the interest rate increased. The sixth factor was the business conditions of banks and other financial institutions. He hoped to see the demand and supply of loanable funds balanced. Amano explained the sixth factor as follows:

> People could save more if the conditions of credit institutions such as banks and the office of postal savings were stable. If the financial institutions could be put in order, people would save more and capital would increase. On one hand, there are those who save money but are unable to use it for production. On the other hand, there are those who have no savings but have the know-how to start a business. Safe intermediaries can play a role for balancing loanable funds and to increase national capital by transforming savings.
>
> (Amano 1902a: 30–1, my translation)

Financial institutions could balance savings and the increment of capital (investment) and attain a macroeconomic equilibrium at a high level. This idea is associated with Keynes's discussion of Say's law ("Supply can create its own demand"). For Amano, banks have to facilitate the efficient allocation of funds from savers to the entrepreneurs who plan to increase their capital installment for future production. In other words, the banking system should be stable to connect savings and investment. In the Edo era, people like Ninomiya engaged in financing among the people whom he knew well, whereas since the Meiji era, the modern banking system matches loanable funds among people who do not know each other. We need to consider institutional differences in comparing Amano and Ninomiya. In a nutshell, many Edokko acted as if they followed Keynes's doctrine of "Demand can create its own supply."

4 Sontoku Ninomiya and modern economics

In the Edo era, the teachings of Sorai Ogyu were regarded by the Tokugawa shogunate as the official doctrine for governing Japan. There were two important ruling institutions at the time. The first was the class system of the four: in hierarchal order, warriors, farmers, artisans and tradesmen. The second was the isolationist policy, which included a ban on the construction of large sailing boats, with the notable exception that allowed for diplomatic relations with the Dutch. Yet, there were a number of thinkers who observed and published findings on economic phenomena, such as the circulation of money and the changes in rice prices, as well as economic activities, such as lending and borrowing, and economic policies undertaken in the name of "political reform."[13] Schaede (1989) clarified that the Dojima Rice Exchange in Osaka was the pioneer of future trading (in rice), established before the Chicago Mercantile Exchange, which started an agricultural commodities exchange. The quality of data relating to rice during the Edo era was so good that Wakita (2001) obtained significant results in his econometric research with the use of an Edo-era data set and a recent technique. In fact, the first comprehensive economic surveys may go back to the Taiko Kenchi, the survey instituted by Hideyoshi Toyotomi in the sixteenth century, which has become the first to provide data of good enough quality to conduct economic research of a high quality (Ichimura 2010; Ikeo 2011b).

Particularly those who studied political economy and political philosophy in English, including T. Amano, should consider *Hotokuki* (The Record of Returning Virtue by Virtue, Tomita 1883) and *Sage Ninomiya's Evening Talks* (Fukuzumi 1884–7, 1893) as Japanese classic works. Fukuzumi (1884–7) and Tomita (1883) were also well read by Japanese entrepreneurs. As previously mentioned, Tomita (1883) was a mandatory book to be read at the Ministry of Agriculture and Commerce (MAC). Fukuzumi (1884–7) supplied the foundations of scientific knowledge, rationale and practical thinking, and Japanese virtue. Out of the 36 volumes of *The Complete Works of Sontoku Ninomiya*, edited by Shintaro Sasai during the period 1927–30, 25 volumes covered the detailed record of *hotoku* activities, namely their investigation in each troubled area or village, detailed data on the economic lives (income, consumption, savings and debt) of the lord and his family, and his people, hearings from the residents as well as the fiscal reconstruction plan of a local economy and Ninomiya's cultivation of work ethics in their mind (Takemura 1997). Tomita (1883) was a concise book giving Ninomiya's personal history as well as the essentials of his reforms and his insights taken from the rational reconstruction activities and the response from the lords and their people.

We can read the imbedded teachings of Ninomiya in Amano's writings, especially in his discourse on thrift and savings and the promotion of business education (emphasizing the importance of moral judgment), although Amano never specifically referred to Ninomiya in his economic literature. Numerous other Japanese authors have discussed Ninomiya's works since Fukuzumi. Kobayashi (2009) compared the wealth of statistical data listed in Ninomiya's *Complete Works* (including current economic conditions, and reform plans for repayment and reconstruction of domain finance) to Cournot's "mathematical economics." It may be an exaggeration to say that Ninomiya is the uncontested pioneer in mathematical economics. Nonetheless, we can boldly attempt a modern interpretation of Ninomiya by highlighting his modernity and rationality and how Amano might read Ninomiya.

We should note that Ninomiya learned Shinto, Buddhist and Confucian doctrines by reading and talking to learned and religious figures, and therefore these Oriental factors can be witnessed in Ninomiya's talks and writings in Japanese. One may find it strange to find Christian terms instead of Oriental ones used in the text of English translations. However, Shinto and Buddhist terms can sometimes be found in place of original Christian terms in Japanese translations of Western classics.

Amano (1890) maintained that we should think twice whether our economic decisions are compatible with moral values probably because he saw the current economic situation changing dynamically over time and business leaders facing new challenges. This has been a Japanese or Oriental tradition because we can find similar thinking in *Sage Ninomiya's Evening Talks* (Fukuzumi 1884–7). We could interpret "the Sutras of Heaven and Earth" in the first and often cited section of "Discourse on Truth" as "observation." Ninomiya emphasized the importance of thinking for oneself and developing understanding on the basis of personal observation. In fact, his teachings were founded on "the Sutras of Heaven and Earth" or his "observation." He included horizontality, verticality, the way of measurement, the timepiece (he used a portable sun watch), a basic cultivation technique, and astronomical and multiplication tables in the "natural laws" or celestial laws that remain unchanged for all times. He said, "I set little value on books" (Fukuzumi 1970: 19). Amano would agree with Ninomiya that it is important to think for oneself without resorting to the views and opinions of men of erudition, and to put one's ideas into action (Fukuzumi 1970: 20). Yet, we should remember that Ninomiya was a great reader himself.

We could compare Ninomiya's concept of "the mind of an impartial and wise person" (found in his letter to the lord of Soma) to Adam Smith's "impartial spectator." Ninomiya said:

> It is impossible to accomplish a great plan for a country if you take the opinions of commonplace people, because a mediocre person cannot have a clear perspective on the situation and can infer only what he is feeling. How could a mediocre person conjecture the mind of an impartial and wise man who devotes himself to assuring the people's security?
>
> (II: 134, my translation)

We need to be sure to consider the state of mind of an impartial and wise man rather than the opinion of mediocre people when we decide state policies. For Ninomiya, the impartial and wise man is not compared to a *Kami* (Shinto) or a god, but he is rather a cultivated human being.

In order to approach Ninomiya's concept of thrift and savings, we have to understand his concept of "the way of man," which is sharply contrasted with "the way of nature." "The way of nature" covers celestial law and "the law of beast." Ninomiya said:

> The way of beast, which people despise, is the way of nature, while the way of man, which they make much of, is an artificial way though it is in compliance with the celestial law.
>
> (Fukuzumi 1970: 40)

> [M]en set up houses to shelter themselves from the elements, have storehouses to keep grains make clothes to keep their bodies safe from cold or heat, and eat rice year in year out. Isn't this an artificial way?... [T]he way of man, which is artificial, dies out if men neglect to keep it going.
>
> (Fukuzumi 1970: 41)

Therefore, Ninomiya criticized a man "who while living in this world looks on leaking roofs with folded arms, remains an unconcerned spectator of ruined roads and does not mind bridges decaying away" (Fukuzumi 1970: 48) by calling him a transgressor (or a sinner) of "the way of man." To keep "the way of man" one should repair leaking roofs, fix roads and reconstruct bridges before they are ruined. Then, we can understand his suggestion for thrift and savings, namely, to become rich. Advocating the importance of concession and savings as the road to the wealth of a nation (or nations), Ninomiya said:

> The people in general call one avaricious or greedy if he spends less than he earns or uses less firewood than he gets. It is a mistake. In "the way of man" people should work diligently against "the way of nature," and therefore, they choose to save. Savings means to forfeit the things of this year to the next. It is a form of concession. Concession of the fortune of parents to their children is based on the way of savings. Therefore, the way of man is the way of savings. It is the road or the great way to the wealth of nations.
>
> (Fukuzumi 2012: 15, my translation)

"The way of savings" was "the way of man" and is therefore artificial. We quote the following passage in which he used a numerical example from the section entitled "Causality of Wealth and Poverty."

> It is not by accident that one becomes rich or poor. Wealth comes from adequate causes, as does poverty, too. It is wrong to think, as people generally do, that wealth finds its way to those who are wealthy. As a matter of fact, it goes to those who are thrifty and industrious. When a man who enjoys an income of 100 yen a month lives on 100 yen a month, neither wealth nor poverty comes to him, but when he lives on 80 or 70 yen a month, wealth is due to him and money accumulates at his house. On the other hand, if he were to live on 120 or 130 yen a month, poverty visits him and money leaves his house. All this difference is due only to whether one lives within or beyond means.
>
> (Fukuzumi 1970: 68–9)

Ninomiya thought that in "the way of man" one should control selfishness, and he prized diligence most of all in his teachings (Fukuzumi 1970: 42). Why did he preach this type of message to the common people? The sage Ninomiya gave a paradoxical explanation and said:

> A commonplace man is the least avaricious. Learning is an art aimed at making men of small avarice to those of great avarice. What is great avarice? It is a desire to make all people happy by giving them enough to eat, plenty of clothing and a comfortable house. It is a desire to bestow on them a great bliss. The way to do this is to open up land, develop natural resources, give good government by wise statesmanship and relieve the masses from distress.... [T]he teaching of sages is aimed at good administration of the state by wise statesmanship as well as at enhancement of happiness of the people at large.
>
> (Fukuzumi 1970: 28–9)

As stated also in Tomita (1883), after the accumulation of savings, with the cooperation of the domain or village leaders, Ninomiya facilitated cooperation to develop new rice fields and to enable public enterprises for irrigation, embankment and dams. He sometimes sent his men to build an individual's house or barn while he just gave an iron-headed hoe to an indebted peasant to cultivate waste land, which was tax free for at least the following five years while normal land tax was 50 percent or less. Tomita (2012: 21) conveyed Ninomiya's sympathetic statement in the village of Aoki: "Sontoku said, 'As I feel the deepest sympathy for you I will give each of you a hoe. With this implement you can get rid of your poverty, pay off your debts, and acquire your wealth.' " Ninomiya always felt sympathy for the people and encouraged them to work hard to get out of troubled situations and then they could enjoy a higher standard of living. Amano in the Meiji era must have learnt from Ninomiya's teachings the importance of savings and its role of increasing "capital." By examining the reform of Soma district, we are able to find a common pattern in Ninomiya's plans. Ninomiya discovered a variety of reasons why these districts were falling into serious trouble and made plans to solve the problems. He analyzed the collected massive amounts of economic and geographic data and calculated the *bundo*, which was actually the combination of the optimal size of public finance and the optimal size of savings and consumption for each economy, or in other words, the combination of the optimal tax and optimal savings ratio. *Bundo* could be translated into "computational general equilibrium" or "sustainable growth path" in modern terminology.

Tomita (1883)[14] and Miyanishi (1956) suggested that Ninomiya and his followers engaged in a comprehensive investigation of troubled domains and villages and made reform and growth plans called *shiho*. Ninomiya's *shiho* program of reconstructing impoverished villages was relatively neglected by the historians of the Tokugawa era who had researched Ninomiya's thought and activities at that time. Therefore, Eiji Takemura (1997) filled the research blank by providing a detailed discussion of the *shiho* program including the cultivation of the inner self through work, the education of financial planning, and the introduction of an award system within public enterprise. We can quote Ninomiya's cultivation of a work ethic and the introduction of incentives and awards from Tomita (2012: 38):

> In every village he taught the people to love one another, and persuaded them of the nobility of work; he helped them to make better roads, to improve their irrigation, to open up new fields, and to amend their condition in various other ways; to widows and orphans and other helpless persons he gave money, from one to five *ryo* [a monetary unit of the Edo era] according to their need; he commended the good and diligent sometimes giving ten or fifteen *ryo* to the specially worthy in industrious villages, by way of encouragement to them and incentive to others.

Indeed, Ninomiya believed that it was necessary first to give the people incentives for working hard and to cultivate a work ethic in people's mind. Therefore, in the case where a large region was in trouble, Ninomiya suggested that the lord pick the better villages first to start his reform program, and to show the performance to the worse ones in order to reform all the villages in the domain (Tomita 2012: 35). Moreover, when the villagers accomplished the hard work, such as the opening of wild land and the construction of dams as he designed, Ninomiya always showed his appreciation by having a decent party with sake and rice cake.

As shown in Najita (2009), Ninomiya's many reform plans commonly included conversion of a high-interest loan into a low-interest loan, and to implement an austerity policy and an agricultural reform plan to build a new system of irrigation including dams and to introduce new cultivation technology in rice farming. Based on the observation by Ninomiya, many impoverished villages and their people were suffering from the burden of paying high-interest rates like 20 percent. If a domain borrowed a hundred *koku* (unit of rice crop) from a merchant, it wasn't enough to repay 20 *koku* (just the interest) every year to clear off the debt. Ninomiya advised the domain to borrow money from Ninomiya himself with no interest, to pay the whole debt back immediately to the merchant, to pay a fifth of the principal, say, 20 *koku* out of 100 *koku*, to him for the next five years and then to donate the same amount as *hotoku-kin* (money for returning virtue) in the sixth year. In the beginning, Ninomiya hastened to raise funds by collecting savings (surplus, loanable funds) from his friends and followers. After he received the principal and the *hotoku-kin* from the first borrower, he could use the funds for his next restoration plan. After paying back to Ninomiya, the domain and its people were supposed to continue positive savings (which might be allowed to reduce lower than the restoration period) and concession to others (based on virtue), enjoy more crop production and a higher living standard. Savings led to a higher living standard and sustainable economic growth. Although we cannot call his finance "loan without interest" in modern terminology, it was a considerably low-interest finance (around six percent or less). It can be said that Ninomiya's reform plans became a good example of scientific thought and the groundwork for private finance, public finance and economic science in Japan after the Meiji era.

It was a rational restoration of the troubled economy with the target of attaining the computational optimal equilibrium both in private and public sectors. Ninomiya must have reached the idea of a harmonious state, namely an equilibrium, in local economy by aggregating individual data. In the Meiji era, Amano came to grasp that a certain level of macroeconomic equilibrium was attained by balancing savings and investment (the increment of capital) through the banking system. It could be said that not only Amano but also Ninomiya reached a concept of a Keynesian macroeconomic equilibrium and Walrasian general equilibrium. Amano must have thought that one must analyze economic data to understand current conditions and make relevant policies. Both Ninomiya and Amano were econometricians rather than mathematical economists.

A significant part of one reform plan based on all-out investigation was usually different from other plans. We should pick up a couple of interesting cases for reference. First, in the reform of the Shimodate district, Ninomiya suggested to the lord that he give up his salary and reduce the salaries of the retainers. Tomita (2012: 34) carried Ninomiya's statement to the lord of Shimodate:

> Sontoku says, "You must resign your salary confessing that the whole distress of the district and of your lord's house is due to your mismanagement of affairs, and expressing your desire to atone for your fault in this manner by adding the whole of your salary to the reform fund, and by devoting all your time and energy to the work of reform. The other retainers can then make no objection to some reduction in their salaries, and some will even follow your example, thinking it not right that they should receive any payment while the chief retainer is receiving nothing."

The persuasion of the lord and retainers was very important to make a successful reform of the domain. In this case, their salaries were too high for the district economy to enjoy a sustainable growth.

Second, in the village of Aoki, Ninomiya proposed and took a Schumpeter-like innovative measure by using a thatched roof in constructing a dam.[15] He carefully studied the water supply of the village and the flow of Sakura River running near the village, and then conceived a plan of constructing a dam and a better system of irrigation. He encouraged the villagers to work very hard, carrying rocks and timber from the hill to the banks of the stream. Then he ordered them first to build a thatched roof over the water. When finished, Ninomiya himself jumped onto the roof and quickly cut several of the ropes. The roof fell down into water where it floated, and he was standing on the roof in safety. He then ordered them to throw stones and branches on top of the roof, from both banks, to sink it as a foundation for their dam. The thatching prevented the fine sand from moving, and no water could get through it. Beforehand, Ninomiya made stonemasons prepare for a dam which had two water gates, "a small one to be opened when the river was slightly swollen, and a large one for use when the water was very high, to prevent floods" (Tomita 2012: 21). He ordered them to construct a stone dam on the thatching foundation. Then the villagers reconstructed their irrigation ditches and founded an excellent system of irrigation which supplied water to not only for their own field but also some to the neighboring village.

Third, it is interesting to note how jealous officials (retainers) acted to prevent Ninomiya from conducting his honest investigation prior to making a rational restoration program. On one occasion Ninomiya managed to turn such a retainer's attention away from the current restoration activities by treating him to sake and fine dishes every day in his home until its completion. The episode states that jealousy could hinder the implementation of a rational reconstruction and scientific activities. Fourth, Ninomiya declined a construction plan of a canal, which he found too difficult. He could say "No" to a lord based on his prior rational investigation (Tomita 2012: 36). There are many other cases from which we can learn lessons.

Fukuzumi (1884–7) and Tomita (1883) carried not only plenty of direct messages originally sent by Ninomiya but also his insightful statements from which later Japanese native speakers could derive modern thinking and interpretation by shedding new light on the text. Takemura (1997) is the first to interpret Ninomiya's reform activities in the language accorded to modern economics such as incentives and macroeconomy.

5 Postface

The teachings of Sontoku Ninomiya could be the nexus linking the Edo and Meiji eras in the history of economics and economic thought in Japan. In fact, the research project on Japan's savings in 1987 managed to grasp the continuity of the two eras by focusing on the difference in economic and financial institutions as well as the teachings of Ninomiya (Ikeo 1988). As expressed in the saying that no Edokko would keep his earnings overnight, Edokko had enough job opportunities to hunt every day and they could enjoy city lives filled with pleasure, reading novels and watching performances. Yet locating the teaching quoted in section 2 in Fukuzumi (1884–7) and paying attention to the changes in financial institutions from the Tokugawa to the Meiji eras, we were able to connect Ninomiya's *suijo* (concession) in the Edo era with the current analysis of savings (Ikeo 1988).

Fukuzumi (1884–7) and Tomita (1883) are Japanese classic works. Ninomiya's *Complete Works* (1927–30) included numerous data on agrarian economy, rates of interest and early modern finance, concession (savings), expenditure in consumption, the construction of a system of irrigation, and therefore it had something to do with research activities in modern economics. Or rather, it can be said that the Japanese picked up the parts of Western political economy which were coherent with traditional Japanese economic thought and established economic science in Japan. The active use of numbers and calculations in economic analysis was a long tradition in Japanese economic thinking and analysis because Ninomiya and other Japanese economic thinkers in the Tokugawa era were strong at dealing with economic data and arithmetic.

Tameyuki Amano and his contemporaries were interested in "Practical Utilization of Knowledge" and "Harmonization of Eastern and Western Cultures." Although he was taught political economy in English by an American, he would probably have read contemporary Japanese writings by Yukichi Fukuzawa and Ukichi Taguchi and the influential *Suggestions for the Promotion of Industrial Enterprises* authored by M. Maeda and his men at the Ministry of Agriculture and Commerce. Amano did not refer to them. Neither did he refer to Ninomiya in his economic literature in spite of the fact that Amano and S. Nishimura's *Elementary Moral Textbook* (1893, 1894) included a story about Ninomiya. Nonetheless, Amano became able to persuade people of the importance of "Practical Utilization of Knowledge" in his economic writings by focusing on Ninomiya's teachings, especially on concession and savings.

Tanzan Ishibashi, a young colleague of Toyo Keizai Shinposha, who had contributed to the establishment of the English journal *The Oriental Economist* in 1934, praised Amano's activities as educator and economic writer in the April 1938 issue as follows:

> A great leader and educator was lost to Japan on March 26 last when Dr. Tameyuki Amano, LL.D., passed away at the age of 79. As a writer and as a teacher, he was an outstanding personality, and his passing is an irreparable loss to this country.... How indelibly he has left his mark on his times may be seen from the fact that the majority of scholars in economics who won distinction through the Meiji and the Taisho eras –1868–1921– were at one time or another his pupils, either in his class rooms or through his written works.
>
> (Ishibashi 1938: 213)

Now Japanese people remember Amano's activities as economist, journalist and educator in the Meiji era. Amano managed to connect Western economic analysis with traditional Japanese economic thinking by utilizing Ninomiya's teachings on *bundo*, *suijo* and *shiho*.

Notes

1 This chapter is based on Ikeo (2012, 2013). Yasutami Suzuki (Kokugakuin University) and a few members of International Ninomiya Sontoku Association (INSA) suggested I examine Tameyuki Amano. I thank Masanori Yokoyama for giving me basic information on Amano, and Kiyoshi Ogasawara and Satoshi Kamikubo for their valuable comments on a draft.

2 See Mitsuhashi (1929), Asakawa and Nishida (1950) and Kinoshita (2012). The English titles of Amano (1886a) and (1902a) were given by Amano himself.

3 Bellah (1957: 130) explained Sontoku Ninomiya as follows:

> Sontoku is noteworthy not only as a religious and ethical teacher but also as a practical man of affairs. On several occasions he was put in charge of feudal estates which were in a sad state of decay and in a few years' time had transformed them into prosperous and economically sound districts. His policies were many but consisted chiefly in insisting on the strictest economy and on the extension of the amount of cultivated land, development of irrigation, etc., by means of the money saved.

Bellah (1957) discussed Ninomiya and Baigan Ishida and tried to shed light on religious aspects of their teachings. T. C. Smith (1959, 1988) searched for origins and sources of modern Japan in early modern agriculture. Hayami *et al.* (2004) collected the English version of research articles on early modern economic activities first published in Japanese. See also Fujimori (2006).

4 Bellah (1957: 130) said *bundo* meant that "more should be accumulated in one year than would be spent in the next, the reserve being kept for emergency or capital accumulation." It was not enough of an explanation for *bundo* because the concepts of modern economics are needed for the English interpretation of *bundo* as discussed in the chapter.

5 Smethurst (2007) is a wonderful biography of Korekiyo Takahashi in English. Smethurst could not discuss Amano in detail, whose house and library, including irreplaceable documents and correspondence, were burned to ashes in the fire following the Great Kanto earthquakes of September 1, 1923.

6 It is interesting to note that the university had been established one year earlier. See also Chuhei Sugiyama and Hiroshi Mizuta (eds) (1988) and Jiro Kumagai (2001).

7 Ernest Francisco Fenollosa was born in Salem, Massachusetts, in 1853, and died in London in 1908. He graduated with highest honors in Philosophy at Harvard College in 1874. Granted one of the Parker Fellowships, he took a two-year postgraduate course in Philosophy. In 1876, he entered the Divinity School, but his interest soon became diverted to aesthetics, and in 1877 he entered the newly founded school at the art museum in Boston. In 1878, he was offered the Professorship at Tokyo University and in August he started to lecture there on the History of Philosophy, Political Philosophy, and Political Economy. (Harvard University Archives, HUG 300 Quinquennial File: Fenollosa). He became well known by introducing Japanese art and Buddhism to the West and opened the Oriental section at the Boston Museum of Fine Art. Also see Yamaguchi (2000).

8 I thank Roger Sandilands, David Mitch and Peter G. Stillman for responding to my query on who was in charge of the course in Political Economy at Harvard around 1878, and for posting the related information and literature in the emailing list SHOE. See also Mason and Lamont (1982).

9 Tanzan Ishibashi graduated from Waseda University's School of Letters in 1908. Joining Toyo Keizai Shinposha in 1911, he began his own study of economics by reading Amano (1902a). He must have read Amano's editorial and other articles for *Toyo Keizai Shinpo* as well. The English version of *Toyo Keizai Shinpo*, *The Oriental Economist*, would be established by Ishibashi in 1934. This magazine caught the attention of the Americans who were concerned about Japanese government policies, especially after Ishibashi was nominated as Finance Minister in 1946. See Chapters 2 and 10, and Ikeo (2011a).

10 The title of the English version is "A Peasant Sage of Japan: The Life and Work of Sontoku Ninomiya," which we refer to Fukuzumi (1970).

11 It is controversial as to how much wood he gathered on the common where he could visit on foot. Sontoku's great-grandson Yasuhiro Ninomiya (2010) has found that collecting firewood on the common was usually banned (for adults) within walking distance from Sontoku's house.

12 See also Sugihara (1987b, 1988, 1990) and Omori (1998). *Toyo Keizai Shinpo* became a weekly in 1919.

13 See Y. Nakamura (1971), Gramlich-Oka and Smits (2010), Gramlich-Oka (2010), Ravina (2010) and Kobayashi (1989).

14 *Hotokuki* (Tomita 1883) was translated into contemporary Japanese and annotated by Norihiko Sasai and published as *Hochu Hotokuki* (A Peasant Sage of Japan with Notes) in 1954. I used the 1954 Japanese edition.

15 Tomita (2012: 20–1) gave a detailed explanation of the construction process and Ninomiya's brilliant guidance on the scene.

9 From the economics of Keynes to Keynesian economics[1]

1 Introduction

Many Japanese who would have liked to actively learn commercial policy and international business environment from the 1880s to the 1920s had read Tameyuki Amano's books or journal articles on economics, policies, banking and savings, which included "Keynesian" macroeconomic arguments three decades before the publication of Keynes's *The General Theory of Employment, Interest and Money* (1936). This is the main reason why quite a number of Japanese naturally took up Keynes's articles, pamphlets and books immediately after their publications. Keynes was one of the contemporary economists for the Japanese who were actively examining the international financial architecture and working on monetary economics and policies, and economic theories from around 1913 to 1941. Thanks to globalization, some Japanese had a chance to meet Keynes in Paris, Leningrad (St. Petersburg) and London, whereas no Japanese had ever met Adam Smith or Karl Marx.[2] Japanese economists and economics students read the writings of these authors for the first time only a long time after their publication.

In the process of writing this survey, I came to realize that this survey eventually traces the transformation from the economics of Keynes to Keynesian economics, and, more importantly, the formation of an international forum for theoretical economists who were the main producers of economic knowledge in the 1930s. As suggested in the title *On Keynesian Economics and the Economics of Keynes*, Axel Leijonhufvud (1968) maintained that the economics of Keynes is different from Keynesian economics. This chapter suggests that Keynesian economics was rapidly formed after 1936 based on the theoretical messages exposed in Keynes (1936) by professional economists. Those who were teaching at universities raised questions relating to Keynes (1936) and discussed related issues in a wider scope with the fellow economists. This group read the international journals in economics and contributed more to scientific journals rather than general magazines.[3]

The spread of Keynesian ideas in Japan has already been discussed several times both in Japanese and English. Section 2 gives a brief survey of the discussion of Keynesian economics in Japan including the introduction of new related facts (and covering the post-World War II period). Section 3 shows how Japanese economists became interested in Keynes's first book *Indian Currency and Finance* (1913). Section 4 discusses the Japanese intellectual connection with Keynes and the formation of international order in the peaceful period of the 1920s. Section 5 shows some of the Keynesian ideas found in the political and journalistic argument against the policy of economizing consumption in 1929–30 (which was eventually stimulated by Tameyuki Amano's macroeconomic argument). Section 6 discusses Finance Minister Korekiyo Takahashi's deficit financing policy in 1932–6 and the important role of the central banker Eigo Fukai as the adviser. Section 7 discusses an apparent change in Keynes's style of writing between *A Treatise on Money* (1930) and *General Theory* (1936), and discusses Kei Shibata's review in detail because Keynes commented on a draft of this review. Section 8 summarizes some conclusions.

2 A survey of Keynesian economics in Japan

To the best of my knowledge, the impact of Keynes's *General Theory* (1936) on Japan was first examined in R. Mikami (1967, in Japanese). *The Encounter with Keynes* edited by T. Hayasaka (1993, in Japanese) included important information about the research of Keynes in Japan, such as his interviews with historical personages who had read Keynes plus his brief history of "Keynes in Japan." Although only part of it was presented in English (Hayasaka 1982) and a more complete version was published much later than initially scheduled, Hayasaka provided K. Hamada with the relevant information for Hamada to write his "The impact of the General Theory" (1986) in English. This allowed E. M. Hadely to use it in her "The diffusion of Keynesian ideas in Japan" (1989). M. Hayashida in his *A Fifty-year History of the Studies of Keynes's General Theory* (1986, in Japanese) surveyed almost all of the books, articles and translations on Keynes and Keynesian economics published in Japan. The index of authors listed 970 Japanese names on 17 pages and the titles of publications, mostly written in Japanese, on 55 pages.

Therefore, we already have some knowledge about the historical development of Keynesian Economics in Japan. We can confirm the following five points.

First, the idea of state intervention in the economic process, which is usually associated with Keynesianism, was not new in Japan, because the government had to create a modern financial architecture and had a strong influence on its economy in the process of industrialization since it began its take-off stage in 1868 (Meiji Restoration). This point is often emphasized as a hallmark of Japan's modernization. In fact, Hadely (1989: 292) writes, "In Japan, the government has been part of the economy from the beginning of its modernization in 1868. Accordingly, the matter of a government role in the economy was close to a nonissue." From a more general perspective, the strong leadership of the government in the economy may be rooted in Oriental tradition, as represented in the saying "The role of the government is making the world better and saving the people." Therefore, it received attention as one of the typical characteristics which could be found in the successful economic development of the newly industrialized countries of East Asia (IBRD 1993).[4] In fact, this tradition is considered to be the root of both the Chinese and Japanese terms for "the subject of economic science," namely *Jing Ji* and *Keizai*, which are written in similar characters (Ye 1997: 39, 53 – Editor's note).

Second, deficit financing (without significant inflation), which is an important hallmark of Keynesian policy, was practiced by Korekiyo Takahashi (1854–1936) as the Finance Minister in his attempt to pull the Japanese economy out of a prolonged slump worsened by the overvalued yen. This policy was enacted in 1932, *four years prior to* the publication of Keynes's *General Theory* (1936). To the best of my knowledge, the Japanologist Jerome B. Cohen was the first to examine Takahashi's fiscal policy with deficit financing and call Takahashi the "Japanese Keynes." Cohen (1950: 110) stated:[5]

> The nadir of the great depression in Japan was reached in the last quarter of 1931, and thereafter the economy expanded. April, 1931, saw the advent of deficit financing; September, 1931, marked the beginning of the Japanese occupation of Manchuria. The gold standard was finally abandoned in December, 1931. Takahashi, finance minister from 1931 to 1936, who has sometimes been called the "Japanese Keynes," advocated deficit financing as a way out of the depression. He regarded 600 million yen as a safe limit for deficits but the militarists needed more for the China campaign they were planning. Takahashi was assassinated in 1931 for resisting further military expenditures, and thereafter the deficit rose.

Cohen was completing his Ph.D. thesis, which was to be published under the title of *Japan's Economy in War and Reconstruction* (1949), before he came to Japan as a vanguard member of the US Tax Reform Mission led by Carl Shoup in 1949. Shoup was an economist specialized in public finance at Columbia University, where Cohen was a graduate student in the field of Japanese studies. Cohen was one of the most responsible scholars who provided the American occupiers and scholars with the information on Japan's fiscal policy and the conditions of the government budget in English.

Following Cohen, Tsutomu Ouchi was the second scholar to pay attention to Takahashi's Keynesian policy but he was more successful in popularizing Takahashi as the Japanese Keynes in his *The Way to Fascism* (1967, in Japanese: 260–1). Takahashi decided to maintain the increment of military expenses and civil engineering expenses by issuing public bonds for the consecutive years. (Ouchi 1967: 254)

> It is interesting to note that the policy of releasing additional purchasing power by an inflationary measure was enacted in Japan prior to the New Deal and the Nazis. Needless to say, neither Hitler nor Roosevelt followed Takahashi.... I do not think that Takahashi was familiar with Keynes's theory because he was assassinated prior to the publication of Keynes's

> *General Theory* (1936).... However, it can be said that Takahashi's observant eye for economic reality had reached the level of Keynes.[6]
>
> (My translation)

T. Ouchi might have known the extensive network for research and policies existed beyond regions at the time and he was right to note the following, "Takahashi was such an avid reader that he might have read early writings of Keynes" (Ouchi 1967: 260). This chapter shows that Keynes's books and pamphlets were widely read in Japan and Chapter 8 argues that Tameyuki Amano was forgotten.

C. P. Kindleberger mentioned Takahashi's fiscal policy in his *The World in Depression, 1929–1939* (1973: 166–7) based on the information supplied by the Japanese economist R. Komiya. A number of scholars referred to Keynesian aspects of Takahashi's fiscal policy.[7] S. Goto (1977, in Japanese) was the first to popularize Takahashi as the Japanese Keynes. D. K. Nanto and S. Takagi gave a paper "Korekiyo Takahashi and Japan's recovery from the Great Depression" to the meeting of the American Economic Association and the summary was included in the 1985 issue of the *American Economic Review* (Nanto and Takagi 1985). There are several biographies written in Japanese of Takahashi, such as Imamura (1958, in Japanese), because of his checkered life from a bitter adolescence in America through his career as Finance Minister and (acting) Prime Minister until the moment of his passing by assassination. Moreover, T. Nakamura (1986, in Japanese: 73–5, 1994, in Japanese: 61) rightly noted that Takahashi's closest adviser was Eigo Fukai (1871–1945), who was the deputy governor of the Bank of Japan and later became its governor (see section 6). Thanks to the publication of Richard J. Smethurst's detailed biography in English *From Foot Soldier to Finance Minister: Takahashi Korekiyo, Japan's Keynes*, many English readers obtained information about Takahashi's life, activities and policymaking groups.

Third, an incomplete version of multiplier analysis, including indirect employment effects triggered by public spending and a numerical example, were also given by Korekiyo Takahashi in November 1929 in order to criticize the current austerity policy implemented to achieve Japan's return to the international gold standard. T. Nakamura (1967, in Japanese: 201–2) pointed out that this was *seven years prior to* the publication of Keynes's *General Theory* (1936). Kindleberger (1973: 166) noted that it was *a few years prior to* Kahn's "The relation of home investment to unemployment" (1933), in which his analytical work clearly showed the process would converge to some finite figure. Yet we will demonstrate in section 5 that Takahashi's numerical example of spending multiplier would explode to infinity although he believed it would not. Moreover, it was pointed out in Nanto and Takagi (1985) that Takahashi's multiplier analysis took place *a few months after* the publication of Keynes and Henderson's *Can Lloyd George Do It?* (1929), in which indirect employment effects first appeared with numerical calculations. Nevertheless, it is noteworthy that both Takahashi and the influential journalist Tanzan Ishibashi clearly understood the paradox of savings, and in 1929 they strongly opposed Japan's return to the international gold standard without a devaluation (see Komiya 1996, in Japanese).

Fourth, the standard version of Keynesian economics became popular in Japan after World War II thanks to the stream of American Keynesian literature accompanied by econometric studies, such as L. Klein's *Keynesian Revolution* (1947). It is epitomized by two theoretical pillars, namely the theory of effective demand determining the level of national income and total employment, and the theory of liquidity preference determining the level of the interest rate. An increasing number of young Japanese economists began to study in the United States from 1950 onward. The empirical studies which had been developed in the 1940s impressed them so deeply that they conducted similar works after they returned to Japan (Chapter 4; Ikeo 1994a, in Japanese; Ikeo 1996a). By the mid 1960s, Keynesian and neoclassical economists outnumbered Marxian economists, who had been the majority in Japanese universities since 1945 (Ikeo 1996c, Ikeo ed. 2000). The Japanese version of P. Samuelson's *Economics* (1948), the standard textbook of Keynesian economics, was published by Shigeto Tsuru (from the sixth edition) for the first time in 1966–7.

Fifth, the case (supported by T. Shionoya 1974, in Japanese) for calling Finance Minister Tanzan Ishibashi a Keynesian is controversial even though he called himself a Keynesian after 1946. The Keynesian part of his inaugural address, which was often quoted, went as follows:

> The most important objective of fiscal, economic policy is the attainment of full employment of all existing productive resources.
>
> Lord Keynes once defined genuine inflation as the inflation that would occur from excessive demand under the full utilization of capital.
>
> We need not worry so much about the government budget deficit or monetary expansion.
>
> (Ishibashi 1970, in Japanese, vol. 13: 188–9, 191, 192; translation based on Hamada 1986: 453)

Although the postwar Japanese economy was suffering from serious inflation, Ishibashi stuck to his own belief in Keynesian policy measures and tried to keep increasing money supply by issuing national bonds through the Reconstruction Finance Corporation. This policy was vehemently criticized by several economists such as Hyoye Ouchi and Hiromi Arisawa, who thought that the policy of stimulating the production capability was necessary at first for the war-torn economy. The economic policy was changed toward the belt-tightening direction after Ishibashi was purged from public service by the Occupation Force, namely the Supreme Commander for the Allied Powers (SCAP). M. Bronfenbrenner, a member of the Shoup Reform Tax Mission, was critical of Ishibashi's Keynesianism. It is worth examining Bronfenbrenner's criticism of Ishibashi's Keynesianism in his "Four positions on Japanese finance" (1950a, 285):

> If the present Japanese government and the dominant Liberal party were operating without consultation with SCAP on economic matters, many believe that there would be a reversion to policies associated with the

> name of Tanzan Ishibashi. Mr. Ishibashi, former editor of the influential *Oriental Economist*, was for a time economic spokesman for Japanese big business. He held the key post of finance minister in the first Yoshida Cabinet during the period of most rapid Japanese postwar inflation but was removed in 1947 under charges of obstructing SCAP policies. The *Oriental Economist* remains the most effective English-language proponent of his views.
>
> His Keynesianism ... is of a fundamentalist variety which takes literally the view that *no* monetary expansion should be considered inflationary so long as production and employment are increasing along with prices. His critics call him an inflationist–more specifically, a profit inflationist.
>
> (Italics in original)

We should discuss the issue of the post-World War II monetary policy in the whole process of the reconstruction of the Japanese economy, such as the price stability, the security of tax revenue and the establishment of fixed-exchange rate for the Japanese yen. As a matter of fact, Ishibashi was purged for reasons not connected directly with his macroeconomic policy but with his leadership of public opinion as the managing editor of the weekly magazine *Toyo Keizai Shinpo* (the Japanese-language equivalent of *The Oriental Economist*, which made Ishibashi well known among the Japan watchers in Western countries, see Chapters 2 and 10).

3 The first attention to Keynes in Japan

As discussed in Chapter 3, in the early 1910s there were only a few Japanese monetary experts in academia and at least three leading Japanese monetary economists of the day became interested in Keynes right after the publication of Keynes's first book *Indian Currency and Finance* (1913). To the best of my knowledge, Kakujiro Yamazaki (1868–1945) of the Imperial University of Tokyo was the first Japanese economist who referred to the book in his scientific paper.[8] From 1913–14, Yamazaki took up Keynes (1913), while he was intensively debating with Masao Kanbe of Kyoto Imperial University and Senjiro Takagi of Keio-gijuku the characteristics of Irving Fisher's plan for a compensated dollar (Chapter 3). The debate among the Japanese economists was somewhat confusing, and shifted to the characteristics of both India's monetary system and the gold exchange standard.

Yamazaki maintained in his "Answers to Professor Takagi on the value of money, II" (1914a, in Japanese) that the adoption of the gold exchange standard, as in India, was primarily aimed at the stability of the external value of currency. Arguing that Britain's monetary situation was uncommon, Yamazaki (1914a, in Japanese: 72–3) quoted from Keynes (1913) as follows: "[F]oreign observers seem to have been more impressed by the fact that the Englishman had sovereigns in his pocket than by the fact that he had a chequebook in his desk" (Keynes 1913: 19; *CW* vol. 1: 14). Next, in his "On the countries with the gold standard without gold currencies, reconsidered" (1914b, in Japanese: 557–8), Yamazaki again quoted from Keynes with a slight modification as follows:

> A gold standard is the rule now in all parts of the world; but a gold currency is the exception.... I think I am right in saying that *there is only one country* in the world in which actual gold coins are the principal medium of exchange.[9]
>
> (Italics added)

Yamazaki had already discussed the related matters intensively in his "On the countries with the gold standard without gold currencies" (1911, in Japanese). Japan's international monetary policy had many similarities with India's because both countries were located far away from the world financial center in London. Both India and Japan had foreign exchange as well as gold reserves at banks abroad including the Bank of England. Otherwise, their theoretical gold points were very high. The difference between the two was that silver coins were circulated in India, while the banknotes convertible to gold were circulated in Japan.

Second, Saichiro Takashima in his *Principles of Money and Prices* (1915, in Japanese) surveyed both the debate in Japan and the extensive literature on money and prices, as shown in Chapter 3. Takashima placed Irving Fisher's (1911) quantity theory of money at the center of his book. However, in the second half of his book, Takashima surveyed four major current monetary topics such as Indian currency and the financial mobilization for World War I. In appendix 1, Takashima mostly translated the first three chapters of Keynes (1913) under the title of "the new trend of the currency system in the leading countries." In the section entitled "The place of gold in the Indian currency system and the criticism of the proposal for circulating gold," Takashima surveyed the discussion of the gold exchange standard based on the evidence provided by Keynes. Takashima confirmed that Kakujiro Yamazaki had discussed the gold exchange standard in 1911 prior to the publication of Keynes's *Indian Currency and Finance* (1913) (see Chapter 3).

The third Japanese economist who paid attention to Keynes was Torajiro Takagaki (1890–1985), a monetary economist who had a keen interest in practical issues such as current monetary conditions and desirable monetary policies. Takagaki started his academic career in 1913, when he graduated from Tokyo College of Commerce (now Hitotsubashi University). He recalled that he was probably advised to read Keynes (1913) by Naozo Igarashi, who was the president for the Indian branch of Yokohama Specie Bank (Hayasaka ed. 1993, in Japanese: 36). Many international bankers must have read Keynes (1913). When he had a chance to study abroad, Takagaki had limited choices due to World War I and studied under Irving Fisher at Yale University. When the ceasefire treaty was signed in November 1918, Takagaki decided to travel to Europe. Fisher advised him to meet Keynes and kindly wrote a reference letter for him to do so. Keynes had been known as the young editor of *Economic Journal* since 1912. Although he did not have a chance to meet Keynes, Takagaki later advised young Japanese to read Keynes carefully and translate his works. For example, Nisaburo Kito translated Keynes's *A Treatise on Money* (1930) and Tsukumo Shionaya translated *General Theory* (1936) under the advice of Takagaki. It is noteworthy that Keynes did not ask any copyright fees but wrote the preface to the Japanese edition when Takagaki wrote to Keynes to get the translation right for *A Treatise on Money* (1930). In the preface, Keynes announced that he had been writing a new book, which was to be published in the form of his *General Theory* (1936).

4 The world-famous economist-journalist Keynes in the 1920s

In the 1920s, Keynes was not only an active economist but also a world-famous journalist who opposed the Treaty of Versailles and the British monetary policy of returning to the gold standard. To the best of my knowledge, there were four intellectual Japanese connections with Keynes (in addition to the correspondence on the translation of his works).[10]

First, Keynes became known to the Japanese more widely by the publication of *The Economic Consequences of Peace* (1919). In 1919, Keynes and 58 Japanese officers, including the chief delegate Kinmochi Saionji and Korekiyo Takahashi, participated in the Paris Peace Conference. However, there was no evidence of Keynes and the Japanese interacting with each other. Keynes left Paris before the conclusion of the conference when he found no room for revision in the draft of the peace treaty in spite of his strong opposition to the punitive reparations imposed on Germany. He quickly wrote the reasons why he resisted the peace treaty and published them as *The Economic Consequences of Peace* in December 1919. Keynes exposed the purpose of the peace treaty which aimed at destroying not only German international trade, coal mining and the iron and steel industry, but also the whole of German industry. It also required Germany to pay reparations in spite of the expectation that Germany would have a trade deficit for at least the next two years due to the import of necessities. In 1920, the Japanese journalist Tanzan Ishibashi summarized Keynes's *The Economic Consequences of Peace* (1919) in the five consecutive issues of a popular weekly *Toyo Keizai Shinpo* (*The Oriental Economist* in unequivocal English, March 27, April 3, 10, 17 and 24; Ishibashi 1971, in Japanese, vol. 3: 146–73), because he agreed with Keynes. In 1919 Ishibashi had already criticized the peace treaty and expected that it would cause problems in the future (May 25, June 5 and 15; Ishibashi 1971, in Japanese, vol. 3: 128–47).

Second, the journalist Keikichi Ishimoto contributed his "The population problem in Japan" to *Reconstruction in Europe* (August 17, 1922), which was under the general editorship of Keynes as a special monthly series to *Manchester Guardian Commercial*. Dozens of experts in economic and social problems from around the world, including Gustav Cassel and Charles Rist, responded to Keynes"s request, and the series was advertised as "the most ambitious journalistic venture of modern times." Ishimoto (1922: 356) reported the population problem in Japan – "the problem presented by a growing population and a static food supply" – in the sixth issue. Based on the investigations made in 1921, he said:

> The population in Japan increases by 600,000 to 700,000 every year. It goes without saying that the situation will become more serious if this state of affairs is left to itself, in view of the fact that Japan is already one of the most densely populated countries on earth.
>
> (Ishimoto 1922: 356)

Ishimoto discussed two ways of seeking a solution, one peaceful and the other not. As to the latter, he judged that such an idea was impossible in the future in view of the international naval holiday decided upon by the Washington Conference in 1921. Then he sought the peaceful method, and listed three alternatives – the importation of foodstuffs, emigration and birth control.[11] First, Ishimoto considered the supply of rice, which was a Japanese staple foodstuff. The statistics of Japan during the last decade showed that the increase in population was 14 percent, in land under cultivation 5 percent, and in rice production 5 percent. Moreover, rice imports had not increased as much as Japan's trade on the whole. He concluded that it would be impossible to anticipate such a fantastic increase in the importation of rice. Second, Ishimoto admitted that it was impossible for 600,000 to 700,000 people in Japan to emigrate to America or Australia because of their policy against emigration, nor to Korea, Manchuria or Siberia because the Japanese emigrants could not compete in wages with native people, nor to Central or South Africa because it was necessary to get enough funds beforehand to emigrate to places far away from Japan. Therefore, Ishimoto found the only way of solving the population question was birth control. Ishimoto drew the following conclusion: "Japan must regulate her population, whether it is moral or immoral to do so" (1922: 356).

Third, the Japanese were deeply interested in the debate over Britain's return to the international gold standard. Although the Japanese government chose not to return to the international gold standard in the face of instability in neighboring countries such as China and Russia in 1919, it was anxious to make such a return when the time was right. The two controversial points in Japan were when to return to the international gold standard and what rate to choose, either the prewar rate or a lower rate. It was well known that Keynes was opposed to Britain's policy of returning to the gold standard. When his articles on the international monetary system which had been written for *Reconstruction in Europe* were collected and published as *A Tract on Monetary Reform* in 1923, it immediately drew the attention of several Japanese economists, and Kanji Okabe and Sunao Uchiyama published the Japanese version in 1924. However, Japan was not at all ready to return to the international gold standard in the aftermath of the major earthquakes which hit the Tokyo metropolitan area and Yokohama in September 1923.

Thus Keynes's activities relating to the gold standard always received serious attention in Japan, because he was a British economist opposing Britain's return to gold. For example, the mathematician Rikitaro Fujisawa briefly referred to Keynes's statement sent by telegram in his own speech at the meeting of the Japan Actuary Society on March 29, 1925 (Fujisawa 1925b, in Japanese). Yet the British government decided to return to the gold standard at the prewar parity in April 1925 despite Keynes's strong opposition and Fujisawa's negative statement (Chapter 3).

Fourth, Tokuzo Fukuda met Keynes in Petrograd in September 1925. The Russian Academy of Sciences celebrated its second centennial anniversary and invited international scholars, including six economists.[12] At the first meeting in the finance ministry, Keynes gave a one-hour speech entitled "Economic Transition." He summarized the current situation of the British economy and tried to give reference points for the Russian people. According to Fukuda (1930, in Japanese: 385), about one half of Keynes's speech in Petrograd was included in the pamphlet *The End of Laissez-faire* (1926). Keynes referred to J. R. Commons's theory of economic development dividing the timeline to the three periods, namely the Age of Scarcity, the Age of Abundance and the Age of Stabilization. Regarding the liberalism developed in Britain as the most beautiful result in the Age of Abundance, Keynes maintained that the Age of Stabilization had come and individual freedom would be decreased. Keynes did not support either state socialism or Italian fascism, and advocated a new liberalism based on individual freedom, which would regulate population and adjust the price level (Fukuda 1930, in Japanese: 385–92).

Following Eli Hecksher's favorable remarks, Fukuda gave critical comments on Keynes's lecture (Fukuda 1930, in Japanese: 389–402; Hayasaka 1993, in Japanese: 244, 266–7; Yoshikawa 1995, in Japanese: 109–11; Nasu 1995, in Japanese: 221). Fukuda disagreed with Keynes in the following way:

> It is wrong to regard the current situation as an economic transition and as a universal phenomenon in the rest of the world outside of Britain. It is a situation unique to the British economy, and should be regarded as a structural change or *strukturell Wandlung* as currently discussed by German authors. It is true that Britain became the richest country in the period which Commons calls the Age of Abundance, thanks to the great increase in the productivity of the country. However, it also owed its prosperity to its massive exploitation of the foreign markets. Therefore, as the remaining countries are catching up with Britain and Eastern people were shaken up, Britain would begin to lose its advantage and share in the world market, especially in the export of coal.
>
> (Fukuda 1930, in Japanese: 391–402, my translation)

Fukuda emphasized that what was happening to the world economy was not an economic transition as claimed by Keynes but a structural change.

As he criticized Keynes, Fukuda was given a chance to deliver a lecture on the current economic situation from his point of view a couple of days after Keynes. Yet Keynes did not show up and therefore Fukuda made a speech in

German under the title of "Das Problem der Productivität" (The problem of productivity) instead of in English as he had prepared. Referring to François Quesnay, Adam Smith and Confucius (who had an influence on Quesnay's economic thought), Fukuda argued that the improvement in economic life depended on the increase in the wealth of the nation, or more exactly, the increase in productivity. Although his remaining report is a little confusing, what Fukuda meant in modern terms was probably that the increase in per capita national wealth or income was necessary to improve economic life given that population was increasing rapidly – rapidly enough to become a serious problem.[13]

5 Argument against the policy of economizing consumption

Many countries around the world were returning to the international gold standard from the mid 1920s, as shown in Chapter 3. Gustav Cassel's idea of purchasing-power parity was the most useful for the discussion about the level of parity that each country should choose through consideration of the difference in the inflation rates among various countries. Cassel's special research paper "The Japanese Currency" (1926) had an influence on the debate about the level of the parity which Japan should choose in returning to the international gold standard. Cassel recommended that Japan should return to the gold standard at the current rate, not the old one, and gave a serious warning.

From 1919 on, Keynes became more and more popular among Japanese journalists, politicians and economists. Keynes wrote pamphlets and gave radio talks in order to criticize the incumbent British government and to affect public opinion on fiscal policy and deficit financing. It seems that Japanese politicians and journalists borrowed Keynes's ideas in their own critical speeches and articles against Japan's belt-tightening policies. They paraphrased Keynes's statements to fit them suitably to the Japanese context and further elaborated Keynes's arguments. Several opposition leaders and journalists, such as Korekiyo Takahashi and Tanzan Ishibashi, criticized the policy of economizing consumption during the period of recovery from the prolonged economic depression which had been caused by the financial panic in 1927.

In July 1929, the new government started serious and concerted efforts for the stabilization of the yen without devaluation. A majority of Japanese economists believed that the chance for Japan to return to the international gold standard at the prewar parity, 49.375 dollars per 100 yen, came when the price level went down due to the 1927 financial panic. At this point it seems that there were no economists who objected to Japan's return to the international gold standard. Japan was taking a similar course to the one taken by Britain and vehemently criticized by Keynes in the mid 1920s, and the course warned against by Cassel.

Korekiyo Takahashi explained the essence of the Keynesian expenditure multiplier theory to criticize the thrift campaign in November 1929. His explanation resembled Keynes and Hubert Henderson's *Can Lloyd George Do It?*, which was published in May 1929. However, Takahashi's "multiplier analysis" is worth quoting in full because it was better and more impressively explained than Keynes and Henderson (Keynes [1931] 1972, vol. 9: 103–6). Takahashi argued as follows (K. Takahashi 1936b, in Japanese: 247–9; summarized in T. Nakamura 1967, in Japanese: 201–2 and Nanto and Takagi 1985: 372; quoted first in T. Nakamura 1978, in Japanese).

> Let us imagine that a parson can spend 50,000 yen every year. If he spends only 30,000 yen and saves 20,000 yen, his own assets will accumulate by 20,000 yen every year. It should be good for his own economic life. From the viewpoint of a nation's economy, however, the increase in saving by 20,000 yen means the decline in consumption demand by 20,000 yen somewhere, and, therefore, it will lead to the decline in the nation's production. Consequently, it is better for the nation's economy that a person who has a budget of 50,000 yen spend all the money.
>
> More frankly, let us suppose, say, a man visited a clubhouse (*machiai*), called up geisha girls and had luxurious dishes, and spent 2,000 yen. Though this cannot be recommended from the viewpoint of public morals, if it happened, the money he would spend would become a part of the salary of the cooks, the payment for the fish, meat, vegetables and seasonings which had been used in the dishes, the coverage of transportation cost, and the profit of the merchants. In turn, the farmers, fisheries and other producers made profits by receiving these payments. Then, the farmers, the fisheries and the merchants would spend their profits on food, clothing and housing. A part of the money paid for the geisha girls' service would be handed over to the geisha girls, and the girls would spend on their food, tax, clothes, cosmetics and others. Let us take an opposite example. What would happen if the man decided not to visit the clubhouse? He would be able to save 2,000 yen and probably make a deposit. But that's all.
>
> Therefore, if the man spent the money at the clubhouse, the money would be in turn handed over to the farmers, the workers, merchants and fisheries, and thus work 20 or 30 times as much in the whole economy. It is good for a man to save 2,000 yen from the individual point of view. However, it is better for a nation's economy that a man spend rather than save, because the same amount of money functions as 20 or 30 times as much. This is the difference between the individual economy and the nation's economy.
>
> (Takahashi's "Austerity policy and the lifting of the gold embargo" 1936b, in Japanese, in his *Zuisoroku*, my translation)

Thus Takahashi mentioned secondary employment effects and used numerical examples. He believed that the spending multiplier would be 20 or 30 (in the last paragraph) without any exact reasoning. However, his numerical example meant that his marginal propensity to consume was assumed to be one and therefore his multiplier process should explode to infinity.

Tanzan Ishibashi discussed "The fallacy of economizing consumption" in his radio talk "Consuming economy and producing economy" on December 14 and

15, 1931. Ishibashi explained the paradox of savings clearly as follows (1971, vol. 8, in Japanese: 498–9):

> Ordinary people believe that consumption is immoral and a negative behavior of losing something. Therefore, they say that they had better decrease consumption and increase so-called savings. This is true without any conditions from the individual point of view, whereas it cannot be accepted without some conditions from the social point of view. The condition is that the saved money should be used for the production of new capital installments. Unused, hoarded money would do more harm than good. If the people in the whole society believe that they save when they only do not spend and store the money, the money withdrawn from circulation will be kept in bankers' safes or individuals' wallets. Then the commodities will not sell well, and the price level will go down. Therefore all the producers will not be able to make a profit and will instead lose money. In turn, producers have no choice but to reduce production in factories, fire employees and cut wages. This is a phenomenon of economic depression.
>
> (My translation)

Thus Ishibashi had a clear idea of the paradox of savings.[14]

In spite of the continuing strong criticism, Finance Minister J. Inoue was not persuaded by "Keynesian" diagnosis and disagreed on the best policy for the depressed economy. He believed that expenses should be cut when revenue declined, and that a policy of belt-tightening was unavoidable. He continued a deflationary policy and rationalized the administrative organization. He cut spending including the military, the salary of government officials, subsidies and pensions. Keynesian fiscal policies deserved consideration for the Japanese government because the policy of sound finance was believed and kept at the time.

6 Korekiyo Takahashi's Keynesian policy

It is well known that Finance Minister Korekiyo Takahashi decided on a Keynesian fiscal policy in 1932, four years prior to the publication of Keynes's *General Theory* (1936). On December 13, 1931, K. Takahashi, at the age of 77, became Finance Minister under the Prime Minister Tsuyoshi Inukai. Supported by Eigo Fukai, the deputy governor of the Bank of Japan (BOJ), Takahashi decided to take an activist policy in fighting against depression, especially to save impoverished farming villages.

First, the Inukai Cabinet decided to re-embargo gold exports immediately on December 13 and not to intervene in the exchange market. Thanks to the embargo on gold exports, the exchange rate against the US dollar went down on average from 2.05 yen in 1931 to 3.56 yen in 1932 and 3.97 yen in 1933, and thereby stimulated Japan's exports. However, capital fled from Japan until the government decided to control foreign exchange. Moreover, Takahashi agreed to stop converting notes into gold after a slight hesitation, and thus Japan abandoned the gold standard completely (Fukai 1941, in Japanese: 260–1).

Second, Takahashi took an easy-money policy. He cut the bank rate to 4.5 percent, raised the limit of fiduciary issue of convertible notes, and cut the tax rate for the note issue above this limit. He then left final "control" of the currency supply to the BOJ's discretion. Fukai thought that in order to stimulate the depressed economy, it was necessary to increase the general purchasing power by releasing funds from the BOJ, as the money supply declined due to the fall in the gold reserve after the lifting of the gold embargo. The BOJ supplied abundant finance to the industrial sectors and stimulated Japan's heavy industries including its colonial ones.

Third, Takahashi expanded government spending not only for relieving rural communities, which were most affected by the economic depression, but also for increased military spending in Manchuria (the northeastern region of China). He made up the shortage of revenue by using deficit finance in order to avoid raising taxes, which he hated. In 1932, the BOJ accepted all of the loans of 200 million yen at a 4.5 percent interest rate and later sold them to commercial banks. It continued to accept almost all of the new government loans for the next dozen years and the cumulative balance of government debt was steadily increased.

From the second and third points, Takahashi's policy was later called "Keynesian policy prior to Keynes." It is important to note that Takahashi's fiscal policy was closely supported by Eigo Fukai. Fukai (1941, in Japanese: 268–9) noted that he and Takahashi maintained close contact with each other after the gold re-embargo. Without the help of an able, influential central banker, Takahashi's deficit financing could not have been put into practice.

> It was the hardest task to work out the problem of how the BOJ would properly provide the extremely contracted monetary situation due to the lifting of the gold embargo with additional currency. It might be the easiest way in which the BOJ would give loans directly to the weakened industries. However, it would reflect on the future course of the business world.... It is opportune for the BOJ to keep close contact with the financial markets by its purchase and sale of government bonds. The BOJ's purchasing government bonds should mean the releasing of funds toward the financial markets, and it should be even better if the BOJ could take operations of selling government bonds at the same time. The BOJ should purchase government bonds in exchange for their funds to achieve the necessary level of currency supply. The BOJ had previously purchased some government bonds under a special consideration of the general financial conditions and the circumstances of a particular bank. I consulted such cases. Finance Minister Takahashi often urged strongly that the BOJ and the financial markets should keep close contact with each other. So I told him that the BOJ's purchase and sale of government bonds should mean the BOJ's contact with the financial markets. Finance Minister Takahashi extended this idea of purchase of negotiable bonds, and invented the idea of issuing government bonds

> directly through the acceptance of the BOJ. His idea of the BOJ's acceptance of new government bonds must be the same as my idea of the BOJ's purchase of negotiable bonds with respect to the supply of currency. This new measure worked in three ways, namely it facilitated the additional supply of currency, the bond issue to finance the Manchurian Incident, and a reduction of the level of interest rates.
>
> (Fukai 1941, in Japanese: 268–9, my translation)

In expression in economics, Takahashi extended Fukai's idea of open market operations with negotiable bonds, and decided to issue government bonds directly through the acceptance of the BOJ. Fukai's contribution to Takahashi's "Keynesian policy prior to Keynes" has been discussed a couple of times (See T. Nakamura 1978, in Japanese: 125–8, 1981, in Japanese, and 1994: 55–67; M. Nakamura 1982, in Japanese: 304–9).

Fukai's career undoubtedly contributed to his comprehension of economic policy. First, in 1904–5, Fukai efficiently assisted Takahashi in floating funds in London, Paris and New York in order to wage the Russo-Japanese War (Fujimura 1992a). Second, in the 1920s, Fukai had contact with the leading economists such as Kakujiro Yamazaki and Seibi Hijikata to exchange information on both the current economic situation and currency policy, and on the latest economic ideas (Fukai 1941, in Japanese: 368–9). Encouraged by Hijikata, Fukai published several books such as *The Adjustment of Currency Value* (1928, in Japanese) and *Monetary Policy after the Lifting of the Gold Embargo* (1929, in Japanese). Third, Fukai attended several international economic conferences. It could be said that he was known abroad as a capable central banker because he was commissioned to contribute his paper "The recent monetary policy of Japan" to the Festschrift volume for Irving Fisher entitled *The Lessons of Monetary Experience* (Gayer 1937; Fukai 1941, in Japanese: 370; Kindleberger 1973: 166). Fukai had an intellectual connection with Keynes because Keynes's "The theory of the rate of interest" was also included in Gayer (1937).

When the balance of debt was estimated to amount to 9.8 billion yen at the end of 1935, K. Takahashi planned to cut military expenses and decided to set the balance under the ceiling of ten billion yen. In November 1935, Takahashi explained the budget of 1936 and vehemently criticized the never-ending expansion of military expenses. On February 26, 1936, Takahashi was assassinated in the uprising of hundreds of young, armed nationalists (see Chapter 3).

7 Keynes's *A Treatise on Money* (1930) and *General Theory* (1936)

From 1930 on, the international community for economists was gradually finding a shape in the establishment of the Econometric Society in 1930 and the three international economics journals, *Zeitschrift für Nationalökonomie* (1930–), *Econometrica* (1933–) and *Review of Economic Studies* (1933–). As shown in Chapter 2, the international network of economists had already been extended to involve Japanese economists by the 1930s (Ikeo 1993a, 1994a, in Japanese; 1996). There is an apparent change in Keynes's own style of writing between *A Treatise on Money* (1930) and *General Theory* (1936). *A Treatise on Money* (1930) was addressed not only to academic economists but also to financiers, bankers and government officials. On the other hand, *General Theory* (1936) was addressed solely to Keynes's fellow economists who had a strong theoretical interest.

It is not surprising that there were two groups of Japanese economists regarding the acceptance of Keynes (1936). One was a group of monetary economists who started to read Keynes's writings from their interest in current international monetary policy problems and accepted his new ideas as the new monetary economics. Most of them were advised by Torajiro Takagaki to pick up Keynes. Another was a group of theoretical economists who started to pay attention to Keynes when his *General Theory* (1936) became available. In other words, they had not read Keynes's other books on monetary problems so closely. They usually criticized Keynes's unfamiliar ideas and each building block of his theory.

On the one hand, Japanese monetary economists preferred *A Treatise on Money* (1930) although they gave high praise to *General Theory* (1936). For example, Nisaburo Kito (1900–47), the most enthusiastic Japanese admirer of Keynes, discussed both books in his *Dynamics of Money and Interest* (1942, in Japanese). The title tells us that N. Kito rated *A Treatise on Money* (1930) higher. He also published the Japanese version of Keynes's *A Treatise on Money* (1930) in five volumes during 1932 and 1934. Keynes in the new preface of the Japanese edition explained his defensive discussion in response to the reviews he had received. He also announced the publication of a short book in the near future, which was to become *General Theory* (1936). Several Japanese scholars ordered copies of the new book on its publication, and began to make their students study this difficult book in seminars a couple of months later.

On the other hand, two Japanese theoretical economists, Kei Shibata (1902–86) and Yasuma Takata (1883–1972), discussed Keynes's *General Theory* (1936) in English as well as Japanese, and contributed their papers in English to *Kyoto University Economic Review*. Three reviews, Kei Shibata (1937, 1939) and Takata (1937), were referred to in D. Dillard's *The Economics of John Maynard Keynes* (1948: 57–8). Dillard (1948: 57–8) stated, "Shibata's articles are excellent." In fact, Shibata's experience and review were worth discussing in detail for two reasons. First, Keynes gave his comments on a draft of the review. Second, some points of Shibata's criticism were typical at the time. For instance, Shibata rejected the paradox of savings.

Shibata was studying under J. A. Schumpeter at Harvard University when Keynes's *General Theory* was published in January 1936. According to Shibata's observation (Shibata 1937: 83),

> [S]o many brilliant economists of the younger generation, whom I happened to meet while traveling in England and [the] United States of America,

> seemed to have been so dazzled by Mr. Keynes' convincing argument as to forget entirely the more fundamental unemployment problem inherent in the capitalist system of production.
>
> (Originally written in English)

Some readers might recall Paul Samuelson's memory of the impact of what has been called "The Keynesian Revolution" in his "Lord Keynes and the General Theory" (1946: 187) as follows:

> The *General Theory* caught most economists under the age of 35 with the unexpected virulence of a disease first attacking and decimating an isolated tribe of South Sea islanders. Economists beyond 50 turned out to be quite immune to the ailment. With time, most economists in-between began to run the fever, often without knowing or admitting their condition.

It is well known that Robert Bryce, a Canadian student, who had attended Keynes's lectures based on the final draft of the *General Theory* (1936) at Cambridge University, introduced Keynes's new theories to Harvard by challenging notable economics professors. Samuelson was a graduate student at Harvard while Shibata was 34 but an analytical Marxian economist.

Early in 1937, Shibata left the United States for England. Shibata carried the reference letter, which was written by Hiroshi Saito, the ambassador to the United States, for Shibata to meet Shigeru Yoshida, the ambassador to the United Kingdom. In London Yoshida asked Shibata to stay in London to attend the coming international economic conference (which was to be canceled) instead of visiting the Kiel Research Institute for Business Cycles. In return, Yoshida agreed to write a letter for Shibata to meet Keynes. Keynes wrote back to Yoshida and told him that he could meet Shibata. Shibata sent both his schedule and his questions about Keynes (1936).[15] Keynes wrote his responses directly on the margins of Shibata's letter of questions in his own handwriting and this might have been very useful for Shibata in exploring the problems. On April 20, 1937, Shibata lunched with Keynes, Lydia Lopokova and an American official at Keynes's house (Shibata 1987, in Japanese: 63). Yet they did not engage in any serious discussion on the *General Theory*.[16] Shibata reported Keynes's cynical comments on Japanese economists: "Whenever my new book is announced, five or six letters come from Japan asking for its translation right. This happens only in Japan" (Shibata 1987, in Japanese: 63; translated into English in Hamada 1986: 464 note 6). Returning to Japan, Shibata completed his "Some questions on Mr. Keynes's general theory of employment, interest and money" (1937) referring to Keynes's reply, although he did not mention his own communication with Keynes. Shibata questioned several aspects of Keynes (1936). Some points of Shibata's criticism are worth reproducing because he made several relevant remarks which represented typical responses to Keynes (1936), and recall for us the disadvantages of Keynesian economics.

First, Shibata (1937: 85) criticized Keynes's aggregate analysis of the employment problem and argued that the volume of employment should depend on the attitude of laborers as follows:

> [T]he volume of employment and the real wages are determined, according to Keynes' equation system, independently of the attitude of labourers towards their supply of labour. But, how is this made possible? Evidently by presupposing a certain given level of money-wages. He asserts "this simplification … is introduced solely to facilitate the exposition" and that "the essential character of the argument is precisely the same whether or not money-wages, etc., are liable to change."… But is it really so? Doesn't the very fact that some assumption as to money-wages is indispensable for the determination of the volume of employment and of real wages necessarily mean that the attitude of the labourers concerning money-wages influences the volume of employment and real wages?
>
> (Originally written in English)

Second, Shibata pointed out that Keynes lacked an idea of technological innovation and assumed a constant ratio between investment goods (new and old) and the volume of the complementary labour. Shibata (1937: 88–90) said:

> Indeed it is one of the greatest faults of the capitalist system of production that such changes in the method of production as will increase the amount of investment in relation to complementary labour are introduced only for the reason that they are more profitable to the entrepreneurs, notwithstanding the fact that these changes diminish the volume of employment.… Mr. Keynes entirely neglects the fact that income is not a simple function of the volume of employment, but is at least a compound function of the volume of employment and the ratio between the volume of employment in general and that in investment goods industries … new investment may not necessarily increase the volume of employment but may possibly decrease it.
>
> (Originally written in English)

Third, Shibata rejected the paradox of savings and believed that the accumulation of capital was funded by saving, no matter if the saving be voluntary or by force (1937: 93). Keynes maintained that a decrease in the propensity to consume would result in a decrease in investment, or in Shibata's terminology, an increase in the propensity to save would result in a decrease in the accumulation of capital. The typical perspective of the loanable fund theory of interest was given by Shibata as follows: "[A]n increase in the propensity to save will tend to increase the reserve funds of banks, inducing banks to lower the rate of interest, and thus encouraging the inducement to capital accumulation" (1937: 94).

Shibata continued to be critical of Keynesian economics after World War II as well. In other words, Shibata (and Yasuma Takata) never converted to Keynesian economics.

8 Some conclusions

Thanks to Tameyuki Amano's macroeconomics, some parts of Keynesian economics were known in Japan prior to the publication of Keynes's *General Theory* (1936). The discussion of Japan's return to the international gold standard or the lifting of the gold embargo around 1930 covered not only Keynes's criticism of Britain's return to the international gold standard but also his proposals for fighting against economic depressions which were to lead important elements of Keynes's *General Theory* (1936). Korekiyo Takahashi and Tanzan Ishibashi, who knew Amano very well, understood the paradox of savings around 1930 although Takahashi's "multiplier analysis" was incomplete in the sense that his multiplier process would explode to infinity. It is also noteworthy that Keynes's writing style changed and his audience shifted to theoretical economists in *General Theory* (1936) from monetary economists in *A Treatise on Money* (1930). Kei Shibata and Yasuma Takata's critical reviews written in English were cited in D. Dillard's *The Economics of John Maynard Keynes* (1948), which was read widely in many countries. Moreover, Shibata rejected the paradox of savings, which was one of the important building blocks of Keynesian macroeconomics.

Notes

1 This chapter is based on Ikeo (1997, 2004a). It has had a long gestation period. Variations of this chapter were presented at the joint meeting of Keizaigakushi Kenkyukai and Keizai Rironshi Kenkyukai at Rikkyo University on December 17, 1994, at the annual meeting of the Japan Society for the History of Economic Thought at Seinan Gakuin University on October 28–29, 1995, at the Second European Conference for the History of Economics in Lisbon on February 8–10, 1996, at the annual meeting of the History of Economics Society at the University of British Columbia in Vancouver in 1996, and at the lunch meeting on the History of Economic Thought at Duke University on September 10, 1996. I thank all the participants for their comments, suggestions and questions. I give special thanks to Robert Dimand, Atsushi Komine, Takeo Minoguchi, Masahiko Nasu, Ikuo Omori, Paul Pecorino, Michalis Psalidopoulos, Bo Sandelin, Hiroshi Yoshikawa, E. Roy Weintraub and the late Martin Bronfenbrenner for their information and comments.

2 I have written "Classical economics in Japan" (Ikeo 1998) and "Adam Smith in Japan" (Ikeo and Wakatabe 2000) at the request of the organizers of the related country study project. See also Sugiyama *et al.* (1993). I wrote "Marxist economics in Japan" (Ikeo 1996b) by receiving comments on earlier editions with reference to several survey articles in Japanese because Marxist and Marxian economists represented the majority in Japanese academia from 1945 until around the mid 1960s. Yet, I realized that there were several schools in the community of Marxian economists and that it was not my job to write a further English survey of their research activities.

3 R. Backhouse (1999) was the collection of the reviews on Keynes's *General Theory* (1936), which appeared in the same year, 1936. He organized them into three groups: reviews published in newspapers; general, literary and professional journals; and specialist academic journals.

4 In the World Bank's policy research report *The East Asian Miracle* (1993 IBRD publication), economic growth was noted in several East Asian countries, and the analysis

of the effect of market-friendly growth policies was the topic of discussion. The detailed analysis of the report had a favorable reception mainly within Japan, but opinions on the economic growth in East Asia were divided amongst economists in the US. Paul Krugman expressed his skeptical view that its growth was caused by the demographic dividend, and furthermore, was merely a result of government authoritarianism. In contrast, Josef Stiglitz adopted a neutral position, perceiving economic growth in East Asia as genuine. Note that they expressed these views outside of scientific journals. Moreover, the UK's Paul Moseley, Jane Harrigan and John Toye (1995), in the World Bank publication "Aid and Power," clarified that the 1993 IBRD publication was supported by the Japanese government's proposals and financial sponsorships. In other words, there was an eagerness to put the Japanese government in the firing line – in terms of public research – when it came to discrepancies between the historical record of the developing country that had shown the most continuous success and the World Bank, with its promotion of poverty countermeasures and "path to liberalization."

In the 1997 East Asian currency crisis, Thailand, Indonesia and South Korea had to accept financial assistance in the form of an "IMF package." Ten years later, at the 2007 Annual Meeting of the Asian Development Bank (ADB), Thai Finance Minister Chalongphob Sussangkarn unambiguously admitted that policies preceding the financial crisis of 1997 had been at fault (the combination of pegging exchange rates and fixing domestic interest rates, which were high). See also Richard Carney (2009) and Takatoshi Ito (2007).

5 Cohen (1950) was published in the fifth volume of the *Journal of Finance*, whose readers were usually business conscious. Cohen referred to Hyoye Ouchi's "Financial and monetary situation in post-war Japan" (1948), which was first presented at "A Symposium on the Democratization of Japan." Ouchi was very critical of the current Finance Minister Tanzan Ishibashi. Both Takahashi and Ishibashi had a close relationship with Tameyuki Amano. H. Ouchi translated Cohen (1949). T. Ouchi was the second son of H. Ouchi.

6 Actually Keynes's *General Theory* was published in January 1936 before Takahashi was assassinated on February 26, 1936.

7 S. Mori's "Fiscal policy of Korekiyo Takahashi, Finance Minister, 1932–36" (1975, in Japanese), S. Sasahara's "Theoretical basis for expansionary policy of K. Takahashi" (1981, in Japanese, 1997, in Japanese), T. Nakamura's "Takahashi's fiscal policy and public investment policy" (1981, in Japanese), M. Nakamura's *The Economic Crisis in Showa* (1982, in Japanese: 298–309), S. Shima's "On Takahashi's fiscal policy" (1983, in Japanese), R. Dimand's *The Origins of the Keynesian Revolution* (1988: 103), R. Komiya's "Keynes and Japan's economic policy" (1996, in Japanese) and others. Y. Cho's *The Showa Crises* (1994 [1973], in Japanese) regarded Keynesianism as managed currency policy and did not refer to (standard) Keynesian economics as defined in this chapter or P. Hall's *The Political Power of Economic Ideas: Keynesianism across Nations* (1989).

8 As seen in Chapter 3, Kakujiro Yamazaki was the best informed monetary economist in Japan from the 1910s through the 1930s. He had close contact with the mathematician Rikitaro Fujisawa and Japanese central bankers including Eigo Fukai in the 1920s and 1930s.

9 The phrase "there is only one country" was modified from the original text "Egypt is now the only country" (Keynes 1913: 71; *CW* vol. 1: 50).

10 K. Yagi's "Japanese translators found in the Keynes paper" (1997, in Japanese) examined the correspondence regarding to the translation rights between Keynes and the Japanese.

11 K. Ishimoto's "The population problem in Japan" (1922) discussed three alternative ways of solving the population question – emigration, the importation of foodstuffs, and birth control in order. I changed the order for logical clarity.

12 M. Yasukawa's "Lord J. M. Keynes and Dr. Tokuzo Fukuda" (1996, in Japanese) confirmed that Fukuda was three people to the left of Keynes in the memorial photograph of 1925 in Petrograd, located in R. Skidelsky's *John Maynard Keynes: The Economist as Saviour 1920–1937* (1992: 220–1).

13 Kaname Akamatsu, one of Fukuda's students, discussed the importance of technological development for continuous economic prosperity (Ikeo 2008).

14 T. Ishibashi (1971, in Japanese, vol. 8: 498) claimed that he repeated the argument which he had made in his radio talk entitled "The social meaning of savings" two years before. However, the list of his lectures (Ishibashi 1972, in Japanese, vol. 15: 186) shows that the talk was broadcast on August 27, 1930, and the draft of the talk was not included in his *Complete Works* (Ishibashi 1970–2, in Japanese).

15 Unfortunately, Shibata later lost his letter of questions with Keynes's answers (Shibata 1987, in Japanese: 60–3).

16 Keynes was not in good health at the lunch. Less than a week later, Shibata (1987, in Japanese: 64) learned from a newspaper that "Mr. Keynes had his brain broken and is hospitalized" (quoted in English).

10 Martin Bronfenbrenner and the reconstruction of the Japanese economy[1]

1 Economists in the twentieth century

This chapter gives an overview of the activities of Martin Bronfenbrenner (1914–97) (and other American officials) relating to the reconstruction of the Japanese economy in the period of 1945–52 by referring to the Bronfenbrenner Papers at Duke University and Carl Shoup's collections at Yokohama National University.

Bronfenbrenner was an American economist who was conversant with Japanese counterparts and well informed in Japan's economics and economy. Among his many publications in academic journals were a series of papers on "economic Japanology," lecture manuscripts for specific audiences unpublished at the time of his death, and his autobiography, which explores the background of his publications on Japan and his related social activities. By using both published and unpublished materials, this chapter aims to examine how he managed to communicate with Japanese economists when he visited Japan (three times) during the period immediately after the conclusion of the Asia-Pacific War (1937–45). It also discusses his caustic criticism of the monetary expansion policy started by Japanese Finance Minister Tanzan Ishibashi to bolster up the national reconstruction strategy based on the so-called priority production system, which itself was based on the so-called Austrian idea of a roundabout method of production (for the increment of productivity). It also sheds light on Bronfenbrenner's other activities in Japan and East Asia as a liaison to the Shoup Tax Reform Mission (1949–50) and a consultant to a UN organization in Bangkok (1951–2).

After 1952, Bronfenbrenner continued his travels in East Asia and helped a number of Japanese economists conducting research in US universities and participating in a conference of the Econometric Society. He stayed at Kobe University from 1963–4 and Kyoto University in 1980, visited Taipei to give lectures in 1979, and gave a series of lectures on "Economic Doctrines" at Nankai University, Tianjin, in 1982. Because of his appointment at the newly established Graduate School of International Politics, Economics and Communication of Aoyama Gakuin University in Tokyo in 1984, American *Eastern Economic Journal* decided to publish "A Conversation with Martin Bronfenbrenner" (1987a), in which he talked about some of his experiences in the 1940s and the early 1950s – how he had learned Japanese during World War II and what he had done in Japan after the end of the Pacific Campaign. After 1984, he resumed intensive communications with his old Japanese friends and, in response to frequent requests, collated his recollections of World War II and the period following and published a selection of them.

Bronfenbrenner returned to the US in 1991.[2] He was elected a distinguished fellow of the American Economic Association (AEA) for 1997 (AEA 1998). After his passing, Craufurd Goodwin wrote his obituary (1998) for the British *Economic Journal*. A round-table session in memory of Bronfenbrenner was organized at the annual meeting of the History of Economics Society in Montreal, Canada, in 1998 (Bronfenbrenner *et al.* 1999). His former Japanese colleague, Hiroshi Ohta, contributed his fond memories of Bronfenbrenner to the special 1999 issue of *Duke Journal of Economics*, which consisted mostly of essays written for the memorial gathering held at Duke University. Bronfenbrenner (1983: 50) described his own principal contributions: "Assisted in keeping general economics alive and making Japanological economics respectable." However, enough has not yet been published on his contributions in these fields or his intellectual connection with Japan. Bronfenbrenner's unfinished autobiography (1997) includes a formerly untold story about how he spent his student life at the University of Chicago in the 1930s and what he thought when he observed Japan's economy and policy during the Occupation period of 1945–52. Thanks to these unpublished materials, we can firmly discuss issues which hitherto were implied in published articles and books but were too indefinite to handle in a scholarly context.

Simultaneously, in order to understand how Bronfenbrenner managed to communicate with Japanese economists right after his first meeting with one in 1945, we should consider the development of a new economic science that makes more use of mathematics and statistics in research as well as the beginning of the age of periodicals with its smooth distribution of internationally oriented economics journals by surface mail starting around 1930. As discussed in Chapter 2, the year 1930 was especially important for the conscious internationalization of the economics profession not only in Japan but also in many countries. Internationally oriented economists swiftly laid a foundation for the formation of their world community after 1930. For economists in Japan and throughout the world, periodicals and journals became more important than published books as a means of professional communication and exchange of new ideas and analytical results. Japanese economists emphasized the impact of the three internationally oriented economics journals, namely *Econometrica* (1933), *Review of Economic Studies* (1933), and *Zeitschrift für Nationalökonomie* (1930). Under their influence, several young Japanese economists were encouraged to become involved in theoretical and mathematical economics rather than alternative non-mathematical approaches. The tendency was not restricted to Japanese economists but also true for the internationally oriented economists such as Henry Schultz, who supervised Martin Bronfenbrenner's thesis at the University of Chicago. There has been an apparent tendency among these scholars to favor the theorizing and modeling of economic ideas and statistical studies of economic issues rather than the descriptive, historical approach to economics.

Section 2 examines Bronfenbrenner's training as a professional economist and his intellectual relationship with the economists at the University of Chicago. His Japanese-related activities are then traced in chronological order, starting with his training as a language officer and his first communication with a Japanese economist at Kyushu University in 1945. He started to pay attention to Ishibashi's monetary policy prior to his second visit to Japan. From 1949–50, he stayed in Tokyo as a tax economist of the Economic and Scientific Section (ESS) and the Finance and Public Finance Section under the Supreme Commander for the Allied Powers (SCAP) as well as a liaison to the Shoup Tax Reform Mission and Japan's Ministry of Finance. He also participated in regular seminars at Hitotsubashi University. In November 1949, he and the ESS staff visited Ryukyu (Okinawa) to monitor its economy. From 1951–2, he joined the Economic Commission for Asia and the Far East (ECAFE), an umbrella organization of the United Nations (UN) in Bangkok, Thailand, which would expand to become the Economic and Social Commission for Asia and the Pacific (ESCAP). In the summer of 1952, he visited Kyoto and gave a series of lectures, thereby establishing intellectual ties with many Japanese economists. Finally, we will draw some conclusions.

2 Training at Chicago and Boulder

Martin Bronfenbrenner was born in Pittsburgh in December 1914. In 1934, he received his A.B. in Political Science and Economics from Washington University (St. Louis) and entered the Graduate School of Economics, the University of Chicago. It is worth noting that the university decided to give the talented 20-year-old a Hillman Fellowship grant and then the University Fellowship for his graduate study of economics. At Chicago, this very brilliant young scholar was taught by outstanding professors such was Frank Knight (1861–1933), Henry Simons (1899–1946), Henry Schultz (1893–1938), Jacob Viner (1892–1970) and Paul Douglas (1892–1976).

Bronfenbrenner also met many promising students who would eventually become more distinguished economists than their professors. Bronfenbrenner (1987a, 1997) listed among his Chicago fellow students four future Nobel Prize winners (Milton Friedman, Paul Samuelson, Herbert Simon and George Stigler), one future Chairman of the Council of Economic Advisers (Herbert Stein), one future President of the University of Rochester and Assistant Secretary of State for Economic Affairs (Allen Wallis), and two future high officials of the United Nations secretariat (Sune Carlson and Jacob Mosak).[3] Bronfenbrenner, full of elitist pride, confidently lived a different professional life from theirs as a general economist with a bird's-eye view of how economies and economics would work and how real institutions would matter in making economic policies.

Bronfenbrenner took Henry Schultz's course. Schultz was known in Japan for his econometric research on demand and supply curves (Schultz 1925, 1927), his theoretical consideration of supply (Schultz 1927), and his discussion of demand and the cobweb theorem (Schultz 1930). Schultz wrote his signature on the title page of his 1928 book and sent it to Eiichi Sugimoto (1901–52, see Chapter 7), which is located in the library of Hitotsubashi University. Bronfenbrenner (1997: 7–3, 4) commented on the professor:

> Professionally, he was its major empiricist, interested in the econometric problems of what demand and supply curves actually looked like, and how they shifted over time. His lectures were largely in the "general equilibrium" tradition, singularly clear, meticulously prepared, and supplemented by blackboard math and diagrams beautifully written or beautifully drawn.

(Bronfenbrenner's biography (1997) was paginated chapter by chapter. Therefore, (7–3, 4) means Chapter 7 and its pages 3 and 4.) Bronfenbrenner and the Japanese economists of his generation came to share the research tradition of Walrasian general equilibrium approach and empirical studies, and the interest in the theory of money. This tendency later helped him share economic knowledge with modern economists during his stay in Japan in the post-World War II period.

Bronfenbrenner completed his 391-page dissertation thesis entitled "Monetary Theory and General Equilibrium," under the strong influence of his supervisor before Schultz's sudden death at 46 in 1938. As suggested in the title, his thesis was a vast survey of his contemporary analytical achievements in general equilibrium approach and the theory of money. His list of references includes books in French including Léon Walras's *Elements d'économie politique pure* (1874–7) and its definitive edition (1924), Italian writings by Luigi Amoroso and Vilfredo Pareto, German articles including Hicks (1933), and Kei Shibata's critical review article (1937) on Keynes (1936).[4] Oskar Lange, another general equilibrium theorist and the future author of *Price Flexibility and Employment* (1944), moved Chicago from Boston in 1938 and suggested that he look up Shibata (1937) (Bronfenbrenner 1987b). Bronfenbrenner's thesis was written prior to the publication of J. R. Hicks's masterpiece *Value and Capital* (1939) although he referred to several of Hicks's journal articles. Later he helped Don Patinkin, who obtained a Ph.D. from the University of Chicago in 1947, to write the manuscript of *Money, Interest, and Prices* (Patinkin 1956). Their related correspondence (The Don Patinkin Papers) tells us that they shared the analytical framework and considered the details of theoretical discussion to be published in Patinkin's new book. Therefore, Bronfenbrenner was a general equilibrium economist, like Hicks and Patinkin, in favor of expressing a coordination of various economic activities via responding price signals in a market economy by using discrete models with the metaphor of a series of theoretical "weeks" in analysis of market coordination of individually made economic decisions in consumption and production. Although he received his Ph.D. from the University of Chicago in June 1939, he felt that, without his mentor, he had become an orphan in the community of economists.

Paul Douglas hired Bronfenbrenner as one of his assistants in statistical studies for estimating the coefficients in Cobb–Douglas production functions (Biddle 2011). In this way Bronfenbrenner gained the skills necessary for collecting research data and the knowledge of real institutions such as trade unions. Douglas had three fields of specialization, namely Labor Economics, Income Distribution, and Comparative Economic Systems. Bronfenbrenner had taken Douglas's course in Comparative Economic Systems, which dealt largely with Marxism, in the spring of his first graduate year and found an overlap with the Comparative Political Systems course he had taken at Washington University. Douglas's *The Theory of Wages* (1934) was basically a theoretical study of the labor share of the income distribution rather than a factual study of the labor market (Bronfenbrenner 1997: 7–4).

It is also important to note that the Keynesian revolution arrived in Chicago and the rest of the US right after the publication of Keynes's *General Theory* in January 1936. Bronfenbrenner (1997: 7–9) explored the Chicago economists' response to Keynes (1936) and, in spite of reading Shibata's critical review, his own conversion to Keynesian came after 1939:

> My graduate-school years spanned the "Keynesian revolution" in macroeconomics – the economic theory of income and employment. When I came to Chicago in 1934, Keynes was known to specialists, but "Keynesianism" meant nothing at all. By the time I took my degree (June 1939), Colonel McCormick of the *Chicago Tribune* had called Keynes "the Englishman who rules America" and "Keynesianism" was a label to conjure with – even among those with no idea of what Keynes had said, what he meant, or how his name should be pronounced.
>
> Copies of Keynes's General Theory of Employment Interest and Money accompanied into Chicago the followers that bloomed in the Spring of 1936. Having already completed course work in that general area but not the comprehensive examination covering it, my immediate reaction was that I had best hurry up and pass that examination before my examiners could hold me responsible for the contents of "Keynes's new book."

The impact of Keynes (1936) was immense. Two decades later the trend of thought changed again and Bronfenbrenner himself re-converted to non-Keynesian.

Bronfenbrenner had experience of working in the public sector: as an economist at the US Treasury in Washington, DC from 1940–1, and as a statistician and analyst at the Federal Reserve Bank in Chicago from 1941–3. The Pacific Campaign of World War II started in December 1941. He decided to volunteer to serve his country before being drafted (Bronfenbrenner 1987a, 1997). It seemed to him in the late fall of 1942 that there were two options open to him: to be a weather officer (meteorologist) or a language officer. After scrutinizing these options more closely, he realized that only the Japanese language was open to him. He enrolled in the Naval Training School in Oriental Languages

(NavTraSch OrLang), which was located on the University of Colorado campus at Boulder and registered for a 15-month intensive course. He was confident with his own language ability (this was why took up Japanese) and Japanese became his third language, with his second being French, and his fourth and fifth being German and Italian (personal communication with Teruko Bronfenbrenner on March 18, 2009). He graduated from the language school around May 1944, three months behind schedule because of a minor illness.

A few months later, he began his work in further language acquisition in Oahu, Hawaii (Bronfenbrenner 1997: 12–1). Bronfenbrenner participated in three translation projects and received frequent assignments to the Iroquois Point camp for prisoner-of-war (POW) interrogation. Although he had not been trained as a *kaiwa* (conversation) specialist in Boulder, before leaving Pearl Harbor he had acquired more self-confidence than his skills would support. His interrogation experience was told in Bronfenbrenner (1987a) and cited in the announcement of his election as a distinguished fellow of the AEA for 1997 (AEA 1998). Therefore, it is well known by American economists.

Bronfenbrenner was eager to keep in contact with economists and went to the University of Hawaii campus in the Manoa Rainforest. Professor Cameron, the Chairman of the Economics Department, was interested in income distribution issues by justifying income inequality because it provided for private charity by increasing scope. He wanted Bronfenbrenner to teach a regular course in Comparative Economic Systems at Hawaii, including Marxism. Although Bronfenbrenner was all set to begin classes in February, the Navy abruptly forbade regularly scheduled outside activities by its personnel.

3 First visit to Kyushu in 1945

The Japanese Emperor's message of the acceptance of unconditional surrender was recorded on disk in a studio on August 14. It was ciphered and wired from Tokyo to military bases inside and outside of Japan shortly before noon on August 15. It was then broadcast by radio throughout mainland Japan and the military fronts. The same contents were deciphered around the time of the conclusion of the radio broadcast at each base. It was the end of the war in East Asia. The people in charge of the bases and private correspondents were informed around August 10 that a very important message from Tokyo would become public on August 15 (Ikeo 2008). On September 2, Mamoru Shigemitsu, leading plenipotentiary of Japan, signed the Instrument of Surrender on the battleship Missouri in Tokyo Bay.

The Allied Powers, led by General Douglas MacArthur, occupied Japan from September 1945 until April 1952. The Occupation period was longer than necessary for disarmament, economic relief and the establishment of democracy in Japan because of the onset of the Cold War in 1947. The Americans or their Allies destroyed facilities capable of making nuclear weapons, and worked painstakingly to calculate how much effort and money they needed to allow Japan to stand on its own and to be incorporated into an international community based on free trade.[5] They also monitored the postwar settlements in East Asia (Far East) and Southeast Asia, conducted a comparative study of the nations in these regions to get a better understanding of them, and tried to promote intra-regional trade (Ikeo 1996). (This concern would lead to the establishment of ECAFE and later ESCAP.)

Bronfenbrenner came to Japan for the first time in the fall of 1945. Like many younger soldiers and officers he arrived in Sasebo, Nagasaki Prefecture, Kyushu (the second largest island of Japan, after Honshu). Nagasaki is the most western prefecture in Japan, the closest to Korea and China. Even now it takes more than two hours by plane from Tokyo to Nagasaki. Nagasaki is a little closer to Beijing and Pyongyang than to Tokyo. Bronfenbrenner's attitude to Japanese intellectuals was probably more cautious and polite than any other non-Japanese. It can be said that he was looking at the human aspects of the Japanese people.

It seems that the American side made a request to the Japanese side to find a Japanese economist in the Kyushu area who could communicate with a Chicago-trained economist. Yukichi Kurimura (1899–1983) was the economist chosen and became the first Japanese modern economist whom Bronfenbrenner encountered on Kyushu. Kurimura, a former student of Yasuma Takata, whom Bronfenbrenner would later call the Japanese Marshall, had published books including *Theory of Monopolistic Prices* (1939) and *Theory of Price* (1941). After meeting Bronfenbrenner, Kurimura published *Price and Money* (1949a), *Production and Distribution* (1949b), and *Economic Measurement* (1949c) when printing companies returned to normal business.[6] Bronfenbrenner visited Kyushu University in Fukuoka. Kurimura was the only Japanese economist that Bronfenbrenner met in 1945. Both modern economists maintained vivid memories of that first dramatic encounter in a chaotic environment. Let us see an observation from Bronfenbrenner (1997: 13–11):

> On my first day off I went there still in full regalia – loaded gun and all – in search of an economist with whom I might talk. A janitor led me from the main gate through dark corridors of dark buildings, windows being still blackened out as air-raid defenses. Eventually we reached an office where a starved-looking professor, perhaps 15 years older than myself, was conducting a seminar for two starved-looking students. Everyone's clothes were patched, and *the room should have been heated but wasn't* [italics added]. When I appeared, the professor thought my mission might be his arrest, and he was visibly shaken. But on his rickety blackboard was written what looked like a Cobb-Douglas production function, and I immediately established my credentials as a student and former assistant of Professor Douglas at Chicago. The professor was Kurimura Yukichi [*sic*], who turned out to be almost the sole non-Marxist in the Kyushu Faculty of Economics as reconstructed under the Occupation. We became friends on the spot, took walks together all over Fukuoka, and discussed the prospects for Japanese economic recovery in pessimistic tones. Later we met from time to time, mainly in Japan but also in America, until shortly before Professor

Kurimura's death in 1983. His talents, incidentally, extended well beyond economics into botany, calligraphy, architectural design, and university administration.

Bronfenbrenner expressed the Cobb-Douglas function as follows:

$$P=bL^{k}C^{j},$$

where *P*, *L* and *C* represent product, labor and capital (or index numbers of these quantities), while *b*, *k* and *j* are determined by the statistical method of least squares. Nine years later, Kurimura (1954) expressed his good impression mutually shared by Bronfenbrenner but he insisted that it was warm enough to do without heating. Their longtime friendship started the moment that they recognized each other as modern economists in the sense of Oskar Lange's terminology. A number of Japanese modern economists, who were doing similar research and teaching as Kurimura, could be found in Kobe, Kyoto, Yokohama, Tokyo and Sendai, whereas Marxist economists, who had been opposed to the war, were rehabilitated in Japanese academia and gained political power. The Americans found Fukuoka the most comfortable place to stay on Kyushu. However, it was decided that Bronfenbrenner was scheduled to return to the US in December 1945. He was transported to Tokyo from Kyushu by slow train stopping at each station for nearly 36 hours. He viewed the scenes of one bombed-out and burnt city after another. His train passed both Hiroshima and Kyoto in the middle of the night. He left Japan on a clear, crisp December morning, aboard the aircraft carrier USS *Lexington*, bound for San Francisco with no stop at Pearl Harbor. He landed at Alameda, on the Oakland side of San Francisco Bay (Bronfenbrenner 1997, 13–15, 16). He worked again as a financial economist at the Federal Reserve Bank in Chicago from 1946–7 and as an associate professor at the University of Wisconsin from 1947–57.

4 The purge of Finance Minister Tanzan Ishibashi and the Dodge Line (1947–9)

By reading Bronfenbrenner's published and unpublished writings, it is possible to ascertain what the Americans were thinking about the policy for the reconstruction of Japan's economy during the Occupation period. Bronfenbrenner's second visit to Japan was brought about by his involvement in the Shoup Tax Reform Mission in 1949 and on this occasion he was stationed mostly in the capital city Tokyo. He acted as a tax economist of the Economic and Scientific Section (ESS) and the Finance and Public Finance (FPF) Section under SCAP, as well as a liaison to the Shoup Tax Reform Mission (1949–50) and Japan's Ministry of Finance (MOF). Prior to his arrival in Japan, he obtained enough information about Japan's economic conditions to grasp the characteristics of Finance Minister Ishibashi's monetary policy, and the nature of the Dodge Line. There are several necessary conditions for a market economy to work efficiently for the allocation of economic resources in a real economy. The implementation of the deflationary Dodge Line fortunately became a prerequisite for the tax reform tasks of the Shoup Mission.

In May 1947, Finance Minister Ishibashi was purged from his public position by SCAP because SCAP believed that his monetary policy was causing the current inflation (not hyperinflation) and disturbing its Occupation policy for the reconstruction of Japan's economy.

Although the postwar Japanese economy was suffering from serious inflation, Ishibashi stuck to his own belief in policy measures and tried to keep increasing money supply by issuing national bonds through the Reconstruction Finance Corporation (*Fukko Kinnyu Kinko*), which was established literally for lending money to those who needed it for economic recovery based on the governmental recovery plan. The bonds were purchased by the Bank of Japan during the period when Ishibashi was Finance Minister. Ishibashi believed that he was implementing the right policy, whether it was called Keynesian or not, for the reconstruction of the Japanese economy. However, this policy was vehemently criticized by several Japanese economists such as Hyoye Ouchi and Hiromi Arisawa, who thought that a policy of stimulating production capability was the first priority for the war-torn economy. Moreover, SCAP regarded the Reconstruction Finance Corporation as the biggest obstacle to the economic recovery process of Japan. After Ishibashi was removed from public service, Japan's economic policy was changed toward the belt-tightening direction and this direction was reinforced by the so-called Dodge Line.

Japanese political scientists like Hiroshi Masuda (1996) put his focus on the purge of Ishibashi not only by scrutinizing related official documents but also by traveling to the US to get direct hearings from some former SCAP officials, and he could find no reason good enough to remove the Finance Minister.

Bronfenbrenner kept his keen interest in inflation theory and later coauthored with F. D. Holzman "Survey of inflation theory" (1963), which established their reputation in the field. Reading the manuscript of the financial history of Japan during the Occupation period (1945–52) edited by Japan's MOF, Bronfenbrenner (1975) confessed that "inflation theorizing" was never monolithic among the economists within SCAP and some Japanese related to SCAP, and he counted at least six different theories: (1) "Ishibashi" Keynesianism; (2) "Vulgar" Marxism; (3) "OPA" direct control; (4) "Sound finance" fiscalism; (5) "Banking school" monetarism; (6) "Old Chicago School" price flexibility. Bronfenbrenner discussed these theoretical positions in the same order.

Let us make a brief summary. (1) He repeated his criticism of Ishibashi's Keynesian views and stated that Ishibashi tried to apply Keynes's macroeconomics not to a depressed economy but to economic recovery without considering any inflation during a postwar period. (2) Marxist economists maintained that prices went up because firms passed the rises in wages on to the prices of products. (3) The US Office of Price Administration (OPA) was in operation during the war and ended in the latter half of 1946. A substantial number of its former officers found positions in Japan. Sincere devotees of OPA doctrine believed that the way to control the price level was to control those individual prices most important in ordinary people's market baskets.[7] (4) According to "Sound finance" fiscalism, deficit financing in the government (public expenditure in excess of tax receipts) was regarded as the main cause of "hyperinflation." The idea was most supported within SCAP and became the basis for the deflationary Dodge Line. (5) "Banking school" monetarism, which was a combination of monetarist doctrine and tight-money policy, became the second basis of the disinflationary program for postwar Japan. It stated that a reduction in money supply was necessary for curbing inflation. (6) "Old Chicago School" price flexibility gave a description of Bronfenbrenner's position. The "old" Chicago monetarists he had in mind were Henry Simon and Lloyd Mints rather than "new" monetarists (Milton Friedman and his disciples). He meant a direct concern with price level as such, rather than with money supply and its growth rate. Firms would then be able to make rational decisions by acting on price flexibility, namely a smooth operation of the price mechanism. It can be said that, by resorting to (4), (5) and (6), SCAP economists were primarily concerned with price stability and expected to see a natural economic recovery occur in the private sector.

As mentioned, after Ishibashi was removed from public service, Japan's economic policy was changed in the belt-tightening direction especially by Josef M. Dodge of the Detroit Bank (later Director of the Budget in the Eisenhower administration), who was sent to Japan to suppress the postwar potential hyperinflation. The Nine-Part Interim Directive on Stabilization (December 11, 1948), which has been called the Dodge Line, directed Japan's government to adopt measures designed to:

(1) achieve a true balance in the consolidated budget at the earliest possible date by stringent curtailing of expenditures and maximum expansion in total government revenues, including such new revenue measures as may be necessary and appropriate;
(2) accelerate and strengthen the program of tax collection and insure prompt, widespread and vigorous criminal prosecution of tax evaders;
(3) assure rigorous limitation of credit expansion to projects contributing to the economic recovery of Japan;
(4) establish an effective program to achieve wage stability;
(5) strengthen and, if necessary, expand the coverage of existing price control programs;
(6) improve the operation of foreign trade controls and tighten existing foreign exchange controls, to the extent that such measures can appropriately be delegated to Japanese agencies;
(7) improve the law effectiveness of the present allocation and rationing system, particularly to the end of maximizing exports;
(8) increase production of all essential indigenous raw materials and manufactured products;
(9) improve efficiency of the food collection program.

Japan's MOF (1976: 395) gave a detailed description of the Dodge Line process, and said, "It was their threat of finalizing aid that forced the Japanese reluctantly to accept the implementation of Dodge's Nine Part Directives." Bronfenbrenner did not go this far. After the implementation of the directive, the prices of commodities on the black markets began to decline and finally the price level was stabilized, but it was accompanied by formidable social instability including massive unemployment.

5 The Shoup Mission in Tokyo, 1949–50

Neither the American nor the Japanese side ever thought that the introduction of several temporary taxation measures to control rampant inflation was sufficient to attain the target of economic reconstruction. They agreed with each other that Japan had to reestablish a robust taxation system with strong authority to secure tax revenue for the achievement of "more sound finance." Based on a natural and mutual agreement between SCAP and the Japanese side, General Douglas MacArthur made Harold Moss, an ESS official, fly to New York to meet Carl S. Shoup, specialist in public finance, at Columbia University, requesting him to form a tax mission to reform the entire Japanese tax system both at central and local levels. Thus Shoup became the chairman of a new Mission with the economist Howard R. Bowen, William Warren, Stanley Surrey, William Vickrey and Bronfenbrenner. Rolland Hatfield (Director of Tax Research, State of Minnesota) and Jerome B. Cohen (specialist in Japanese economic institutions) also joined the Mission.[8] They arrived in Tokyo in the spring of 1949 and the four volumes of the *Shoup Report* were nearly completed around the time that Bronfenbrenner arrived in Japan after a long voyage across the Pacific Ocean.[9]

Although he did not add his signature to the report, Bronfenbrenner acted as if he had been a formal member of the Shoup Mission because he was asked to join the mission in Japan and stay on in Tokyo after its departure. Thus he officially became a tax economist in the Public Finance Division of the Economic and Scientific Section of SCAP, his appointment to last for two years. He acted both as a revenue estimator by visiting various scenes of tax estimation and as liaison between the Shoup Mission, which was back in the US, the Public Finance Division of SCAP and Japan's MOF. Prior to leaving the US, he shared with Shoup the ideas on the basic principles of taxation such as "Fairness (Equity), Economic Efficiency, and Administrative Feasibility."[10] He was delighted to get a chance to improve his Japanese and to visit Japan for a second time (Bronfenbrenner 1997, 14–17).

In Japan, the mission members, full of research enthusiasm, were all excited by the challenge of tax reform and believed that they were trying to implement an ideal tax system on the clean slate of a non-Western country. Bronfenbrenner (1957: 237) tells us of their excitement:

> The Shoup tax reform is interesting, then, as a case study of the accomplishments of a Western tax mission in a short period under (nearly) ideal

conditions. It is interesting more particularly to Americans as a case study of an Occupation-sponsored, economic reform in Japan.

In writing a tax reform recommendation report, they were very cautious of not proposing an unworkable idea not worth the paper it was written on. They referred to the currently existing US tax system and imagined being able to reform it and establish a new, ideal one. Then they recommended that Japan establish the best tax system that they could imagine as reform missionaries.

Right after the release of the *Shoup Report*, which was not regarded as a report by the Japanese side but as a tax reform recommendation, in August 1949, Japanese tax officials (including MOF bureaucrats), business leaders and public finance specialists (including tax law specialists and economists) read it carefully and put it through a series of examinations and discussions. Later, the Japanese official assessments of the recommendation and its implementation were made public by the release of MOF (1976, 1977, 1990, 1997), and recent scholarly studies were conducted by Hiromitsu Ishi (2001, 2008) and the special issue "The significance and problems of the Shoup Recommendations: examinations after 50 years' of *Japanese Tax Law Review*" (2000).[11] The related historical materials, such as official documents, the timely commentaries released by stakeholders and the articles carried in newspapers and magazines, were collected in Yukihiro Fukuda *et al.* (eds) (1985) and Ichiro Inoue (ed.) (1988). Shoup (1988), Bronfenbrenner (1950b, 1957), and Bronfenbrenner and Kogiku (1957) may be included in the assessments by the American side.

Let us see the fundamental substantive points of the recommendations summarized by Bronfenbrenner (1997, 15–3).

(1) Retention of a direct rather than an indirect tax system, with a high degree of income tax progression. This represents a break with Japan's prewar tax tradition, but continues previous Occupation policies, and is based on contemporary (1940s) American practice.
(2) Introduction of numerous refinements, both substantive and administrative, designed to reduce evasion and avoidance, and at the same time to increase progressivity. Many of these had been developed by Professor William Vickrey (a Mission member) and adapted from Vickrey's *Agenda for Progressive Taxation* (1947).
(3) A shift in tax receipts from the central to the local government bodies to give the latter more revenue sources independent of Tokyo as the financial basis for local autonomy.
(4) Revaluation of individual and corporate assets to take account of wartime and postwar inflation, and permit realistic provision for depreciation reserves and eventual replacement of capital.

In reality, Japan's Yoshida Cabinet and the ruling Liberal Party considered the Shoup proposals "too theoretical," namely too complex for practical administration in Japan, although they shared the American Occupation's interest in tax reform. As Bronfenbrenner (1997: 15–3) knew, the Japanese side would have preferred greater encouragement for saving and investment, and less concern with effects upon the distribution of income and wealth. Somehow or other, the Shoup Recommendation was almost entirely implemented in both the 1949 supplementary budget and the 1950 budget (Bronfenbrenner's activities will be mentioned below). However, right after the Peace Conference in San Francisco in September 1951, Japan's government was given back the real power for its economic policies and began to abolish parts of the "reforms" enforced by the visitors from outside during the Occupation. The government began to utilize tax measures for the implementation of the policy targets such as "Increase in Savings, Capital Accumulations, and Industrial Development," which was not in accord with American practice and was strongly reproved of by the Shoup Mission. Therefore, the postwar Japanese tax system was sometimes regarded as a detachment process from the Shoup Tax Recommendations.

With regard to the summary of the aftermath of the Shoup tax reform and the following modifications, *The Japanese Tax System* (2001) authored by Hiromitsu Ishi, the public finance specialist who for a long time led the discussion of tax policy in Japan, gave a lucid explanation from the Japanese side. Referring to Bronfenbrenner (1950b) and Bronfenbrenner and Kogiku (1957), Ishi (2001, 29–30) stated:

> From the beginning ... some of the Shoup tax plans were criticized as being too theoretical to be carried out, given the state of socio-economic development in postwar Japan. No doubt, the Mission thought of tax reform primarily in terms of US practice and experience. This was apparent in such matters as the treatment of capital gains taxation or the emphasis on "local autonomy." Accordingly, modifications to the Shoup tax system were implemented shortly after 1950.
>
> Two tendencies emerged from these modifications. One was the revival of the old system: equity was sacrificed for the convenience of incentives and administration. The other was the reduction of the tax burden of firms, especially big businesses. The goal of this trend was to give priority to the restoration of the postwar economy and the promotion of capital accumulation....
>
> The most symbolic modification of the Shoup system occurred with the repeal of full taxation on capital gains from sales of securities in 1953.... The net worth and accession taxes were abolished in 1953 because of inadequate revenues. *The value added tax was not even brought into operation....*
>
> When the Japanese government departed from the Shoup system, its departure was not in the direction of further experimentation, but towards a return to prewar traditions and practices which it considered particularly suitable to the Japanese economic situation. Thus, the tax innovations advocated in the Shoup Report were disregarded.
>
> (Italics added)

We need to pay attention to the argument of the value-added tax (VAT) system. As emphasized in Bronfenbrenner (1950b, 1997), the Shoup Mission confidently recommended the introduction of VAT at local level. In fact, Bronfenbrenner (1950b: 298) shed light on the importance of value-added sales tax and defined it as "a system of sales taxation to be applied at each stage of production on the part of the product's value which originates at that specific stage." VAT was supposed to become the principal independent revenue source for the Japanese prefectures (*ken*, *do* and *fu*), which are usually smaller than American states and rather larger than the average American county. As mentioned in the above quotation from Ishi (2001), although Japan's Local Tax Law of 1950 represented its first detailed overall application of a VAT system, the effective date of the new law was postponed twice to 1952 and then it was abolished due to the endless controversy over the characteristics and viability of VAT in Japan. Later Bronfenbrenner (1963: 296) pointed out that the Japanese term "*fuka-kachi*" was created by translating "value-added" because there was no corresponding term in the Japanese dictionary. Japanese local officials simply lacked the authority of experience in collecting taxes at various production stages. The owners of mom-and-pop stores did not make it a rule to keep books (personal communication with Bronfenbrenner *c.* 1987).

Bronfenbrenner (1997: 15–5) wrote about the political results of the Shoup proposal:

> The proposed value-added tax (VAT) was a greater failure. It passed the Diet in 1950, with its application postponed to 1951. The postponement was later repeated in 1951. When the Occupation ended in 1952, the prefectural VAT of the Shoup Mission was quietly forgotten. After its widespread adoption in Europe VAT has received renewed attention in Japan, but only at the national level. A form of it was adopted in 1989.

If the VAT system had been adopted, Japan's current public deficit and the stock of national bonds might have been much smaller than the present amount (even before the major earthquakes hit the Tohoku and Kanto regions of Japan on March 11, 2011).

On weekdays except Wednesdays, Bronfenbrenner assumed a job as a revenue estimator with the help of Taro Yamane, who was born in New York and was a graduate in Economics of Hitotsubashi University, Tokyo. Yamane knew both languages and gave Bronfenbrenner a lot of help. He would later obtain his Ph.D. at Wisconsin University and become known as the author of textbooks in mathematics and statistics for economists (Yamane 1962, 1967).[12] Returning to Japan, he was appointed as professor at Aoyama Gakuin University, and was responsible for recruiting Bronfenbrenner as an English-speaking professor to teach international economics, just before his passing in 1979.

6 The Dodge Line and tax reform

The understanding and evaluations of the projects executed during the Occupation might differ between the people in power during occupation and the people in the occupied country. Bronfenbrenner discussed this kind of problem in his paper strangely titled "Balm for the visiting economist" (1963) by pointing out the perception gaps of postwar reforms conducted during the Occupation period between the outside visitors drafting reforms and the domestic officials implementing the reforms. Bronfenbrenner (1963: 295) said:

> Ranking high among SCAP's weakness was its early loss of the sympathy of all substantial groups of Japanese intellectuals.... In the Economic and Scientific Section of SCAP there was pervasive underestimate and mistrust of the Japanese academic and civil service counterparts of the top Occupationaries.

Therefore, it is very interesting to see the visitor's understanding of the close relationship of two missions, namely the disinflationary Dodge Line and the Shoup Tax Reform Mission. Bronfenbrenner (1950b) believed that the problems of Japanese financial reconstruction involved issues which transcend American interest in Japan and are worthy of consideration in a broader setting. It is worth quoting from Bronfenbrenner (1997: 15–2, 3):

> It is never easy, even for an Occupation independent of popular votes, to stop a major inflation in its tracks by methods short of Nazi or Stalinist dictatorship. SCAP in 1949 was in the position of doing precisely that, after three years or more of feckless piddling with the inflation problem, by the combined efforts of its own Finance and Public Finance Divisions and a number of outside consultants. The most important of these latter were Joseph Dodge, a Detroit banker of orthodox leanings ([former US Secretary of the Treasurer] Andrew Mellon model), Ralph Young of the Federal Reserve [of New York], and of course Professor Shoup himself.

Ralph Young visited Japan for the consultation of the exchange rate for Japan to join the Bretton Woods par value system, which was supported by the International Monetary Fund (IMF). Then Bronfenbrenner discussed the following four points of SCAP's famous (or infamous) Nine-Part Interim Directive on Stabilization (the price stability and eventual self-sufficiency) in Japan. They were closely related to his assignment. Bronfenbrenner (1997: 15–2) summarized:

(1) Restraint on public expenditures, with the exception (in practice) of "Termination of War Expenditures" (logistical support of the Occupation itself).
(2) Restraint on the growth of the currency component of the money supply (although the bank-deposit component remained quite free to expand).
(3) Drastic increase in tax collections from both direct and indirect taxed, and at both national and local levels.

(4) A balance, or some would say an overbalance or surplus, in the Central Government budget, including both the general account and the myriad of special accounts (some of them secret) in which deficits had previously been concealed.

Bronfenbrenner felt compassion for Japanese ordinary people, who hoped for "Tax Reduction" from the bottom of their hearts. However, it was somewhat different from the target of the Shoup Mission, which aimed to reform the entire tax system to increase tax revenue for the government. Bronfenbrenner (1997: 15–2) lamented:

> As far as the Japanese were concerned, the Mission merely shifted the total around from one tax to another, one income bracket to another, or one government unit to another, without reducing its total. (For some people that was enough to condemn it!)

Therefore, Bronfenbrenner realized that the reduction of public expenditure by conducting the Dodge Line was really necessary for the balance of the public budget.

7 Fixing the Ryukyuan yen in Okinawa, November 1949

In August 1947, private firms resumed trade with the rest of the world under governmental control like foreign exchange control. In April 1949, the Japanese yen became convertible into foreign currencies by fixing the single exchange rate at 1 dollar=360 yen, instead of complex, multiple rates set for various trade items. This was the first, important step forward in introducing foreign capital into a war-torn country like the Japan of the day. The Japanese economy started to make a recovery by increasing private trade and it was realized by both SCAP and the Japanese side that international trade in the private sector was critically important for an economic recovery.

In November 1949, Bronfenbrenner (Public Finance Section) and other SCAP economists (Economic and Scientific Section) were sent to Okinawa for ten days on a SCAP Mission to produce for the Ryukyu Islands the same speed of monetary and fiscal disinflation that Japan was achieving (Bronfenbrenner 1997: 15–18). Okinawa is the largest island of Okinawa Prefecture, which was called the Ryukyus at the time. Their mission chief, a Wisconsin trained Ph.D., was supposed to report to SCAP on reasons why the recovery of the Ryukyus was lagging behind that of the Japanese mainland, and needed to report on the extent to which the disinflationary perestroika of the Dodge Line might be applied there (Bronfenbrenner 1990).

Landed in Okinawa, they were confronted with the economic conditions of the area. It specialized in subtropical agriculture and had no industrial base worth mentioning. Bronfenbrenner's main target was supposed to be the Ryukyuan tax system but he realized that the problem of the exchange rate of the Ryukyuan yen with both the US dollar and the Japanese yen was the most urgent and serious. Because no one else was willing to fix an exchange rate for the Ryukyuan yen, he spent most of his time on that problem. By using the rudimentary price statistics for around ten key commodities, he compared the "weighted average of these prices" between Okinawa and the mainland and decided that one Ryukyuan yen had the approximate purchasing power of three Japanese yen. Referring to an elementary purchasing-power parity theory of foreign exchange rates, he suggested that the US dollar should equal 120 Ryukyuan yen, since the price of the dollar was set at 360 yen in April of the year. His suggested exchange rate for the Ryukyuan yen was adopted by SCAP and the rate was used until 1958, when the Ryukyuan yen was abolished and the islands adopted US currency for the few remaining years of American rule. Bronfenbrenner (1997, 15–9) proudly said, "I am thus one of the few international (or other) economists to have set an exchange rate by himself, more or less successfully." The doctrine of purchasing-power parity worked in deciding the exchange rates. His experience in Okinawa was made public for the first time in his "An airport economist in the Ryukyus (November 1949)" (1990) and a detailed description was given his autobiography (1997).

It is worth mentioning the two economic problems in Okinawa summarized by Bronfenbrenner (1997: 15–18, 9). First, wages on US projects were much lower than on the mainland. This problem was resolved to some degree by evaluating the Ryukyuan yen to the triple value. Second, although the Ryukyuan balance of payments with the US was strongly positive due to American employment of native labor, the dollar balances were simply accumulating in the Ryukyuan account in Washington, DC. The second problem remained unresolved although most of the mission members felt it strange that Ryukyuan balances in Washington were not spent for consumer goods, especially for clothing and building materials in short supply. Their stay in Okinawa was too short to deal with all the problems which the region had been suffering since the Occupation period.

However, a number of incidents forced Bronfenbrenner to return to the US earlier than the original plan of a two-year stay in Japan. He waited for some original members of the Shoup Mission to revisit Tokyo. After meeting them, he left Japan from Haneda Airport while Teruko, his future wife, saw him off on August 12, 1950. In March 1951, Isamu Yamada was invited to the Cowles Commission at Chicago because William B. Simpson, a member of the Econometric Society, visited Japan in the spring of 1947. Yamada managed to communicate with many economists in the United States until June 1951 and established a close tie with members of the Econometric Society (Chapter 7; Ikeo 2011a). Yamada carried a private massage for Martin from Teruko and later helped Teruko travel to Wisconsin. In September 1951, the Treaty of Peace with Japan was signed in San Francisco to bring Japan formally back to the international community (to be enacted in April 1952).

It is noteworthy that Shigeto Tsuru played a pivotal role in creating intellectual connections between the Americans and the Japanese. He served as a high-level consultant to SCAP and worked for the Economic Stabilization Board (ESB) of Japan's government. Tsuru published the Japanese summary of this Tax Mission with finance bureaucrats including Keiichiro Hirata. Moreover, Tsuru and economic bureaucrats including Saburo Okita coauthored the first white paper on the Japanese economy in 1947. Okita and many other government officials were trained as economists through doing jobs in the ESB. Later Okita was sent to the Economic Commission for Asia and the Far East (ECAFE) in Bangkok and met Bronfenbrenner.

8 ECAFE in Bangkok, 1951–2

Returning to the US, Martin Bronfenbrenner resumed teaching economics at Wisconsin. However, he searched for an opportunity to visit Japan and stay somewhere in East Asia. In 1951, he helped Yang Shu-chin, a Chinese student in International Economics at Wisconsin, get a position with the Economic Commission for Asia and the Far East (ECAFE, later ESCAP). ECAFE was established in 1947 as the regional development arm of the United Nations (UN) in order to seek to overcome some of the region's greatest challenges including regional trade. Its initial history was a little complicated but confirmed on the occasion of its sixtieth anniversary in 2007 (ESCAP 2007). It was established in 1947 in Shanghai, China, to assist in postwar economic reconstruction, and moved its headquarters to Bangkok in January 1949. ECAFE would later be enlarged and reorganized to focus on a wider coverage of the economic and social activities in a wider region and renamed the Economic and Social Commission for Asia and the Pacific (ESCAP). Palamadai S. Lokanathan, an Indian economist, was appointed the First Executive Secretary of ECAFE to head the Shanghai headquarters. Shu-chin wrote his doctoral dissertation on the complex Thai system of multiple currencies. Then, thanks to the efforts of Shu-chin and his wife Nancy, Bronfenbrenner was able to find a position as ECAFE consultant in 1951 (Bronfenbrenner 1997: 16–14).

When Bronfenbrenner joined ECAFE, its community was small but professional, and subdivided into three groups. The largest of these was Indian and the second in size and standing was Chinese. Bronfenbrenner belonged to the smallest Anglo-American group, but he was proud of the group because they had the closest ties to the Thai government and international business. Bronfenbrenner's job was to study the developing trade relations between Japan and the "ECAFE region" of South and Southeast Asia. He also noted that these relations could barely be called embryonic in 1951–2 although it was to become more important around 1960 (Bronfenbrenner 1997: 17–13).

As mentioned, Bronfenbrenner came to know Saburo Okita, who was appointed a chief economic analyst for ECAFE from 1952–3. He spoke English fluently and represented "the able Japanese bureaucracy" for a long time although Bronfenbrenner's following statement reflected his later image of the older Okita instead of the younger in Bangkok (Bronfenbrenner 1997: 17–7).

> The most eminent visitor was Dr. Okita Saburo [*sic*] of the Japanese Economic Stabilization Board, a planner of the future Japanese "miracle" and later foreign Minister of his country. Shu-chin himself, with his new Wisconsin doctorate, was the best member of a regular staff top-heavy with Chinese refugee bankers and retired civil servants whose methodology seemed to be the accumulation of as many numbers with as little explanation as possible.
>
> Japanese data being so shaky, my job was shifted to the editorial revision which became rewriting of large sections of ECAFE's Annual Report for the previous year (1951). Here my U.S. Treasury experience helped me; each member Government had veto rights over any reference to its country, so I did my best to avoid both outright lies and the whole truth.... In those days the main criterion of good economic policy was still the minimization of inflation; growthmanship was only a distant second.

ECAFE raised the economists who could make a professional study of this region and communicate with the economists in other regions. For example, ECAFE-related economists participated in the first round-table conference which was organized and held in Gamagori, Japan, in April 1960, and hosted by the International Economic Association (IEA, headquartered in Paris) and leading Japanese economists. Papers such as "Supply of entrepreneurs and technologists with special reference to India" by Lokanathan (National Council of Applied Economic Research, New Delhi), "Capital supply and economic growth: Sources of savings" by Shu-chin Yang (ECAFE), and "Choice of techniques: Japan's experience and its implications" by Okita (Economic Planning Agency, Tokyo) were presented and later included in the Proceedings *Economic Development with Special Reference to East Asia* (Berrill ed. 1964).

9 Some conclusions

One of Bronfenbrenner's first and most important missions in post-World War II Japan was to meet several Japanese modern economists and try to communicate with them on economic issues based on a common knowledge of economics. Many Japanese economists still remember his activities in Japan and some of them told the author not to forget that he stayed at Kobe University from 1963–4 and Kyoto University (Research Center of Southeast Asia) in 1980. At one time or another, he met almost all Japanese modern economists (in the terminology of Oskar Lange). In professional economics journals Bronfenbrenner published not only articles on inflation and distribution theory but also on Japan's economy and economics. He was active in both the academic world of traditional theoretical research and the real world of economic policymaking exemplified in exchange rate adjustments and implementations of tax reform recommendations. He also conducted empirical studies as an application of economic theory using economic data and statistical analysis with reference to knowledge of institutions (such as trade unions) changing over time. He was proud of being a general economist, as he called himself (Bronfenbrenner 1983), although the general trend was the subdivision of economics into more specific fields and increasing specialization within those fields.

It is worth re-evaluating Bronfenbrenner's observation of the Japanese economy and his analysis of American economic recovery policies as they afford a glimpse of how the situation in Japan appeared to those on the outside. The American occupationaries came to realize that a broader perspective was really needed for making policies for a national economy to make a recovery from a devastating situation. Bronfenbrenner closely analyzed Japan's monetary policy, the enforcement of reflationary policy, the implementation of the Shoup tax reform recommendation and its aftermath. He also realized that the establishment of a unified exchange rate promoted external trade and domestic economic recovery. He managed to fix the Ryukyuan yen by referring to the doctrine of purchasing-power parity. He contributed to human resource development, which was necessary for the smooth expansion of regional trade in the headquarters of ECAFE, Bangkok. Some Japanese economists believed that the Americans might have gotten new insight into economic knowledge and actual policy implementation by conducting their missions for the recovery and reconstruction of a national economy and that the insight might have led to forming IMF policies such as the Structural Adjustment Facility (SAF, 1986) and the Enhanced Structural Adjustment Facility (ESAF, 1987).

Personal communication

Teruko Bronfenbrenner, Durham, North Carolina, March–June 2009

Notes

1 This chapter is based on Ikeo (2011a).

2 In the early 1990s, Bronfenbrenner occasionally taught freshmen an introductory course in economics at Duke University because he believed that this was how an economist should live. He donated to Duke University his library of books, reprints, memorial collections written mainly in Japanese such as Shibata (1987) and manuscripts of his lectures.

3 Bronfenbrenner was most dazzled by Samuelson, who was an undergraduate student taking (or auditing) graduate courses like Schultz's in mathematical economics. Bronfenbrenner (1997, 7–11) said, "Overworked by the brilliance of the undergraduate Samuelson, I had been reassured by [Paul] Douglas that 'You needn't be a Samuelson to get along in Economics' – the best academic advice that I have ever received." Bronfenbrenner's autobiography (1997) was paginated chapter by chapter. Therefore, (7–11) means Chapter 7 and its page 11.

4 Lange replaced Schultz teaching economic theory and mathematical economics. He had a socialist inclination in the debate over economic calculations in a socialist economy and published his *On the Economic Theory of Socialism* (1938). He was at the University of Chicago from 1939–45. He was interested in reading Shibata's papers which appeared in *Kyoto University Economic Review* in the 1930s. Lange was the first Western economist who paid attention to Shibata. Lange in his "Marxian economics and modern economic theory" (1935) had referred to Shibata's "Marx's

analysis of capitalism and the general equilibrium theory of the Lausanne School" (1933). Lange basically called Walrasian general equilibrium theory "modern economic theory." Lange served as the first ambassador of socialist Poland (the People's Republic of Poland) to the US from 1945–6, and as the first delegate of Poland to the UN Security Council from 1946–7. (See Emmett ed. 2010; Walter D. Fisher, 1966; Kowalik 1987.)

5 According to James Abegglen (1926–2007), who arrived as a member of the United States Marine Corps in Sasebo, what they were doing was fieldwork similar to anthropologists' research methods (personal communication with Abegglen, 2000). Anthropologists tend to understand the value in a targeted non-Western or uncivilized society.

6 At the time, the word "econometrics" was translated into a couple of Japanese phrases such as "*keizai sokuteigaku*", "*ekonometorikkusu*" and "*keiryo keizaigaku*," which is the current preferred term.

7 John Kenneth Galbraith (1908–2006), a former head of OPA, visited Japan for the first time in the fall of 1945 as one of the leaders of the United States Strategic Bombing Survey team (Pacific). He reunited and established a firm friendship with Shigeto Tsuru, who had been trained at Harvard in the 1930s, although he was busy looking over Japan and its neighbors from an airplane. Galbraith made his second visit to Japan as the US ambassador to India in 1963. In 1968, he participated in the Symposium on Asian Development, held in Japan. Japanese intellectuals learned the American attitude toward Asia from the summary and a series of commentaries which appeared in a newspaper. The newspaper anticipated that major changes might occur in US foreign policy toward two Chinas in the new future. He continued to observe the changes in Japan and its economy by making visits in 1977, 1982, 1985, etc. (see Ikeo 2003b).

8 The formal members of the tax mission, and their professional connections, were as follows: Carl S. Shoup, School of Business and Graduate Faculty of Political Science, Columbia University, (Director of the Tax Mission); Howard R. Bowen, College of Commerce and Business Administration, University of Illinois; Jerome B. Cohen, Department of Economics, College of the City of New York; Rolland F. Hatfield, Director of Tax Research, Department of Taxation, St. Paul, Minnesota; Stanley S. Surrey, School of Jurisprudence, University of California, Berkeley, California; William Vickrey, Graduate Faculty of Political Science, Columbia University; and William C. Warren, School of Law, Columbia University (Foreword to the Report on Japanese Taxation by the Shoup Mission, 1949).

9 Although Bronfenbrenner (1997: Chapter 14) said he landed at Haneda Airport, he traveled by ship from the US to Japan according to his letter to Carl Shoup of August 12, 1949. He came into contact with Shoup at the 1947 AEA meeting and tried to find an opportunity to revisit Japan (Shoup's letter to Bronfenbrenner of February 17, 1949). Shoup and Harold Moss decided to assign him as a liaison (their correspondence in March 1949). The related correspondence is located in the Mission Correspondence in the Shoup Collection at Yokohama National University.

10 It was articulated very clearly later by Shoup. With regard to the new Japanese version of their tax report, Shoup (1985: 5) said:

> The members of the tax Mission hoped that their work would prove useful over a span of time as well as at the moment. For that reason, the basic principles of taxation were emphasized, notably fairness (equity), economic efficiency, and administrative feasibility. The fact that a new translation is now deemed worthwhile indicates this emphasis was proper.

We certainly know that only Bronfenbrenner could examine the quality of the new Japanese translation compared with the quick work done in 1949.

11 Included papers (in Japanese) were: Hiroshi Kaneko's "Historical significance of the Shoup Recommendations," Shigeki Morinobu's "Japanese tax system after comprehensive tax reform and the Shoup Recommendations," Konosuke Kimura's "Legal relationships on the fiscal administrative proceeding: The Shoup recommendations as a starting point," and Shibuya Masahiro's "Individual income tax in the Shoup Report: Focusing on capital gains."

12 American historian of economics E. Roy Weintraub (1991a) has referred to Taro Yamane's textbook on mathematical economics (1962). Japanese students like young Takashi Negishi read textbooks in mathematics for economics written by the mathematician Hibino (1949), which had been printed multiple times. Young Negishi saw Hibino attending an annual meeting of the Japanese Economic Association at the receptionist desk one time (personal communication with Negishi).

References

David M. Rubenstein Rare Book & Manuscript Library, Duke University, Durham, North Carolina, USA, (http://library.duke.edu/specialcollections/collections/economists/).

The Don Patinkin Papers, 1870–1995.

The Kenneth J. Arrow Papers, 1939–2011.

The Martin Bronfenbrenner Papers, 1939–95 and undated.

The Nicholas Georgescu-Roegen Papers, 1944–94.

The Oskar Morgenstern Papers, 1866–1992 and undated.

Yasui Library, Department of Economics, Saitama University, Saitama Prefecture, Japan, (www.eco.saitama-u.ac.jp/~siryo3/fornew.html).

Harvard University Archives, Harvard University, Boston, Mass., US.

Adelman, Irma and Sherman Robinson (1989) Income distribution and development. In Chapter 19 of *Handbook of Development Economics*, Volume II, edited by Hollis Chenery and T. N. Srinivasan. Amsterdam: Elsevier, pp. 950–1003.

Akimaru, J. (ed.) (1941) Eibei Gassaku Keizai Kosenryoku (The Allied Economic Power of the UK and the USA during a War). Tokyo: The Library of the Economics Department, University of Tokyo.

Alexandroff [Alexandrov], P. S. and H. Hopf (1935) *Topologie I* (Topology I). Berlin: Julius Springer.

Allais, M. (1943) *Traité d'économie pure* (Treatise on Pure Economics). Paris: Imprimerie nationale.

Allen, G. C. (1983) *Appointment in Japan: Memories of Sixty Years*. London: Athlone Press.

Allen, R. G. D. (1936) Professor Slutsky's theory of consumers' choice. *Review of Economic Studies*, 3: 120–9.

Allen, R. L. (1991) *Opening Doors: The Life and Work of Joseph Schumpeter*, ten vols. New Brunswick and London: Transaction Publishers.

Amano, Tameyuki (1886a) *Keizaigenron* (Theory of Political Economy). Tokyo: Fuzanbo.

Amano, T. (1886b) *Shoseihyojun* (The Principles of Commercial Legislation). Tokyo: Fuzanbo.

Amano, T. (1890) *Keizaigaku Kenkyuho* (Methodology of Economics). Tokyo: Hakubunkan.

Amano, T. (1901) *Kinkenchochiku Shinron* (Discourse on Thrift and Savings). Tokyo: Hoeikanshoten.

Amano, T. (1902a) *Keizaigaku Koyo* (Outline of Economics). Tokyo: Toyo Keizai Shinposha.

Amano, T. (1902b) *Outline of Economics* (Chinese edn.). Shanghai: Bureau for Translation of Civilized Books.

Amano, T. (1902c) *Gakuri to jissai* (Theory and practice), lecture at Waseda University, October. In Amano (1910) *Keizaisakuron* (Discourse on Economic Policy). Tokyo: Jitsugyononihonsha, pp. 914–30.

Amano, T. (1910) *Keizaisakuron* (Discourse on Economic Policy). Tokyo: Jitsugyononihonsha.

Amano, T. and Shigeki Nishimura (eds) [1893] (1894) *Shogakushushinkei: Nyumon: Jinjokaseitoyo* (Elementary Moral Textbook for Lower Grades). Tokyo: Fuzanbo.

Amano, T. and Shigeki Nishimura (eds) (1894) *Shogakushushinkei: Kotokaseitoyo* (Elementary Moral Textbook for Upper Grades). Tokyo: Fuzanbo.

Amemiya, Takeshi (1973) Regression analysis when the dependent variable is truncated normal. *Econometrica*, 41: 997–1016.

Amemiya, T. (2009) Thirty-five years of Journal of Econometrics. *Journal of Econometrics*, 148(2): 179–85.

Amemiya, T., and J. L. Powell (2007) The ET Interview: Takeshi Amemiya (interviewed by James L. Powell). *Econometric Theory*, 23: 155–81.

American Economic Association (AEA) (1998) Martin Bronfenbrenner, Distinguished Fellow 1997. *American Economic Review*, 88 (June), frontispiece.

Amonn, A. (1924) Cassels System der theoretischen Nationalökonomie (Cassel's economic system). *Archiv für Sozialwissenschaft und Sozialpolitik*, 51: 1–87 and 322–61.

Amonn, A. (1927) [1911] *Objekt und Grundbegriffe der theoretischen Nationalökonomie* (Object and Basic Concepts of Economics). Second edn. Leipzig: F. Deuticke. Trans. by T. Yamaguchi as *Riron Keizaigaku no Taisho to Kiso Gainen*. Tokyo: Yuhikaku, 1937. Reprint, 1950.

Amonn, A. (1932) Die Historie der Grenznutzentheorie (The History of Marginal Utility Theory, unpublished except in Japanese) abridged by R. Kusui. In *Gendai Keizaigaku* (Contemporary Economics), vol. 27. Tokyo: Nihon Hyoronsha, 1932.

Andronow, A. A. and C. E. Chaikin (1949) [1937] *Theory of Oscillations*. English edn. edited by S. Lefschetz. Princeton: Princeton University Press.

Aoyama, Hideo (1937) Dotairiron no tokeitekikiso (Statistical foundations for a macrodynamic theory of the business cycle, with special attention to Frisch's theory). *Annual Report of Japan Statistical Society*, 5: 93–102.

Aoyama, H. (1938a) Seigakuteki ippankinkoron to dogakuka no mondai (The static theory of general equilibrium and its dynamization). *Keizai Ronso*, 47(3). In Aoyama (1958) *Hendo Riron no Kenkyu* (A Study on the Theory of Economic Fluctuation), vol. 1. Tokyo: Sobunsha.

Aoyama, H. (1938b) Mirudaru no keizai hendo riron (Myrdal's theory of economic fluctuation). *Keizai Ronso*, 47(4). In Aoyama (1953) *Kenburijji Gakuha oyobi Hokuo Gakuha no Keizai Riron* (The Cambridge and Scandinavian School on the Theory of Economic Fluctuation). Tokyo: Sobunsha.

Aoyama, H. (1939) Robatoson no bukka hendo riron (Robertson on the theory of price changes). *Keizai Ronso*, 49(2). In Aoyama (1953) *Kenburijji Gakuha oyobi Hokuo Gakuha no Keizai Riron* (The Cambridge and Scandinavian School on the Theory of Economic Fluctuation). Tokyo: Sobunsha.

Aoyama, H. (1940a) A critical note on D. H. Robertson's theory of savings and investment. *Kyoto University Economic Review*, 16(1): 49–73, 16(2): 64–81.

Aoyama, H. (1940b). R. Frisch's sokan kankei riron (R. Frisch's confluence analysis). *Annual Report of Japan Statistical Society*, 8: 87–102.

Aoyama, H. (1942) Gendai keiki riron niokeru hanro hosoku no mondai (On the law of market in the contemporary theories of business cycles). *Nihon Keizai Gakkai Nenpo*, (2). In Aoyama (1958) *Hendo Riron no Kenkyu* (A Study on the Theory of Economic Fluctuation), vol. 2. Tokyo: Sobunsha.

Aoyama, H. (1953) *Kenburijji Gakuha oyobi Hokuo Gakuha no Keizai Riron* (The Cambridge and Scandinavian School on the Theory of Economic Fluctuation). Tokyo: Sobunsha.

Aoyama, H. (1958) [1949] *Keizai Hendo Riron no Kenkyu* (A Study on the Theory of Economic Fluctuation), two vols. Tokyo: Sobunsha.

Arrow, K. J. (1951) An extension of the basic theorems of classical welfare economics. In J. Neyman (ed.) (1951) *Proceedings of the Second Berkeley Symposium on Mathematical Statistics and Probability*. Berkeley and Los Angeles: University of California Press.

Arrow, K. J. (1968) Economic equilibrium. In *International Encyclopedia of the Social Sciences*. New York: Macmillan and the Free Press, 4, pp. 376–86.

Arrow, K. J. (1995) Foreword to Shepherd (ed.) (1995).

Arrow, K. J. (2001) The five most significant developments in economics of the twentieth century. *European Journal of the History of Economic Thought*, 8: 298–304.

Arrow, K. J., H. D. Block and Leonid Hurwicz (1959) On the stability of the competitive equilibrium, II. *Econometrica*, 27: 82–109.

Arrow, K. J. and Gerard Debreu (1954) Existence of an equilibrium for a competitive economy. *Econometrica*, 22: 265–90.

Arrow, K. J. and Frank Hahn (1971) *General Competitive Analysis*. Amsterdam: North-Holland.

Asakawa, Eijiro and Nagatoshi Nishida (1950) *Amano Tameyuki* (Tameyuki Amano). Tokyo: Jitsugyo no Nihonsha.

Aspray, W. (1990) *John von Neumann and the Origins of Modern Computing*. Cambridge, Mass.: MIT Press.

Backhouse, R. (ed.) (1999) *Keynes: Contemporary Responses to the General Theory*. South Bend, Ind.: St. Augustine's Press.

Bank of Japan (BOJ 1993) *Nihon Kinyu Nenpyo, Meiji Gannen kara Heisei Yonen* (Chronological Table of Japanese Finance, 1868–1992). Tokyo: Nihon Ginko Kin'yu Kenkyujo.

Bank of Japan, Editorial Committee for A Hundred Year History (BOJ 1982–4) *Nihon Ginko Hyakunenshi* (A Hundred History of the Bank of Japan), seven vols. Tokyo: Nihon Ginko.

Barbour, D. M. (1913) *The Influence of the Gold Supply on Prices and Profits*. London: Macmillan.

Barker, D. A. (1913) *The Theory of Money*. Cambridge: Cambridge University Press.

Baumol, W. J. and S. M. Goldfeld (1968) *Precursors in Mathematical Economics*. LSE series of reprints of scarce works on political economy, No. 19. London: London School of Economics.

Bausor, Randall (1995) Liapunov techniques in economic dynamics and classical thermodynamics: a comparison. In *Measurement, Quantification and Economic Analysis: Numeracy in Economics*, edited by Ingrid H. Rima. London and New York: Routledge, pp. 396–405.

Beasley, W. G. (1990) *The Rise of Modern Japan*. Tokyo: Charles E. Tuttle Company.

Begle, E. G. (1950) A fixed point theorem. *Annals of Mathematics*, 51(3): 544–50.

Bellah, Robert Neelly (1957) *Tokugawa Religion: The values of pre-industrial Japan*. Glencoe, Ill.: Free Press.

Bendix, L. (1915) Germany's financial mobilization. *Quarterly Journal of Economics*, 30: 724–47.
Berrill, Kenneth (ed.) (1964) *Economic Development with Special Reference to East Asia: Proceedings of a Conference held by the International Economic Association* (IEA), Paris: IEA First Published. Reprint, London: Macmillan, Tokyo; Yushodo and New York: Stockton Press, 1986.
Biddle, Jeff (2011) The introduction of the Cobb-Douglas regression and its adoption by agricultural economists. In Boumans, Dupont-Kieffer and Qin (eds) (2011) *Histories on Econometrics*. Durham, NC: Duke University Press, pp. 235–57.
Black, R. D. C., A. W. Coats and C. Goodwin (eds) (1973) *The Marginal Revolution in Economics*. Durham, NC: Duke University Press.
Blaug, Mark (1998) *Great Economists since Keynes: An Introduction to the Lives and Works of One Hundred Modern Economists*. Second edn. Cheltenham, UK and Northampton, Mass.: Edward Elgar.
Blaug, M. (2003) The formalist revolution of the 1950s. In Warren J. Samuels, Jeff E. Biddle and John B. Davis (eds) *A Companion to the History of Economic Thought*. Malden, Mass.: Blackwell Publishing.
Border, Kim C. (1985) *Fixed Point Theorems with Applications to Economics and Game Theory*. New York: Cambridge University Press.
Boumans, Marcel, Ariane Dupont-Kieffer and Duo Qin (eds) (2011) *Histories on Econometrics*. Durham, NC: Duke University Press.
Bowley, A. L. (1924) *Mathematical Groundwork of Economics*. Oxford: Clarendon Press. Chapter 1, trans. S. Narumi, 1926.
Bridel, Pascal (2011) *General Equilibrium Analysis: A Century after Walras*. New York: Routledge.
Bronfenbrenner, June, Urie Bronfenbrenner, Bruce Fitzgerald, Craufurd D. Goodwin, Samuel Hollander, Tamotsu Matsuura, Warren J. Samuels, Werner Sichel, E. Roy Weintraub and Laurence S. Moss (1999) Dr. Martin Bronfenbrenner (1914–97): scholar, critic, cynic, and comrade-in-arms. *American Journal of Economics and Sociology*, 58(3): 491–522.
Bronfenbrenner, Martin, on the website of Duke University, Department of Economics. http://econ.duke.edu/about/history/individuals/martin-bronfenbrenner, (accessed on August 31, 2013). Bronfenbrenner, M. (1950a) Four positions on Japanese finance. *Journal of Political Economy*, 58(4): 281–8. Also in Bronfenbrenner's *Keizaigaku Tokoro-Dokoro*. Tokyo: Aoyama Gakuin University, 1988.
Bronfenbrenner, M. (1950b) The Japanese value-added sales tax. *National Tax Journal*, 3(4): 298–313.
Bronfenbrenner, M. (1956) Economic thought and its application and methodology in the East: the state of Japanese economics. *American Economic Review*, 46: 389–98.
Bronfenbrenner, M. (1957) The aftermath of the Shoup tax reform, Part I and Part II. *National Tax Journal*, 10(3): 236–54 and 10(4): 345–60.
Bronfenbrenner, M. (1963) Balm for the visiting economist. *Journal of Political Economy*, 71: 293–7.
Bronfenbrenner, M. (1975) Inflation theories of the SCAP period. *History of Political Economy*, 7: 137–55.
Bronfenbrenner, M. (1981) Professor Takata Yasuma, A foreigner's recollections. In Takata Yasuma Memorial Committee (ed.) (1981) *Takata Yasuma Sensei no Shogai to Gakusetsu* (Yasuma Takata: His Life and Theory). Tokyo: Sobunsha.
Bronfenbrenner, M. (1983) Bronfenbrenner, Martin. In Mark Blaug and Paul Sturges

(eds) *Who's Who in Economics: A Biographical Dictionary of Major Economists, 1700–1981*, Cambridge, Mass.: MIT Press, p. 50.

Bronfenbrenner, M. (1987a) A Conversation with Martin Bronfenbrenner. *Eastern Economic Association*, 13(January/March 1987): 1–6.

Bronfenbrenner, M. (1987b) Kei Shibata: an appreciation. In *Odo wo iku: Shibata Kei tsuito bunshu*, Tokyo: Nihonkeizaihyoronsha, 1987.

Bronfenbrenner, M. (1988) *Here and There in Economics* (Keizaigaku Tokoro-Dokoro). Tokyo: Aoyama Gakuin University School of International Politics, Economics, and Business.

Bronfenbrenner, M. (1990) An airport economist in the Ryukyus (November 1949). *The Ryukyuanist* (Newsletter of the International Society for Ryukyuan Studies), 9: 4–5.

Bronfenbrenner, M. (1997) Marginal Economist. Unpublished autobiography in the Bronfenbrenner Papers, David M. Rubenstein Rare Book & Manuscript Library, Duke University Library.

Bronfenbrenner, M. and Franklyn D. Holzman (1963) Survey of inflation theory. *American Economic Review*, 53: 593–661.

Bronfenbrenner, M. and K. Kogiku (1957) The aftermath of the Shoup Tax Reforms. Part I and II. *National Tax Journal*, 5: 236–54 and 345–60.

Brouwer, L. E. J. (1911) Über eineindeutige, stetige Transformationen von Flachen in sich (On the unique, steady transformation from a plane into itself). *Mathematische Annalen*, 70: 176–80.

Brouwer, L. E. J. (1912) Über Abbildung von Mannigfaltigkeiten (On mappings from manifolds). *Mathematische Annalen*, 71: 97–115.

Brouwer, L. E. J. (1913) Intuitionism and formalism. *Bulletin of American Mathematical Society*, (20)2: 81–96. An English translation of Brouwer's inaugural address as professor of mathematics at Amsterdam.

Brown, A. and A. Deaton (1972) Models of consumer behavior: A survey. *Economic Journal*, 82: 1145–236.

Bullock, C. J. (1919) Prefatory statement. *Review of Economic Statistics*, 1: 3.

Bushaw, D. W. and R. W. Clower (1954) Price determination in a stock-flow economy. *Econometrica*, 22: 328–43.

Cairnes, John Elliott (1875) *The Character and Logical Method of Political Economy*. Second edn. London: Macmillan and Co., and New York: Harper. First edn., 1857.

Carney, Richard (ed.) (2009) *Lessons from the Asian Financial Crisis*. London, New York: Routledge.

Cassel, Gustav (1899) Grundriss einer elementaren Preislehre (Introduction to the theory of price). *Zeitschrift für die gesamte Staatwissenschaften*, 55: 395–458.

Cassel, G. (1918) Abnormal deviations in international exchanges. *Economic Journal*, 29: 413–15.

Cassel, G. (1921a) *The World's Monetary Problems. Two memoranda presented to the International Financial Conference of the League of Nations in Brussels in 1920 and to the Financial Committee of the League of Nations in September 1921*. London: Constable and Company Limited. Trans. by T. Tamura and H. Mori as *Sekai no Kahei Mondai*, Tokyo: Nihon Hyoronsha, 1928.

Cassel, G. (1921b) [1918] *Theoretische Sozialökonomie*. Second edn. Leipzig: C. F. Winter. Trans. by S. Ono as *Shakai Keizaigaku Genron*. Tokyo: Iwanami Shoten, 1926.

Cassel, G. (1922) *Money and Foreign Exchange after 1914*. London: Constable.

Cassel, G. (1923) [1918] *The Theory of Social Economy*. Trans. from the enlarged second

German 1921 edn. of *Theoretische Sozialökonomie* by Joseph McCabe, with the collaboration of the author. London: T. F. Unwin, Ltd.

Cassel, G. (1926) The Japanese currency. The study made on behalf of A.-B. Svenska Kullagerfabriken SKF. Economics Department Library, University of Tokyo (donated by K. Yamazaki). Trans. as Nihon-en nitsuite in *Tokyo Ginko Tsushinroku*, 81(483): 492–8, 1926.

Cassel, G. (1927) [1918] *Theoretische Sozialökonomie*. Fourth edn. Leipzig: A. Deichert-sche Verlagsbuchhandlung Dr. Werner Scholl.

Cassel, G. (1932) *The Theory of Social Economy*. Trans. from the manuscript of the fifth German edn. (1932) of *Theoretische Sozialökonomie* by S. L. Barron. New York: Harcourt, Brace & Company, 1932. Reprint, New York: Augustus M. Kelley, 1976.

Cassel, G. (1941–2) *I Fornuftests Tjanst* (In the Service of Reason). Two vols. Stockholm: Natur och Kultur.

Chamberlin, E. H. (1933) *Theory of Monopolistic Competition*. Cambridge, Mass.: Harvard University Press. Trans. by H. Aoyama as *Dokusenteki Kyoso no Riron*. Tokyo: Shiseido, 1966.

Chayanov, A. V. (1923) *Die Lehre von der bäuerlichen Wirtschaft* (The Principles of Family Business). Berlin: Parey. Trans. by H. Isobe and T. Sugino as *Shono Keizai no Genri*, Tokyo: Toko Shoin, 1927.

Chipman, J. S. (1950) The multi-sector multiplier. *Econometrica*, 18: 355–74.

Cho, Y. [1973] (1994) *Showa Kyoko* (The Showa Crises). Tokyo: Iwanami Shoten.

Cho, Y. (ed.) (1974) *Ishibashi Tanzan: Hito to Shiso*. Tokyo: Toyo Keizai Shinposha.

Coats, A. W. (ed.) (1996) *The Post-1945 Internationalization of Economics*. Annual Supplement to Volume 28 of the *History of Political Economy*. Durham, NC: Duke University Press.

Coats, A. W. Bob (ed.) (2000) *The Development of Economics in Western Europe since 1945*. London: Routledge.

Cohen, Jerome B. (1949) *Japan's Economy in War and Reconstruction*. Minneapolis: University of Minnesota Press. Trans. as *Senji Sengo no Nihon Keizai*, two vols, by H. Ouchi, Tokyo: Iwanami Shoten, 1950–1.

Cohen, Jerome B. (1950) Fiscal policy in Japan. *The Journal of Finance*, 5: 110–25.

Cohn, A. (1922) Über die Anzahl der Wurzeln einer algebraischen Gleichung in einem Kreise (On the number of roots of an algebraic equation in a domain). *Mathematische Zeitschrift*, 14: 110–48.

Conant, C. A. (1914) Currency policy and the European War. *Journal of Political Economy*, 18: 717–35.

Corry, L. (1996) *Modern Algebra and the Rise of Mathematical Structure*. Basel: Birkhauser Verlag.

Cournot, A. (1838) *Recherches sur les principes mathématiques de la théorie des richesses*. Paris. Trans. by Nathaniel T. Bacon as *Researches into the Mathematical Principles of the Theory of Wealth*, with a bibliography of mathematical economics by Irving Fisher. Reprint of the 1927 edition, New York: A. M. Kelley, 1971. Trans. by I. Nakayama as *Tomi no Riron no Sugakuteki Genri ni kansuru Kenkyu*, Tokyo: Dobunkan, 1936.

Cowles, A. (1939) Letter to K. Shibata, October 14. In Shibata (1934–79). Correspondence. Department of Economics, Kyoto University.

Cowles, A. (1960) Ragner Frisch and the foundation of the Econometric Society. *Econometrica*, 28: 173–4.

Craver, Earlene (1986) The emigration of the Austrian economists. *History of Political Economy*, 18(1): 1–32.

Craver, E. and A. Leijonhufvud (1987) Economics in America: the Continental influence. *History of Political Economy*, 19(2): 173–82.

Cunning, Jan Willem and Michiel A. Keyzer (1995) Applied general equilibrium models for policy analysis. In Chapter 35 of *Handbook of Development Economics*, Volume IIIA, edited by Jere Behrman and T. N. Srinivasan. Amsterdam: Elsevier, pp. 2025–107.

Debreu, G. (1951) The coefficient of resource utilization. *Econometrica*, 19: 273–92.

Debreu, G. (1959) *Theory of Value*. New Haven and London: Yale University Press. Trans. by T. Maruyama as *Kachi no Riron*. Tokyo: Toyo Keizai Shinposha, 1977.

Debreu, G. (1982) Existence of competitive equilibrium. In Vol. 2 of K. J. Arrow and M. D. Intriligator (eds) *Handbook of Mathematical Economics*. Amsterdam: North-Holland, pp. 697–743.

Debreu, G. (1987) Existence of competitive equilibrium. In J. Eatwell, M. Milgate and P. Newman (eds) (1987) *The New Palgrave: A Dictionary of Economics*. London and Tokyo: Macmillan and Maruzen, vol. 2, pp. 216–19.

Debreu, G. (1991) The mathematization of economic theory. *American Economic Review*, 81: 1–7.

De Vries, B. A. (1996) The World Bank as an international player in economic analysis. In Coats (ed.) (1996) *The Post-1945 Internationalization of Economics*. Annual Supplement to Volume 28 of the *History of Political Economy*. Durham, NC: Duke University Press, pp. 225–44.

Dillard, D. (1948) *The Economics of John Maynard Keynes*. New York: Prentice Hall. Trans. by Y. Okamoto as *J. M. Keinzu no Keizaigaku*. Tokyo: Toyo Keizai Shinposha, 1950.

Dimand, R. W. (1988) *The Origins of the Keynesian Revolution*. Cheltenham, UK: Edward Elgar.

Dore, M., S. Chakravarty and R. Goodwin (eds) (1989). *John von Neumann and Modern Economics*. Oxford: Clarendon Press.

Dore, R. and R. Sinha. (1987) *Japan and World Depression: Then and Now*. London: Macmillan.

Douglas, Paul H. (1934) *The Theory of Wages*. New York: Macmillan.

Dupuit, A. J. È. J. (1844) De la measure de l'utilité des travaux publics (On the measurement of the utility of public works). *Annales des Ponts et Chaussées*, 2e semestre, 332–75. Trans. by I. Nakayama as Kokyoteki romu riyo no sokutei nitsuite, *Shogaku Kenkyu*, 4(1), 1924. In Nakayama (1972–3) *Nakayama Ichiro Zenshu* (Complete Works of Ichiro Nakayama), Tokyo: Kodansha, Vol. 3. Trans. by K. Kurita, Tokyo: Nihonkeizaihyoronsha, 2001.

Dupuit, A. J. È. J. (1849) De l'influence des péages sur l'utilité des vois de communication (On tolls and transport charges). *Annales des Ponts et Chaussées*, 1er semestre, 170–248. Trans. by I. Nakayama as Kotsu kikan no riyo ni oyobosu shiyoryo no eikyo nitsusite, *Shogaku Kenkyu*, 4(2–3), 1924. In Nakayama (1973) *Nakayama Ichiro Zenshu* (Complete Works of Ichiro Nakayama), Tokyo: Kodansha., Vol. 3. Trans. by K. Kurita, Tokyo: Nihonkeizaihyoronsha, 2001.

Eatwell, J., M. Milgate and P. Newman (eds) (1987) *The New Palgrave: A Dictionary of Economics*. London and Tokyo: Macmillan and Maruzen.

Econometric Society (1953) Report of the Chicago meeting (The Econometric Society), December 27–9, 1952. *Econometrica*, 21(3): 463–90.

Edgeworth, F. Y. (1881) *Mathematical Psychics*. London, reprint, New York: Augustus M. Kelley, 1967.

Eguchi, Hidekazu (1976) Econometric modeling at Bank of Japan. *Proceedings of the First Pacific Basin Central Bank Conference on Econometric Modeling*. San Francisco: Reserve Bank of San Francisco.

Eichengreen, B. (1995) [1992] *Golden Fetters: The Gold Standard and the Great Depression, 1919–1939*. New York and Oxford: Oxford University Press.

Eilenberg, S. and D. Montgomery (1946) Fixed point theorems for multi-valued transformations. *American Journal of Mathematics*, 68: 214–22.

Emmett, Ross B. (ed.) (2010) *The Elgar Companion to the Chicago School of Economics*. Cheltenham, UK and Northampton, Mass.: Edward Elgar.

ESCAP (2007) *The First Parliament of Asia: Sixty Years of the Economic and Social Commission for Asia and the Pacific (1947–2007)*. Bangkok: Economic and Social Commission for Asia and the Pacific (ESCAP), www.unescap.org (accessed on August 31, 2013).

Evans, G. C. (1930) *Mathematical Introduction to Economics*. New York: McGraw-Hill.

Fischer, S. (1987) Paul Anthony Samuelson. In J. Eatwell, M. Milgate and P. Newman (eds) (1987) *The New Palgrave: A Dictionary of Economics*. London and Tokyo: Macmillan and Maruzen, vol. 4, pp. 234–41.

Fisher, I. (1911) *The Purchasing Power of Money*. New York: Macmillan. Reprint, New York: Augustus M. Kelley, 1963. Trans. by K. Kinbara as *Kahei no Kobairyoku*, Tokyo: Kaizosha, 1936.

Fisher, I. (1912a) *Elementary Principles of Economics*. New York: Macmillan.

Fisher, I. (1912b) The "equation of exchange" for 1911, and forecast. *American Economic Review*, 2: 302–13, June.

Fisher, I. (1912c) International Conference regarding the Cost of Living. Report, n.p., September 26, 1912.

Fisher, I. (1912d) A more stable gold standard. *Economic Journal*, 22: 570–6, December.

Fisher, I. (1913a) A compensated dollar. *Quarterly Journal of Economics*, 28: 213–35.

Fisher, I. (1913b) Standardizing the dollar. *American Economic Review*, 3(1) Supplement: 20–8.

Fisher, I. (1925) [1892] *Mathematical Investigations in the Theory of Value and Prices*. New Haven: Yale University Press, 1925. Trans. by M. Hisatake as *Kachi to Kakaku no Riron no Sugakuteki Kenkyu*, Tokyo: Shokabou, 1933.

Fisher, Walter D. (1966) Oskar Ryszard Lange, 1904–1965. *Econometrica*, 34: 733–78.

Friedman, M. (1955) Léon Walras and his economic system. *American Economic Review*, 45: 900–9.

Frisch, R. (1929) Statikk og dynamikk (Statics and dynamics). *Nationalökonomisk Tidsskrift*, 67: 321–79.

Frisch, R. (1933) Propagation problems and impulse problems in dynamic economics. In *Economic Essays in Honour of Gustav Cassel* (1933). London: George Allen & Unwin.

Frisch, R. and H. Holme (1935). The characteristic solutions of a mixed difference and differential equation occurring in economic dynamics. *Econometrica*, 3: 225–39.

Frobenius, G. (1908) Über Matrizen aus positiven Elementen (On the matrices with positive elements). *Sitzungsberichte der Königlich Preussischen Akademie der Wissenschaften*, 471–6.

Frobenius, G. (1909) Über Matrizen aus positiven Elementen, II (On the matrices with positive elements, II). *Sitzungsberichte der Königlich Preussischen Akademie der Wissenschaften*, 514–18.

Frobenius, G. (1912) Über Matrizen aus nicht negativen Elementen (On the matrices with non-negative elements). *Sitzungsberichte der Königlich Preussischen Akademie der Wissenschaften*, 456–77.

Fujimori, Kaoru (2006) Ninomiya Sontoku (1787–1856). *Encyclopedia of Shinto*, Kokugakuin University, http://eos.kokugakuin.ac.jp/modules/xwords/entry.php?entryID=523 (accessed on March 29, 2013).

Fujimura, Kinichro (1992a) *Takahashi Korekiyo to Kokusai Kin'yu, I* (Korekiyo Takahashi and International Finance I: The Russo-Japanese War and His Diary on the Issuance of Bonds Abroad). Tokyo: Fukutake Shoten.

Fujimura, K. (1992b) *Takahashi Korekiyo to Kokusai Kin'yu, II* (Korekiyo Takahashi and International Finance II: The Connection of Financial Commissioners and Sir Leith-Ross). Tokyo: Fukutake Shoten.

Fujisawa Memorial Committee (FMC 1934–5). *Fujisawa Hakushi Ibunshu* (The Collected Essays of the Late Dr. Fujisawa). Three vols. Tokyo: Fujisawa Hakushi Kinenkai, Tokyo Daigaku Sugakuka.

Fujisawa, Rikitaro (1889) *Seimei Hokenron* (Life Insurance). Tokyo: Bunkaido.

Fujisawa, R. (1903) Joint-metallism: An essay on a new monetary system (in English). Mimeo, private circulation. In Fujisawa Memorial Committee (1935) vol. 3, pp. 187–210.

Fujisawa, R. (1906) Hojokahei ginka kaichu no gi ni tsukite (On the remintage of subsidiary silver coins). *Kokka Gakkai Zasshi* 20(3). In Fujisawa Memorial Committee (1934) vol. 1, pp. 299–309.

Fujisawa, R. (1925a) Tsuka no kachi no hendo oyobi choki taishaku no kessai ni tsukite (On the changes in the value of currency and the payment of a long term loan). *Kokka Gakkai Zasshi*, 39(6). In Fujisawa Memorial Committee (1934) vol. 1, pp. 353–78.

Fujisawa, R. (1925b) Kinhoni heno keiro (The way to the gold standard). *Kokka Gakkai Zasshi*, 39(11). In Fujisawa Memorial Committee (1934) vol. 1, pp. 379–409.

Fujiwara, Matsusaburo (1925) Über die Bezoutiante zweier Polynome (On the Bezout-type binomial expression). *Japanese Journal of Mathematics*, 2: 9–12.

Fujiwara, M. (1926) Über die algebraischen Gleichungen, deren Wurzeln in einem Kreise oder in einer Halbebene liegen (On algebraic equations whose root lies in a domain or on half line). *Mathematische Zeitschrift*, 24: 161–9.

Fujiwara, M. (1928–9) *Daisugaku* (Algebra), two volumes. Tokyo: Uchidarokakuho, the sixth edn., 1948.

Fujiwara, M. (1934–9) *Bibun Sekibungaku* (Calculus), two volumes. Tokyo: Uchidarokakuho.

Fujiwara, M. (1935) Obituary note. Tsuruichi Hayashi. *Tohoku Mathematical Journal*, 41: 265–89.

Fukai, Eigo (1922) Jenoa kaigi ni tsukite (A report on the Genoa conference). *Ginko Tsushinroku*, 74(444): 396–400(26–30).

Fukai, E. (1928) *Tsuka Chosetsuron* (The Adjustment of Currency Value). Tokyo: Nihon Hyoronsha.

Fukai, E. (1929) *Kinkaikin ni tomonau Tsukaseisaku* (Monetary Policy after the Lifting of the Gold Embargo). Tokyo: Ginko Kyokai.

Fukai, E. (1937) The recent monetary policy of Japan. In Gayer (ed.) (1937) *The Lessons of Monetary Experience: Essays in Honor of Irving Fisher*. New York: Rinehart and Company, pp. 379–95.

Fukai, E. (1941) *Kaiko Shichijunen* (My Seventy Years in Retrospect). Tokyo: Iwanami Shoten.

Fukuda, Tokuzo (1900) Die gesellschaftliche und wirtschaftliche Entwicklung in Japan

(Social and Economic Development in Japan). In Münchener Volkswirtschaftliche Studien (Munich Studies of National Economies) edited by L. Brentano and W. Lotz. Stuttgart: J. G. Cotta.

Fukuda, T. (1913) Jo (Introduction) to the Japanese version of W. S. Jevons (1871).

Fukuda, T. (1925) *Keizaigaku Kogi* (Lectures on Economics). Revised edn., Tokyo: Dobunkan.

Fukuda, T. (1930) *Kosei Keizai Kenkyu* (A Study of Welfare Economics). Tokyo: Toko Shoin.

Fukuda, Yukihiro and the Research Group of the Shoup Tax System (eds) (1985) *Shoup no Zeisei Kankoku* (Shoup's Tax Report). Tokyo: Kasumi Shuppankai.

Fukuzumi, Masae (Shokei) (1884–7) *Ninomiya-o Yawa* (Sage Ninomiya's Evening Talks). Japanese binding, Shizuoka: Shizuoka Hotokusha. Popular edition, Shizuoka: Hotoku Library, 1893. Modern trans. by K. Kota, Tokyo: Chuokoronsha, 1970. Reprint, 2012.

Fukuzumi, M. (1970) [1937] *Sage Ninomiya's Evening Talks*. Trans. by Isoh Yamagata from (Fukuzumi 1893). Westport, Conn.: Greenwood Press. The Tokuno Kyokai, 1937.

Fukuzumi, M. (2012) *Ninomiya-o Yawa* (Sage Ninomiya's Evening Talks), edited by Kota Kodama with an introduction by Tadashi Kobayashi. Tokyo: Chuokoronsha.

Furuya, Hiroshi (1949) Keizai kinko no antei bunseki (Stability analysis of economic equilibrium). In *Riron Keizaigaku no Shomondai* (Problems in Theoretical Economics), edited by T. Yanaihara. The Economics Department of the University of Tokyo. Tokyo: Yuhikaku.

Gale, D. (1955) The law of supply and demand. *Mathematica Scandinavia*, 3: 155–69. Also in Newman (ed.) (1968) *Readings in Mathematical Economics*, vol. 1, *Value Theory*. Baltimore: Johns Hopkins University Press.

Gayer, A. D. (ed.) (1937) *The Lessons of Monetary Experience: Essays in Honor of Irving Fisher*. New York: Rinehart and Company. Reprint, New York: Augustus M. Kelley, 1970.

Goodwin, Craufurd (1998) Martin Bronfenbrenner, 1914–1997. *Economic Journal*, 108 (November): 1775–80.

Gossen, H. H. (1854) *Entwicklung der Gesetze des menschlichen Verkehrs und der daraus fliessenden Regeln für menschliches Handeln*. Brunswick: Vieweg. Trans. by S. Tedzuka included in Tedzuka (1920) *Gossen Kenkyu* (A Study of Gossen). Tokyo: Dobunkan, and by Y. Ikeda, Tokyo: Nihonkeizaihyoronsha, 2002. Trans. by R. C. Blitz (with introduction by N. Georgescu-Roegen) as *The Laws of Human Relations and the Rules of Human Action Derived Therefrom*. Cambridge, Mass.: MIT Press, 1983.

Goto, S. (1977) *Takahashi Korekiyo: Nihon no Keinzu* (Korekiyo Takahashi: The Japanese Keynes). Tokyo: Nihon Keizai Shinbunsha.

Gramlich-Oka, Bettina (2010) A domain doctor and Shogunal policies. In Gramlich-Oka and Smits (eds) (2010) *Economic Thought in Early Modern Japan*. Leiden and Boston: Brill, pp. 111–56.

Gramlich-Oka, Bettina and Gregory Smits (eds) (2010) *Economic Thought in Early Modern Japan*. Leiden and Boston: Brill.

Granger, C. W. J. and M. Hatanaka (1964) *Spectral Analysis of Economic Time Series*. Princeton: Princeton University Press.

Gustafsson, B. (1987) Gustav Cassel. In J. Eatwell, M. Milgate and P. Newman (eds) (1987) *The New Palgrave: A Dictionary of Economics*. London and Tokyo: Macmillan and Maruzen, vol. 1, pp. 375–7.

Haavelmo, T. (1944) The probability approach in econometrics. *Econometrica*, 12 (supplement): 1–118.

Hadely, E. M. (1989) The diffusion of Keynesian ideas in Japan. In Hall (ed.) (1989) *The Political Power of Economic Ideas: Keynesianism across Nations*. Princeton: Princeton University Press, pp. 291–309.

Haga, Hanjiro (1951) Kokusai boeki no antei joken (Stability conditions for international trade). *Keizaigaku Ronshu*, 20: 45–66.

Hagemann, H. (2000) Development of economics in Germany. In Coats (ed.) (2000) *The Development of Economics in Western Europe since 1945*. London: Routledge, pp. 113–28.

Hagemann, H. and C.-D. Krohn (1992) *Die Emigration deutschsprachiger Wirtschaftswissenschaftler nach 1933: Biographische Gesamtübersicht* (The Emigration of German-speaking Economists after 1933: Biographical Survey). 2. Erw. Auflage. Universität Hohenheim.

Hagemann, H. and C.-D. Krohn (1999) *Biographisches Handbuch der deutschsprachigen wirtschaftswissenschaftlichen Emigration nach 1933* (Biographical Handbook on the Emigration of German-speaking Economists after 1933). Two vols. Munich: K. G. Saur.

Hall, P. (ed.) (1989) *The Political Power of Economic Ideas: Keynesianism across Nations*. Princeton: Princeton University Press.

Hamada, Koichi (1986) The impact of the General Theory. *Eastern Economic Journal*, 12(4): 451–66.

Hansen, A. H. (1953) *A Guide to Keynes*. New York: McGraw-Hill. Trans. by Y. Oishi as *Keinzu Keizaigaku Nyumon*. Tokyo: Tokyo Sogensha, 1956.

Harvey, A. C. (1989) *The Econometric Analysis of Time Series*. Cambridge, Mass.: MIT Press.

Hatanaka, Michio (1952) Note on consolidation within a Leontief system. *Econometrica*, 20(2): 301–3.

Hatanaka, M. (1963) Review of Yamada 1963. *Econometrica*, 31: 279–80.

Hatanaka, M. (1975) On the global identification of the dynamic simultaneous equations model with stationary disturbances. *International Economic Review*, 16(3): 545–54.

Hatanaka, M., K. Maekawa and K. Tanaka (1990) Interview: Professor Michio Hatanaka. *Econometric Theory*, 6(3): 385–402.

Hayakawa, Miyoji (1933) Sulla distribuzione dei terreni agrai Giappone del 1908 al 1930 (On the distribution of agricultural land in Japan from 1908 till 1930). *Giornale degli economisti e rivista di statistica*, 73(9): 639–44.

Hayakawa, M. (1951) The application of Pareto's law of income to Japanese data. *Econometrica*, 19(2): 174–83.

Hayami, Akira, Osamu Saito and Ronald P. Toby (eds) (2004) *Emergence of Economic Society in Japan, 1600–1859*. Oxford: Oxford University Press.

Hayasaka, Tadashi (1971–2) Nihon keizaigakushi no shodanmen (Various aspects of Japanese economic thought in retrospect). *Keizai Semina*. Tokyo: Nihon Hyoronsha.

Hayasaka, T. (1972) Amano Tameyuki to J. S. Mill (Tameyuki Amano and J. S. Mill: an introduction). *Journal of Liberal Education* (University of Tokyo), 4: 143–62.

Hayasaka, T. (1982) The reception and influence of modern economics in Japan: the main connection with the economics of Keynes. Paper presented at the annual meeting of the History of Economics Society.

Hayasaka, T. (1993) Wagakuni heno Keinzu donyu ryakushi (The introduction of Keynes into Japan: a brief history). In Hayasaka (ed.) (1993) *Keinzu tono Deai* (The Encounter with Keynes: The Introduction of Keynesian Ideas into Japan). Tokyo: Nihonkeizaihyoronsha, pp. 239–70.

Hayasaka, T. (ed.) (1993) *Keinzu tono Deai* (The Encounter with Keynes: The Introduction of Keynesian Ideas into Japan). Tokyo: Nihonkeizaihyoronsha.

Hayasaka, T. and H. Arisawa (1983) Senchusengo no keizai to keizaigaku (The economy and economics during and after WWII). *Shukan Toyo Keizai*, special issue, *Kindai Keizaigaku Shirizu*, No. 65, February 9.

Hayashida, M. (1986) *Keinzu Ippan Riron Kenkyu Gojunenshi* (A Fifty-year History of the Studies of Keynes's General Theory). Tokyo: Taga Shuppan.

Hayek, F. (1941) *Pure Theory of Capital*. London: Routledge & Kegan Paul. Trans. by T. Ichitani as *Shihon no Junsui Riron*, Tokyo: Jitsugyononihonsha, 1944.

Heertje, A. (1987) Joseph Alois Schumpeter. In J. Eatwell, M. Milgate and P. Newman (eds) (1987) *The New Palgrave: A Dictionary of Economics*, vol. 4. London and Tokyo: Macmillan and Maruzen, pp. 263–6.

Heertje, A. (ed.) (1999) *The Makers of Modern Economics*, vol. 4. Cheltenham, UK: Edward Elgar.

Hibino, Isao (1949) *Keizairiron no Sugakutekikiso* (Mathematical Foundations for Economic Theory). Tokyo: Dobunkan.

Hicks, J. R. (1933) Gleichgewicht und Konjunktur. *Zeitschrift für Nationalökonomie*, 4(4): 441–55.

Hicks, J. R. (1934) Léon Walras. *Econometrica*, 2: 338–48.

Hicks, J. R. (1937) *Théorie mathématique de la value en régime de libre concurrence* (Mathematical Theory of Value under the Regime of Free Competition). Paris: Hermann & C. Éditeurs.

Hicks, J. R. (1939) *Value and Capital*. Oxford: Oxford University Press. The second edn., 1946. Trans. by T. Yasui and H. Kumagai as *Kachi to Shihon*, Tokyo: Iwanami Shoten, 1951.

Hicks, J. R. (1945) *The Social Framework of the American Economy*. New York: Oxford University Press.

Hicks, J. R. (1951) A comment on Mr. Ichimura's definition. *Review of Economic Studies*, 47: 184–7.

Hicks, J. R. and R. G. D. Allen (1934) A reconsideration of the theory of value. *Economica*, New Series, 1: 52–76, 196–219.

Hijikata, Seibi (Narumi) (1929) *Kin Kaikin* (The Lifting of the Gold Embargo). Tokyo: Nihon Hyoronsha.

Hildenbrand, W. and H. Sonnenschein (eds) (1991) *Handbook of Mathematical Economics*, Vol. IV. Amsterdam: North-Holland.

Hirata, Tomitaro (1957) Tameyuki Amano. In *Social Sciences in Modern Japan and Waseda University*, edited by the Committee for the Publication of the Memorial Volume of the 75th Anniversary of Waseda University.

Hirowatari, Shiro (1924) *Soyeda Juichi-kun Shoden* (Biography of Juichi Soyeda). Tokyo: Jitsugyodoshikai.

Hisaki, Yukio (1984) Shishinkyokasho hyosetsu jiken (The plagiarism in moral textbooks in 1894). *Yokohama National University Journal of Education*, 24: 1–29.

Hisatake, Masao (1942) Koyo keisoku riron no hatten (The theoretical development of how to measure utility). *Hitotsubashi Ronso*, 4: 72–98.

Hisatake, M. (1959) A reconsideration on the concept of utility. *Annals of the Hitotsubashi Academy*, 10: 171–80.

Hutchison, Terence (2000) *On the Methodology of Economics and the Formalist Revolution*. Cheltenham, UK: Edward Elgar.

Hurwitz, A. (1895) Über die Bedingungen, unter welchen eine Gleichung nur Wurzeln mit negative reelen Theilen besitzt (On the conditions that an algebraic equation has only roots with negative real parts). *Mathematische Annalen*, 46: 273–84.

Ichimura, Hidehiko (2010) Mikuro jissho bunseki no shinten to kongo no tenbo (Development of Microeconometrics and Its Future). In *A Seventy-Five-Year History of the Japanese Economic Association*, edited by the Japanese Economic Association. Tokyo: Yuhikaku.

Ichimura, Shinichi (1951) A critical note on the definition of related goods. *Review of Economic Studies*, 47: 179–83.

Ichimura, S. (1957) *Nihon Keizai no Kozo* (The Structure of the Japanese Economy: An interindustry analysis). Tokyo: Sobunsha.

Ichimura, S. (1991) Letter to A. Ikeo (in Japanese), November 12.

Ichimura, S. (2010) A historic survey of macroeconometric models in Japan. In *Macro-Econometric Analyses of the Japanese Economy*, edited by S. Ichimura and L. R. Klein. Singapore: World Scientific, pp. 1–29.

Ichimura, S. and N. Kamakura (1951) *Kokuminshotoku to Shigen* (National Income and Resources). Tokyo: Kobunndo.

Iiduka, N. and M. Kawagoe (2009) How different are non-specialists' forecasts from specialists? ESRI Discussion Paper Series No. 227, Tokyo.

Ikeo, Aiko (1988) Chochiku no rirontekimonogatari to sono rekishi (Savings in Japan, a history from an economic theoretical perspective), *Money and Affluence*, edited by the Research Center for Savings and Economy. Tokyo: Society for the Promotion of Postal Savings, pp. 41–86.

Ikeo, A. (1990) Japanese economics from another sociological perspective. *Kokugakuin Keizaigaku*, 39: 112–28.

Ikeo, A. (1991) The introduction of the general equilibrium theory in Japan: a comparison with the English-speaking world. *Kokugakuin Keizaigaku*, 38: 430–80.

Ikeo, A. (1993a) Japanese modern economics, 1930–1945. In *Perspectives in the History of Economic Thought*, vol. 9, edited by R. F. Hébert. Aldershot and Brookfield, Vt., pp. 192–202.

Ikeo, A. (1993b) Komeshijo nitsuiteno tokeiteki-kenkyu (Early econometric works on rice). *The Annual Bulletin for the Japanese Society of the History of Economic Thought*, (31): 80–9.

Ikeo, A. (1994a) *Nijisseiki no Keizaigakusha Netowaku* (The Network of Economists in the Twentieth Century: The Development of Economics as Viewed from Japan). Tokyo: Yuhikaku.

Ikeo, A. (1994b) When economics harmonized mathematics in Japan: a history of stability analysis. *European Journal of the History of Economic Thought*, 1(3): 577–99. www.tandfonline.com.

Ikeo, A. (1996a) The advent of marginalism in Japan. *Research in the History of Economic Thought and Methodology*, 14: 217–45.

Ikeo, A. (1996b) Marxist economics in Japan. *Kokugakuin Keizaigaku*, 44(3/4): 425–51.

Ikeo, A. (1996c) The internationalization of economics in Japan. In Coats (ed.) (1996) *The Post-1945 Internationalization of Economics*. Annual Supplement to Volume 28 of the *History of Political Economy*. Durham, NC: Duke University Press, pp. 121–39.

Ikeo, A. (1997) Keynes and Keynesian economics in pre-WWII Japan. *Nihon Bunka Kenkyujo Kiyo* (Kokugakuin University), (80): 271–308.

Ikeo, A. (1998) Classical economics in Japan. In *The Elgar Companion to Classical Economics*, edited by H. Kurz and N. Salvadori. Cheltenham, UK: Edward Elgar.

Ikeo, A. (1999) Monetary Economics and Policy in Pre-WWII Japan. Presented at the 12th World Congress of the International Economic Association, Buenos Aires, August 23–7, 1999.

Ikeo, A. (2000) Scientific research and internationalization. In Ikeo (ed.) (2000) *Japanese Economics and Economists since 1945*. London: Routledge. Japanese version as *Nihon no Keizaigaku to Keizaigakusha*, Tokyo: Nihonkeizaihyoronsha, 1999, pp. 15–49.

Ikeo, A. (2001) History of Japanese economic thought. *Keizaigakushigakkai Nenpo* (Annals of the Japanese Society for the History of Economic Thought) (38): 94–102.

Ikeo, A. (2002a) *Japanese Economics in the International Context: The Internationalization of Economics in the Twentieth Century*. Dissertation paper. Waseda University Library. http://wine.wul.waseda.ac.jp.

Ikeo, A. (2002b) A History of Economics in Japan. In *The Future of the History of Economics*, Annual Supplement to Volume 34 of the *History of Political Economy*, edited by E. Roy Weintraub. Durham, NC: Duke University Press, pp. 165–75.

Ikeo, A. (2003a) Nihon niokeru keizaigaku no kokusaika (Internationalization of economics in Japan: Discussion of international monetary standard). *The Bulletin of the Graduate School of Commerce* (Waseda University), 57: 1–11.

Ikeo, A. (2003b) Kyojin Galbraith-"Fukakujitsusei no jidai" no teigen (John K. Galbraith in Japan). *Kokusai Koryu*, 100: 77–83.

Ikeo. A. (2004a) Keinzu no keizaigaku kara keinzu keizaigaku he: Nihon no baai (From the Economics of Keynes to Keynesian Economics in Japan). *Waseda Shogaku* (Waseda University), 402: 567–603.

Ikeo, A. (2004b) Keizaigaku no rekishi to tenboronbun, relating to Negishi (2003) Kinko no anteisei: 40-yonengno kaiko (Stability of equilibrium: A retrospect in forty years), (a history of economics and a survey article). *The Annals of the Japanese Society of the History of Economic Thought*, 46: 97–9.

Ikeo, A. (2006) *Nihon no Keizaigaku* (A History of Economics in Japan: The Internationalization of Economics in the Twentieth Century). Nagoya: Nagoya University Press.

Ikeo, A. (2008) *Akamatsu Kaname* (Kaname Akamatsu: Surpass My Economic System). Tokyo: Nihonkeizaihyoronsha.

Ikeo, A. (2009) Negishi's general equilibrium approach to trade theory: Trade between similar countries and infant industry protection. In Ikeo and Kurz (eds) (2009) *A History of Economic Theory: Essays in Honor of Takashi Negishi*. London: Routledge.

Ikeo, A. (2011a) M. Bronfenbrenner to sengonihonkeizai no saiken (Martin Bronfenbrenner and the reconstruction of the Japanese economy (1947–1952). *History of Japanese Economic Thought*, 11: 39–56.

Ikeo, A. (2011b) A history of Japanese developments in econometrics. *Histories on Econometrics*, annual supplement to volume 43, *History of Political Economy*, edited by Marcel Boumans, Arian Dupont-Kieffer and Duo Qin. Durham, NC: Duke University Press, pp. 188–210.

Ikeo, A. (2012) Amano Tameyuki to makurokeizaigaku no keisei (Tameyuki Amano and his Theory of Political Economy: His Contribution to Macroeconomic Analysis), *Waseda Commercial Review*, 431: 349–87.

Ikeo, A. (2013) Amano Tameyuki to Ninomiya Sontoku no Kyogi (Tameyuki Amano and the Teachings of Sontoku Ninomiya) to be published in *Hotoku Studies*, International Ninomiya Sontoku Association.

Ikeo, A. (ed.) (2000) [1999] *Japanese Economics and Economists since 1945*. London: Routledge. Japanese version as *Nihon no Keizaigaku to Keizaigakusha*. Tokyo: Nihonkeizaihyoronsha, 1999.

Ikeo, A. and H. D. Kurz (2009) *A History of Economic Theory: Essays in Honor of Takashi Negishi*. London: Routledge.

Ikeo, A. and M. Wakatabe (2000) Adam Smith in Japan, reconsidered from a non-Marxian perspective. In *Adam Smith across Nations*, edited by Cheng chung Lai. New York: Oxford University Press, pp. 207–18.

Imamura, T. (1958) *Takahashi Korekiyo* (Korekiyo Takahashi). Tokyo: Jijitsushinsha.

Ingrao, B. and G. Israel (1990) [1987] *The Invisible Hand: Economic Equilibrium in the History of Science*. Trans. by I. McGilvray. Cambridge, Mass.: MIT Press.

Inoue, Ichiro (ed.) (1988) *Shoup no Zeisei Kankoku: Shimbunshiro hen* (Shoup's Tax Report: Articles in Newspapers). Tokyo: Kasumi Shuppansha.

Inoue, Takutoshi and Kiichiro Yagi (1998) Two inquirers on the divide: Tokuzo Fukuda and Hajime Kawakami. In Sugihara and Tanaka (eds) (1998) *Economic Thought and Modernization in Japan*. Cheltenham, UK: Edward Elgar, pp. 60–77.

International Bank for Reconstruction and Development (IBRD) (1993) *The East Asian Miracle: Economic Growth and Public Policy*. New York: Oxford University Press.

International Statistical Institute (ISI) (1933) *Dai-19kai Kokusaitokeikyokai Kaigi Hokoku* (*Report of the Nineteenth Meeting of the International Statistical Institute*), edited by the Local Organizing Committee. Tokyo: The Local Organizing Committee of the ISI Meeting.

Ishi, Hiromitsu (2001) *The Japanese Tax System*. Third edn. Oxford: Oxford University Press.

Ishi, H. (2008) *Gendai Zeisei Kaikakushi* (A History of the Japanese Tax System, 1945–*c.*1990). Tokyo: Toyo Keizai Shinposha.

Ishibashi, Tanzan (1929) *Kinkaikin no Eikyo to Taisaku* (The Lifting of the Gold Embargo, Its Influence and Measures: A Proposal of the New Parity). Tokyo: Toyo Keizai Shuppanbu.

Ishibashi, T. (1938) Death of Dr. Amano. *The Oriental Economist*, 5(4): 213–14.

Ishibashi, T. (1941) Japan-Manchoukuo industrialization. *The Oriental Economist*, 8(2): 82–5.

Ishibashi, T. (1942) Economic Magazines in Japan. *The Oriental Economist*, 9(1): 26–9.

Ishibashi, T. (1970–2) *Ishibashi Tanzan Zenshu* (The Complete Works of Tanzan Ishibashi). Fifteen volumes. Tokyo: Toyo Keizai Shinposha.

Ishimoto, K. (1922) The population problem in Japan. *Reconstruction in Europe*, (6): 356.

Ishihara, M. (2008) The Reasons for the Establishment of American Culture Centers [in Japanese]. Library and Information Science website, www.mslis.jp/am2008yoko/12_ishihara.pdf (accessed on December 9, 2013).

Ito, Takatoshi (2007) Asian currency crisis and the IMF, 10 years later. *Asian Economic Policy Review*, 2: 6–49.

Iwata, Kikuo (ed.) (2004) *Show-kyoko no Kenkyu* (A Research on the Show Depression, 1930–1931). Tokyo: Toyo Keizai Shinposha.

Japanese Econometric Society (1951) Report of the Tokyo Meeting, October 8–9, 1950. *Econometrica*, 19: 220–3.

Japanese Econometric Society (1952) Report of the Tokyo Meeting, November 11–12, 1951. *Econometrica*, 20: 502.

Japanese Econometric Society (1956) Gakkai shosoku (Report of activities). *Bulletin*

(Japan Union of Associations of Economic Sciences, now the Union of National Economic Associations in Japan), 7: 136–7.

Japan Statistical Society (ed.) (1944) *Kokumin Shotoku to Sono Bunpu* (National Income and its Distribution). Tokyo: Nihonhyoronsha.

Jevons, H. S. (1917) Editorial foreword. *Indian Journal of Economics*, 1: 1–4.

Jevons, W. S. (1871) *The Theory of Political Economy*. London: Macmillan. Fourth edn., 1911. Trans. by S. Koizumi (with an introduction by T. Fukuda) as *Keizaigaku Junri*, Tokyo: Dobunkan, 1913. Revised translation by S. Koizumi, T. Terao and K. Nagata as *Keizaigaku no Riron*, Tokyo: Nihon Hyoronsha, 1944. Further revised translation by S. Koizumi, T. Terao and K. Nagata, Tokyo: Nihonkeizaihyoronsha, 1981.

Johnson, W. E. (1913) The pure theory of utility curves. *Economic Journal*, 23: 483–513.

Kahn, R. (1933) The relation of home investment to unemployment. *Economic Journal*, 42: 173–93.

Kakutani, Shizuo (1941) A generalization of Brouwer's fixed point theorem. *Duke Mathematical Journal*, 8: 457–9.

Kaldor, Nicholas (1934) A Classificatory Note on the Determinateness of Equilibrium. *Review of Economic Studies*, 1(2): 122–36.

Kalecki, M. (1935) A macrodynamic theory of business cycles. *Econometrica*, 3(3): 327–44.

Kalkmann, Ph. (1901) Hollands Geldwesen im 19. Jahrhundert (The financial system in the Netherlands in the nineteenth century). *Schmollers Jahrbuch für Gesetzebung, Verwaltung und Volkswirtschaft im Deutchen Reich*, 25: 3–66.

Kamiya, K. (1941) Nogyorodo no seisansei nitsuite (On the productivity of rice farming). *Journal of Rural Economics*, 17: 363–88.

Kanazashi, Motoi (1991) Schumpeter chosaku mokuroku (Bibliography of the writings of Joseph Alois Schumpeter). *Shogaku Shushi* (Nihon University), 61: 59–95.

Kanazawa, Ikuko (2011) *Fukudo Tokuzo Shoshi* (Bibliography of Tokuzo Fukuda). Tokyo: Nihonkeizaihyoronsha.

Kanbe (Kambe), Masao (1913a) Kinzoka no kaheijono akueikyo wo jokyosuru hosaku ni tsukite (On the plan of eliminating the bad effect of the increase in gold production on money). *Hogaku Shinpo*, 23(3): 23–33, March.

Kanbe, M. (1913b) Fi-shi choseikaheian no hihyo no hihyo no hihyo (Comments on the comments on the comments on Fisher's compensated dollar plan). *Kokka Gakkai Zasshi*, 27(8): 1189–1204, August.

Kato, Toshihiko (ed.) (1983) *Nihon Kin'yuron no Shitekikenkyu* (Historical Development of Monetary Economics in Japan). Tokyo: Tokyo Daigaku Shuppankai.

Katsura, Marquis, Baron Sakatani, S. Naruse and O. M. W. Sprague (1911). The Banking System of Japan. In US National Monetary Commission's Banking in Russia, Austro-Hungary, the Netherlands, and Japan, pp. 119–214, accessed December 10, 2013 from the Fraser Federal Reserve Archive http:fraser.stlouisfed.org/publication/?pid=612.

Kawai, E. (1969) *Kwai Eijiro Zenshu* (Complete Works of Eijiro Kawai), vol. 22, *Nikki* (Diary), edited by Shakai Shiso Kenkyukai. Tokyo: Shakai Shishosha.

Kawamata, Masahiro (2000) Scientific contributions to international journals. In Ikeo (ed.) (2000) *Japanese Economics and Economists since 1945*. London: Routledge, pp. 93–122.

Kawamata, M. (2009) The Negishi method in the history of general equilibrium theory. In Ikeo and Kurz (eds) (2009) *A History of Economic Theory: Essays in Honor of Takashi Negishi*. London: Routledge, pp. 120–36.

Kehoe, T. J. (1991) Computation and multiplicity of equilibrium. In Hildenbrand and

Sonnenschein (eds) (1991) *Handbook of Mathematical Economics*, Vol. IV, Amsterdam: North-Holland, pp. 2049–143.

Kenjo, Teiji (2009) *Kindai Hotokushiso to Nihonshakai* (Modern Hotoku Thoughts and Japanese Society). Tokyo: Periokansha.

Keynes, John Maynard (1913) *Indian Currency and Finance*. London: Macmillan. *The Collected Writings of John Maynard Keynes*, London: Macmillan (hereafter, *CW*) vol. 1, 1971. Trans. by Y. Noritake and S. Katayama as *Indo no Tsuka to Kinyu*, Tokyo: Toyo Keizai Shinposha, 1977.

Keynes, J. M. (1919) *The Economic Consequences of Peace*. London: Macmillan. *CW* vol. 2, 1971. Trans. by T. Hayasaka as *Heiwa no Keizaiteki Kiketsu*, Tokyo: Toyo Keizai Shinposha, 1977.

Keynes, J. M. (1923) *A Tract on Monetary Reform*. London: Macmillan. *CW* vol. 4, 1971. Trans. by K. Okabe and N. Uchiyama as *Kahei Kaikaku Mondai*, Tokyo: Iwanami Shoten, 1924. Trans. by T. Nakauchi as *Kahei Kaikakuron*, Tokyo: Toyo Keizai Shinposha, 1978.

Keynes, J. M. (1926) *The End of Laissez-faire*. London: Hogarth Press. In Keynes [1931] (1971) *Essays in Persuasion*. London: Macmillan. *CW* vol. 9, 1972, pp. 272–94.

Keynes, J. M. (1930) *A Treatise on Money*. Two volumes. London: Macmillan. *CW* vols 5–6, 1971. Trans. by N. Kito as *Kaheiron*, five volumes, Tokyo: Dobunkan, 1952–3. Trans. by A. Koizumi and K. Nagasawa as *Kaheiron*, Tokyo: Toyo Keizai Shinposha, 1979–80.

Keynes, J. M. (1931) *Essays in Persuasion*. London: Macmillan. *CW* vol. 9, 1972. Trans. by S. Kunigo as *Settoku Hyoronshu*, Tokyo: Perikansha, 1969. Trans. by Y. Miyazaki as *Settoku Ronshu*, Tokyo: Toyo Keizai Shinposha, 1981.

Keynes, J. M. (1936) *The General Theory of Employment, Interest and Money*. London: Macmillan. *CW* vol. 7, 1971. Trans. by T. Shionoya as *Koyo Rishi oyobi Kahei no Ippan Riron*, Tokyo: Toyo Keizai Shinposha, 1941. Trans. by Y. Shionoya as *Koyo Rishi oyobi Kahei no Ippan Riron*, Tokyo: Toyo Keizai Shinposha, 1983.

Keynes, J. M. (1937) The theory of the rate of interest. In Gayer (ed.) (1937) *The Lessons of Monetary Experience: Essays in Honor of Irving Fisher*. New York: Rinehart and Company, pp. 145–52. Also in *CW* vol. 14.

Keynes, J. M. and H. Henderson (1929) *Can Lloyd George Do It?* London: The Nation and Athenaeum. Included in J. M. Keynes's *Essays in Persuasion*. London: Macmillan, 1931. In *CW* vol. 9, pp. 86–125.

Kindleberger, C. P. (1973) *The World in Depression, 1929–1939*. Berkeley and Los Angeles: University of California Press. Trans. by T. Ishizaki and I. Kimura as *Dai Fukyo ka no Sekai*. Tokyo: Tokyo Daigaku Shuppankai, 1982.

Kinoshita, Keita (2012) 2011nendo Shukikikakuten, Waseda Shison seitan 150 Shunenkinen Amano Tameyuki to Waseda Daigaku ten (The Sesquicentennial Anniversary of Four Masters at Waseda, Tameyuki Amano and Waseda University: The Autumn Event of 2011). *History of Waseda University*, 43: 191–207.

Kito, Nisaburo (1942) *Kahei to Rishi no Dotai* (Dynamics of Money and Interest). Tokyo: Iwanami Shoten.

Klein, Judy L. and Mary S. Morgan (eds) (2001) *The Age of Economic Measurement*. Durham, NC and London: Duke University Press.

Klein, Lawrence Robert (1947) *Keynesian Revolution*. New York: Macmillan. Trans. by M. Shinohara and K. Miyazawa as *Keinzu Kakumei*. Tokyo: Yuhikaku, 1952.

Klein, L. R. (1961) A Model of Japanese Economic Growth, 1878–1937. *Econometrica*, 29: 277–92.

Klein, L. R. and Michio Morishima (1960) Editorial foreword. *International Economic Review*, 1: 1–2.

Klein, Morris (1972) *Mathematical Thought from Ancient to Modern Times*. Volume 3. Oxford: Oxford University Press.

Kobayashi, Tadashi (1989) *Nihon Hoken Shiso no Seisei to Tenkai* (Historical Development of Japanese Insurance Thought). Tokyo: Toyo Keizai Shinposha.

Kobayashi, Tadashi (2009) *Ninomiya Sontoku* (Sontoku Ninomiya). Kyoto: Minerva Shobo.

Koda, Rohan (1891) *Ninomiya Sontoku-o* (Sage Sontoku Ninomiya). Tokyo: Hakubunkai.

Kojima, Osamu (ed.) (1979) *Kaikeishi oyobi Kaikeigakushi* (The History of Accounting). Volume 6 of *Taikei Kindai Kaikeigaku* (The System of Modern Accounting). Tokyo: Chuo Keizaisha.

Komine, T., K. Ban, M. Kawagoe and H. Yoshida (2009) What have we learned from a survey of Japanese professional forecasters? Taking Stock of Four Years of ESP Forecast Experience. ESRI Discussion Paper Series No. 214, Tokyo.

Komiya, Ryotaro (1996) Keinzu to Nihon no keizai seisaku (Keynes and Japan's economic policy). In *Keynes ha hontoni Shindanoka* (Is Keynes Really Dead?) edited by H. Kanamori and the Japan Center for Economic Research. Tokyo: Nihon Keizai Shimbunsha.

Kondo, Yasuo (1928) *Chunen Koritsukoku no Kenkyu* (A Study of Thünen's Isolated Country). Tokyo: Chikyu Shuppan.

Koopmans, Tjalling Charles (ed.) (1951) *Activity Analysis of Production and Allocation*. New York: Wiley.

Kowalik, Tadeusz 1987 [2008] Lange, Oskar Ryszard (1904–1965). In J. Eatwell, M. Milgate and P. Newman (eds) (1987) *The New Palgrave: A Dictionary of Economics*. London and Tokyo: Macmillan and Maruzen. Available in the 2008 edn.

Kumagai, Jiro (2001) Orchestrating economic ideas: The formation and development of economic societies in modern Japan. In *The Spread of Political Economy and the Professionalisation of Economists: Economic Societies in Europe, America and Japan in the Nineteenth Century*, edited by M. M. Augello and M. E. L. Guidi. London: Routledge.

Kurimura, Yukichi (1939) *Dokusen Kakaku no Riron* (Theory of Monopolistic Prices). Tokyo: Nihonhyoronsha.

Kurimura, Y. (1941) *Kakaku no Ippan Riron* (Theory of Price). Tokyo: Nihonhyoronsha.

Kurimura, Y. (1949a) *Kakaku to Kahei* (Price and Money). Tokyo: Seki Shoin, August.

Kurimura, Y. (1949b) *Seisan to Bunpai* (Production and Distribution). Tokyo: Zoshindo, September.

Kurimura, Y. (1949c) *Keizai Sokuteigaku* (Economic Measurement). Tokyo: Nihonhyoronsha, November.

Kurimura, Y. (1954) Statement Regarding My Friendly Relations with Mr. Martin Bronfenbrenner. A document in the Bronfenbrenner Papers, Duke University.

Kurz, H. D. and N. Salvadori (1993) Von Neumann's growth model and the "classical" tradition. *European Journal of the History of Economic Thought*, 1(1): 129–60.

Kyoto University Economic Review, Editorial Committee (1926) Editorial foreword. *Kyoto University Economic Review*, 1: i–iii.

Laband, D. N. and M. J. Piette (1994) The relative impacts of economics journals: 1970–1990. *Journal of Economic Literature*, 32: 640–66.

Lange, Oskar (1935) Marxian economics and modern economic theory. *Review of Economic Studies*, 2: 189–201.

Lange, O. (1938) *On the Economic Theory of Socialism*. Minneapolis: University of Minnesota Press.

Lange, O. (1944) *Price Flexibility and Employment*. Chicago: University of Chicago Press.

Laughlin, J. L. (1903) *The Principles of Money*. New York: C. Scribner's Sons.

Lederer, Emil and Emy Lederer-Seidler (1929) *Japan-Europa: Wandlungen im Fernen Osten*. Frankfurt am Main: Frankfurter Societäts-Druckerei. Revised English edition as *Japan in Transition*. New Haven: Yale University Press. London: H. Milford, Oxford University Press, 1938.

Lefschetz, Solomon (1949) *Introduction to Topology*. Princeton: Princeton University Press.

Leijonhufvud, Axel (1968) *On Keynesian Economics and the Economics of Keynes*. Oxford: Oxford University Press. Trans. by T. Negishi and the Study Group of Keynes within the Bank of Japan as *Keinjian no Keizaigaku to Keinzu no Keizaigaku*, Tokyo: Toyo Keizai Shinposha, 1978.

Leonard, Robert (2010) *Von Neumann, Morgenstern, and the Creation of Game Theory: From Chess to Social Science, 1900–1960*. New York: Cambridge University Press.

Leontief, Wassily W. (1941) *The Structure of American Economy, 1919–1939: An empirical Application of Equilibrium Analysis*. Cambridge, Mass.: Harvard University Press. Second edn., New York: Oxford University Press, 1951.

Liapunov, A. M. (1907) [1892] Problème général de la stabilité du mouvement, *Annales de la Faculté des Sciences de Toulouse*, 9. In Russian, 1892. Reprint, Princeton.: Princeton University Press, 1947. *Stability of Motion* trans. by F. Abramovici and M. Shimshoni, New York and London: Academic Press, 1966.

Lie, Q. (1997) The "New Education" and Chinese revolution in the 1920s. In Ikeo (ed.) (1997) *Economic Development in Twentieth Century East Asia: The International Context*. London: Routledge, pp. 66–84.

Liénard, A. and Chipart (1914) Sur le signe de la partie réele des racines d'une équation algébrique (On the sign of the real part of the roots of an algebraic equation). *Journal de mathématiques pures et appliquées*, 6e série, Tome 10: 291–346.

Lindahl, Erik Robert (1930) [1929] *Penningpolitikens Medel* (The Means of Monetary Policy). Lund: Gleerup. In Lindahl (1939) *Studies in the Theory of Money and Capital*. London: George Allen & Unwin.

Lindahl, E. R. (1939) *Studies in the Theory of Money and Capital*. London: George Allen & Unwin. Trans. by M. Hara as *Kahei oyobi Shihon Riron no Kenkyu*, Tokyo: Bungado Shoten, 1962.

Liu, T.-C. (1960) Underidentification, structural estimation, and forecasting. *Econometrica*, 28: 855–65.

Maas, Harro and Mary S. Morgan (eds) (2012) *Observing the Economy: Historical Perspectives*. Durham, NC and London: Duke University Press.

Maeda, Masana and his men (1884) *Kogyo Iken* (Suggestions for the Promotion of Industrial Enterprises). Ministry of Agriculture and Commerce.

Marshall, Alfred (1890) *Principles of Economics*. London: Macmillan. Trans. by K. Otsuka as *Keizaigaku Genri* from the seventh edition, Tokyo: Sato Shuppanbu, 1919. Trans. by K. Baba as *Keizaigaku Genri* from the ninth edition, Tokyo: Toyo Keizai Shinposha, 1965–7.

Marshall, A. (1926) *Official Papers by Alfred Marshall*, edited by J. M. Keynes. London: Macmillan and Co.

Marx, Karl (1867–94) *Das Kapital*. Three volumes. Hamburg: Meissner, 1911–19.

Mas-Colell, A. and W. R. Zame (1991) Equilibrium theory in infinite dimensional space. In Hildenbrand and Sonnenschein (eds) (1991) *Handbook of Mathematical Economics*, Vol. IV. Amsterdam: North-Holland, pp. 1835–98.

Mason, Edward S. and Thomas S. Lamont (1982) The Harvard Department of Economics from the beginning to World War II. *Quarterly Journal of Economics*, 97(3): 383–433.

Masuda, Hiroshi (1996) *Koshoku Tsuiho* (The Oust from Public Office: A Study of the Three Major Purges). Tokyo: Tokyo Daigaku Shuppankai.

Matsuda, Yoshiro (1972) Nihon keizai no keiryo bunseki (An Econometric Analysis of the Japanese Economy). In *Keiryo Keizaigaku Kogi* (Lectures on Econometrics), edited by I. Yamada. Tokyo: Seirinshoinshinsha.

Matsuura, Tamotsu (1973) Marginalism in Japan. In R. D. C. Black, A. W. Coats and C. Goodwin (eds) *The Marginal Revolution in Economics*. Durham, NC: Duke University Press, 1973.

Mathematical Society of Japan, Editorial Committee of A Hundred Year History of Mathematics in Japan (MSJ) (ed.) (1983–4) *Nihon no Sugaku 100-nenshi* (A Hundred Year History of Mathematics in Japan), two volumes. Tokyo: Iwanami Shoten.

Mayer, H. (1930) Zur Einfürung (Introduction). *Zeitschrift für Nationalökonomie*, 1: 1–3.

McKenzie, Lionel (1954) On equilibrium in Graham's model of world trade and other competitive systems. *Econometrica*, 13: 54–71.

McCraw, Thomas K. (2007) *Prophet of Innovation: Joseph Schumpeter and Creative Destruction*. Cambridge, Mass.: Belknap Press of Harvard University Press.

Meade, J. E. and R. Stone (1944) *National Income and Expenditure*. Oxford: Oxford University Press.

Menger, Carl (1871) *Grundsätze der Volkswirtschaftslehre*. Vienna: Braumüller. Trans. by T. Yasui as *Kokumin Keizaigaku Genri*, Tokyo: Nihon Hyoronsha, 1937. Revised trans. by T. Yasui and K. Yagi, Tokyo: Nihonkeizaihyoronsha, 1999. *Principle of Economics*, trans. and edited by James Dingwall and Bert F. Hoselitz, with an introduction by Frank H. Knight. Glencoe, Ill.: Free Press, 1950. New York and London: New York University Press, 1981.

Menger, Karl (1928) Bemerkung zu Grundlagenfragen I und II-IV. *Jahresbericht der deutschen Mathematiker Vereinigung*, 37: 213–26 and 299–325. Modified English version as An intuitionistic-formalistic dictionary of set theory. Also in Menger (1979a) *Selected Papers in Logic and Foundations, Didactics, Economics*. Holland: D. Reidel Publishing Company.

Menger, K. (1930) Der Intuitionismus (On intuitionism). *Blatter für deutsche Philosophie*, 4: 311–25. English version as On intuitionism, in Menger (1979a) *Selected Papers in Logic and Foundations, Didactics, Economics*. Holland: D. Reidel Publishing Company, pp. 46–58.

Menger, K. (1973) Austrian marginalism and mathematical economics. In *Carl Menger and the Austrian School of Economics*, edited by J. R. Hicks and W. Weber. Oxford: Clarendon Press, pp. 38–60.

Menger, K. (1979a) *Selected Papers in Logic and Foundations, Didactics, Economics*. Holland: D. Reidel Publishing Company.

Menger, K. (1979b) [1978] My memories of L. E. J. Brouwer. In Menger (1979a) *Selected Papers in Logic and Foundations, Didactics, Economics*. Holland: D. Reidel Publishing Company, pp. 237–55.

Menger, K. (ed.) (1931–37) *Ergebnisse eines Mathematische Kolloquiums* (Proceedings of a Mathematical Colloquium). Vienna. (Hebt 1–5, Leibzig and Vienna: Franz Deutick, 1935).

Metzler, L. A. (1945) Stability of multiple markets: the Hicks conditions. *Econometrica*, 13: 277–92.

Metzler, M. (2002) American bankers and the restoration of the Japanese gold standard, 1927–1929. Mimeo. Department of History, Oakland University.

Midutani (Mizutani), Kazuo (1935) Kori keizaigaku no igi oyobi sono hoho (The significance of axiomatic economics and its method). *Kokumin-keizai Zasshi*, 58: 209–30. In Midutani (1956) *Sugakuteki Shii to Keizai Riron* (Mathematical Thinking and Economic Theory). Osaka: Shigensha, pp. 173–91.

Midutani, K. (1939) Cassel-Schlesinger no seisan-hoteishiki no ichiikai nikansuru Wald no kaiho to sono hihyo (Comments on Wald's proof of the uniqueness of the solution for the Cassel-Schlesinger system of production). In *Keizaigaku Keizaishi no Shomondai: Sakanishi Yoshizo Hakushi Kanreki Shukuga Ronshu* (Problems in Economics and Economic History: Festschrift in honor of Dr. Yoshizo Sakanishi for Memorial of his Sixtieth Birthday), edited by Sakanishikai. Tokyo: Iwanami Shoten. Reprinted in Midutani (1956) *Sugakuteki Shii to Keizai Riron* (Mathematical Thinking and Economic Theory). Osaka: Shigensha, pp. 173–191.

Midutani, K. (1956) *Sugakuteki Shii to Keizai Riron* (Mathematical Thinking and Economic Theory). Osaka: Shigensha.

Mikami, Ryuzo (1967) Nihon ni okeru Keinzu keizaigaku no donyu (The introduction of Keynesian economics into Japan). In *Keinzu Keizaigaku* (Keynesian Economics), edited by M. Ito. Tokyo: Toyo Keizai Shinposha, pp. 195–220.

Mill, John Stuart (1848) *Principles of Political Economy: with some of their applications to social philosophy*. London: J. W. Parker. Seventh edn., 1871.

Mill, John Stuart (1884) *Principles of Political Economy*, abridged, with critical, bibliographical, and explanatory notes, and a sketch of the history of political economy by J. Laurence Laughlin, New York: D. Appleton. Translated into Japanese by Tameyuki Amano as *Kotokeizaigenron*, Fuzanbo, 1891.

Mimura, Yukio (1933) Berurin Viin Ryo-Daigaku Inshoki (An impression on the University of Berlin and the University of Vienna). *Iwanami Koza Sugaku*, supplement. Tokyo: Iwanami Shoten.

Ministry of Finance (MOF), Japan (ed.) (1976) *Showa Zaiseishi: Shusen kara kowa made* (Financial History, 1945–1952), vol. 3 *America no Senryo Seisaku* (America's Occupation Policy). Tokyo: Toyo Keizai Shinposha.

Ministry of Finance (MOF), Japan (ed.) (1977) *Showa Zaiseishi: Shusen kara kowa made* (Financial History, 1945–1952), vols 7–8. *Sozei* (Tax). Tokyo: Toyo Keizai Shinposha.

Ministry of Finance (MOF), Japan (ed.) (1990) *Showa Zaiseishi, 1952–1973* (Financial History, 1952–1973), vol. 6. *Sozei* (Tax). Tokyo: Toyo Keizai Shinposha.

Ministry of Finance (MOF), Japan (ed.) (1997) *Showa Zaiseishi, 1952–1973* (Financial History, 1952–1973), vol. 7. *Kokusai* (National Bond). Tokyo: Toyo Keizai Shinposha.

Minoguchi, Takeo, Tamotsu Nishizawa and Aiko Ikeo (2000) From reconstruction to rapid growth. In Ikeo (ed.) (2000) *Japanese Economics and Economists since 1945*. London: Routledge, pp. 210–54.

Mirowski, P. (1984) Physics and the "marginalist revolution." *Cambridge Journal of Economics*, 8: 361–79.

Mirowski, P. (1989) *More Heat than Light*. Cambridge, Mass.: Cambridge University Press.

Mirowski, P. (1991) The when, the how and the why of mathematical expression in the history of economic analysis. *The Journal of Economic Perspectives*, 5: 145–57.

Mises, L. von (1909) The foreign exchange policy of the Austro-Hungarian Bank. *Economic Journal*, 19: 201–11.

Mitsuhashi, Takeo (1929) Keizaibunkennenpo (Table of economic Literature). In *Meiji Bukka Zenshu*, vol. 9 (Economics), edited by Sakuzo Yoshino. Tokyo: Nihonhyornsha, pp. 519–45.

Miyanishi, Kazumi [1956] (2001) *Hotokushihoshi* (A History of Hotoku Shiho). Odawara: Ichien Yugokai.

Miyajima Hideaki and Shunsuke Hanai (2004) Shogakubu enkakushi (A history of the School of Commerce: from the foundation to WWII). In *A Hundred-year History of the School of Commerce*, Waseda University). Tokyo: Waseda University, School of Commerce, pp. 2–95.

Moore, H. L. (1914) *Economic Cycles: Their Law and Cause*. New York: Macmillan. New York: A. M. Kelley, 1967. Trans. by T. Ninagawa, *Keizai Junkanki no Tokeiteki Kenkyu*, Tokyo: Daitokaku, 1928.

Moore, H. L. (1917) *Forecasting the Yield and the Price of Cotton*. New York: Macmillan. New York: A. M. Kelley, 1967.

Moore, H. L. (1929) *Synthetic Economics*. New York: Macmillan. New York: A. M. Kelley, 1967.

Morgan, Mary S. (2012) *The World in the Model: How Economists Work and Think*. Cambridge and New York: Cambridge University Press.

Morgenstern, O. (1976) The collaboration between Oskar Morgenstern and John von Neumann on the theory of games. *Journal of Economic Literature*, 14(3): 805–16.

Mori, K. (1922) Jenoa kaigi ni tsukite (On the Genoa conference). *Ginko Tsushinroku*, 74(442): 43–50.

Mori, S. (1975) Zosho Takahashi Korekiyo no Zaisei Seisaku (Fiscal policy of Korekiyo Takahashi, Finance Minister, 1932–36). *Shokei Ronso* (Kanagawa University), 10: 1–42.

Morishima, M. (1949) Seigakuteki antei joken to dogakuteki antei joken (Static and dynamic stability conditions). *Shakai Kagaku Hyoron*, 3: 136–47.

Morishima, M. (1950a) Antei joken: Keinzu taikei ni sokushite (Stability conditions for Keynesian system). *Kikan Riron Keizaigaku* (Economic Studies Quarterly), 1: 98–108.

Morishima, M. (1950b) Canonical System no antei joken (Stability conditions for canonical system). *Kindai Keizai Riron Kenkyu* (Studies on Modern Economic Theory), 1(2).

Morishima, M. (1950c) *Dogakuteki Keizai Riron*. Tokyo: Kobundo. *Dynamic Economic Theory*. Cambridge: Cambridge University Press, 1996.

Morishima, M. (1961) A historical note on Professor Sono's theory on separability. *International Economic Review*, 2: 272–5.

Morris-Suzuki, T. (1989) *A History of Japanese Economic Thought*. London and New York: Routledge. Trans. by T. Fujii as *Nihon no Keizai Shiso*, Tokyo: Iwanami Shoten, 1991.

Moseley, P., J. Harrigan and J. Toye (1995) *Aid and Power: The World Bank & Policy-based Lending*. Volume 1. *Analysis of Policy Proposals*. Second edn. London: Routledge.

Muto, Isao (1993) Wien no surikeizaigaku to Hilbert-shugi (Mathematical economics in Vienna and Hilbert's view of mathematics). *Mita-gakkai Zasshi*, 86(1): 70–99.

Myrdal, G. (1927) *Prisbildningsproblemet och föränderligheten* (The Problem of Price Formation and Changeability). Uppsala and Stockholm: Almqvist & Wiksell.

Myrdal, G. (1931) Om penningteoretisk jämvikt (On monetary equilibrium). *Ekonomisk Tidskrift*, 33: 191–308. Der Gleichgewichtsbegriff als Instrument der geldtheoretischen Analyse (The concept of equilibrium as an instrument for monetary analysis). In *Beiträge zur Geldtheorie* (Contributions to Monetary Economics), edited by F. A. Hayek.

Vienna: Julius Springer, 1933. *Monetary Equilibrium*. London: W. Hodge. 1939. Trans. by S. Sobajima as *Kaheiteki Kinkoron*, Tokyo: Jitsugyononihonsha, 1943.

Najita, Tetsuo (2009) *Ordinary Economies in Japan: A Historical Perspective, 1750–1950*. Berkeley and Los Angeles: University of California Press.

Nakamura, M. (1982) *Showa no Kyoko* (The Economic Crisis in Showa). Tokyo: Shogakukan.

Nakamura, T. (1967) *Keizai Seisaku no Unmei* (The Destiny of Economic Policy). Tokyo: Nihon Keizai Shimbunsha.

Nakamura, T. (1978) *Nihon Keizai* (The Japanese Economy). Tokyo: University of Tokyo Press.

Nakamura, T. (1981) Takahashi zaisei to kokyo toshi seisaku (Takahashi's fiscal policy and public investment policy). In *Senkanki no Nihon Keizai Bunseki* (The Analysis of the Japanese Economy in the Interwar Period), edited by T. Nakamura. Tokyo: Yamakawa Shuppansha.

Nakamura, T. (1986) *Showa Keizaishi* (Economic History of the Showa Era). Tokyo: Iwanami Shoten.

Nakamura, T. (1994) *Lectures on Modern Japanese Economic History*. Tokyo: LTCB International Library Foundation. The English version of Nakamura (1986) *Showa Keizaishi* (Economic History of the Showa Era). Tokyo: Iwanami Shoten.

Nakamura, Yukihiko (ed.) (1971) *Ando Shoeki, Tominaga Chuki, Miura Baien, Ishida Baigan, Ninomiya Sontoku, Kaiho Seiryo shu* (A Collection of Shoeki Ando, Chuki Tominaga, Baien Miura, Baigan Ishida, Sontoku Ninomiya, Seiryo Kaiho). Tokyo: Chikuma Shobo.

Nakayama, Ichiro (1933) *Junsui Keizaigaku* (Pure Economics). Tokyo: Iwanami Shoten. Reprinted in Nakayama (1972–3) vol. 1 *Nakayama Ichiro Zenshu* (Complete Works of Ichiro Nakayama). Tokyo: Kodansha.

Nakayama, I. (1970) Kindai keizaigaku nitsuite (On modern economics). *Kikan Riron Keizaigaku* (Economic Studies Quarterly), 21. In Nakayama (1972) *Nakayama Ichiro Zenshu* (Complete Works of Ichiro Nakayama), vol. 6, pp. 293–311.

Nakayama, I. (1972–3) *Nakayama Ichiro Zenshu* (Complete Works of Ichiro Nakayama), 18 volumes and supplement. Tokyo: Kodansha.

Nakayama, I. (1979) *Wagamichi Keizaigaku* (My Path to Economics). Tokyo: Kodansha.

Nanto, D. K. and S. Takagi (1985) Korekiyo Takahashi and Japan's recovery from the Great Depression. *American Economic Review*, 75(2): 369–74.

Narumi, S. (1934) Jo (Introduction to Yamada: 1934). *Shogyo Keizai Ronso* 12: 255–6.

Nash, J. F., Jr. (1950a) The bargaining problem. *Econometrica*, 18(2): 155–62. Also in Nash (1996) *Essays on Game Theory*. Cheltenham, UK: Edward Elgar.

Nash, J. F., Jr. (1950b) Equilibrium points in n-person games. *Proceedings of the National Academy of Sciences*, 36: 48–9. Also in Nash (1996) *Essays on Game Theory*. Cheltenham, UK: Edward Elgar.

Nash, J. F., Jr. (1951) Non-cooperative games. *Annals of Mathematics*, 54(2): 286–95. Also in Nash (1996) *Essays on Game Theory*. Cheltenham, UK: Edward Elgar.

Nash, J. F., Jr. (1953) Two-person cooperative games. *Econometrica*, 21(1): 128–40. Also in Nash (1996) *Essays on Game Theory*. Cheltenham, UK: Edward Elgar.

Nash, J. F., Jr. (1996) *Essays on Game Theory*. Introduction by K. Binmore. Cheltenham, UK: Edward Elgar.

Nasu, M. (1995) *Jitsumuka Keinzu* (Keynes as a Practitioner). Tokyo: Chuo Koronsha.

Negishi, Takashi (1960) Welfare economics and existence of an equilibrium for a competitive economy. *Metroeconomica*, 12: 92–7.

Negishi, T. (1961) Monopolistic competition and general equilibrium. *Review of Economic Studies*, 28: 196–201. Also in Negishi (1994a) *General Equilibrium Theory* (Volume 1 of The Collected Essays of Takashi Negishi). Cheltenham, UK: Edward Elgar.

Negishi, T. (1962) The stability of a competitive economy: a survey article. *Econometrica*, 30: 635–69. Also in Negishi (1994a) *General Equilibrium Theory* (Volume 1 of The Collected Essays of Takashi Negishi). Cheltenham, UK: Edward Elgar.

Negishi, T. (1972) Yasui Takuma kyoju to ippan kinkoron no hatten (Takuma Yasui and the development of general equilibrium theory). *Economic Studies Quarterly*, 23: 19–37.

Negishi, T. (1990a) Studies of von Thünen in Japan. *Japan and the World Economy*, 2: 199–209. Also in T. Negishi (1994b) *The History of Economics* (Volume 2 of The Collected Essays of Takashi Negishi). Cheltenham, UK: Edward Elgar.

Negishi, T. (1990b) Letter to A. Ikeo (in Japanese). June 29, 1990.

Negishi, T. (1990c) Recorded message to A. Ikeo (in Japanese). September 12, 1990.

Negishi, T. (1994a) *General Equilibrium Theory* (Volume 1 of The Collected Essays of Takashi Negishi). Cheltenham, UK: Edward Elgar.

Negishi, T. (1994b) *The History of Economics* (Volume 2 of The Collected Essays of Takashi Negishi). Cheltenham, UK: Edward Elgar.

Negishi, T. (1995) Böhm-Bawerk and Shibata on power or market. *Journal of Economics* (Zeitschrift für Nationalökonomie), 61: 281–99. Also in Negishi (2000) *Economic Thought from Smith to Keynes*. (Volume 3 of The Collected Essays of Takashi Negishi) Cheltenham, UK: Edward Elgar.

Negishi, T. (1996) Takuma Yasui and general equilibrium theory. *Japanese Economic Review*, 47(3): 227–34. Also in Negishi (2000) *Economic Thought from Smith to Keynes*. (Volume 3 of The Collected Essays of Takashi Negishi) Cheltenham, UK: Edward Elgar.

Negishi, T. (1998) General equilibrium theory and beyond: Yasuma Takata and Kei Shibata. In Sugihara and Tanaka (eds) (1998) *Economic Thought and Modernization in Japan*. Cheltenham, UK: Edward Elgar, pp. 97–116. Also in Negishi (2000) *Economic Thought from Smith to Keynes*. (Volume 3 of The Collected Essays of Takashi Negishi) Cheltenham, UK: Edward Elgar.

Negishi, T. (2000) *Economic Thought from Smith to Keynes*. (Volume 3 of The Collected Essays of Takashi Negishi) Cheltenham, UK: Edward Elgar.

Negishi, T. (2003) Kinko no anteisei: 40-yonengno kaiko (Stability of equilibrium: A retrospect in forty years). *Annals of the Society of the History of Economic Thought*, 45: 78–85.

Negishi (2008) Unnoticed predecessors of the early Negishi theorems. *International Journal of Economic Theory*, 4: 167–73.

Negishi, T. (2012) Ippankinkoron kara Keizaigakushi e (From general equilibrium Theory to the History of Economics). Kyoto: Mineruvashbo.

Negishi, T. and A. Ikeo (1999) Aoyama Hideo kyoju to keizaigaku (Hideo Aoyama on Economics). In *Aoyama Hideo Sensei no Gakumon to Kyoiku*, edited by Aoyama Hideo Chosakushu Kankokai. Tokyo: Shobunsha.

Neisser, H. (1932) Lohnhöhe und Beschäftigungsgrad im Marktgleichgewicht (Wages height and employment rates in market equilibrium). *Weltwirtschaftliches Archiv*, 36: 413–55.

Neubauer, J. (1930) Die Casselsche Preistheorie (Cassel's theory of price). *Zeitschrift für die gesamte Staatswissenschaft*, 89(1): 53–79.

Neumann, John von (1928) Zur Theorie der Gesellschaftsspiele. *Mathematische Annalen*, 100: 295–320. Also in Neumann (1961–3) vol. 6, pp. 1–26, On the theory of games and strategy, trans. by S. Bargmann in *Annals of Mathematics Studies*, 40: 13–42, 1959.

Neumann, J. von (1937) Über ein ökonomisches Gleichungssystem und eine Verallgemeinerung des Brouwerschen Fixpunktsatzes. *Ergebnisse eines Mathematische Kolloquiums*, 8: 73–83. Trans. as A model of general equilibrium. *Review of Economic Studies*, 13: 1–9, 1945–6.

Neumann, J. von (1961) [1947] The mathematician. In R. B. Heywood (ed.) *The Works of Mind*, Chicago: University of Chicago Press. Also in vol. 1 of J. von Neumann's *Collected Works of John von Neumann*, edited by A. H. Taub. Oxford: Pergamon Press, 1961. pp. 1–9.

Neumann, J. von and O. Morgenstern (1944) *Theory of Games and Economic Behavior*. Princeton: Princeton University Press. Second edn., 1947. Trans. by H. Ginbayashi, K. Hashimoto and T. Miyamoto as *Futari Gemu no Riron*. Tokyo: Tokyo Tosho, 1972.

Newman, P. (1968) *Readings in Mathematical Economics*, vol. 1, *Value Theory*. Baltimore: Johns Hopkins University Press.

Nicholson, J. S. (1914) The report on Indian finance and currency in relation to the gold exchange standard. *Economic Journal*, 35: 236–47.

Nicola, PierCarlo (2000) *Mainstream Mathematical Economics in the 20th Century*. Berlin: Springer.

Niehans, J. (1990) *A History of Economic Theory*. Baltimore and London: Johns Hopkins University Press.

Nikaido, Hukukane (1954a) Zusatz und Berichtigung für meine Mitteilung "Zum Beweis der Verallgemeinerung des Fixpunktsatzes" in diesen Reports (trans. by S. Ikehara into German, a supplement and correction to my report "Proofs of the generalization of fixed point theorems"), Bd. 5, N. 1. *Kodai Mathematical Seminar Reports*, 6.1: 11–12.

Nikaido, H. (1954b) On von Neumann's minimax theorem. *Pacific Journal of Mathematics*, 4(1): 65–72.

Nikaido, H. (1954c) Note on the general economic equilibrium for nonlinear production functions. *Econometrica*, 22(1): 49–57.

Nikaido, H. (1956) On the classical multilateral exchange problem. *Metroeconomica*, 8: 135–45. Also in Newman (1968) *Readings in Mathematical Economics*, vol. 1, *Value Theory*. Baltimore: Johns Hopkins University Press.

Nikaido, H. (1959) Coincidence and some systems of inequalities. *Journal of the Mathematical Society of Japan*, 11(4): 354–73.

Nikaido, H. (1968) *Convex Structure and Economic Theory*. New York and London: Academic Press.

Nikaido, H. (1970) [1960] *Introduction to Sets and Mappings in Modern Economics*. Amsterdam: North-Holland. Trans. by K. Sato from *Gendai Sugaku no Suriteki Hoho*. Tokyo: Iwanami Shoten, 1960.

Nikaido, H. (1991) Letter to A. Ikeo (in Japanese), November 22.

Nikaido, H. (1996–7) Correspondence with A. Ikeo (in Japanese).

Ninomiya, Sontoku (1927–30) *Ninomiya Sontoku Zenshu* (The Complete Works of Sontoku Ninomiya), edited by Shintaro Sasai and the Editorial Committee, 36 volumes. Kakegawa: Ninomiya Sontoku Igyosenyokai.

Ninomiya, Yasuhiro (2010) *Ninomiya Kinjiro Seiden* (The Biography of Kinjiro Ninomiya). Kashiwa, Chiba Prefecture: Research Institute of Moralogy.

Nishikawa. K. (1979) Nihon kaikeishi: yoshikiboki no wagakuni heno donyu (The history of Japanese accounting: the introduction of Western bookkeeping into Japan). In O. Kojima (ed.) (1979) *Kaikeishi oyobi Kaikeigakushi* (The History of Accounting). Tokyo: Chuo Keizaisha, pp. 284–309.

Nishizawa, T. (2001) Lujo Brentano, Alfred Marshall, and Tokuzo Fukuda: the reception and transformation of the German Historical School in Japan. In Y. Shionoya (ed.) (2001) *The German Historical School: The Historical and Ethical Approach to Economics*. London: Routledge.

Noguchi, A. (2000) External liberalization and industrial policy. In Ikeo (ed.) (2000) *Japanese Economics and Economists since 1945*. London: Routledge, pp. 255–80.

Ohara Institute for Social Research, Hosei University (ed.) (1971) *Ohara Shakai Mondai Kenkyujo Gojunenshi* (A Fifty-year History of the Ohara Institute for Research Study). Tokyo: Hosei Daigaku Shuppankyoku.

Ohkawa, Kazushi (1957) *The Growth Rate of the Japanese Economy since 1878*. Tokyo: Kinokuniya.

Ohkawa, K., M. Shinohara and M. Umemura (eds) (1965–85) *Estimates of Long-Term Economic Statistics of Japan since 1868*. Tokyo: Toyo Keizai Shinposha.

Ohlin, B. (1937) Some notes on the Stockholm theory of savings and investment. *Economic Journal*, 47: 53–69, 221–40.

Ohta, Hiroshi (1999) A Tribute to Martin Bronfenbrenner: "Tanoshikatta." *Duke Journal of Economics*, XI, spring 1999. http://econ.duke.edu/about/history/individuals/martin-bronfenbrenner (accessed December 11, 2013).

Okada, Junichi (1975) Keizaigakusha toshiteno Amano Tameyuki (The establishment of economic science in Japan). *Waseda Commercial Review*, (249): 43–66.

Omori, Ikuo (1998) For diffusing economic knowledge: Tokyo Senmon Gakko (Waseda), in Sugiyama and Mizuta (eds) (1988) *Enlightenment and beyond: political economy comes to Japan*. Tokyo: University of Tokyo Press, pp. 171–87.

Oslington, P. (2000) Japanese contributions to the theory of international trade. *Japanese Economic Review*, 51(3): 334–48.

Ouchi, Hyoye (Hyoe) (1948) Financial and monetary situation in post-war Japan. Tokyo: Nihon Taiheiyo Mondai Chosakai (Japan Institute of Pacific Studies), distributed by International Pub. Co.

Ouchi, Tsutomu (1967) *Fashizumu heno Michi* (The Way to Fascism). Tokyo: Chuo Koronsha.

Pareto, V. (1906) *Manuale di economic politica. Manuel d'économie politique*, 2e éd., 1909. *Manual of Political Economy*, trans. by A. S. Schwier. New York: Kelley, 1971. The mathematical appendix, trans. by M. Hayakawa, 1931.

Patinkin, Don (1956) *Money, Interest, and Prices: An integration of monetary and value theory*. Evanston, Ill.: Row, Peterson. Second edn., New York: Harper & Row, 1965.

Penrose, E. F. (1987) Memoirs of Japan, 1925–30. In Dore and Sinha (1987) *Japan and World Depression: Then and Now*. London: Macmillan.

Physical Society of Japan (PSJ) (1978) *Nihon no Butsurigakushi* (The History of Physics in Japan). Two volumes. Tokyo: Tokai Daigaku Shuppankai.

Picard, Emile (1908) *Traité d'analyse*, 2e éd., Tome 3. Reprint, Sceaux, France: Éditions Jacques Gabay, 1991.

Plenge, J. (1913) *Von der Diskontpolitik zur Herrschaft über den Geldmarkt*. Berlin: Julius Springer.

Poincaré, Henri (1892) *Les méthodes nouvelles de la mécanique céleste*. *New Methods of Celestial Mechanics*, edited and introduced by Daniel L. Goroff. Woodbury, NY: American Institute of Physics, 1993.

Polak, J. J. (1996) The contribution of the International Monetary Fund. In Coats (ed.) (1996) *The Post-1945 Internationalization of Economics*. Annual Supplement to Volume 28 of the *History of Political Economy*. Durham, NC: Duke University Press, 211–24.

Punzo, L. F. (1989) Von Neumann and Karl Menger's Mathematical Colloquium. In Dore, Chakravarty and Goodwin (eds) (1989) *John von Neumann and Modern Economics*. Oxford: Clarendon Press, pp. 29–65.

Punzo, L. F. (1991) The School of mathematical formalism and the Viennese circle of mathematical economists. *Journal of the History of Economic Thought*, 13(1): 1–18.

Ravina, Mark J. (2010) Confucian banking: The community granary (Shaso) in rhetoric and practice. In Gramlich-Oka and Smits (eds) (2010) *Economic Thought in Early Modern Japan*. Leiden and Boston: Brill, pp. 179–204.

Reid, C. (1986) [1970–6] *Hilbert-Courant*. New York: Springer-Verlag. Trans. by K. Iyanaga as *Hiruberuto*, Tokyo Iwanami Shoten, 1972. Trans. by M. Kato as *Kuranto*, Tokyo Iwanami Shoten, 1978.

Ricci, Umberto (1930) Die synthetische ökonomie von Henry Ludwell Moore. *Zeitschrift für Nationalökonomie*, 1(5): 649–68.

Robertson, D. H. (1932) [1926] *Banking Policy and the Price Level: An Essay in the Theory of the Trade Cycle*. London: P. S. King & Son. Trans. by H. Takada as *Ginko Seisaku to Kakaku Suijun*, Tokyo: Genshodo Shoten, 1955.

Robertson, D. H. (1933) Saving and hoarding. *Economic Journal*, 43: 399–413.

Robinson, J. (1933) *The Economics of Imperfect Competition*. London: Macmillan. Trans. by Y. Kato as *Fukanzen Kyoso no Keizaigaku*, Tokyo: Bungado Shoten, 1956.

Robinson, Sherman (1989) Multisectoral models. In Chapter 18 of *Handbook of Development Economics*, Volume II, edited by Hollis Chenery and T. N. Srinivasan. Amsterdam: Elsevier, pp. 885–947.

Routh, E. J. (1877) *A Treatise on the Stability of a Given State of Motion*. London: Macmillan and Co.

Routh, E. J. (1907) *Advanced Rigid Dynamics*, sixth edn. Cambridge: Cambridge University Press.

Samuelson, P. A. (1941a) The stability of equilibrium: comparative statics and dynamics. *Econometrica*, 9: 97–120.

Samuelson, P. A. (1941b) Conditions that the roots of a polynomial be less than unity in absolute value. *Annals of Mathematical Statistics*, 12: 360–64.

Samuelson, P. A. (1942) The stability of equilibrium: linear and nonlinear systems. *Econometrica*, 10: 1–25.

Samuelson, P. A. (1944) The relation between Hicksian stability and true dynamic stability. *Econometrica*, 12: 256–7.

Samuelson, P. A. (1946) Lord Keynes and the General Theory. *Econometrica*, 14: 187–200.

Samuelson, P. A. (1947) *Foundations of Economic Analysis*. Cambridge, Mass.: Harvard University Press. Enlarged Edition, 1983. Trans. by R. Sato as *Keizai Bunseki no Kiso*, Tokyo: Keiso Shobo, 1967, 1986.

Samuelson, P. A. (1948) *Economics*. New York: McGraw-Hill. Trans. by S. Tsuru as *Keizaigaku* from the sixth edn., Tokyo: Iwanami Shoten, 1966–7. From the ninth edn., 1974. From the eleventh edn., 1981.

Sapolsky, H. M. (1990) *Science and the Navy*. Princeton: Princeton University Press.

Sasahara, Shogo (1981) Sekkyokuteki keikiseisaku no rironteki kiso (Theoretical basis for expansionary policy of K. Takahashi). *Chuo Daigaku Keizai Kenkyujo Nenpo* (Chuo University), 12: 201–26.

Sasahara, S. (1997) Senkanki Nihon no keiki seisakuron (Controversy over the policy for economic recovery in interwar Japan). *Keizaigakusi Gakkai Nenpo* (The Society for the History of Economic Thought, Japan) 35: 1–14.

Sasaki, C. (1994) The adoption of Western mathematics in Meiji Japan, 1853–1903. In C. Sasaki, M. Sugiura and J. W. Dauben (eds) (1994) *The Intersection of History and Mathematics*. Basel: Birkhäuser Verlag, pp. 165–86.

Sasaki, C., M. Sugiura and J. W. Dauben (eds) (1994) *The Intersection of History and Mathematics*. Basel: Birkhäuser Verlag.

Sato, Kazuo (1991) Econometric Models of the Japanese Economy. In *A History of Macroeconometric Model-Building*, edited by R. G. Bodkin, L. R. Klein and K. Marwah. Brookfield, Vt.: Edward Elgar.

Sato, K. (ed.) (1980) *Industry and Business in Japan*. Armonk, NY: M. E. Sharpe; London: Croom Helm, *c.*1980.

Sato, K. (ed.) (1984) *The Anatomy of Japanese Business*. Armonk, NY: M. E. Sharpe; London: Croom Helm.

Sato, K. (ed.) (1999) *The Transformation of the Japanese Economy*. Armonk, NY: M. E. Sharpe.

Schaede, Ulrike (1989) Forwards and futures in Tokugawa-period Japan: A new perspective on the Dojima rice market. *Journal of Banking & Finance*, 13: 487–513.

Scherer, F. M. (2000) The emigration of German-speaking economists after 1933. *Journal of Economic Literature*, 38: 614–26.

Schlesinger, K. (1933) Über die produktionsgleichungen der ökonomischen Wertlehre (On the equation of production in the theory of value). In K. Menger (ed.) (1933) *Ergebnisse eines Mathematischen Kolloquiums*. Leipzig and Vienna: Franz Deuticke.

Schmidt, C. (2000) Economics in France: a manifold system. In Coats (ed.) (2000) *The Development of Economics in Western Europe since 1945*. London: Routledge, pp. 129–47.

Schultz, Henry (1925) The statistical law of demand as illustrated by the demand for sugar. *Journal of Political Economy*, 33: 481–504 and 577–631.

Schultz, Henry (1927) Theoretical consideration relating to supply. *Journal of Political Economy*, 35: 437–64.

Schultz, Henry (1928) *Statistical Laws of Demand and Supply, with Special Application to Sugar*. Chicago: University of Chicago Press.

Schultz, H. (1930) *Der Sinn de statistischen Nachfragekurven* (The meaning of demand curves). Bonn: Kurt Schroeder.

Schultz, H. (1935) Interrelations of demand, price, and income. *Journal of Political Economy*, 43: 433–81.

Schumpeter, Elizabeth Boody (ed.) (1940) *The Industrialization of Japan and Machukuo, 1930–1940: Population, Raw Material and Industry*. New York: Macmillan.

Schumpeter, Joseph Alois (1908) *Das Wesen und der Hauptinhalt der theoretischen Nationalökonomie* (The Essence and Main Content of Economics). Leipzig: Duncker & Humblot. Trans. by T. Kimura and T. Yasui as *Riron Keizaigaku no Honshitsu to Shuyo Naiyo*, Tokyo: Nihon Hyoronsha, 1936. Trans. by Bruce A. McDaniel, *The Nature and Essence of Theoretical Economics*, Edison, NJ: Transaction Publishers, 2009.

Schumpeter, J. A. (1912) *Theorie der wirtschaftlichen Entwicklung*. Leipzig: Duncker & Humblot. Second edn., Munich and Leipzig: Duncker & Humblot, 1926. Trans. by Redvers Opie as *The Theory of Economic Development: An Inquiry into Profits, Capital, Credit, Interest, and the Business Cycle*, Cambridge, Mass.: Harvard

University Press, 1934. Trans. by I. Nakayama and S. Tobata as *Keizai Hatten no Riron*, Tokyo: Iwanami Shoten, 1937.

Schumpeter, J. A. (1931a) The theory of business cycle. *Keizaigaku Ronshu* (University of Tokyo), 1: 1–18.

Schumpeter, J. A. (1931b) The present state of international commercial policy. *Kokumin Keizai Zasshi*, 50: 481–506.

Schumpeter, J. A. (1931c) The present state of economics or on systems, schools and methods. *Kokumin Keizai Zasshi*, 50: 679–705.

Schumpeter, J. A. (1933) The common sense of econometrics. *Econometrica*, 1: 5–12.

Schumpeter, J. A. (1942) *Capitalism, Socialism and Democracy*. New York: Harper & Brothers. Trans. by I. Nakayama and S. Tobata as *Shihonshugi, Shakaishugi, Minshushugi*, Tokyo: Toyo Keizai Shinposha, 1961–2.

Schumpeter, J. A. (1954) *History of Economic Analysis*. New York: Oxford University Press. Trans. by S. Tobata as *Keizai Bunseki no Rekishi*, seven vols. Tokyo: Iwanami Shoten, 1955–62.

Schumpeter, J. A. (1982) [1931] The "crisis" in economics fifty years ago. *Journal of Economic Literature*, 20(3): 1049–59.

Schumpeter, J. A. (1991a) [1931] Recent development of political economy. *Kobe University Economic Review*, 28: 1–15.

Schumpeter, J. A. (1991b) [1932] Recent development of political economy. In Schumpeter (1991c) *The Economics and Sociology of Capitalism*, edited by R. Swedberg. Princeton: Princeton University Press, pp. 284–97.

Schumpeter, J. A. (1991c) *The Economics and Sociology of Capitalism*, edited by R. Swedberg. Princeton: Princeton University Press.

Schur, J. (1918) Über Potenzreichen, die im Innern des Einheitskreises beschränkt sind (On the potential which is limited in a unit circle). *Journal für die reine und angewandte Mathematik*, 148: 122–45.

Schwödiauer, G. (1987) Karl Menger. In J. Eatwell, M. Milgate and P. Newman (eds) (1987) *The New Palgrave: A Dictionary of Economics*. London and Tokyo: Macmillan and Maruzen, vol. 3, pp. 444–5.

Seki, T. (1986) Surikeizaigaku (Mathematical economics). In *Hitotsubashi Daigaku Gakumon-shi*. Tokyo: Hitotsubashi University, pp. 323–75.

Seligman, Edwin R. A. (1905) *Principles of Economics, with special reference to American conditions*. New York and London: Longmans, Green and Co. Trans. by Y. Ishikawa as *Keizaigenron*, from the fourth edn. Tokyo: Genshodo, 1912.

Senn, P. R. (1987) What has happened to Gustav von Schmoller in English? *History of Economics Society Bulletin*, 11: 252–94.

Shepherd, G. B. (ed.) (1995) *Rejected: Leading Economists Ponder the Publication Process*. Arizona: Thomas Horton and Daughters.

Shibata, Kei (1930) Kasseru-shi no "kakaku keisei no kiko" no ginmi (An examination of "the mechanism of price formation" as explained by Mr. Cassel). *Keizai Ronso*, 30: 916–36.

Shibata, K. (1933) Marx's analysis of capitalism and the general equilibrium theory of the Lausanne School. *Kyoto University Economic Review*, 8(1): 107–36.

Shibata, K. (1934–79) Correspondence. Department of Economics, Kyoto University.

Shibata, K. (1937) Some questions on Mr. Keynes's general theory of employment, interest and money. *Kyoto University Economic Review*, 12(1): 83–96.

Shibata, K. (1939) Further comments on Mr. Keynes' general theory. *Kyoto University Economic Review*, 14(3): 45–72.

Shibata, K. (1987) *Keizai no Hosoku wo Motomete* (My Quest for Economic Laws). Tokyo: Nihonkeizaihyoronsha.

Shima, K. (1983) Iwayuru Takahashi zaisei nitsuite (On Takahashi's fiscal policy). *Kinyu Kenkyu* (Bank of Japan) 2(2): 83–124.

Shionoya, Tsukumo (1974) Ishibashi-shi to Keinzu (Mr. Ishibashi and Keynes). In Y. Cho (ed.) (1074) *Ishibashi Tanzan: Hito to Shiso*. Tokyo: Toyo Keizai Shinposha, pp. 158–63.

Shionoya, Yuichi (1990) Instrumentalism in Schumpeter's economic methodology. *History of Political Economy*, 22(2): 187–222.

Shionoya, Y. (1995) *Schumpeter and the Idea of Social Science: Metatheoretical Study*. Cambridge: Cambridge University Press.

Shionoya, Y. (ed.) (2001) *The German Historical School: The Historical and Ethical Approach to Economics*. London: Routledge.

Shiroyama, Saburo (1996) *Hana Useteha Omoshirokarazu* (Unexcited When the Flower is Gone: Professor Yamada's Way of Living and Thinking). Tokyo: Kadokawa Shoten.

Shiroyama, Tomoko (2008) *China during the Great Depression: market, state, and the world economy, 1929–1937*. Cambridge, Mass.: Harvard University Asia Center, distributed by Harvard University Press.

Shizume, Masato (2009) *Sekai Kyoko to Keizai Seisaku* (Japan's Economic Policies during the Great Depression: A Lesson of a Small Open Economy for the Contemporary). Tokyo: Nihon Keizai Shinposha.

Shoup, S. Carl (1985) Preface to Y. Fukuda and the Research Group of the Shoup Tax System (eds) (1985) *Shoup no Zeisei Kankoku* (Shoup's Tax Report). Tokyo: Kasumi Shuppankai, pp. 5–6.

Shoup, S. Carl (1988) The tax mission in Japan, 1949–1950. Presented at the Conference on Lessons from Fundamental Tax Reform in Developing Countries, Washington, DC, April 1988.

Shoup Kankoku 50nen no kiseki to kadai (The Significance and Problems of the Shoup Recommendations: Examinations after 50 years), Special Issue of *Sozeiho Kenkyu* (Japanese Tax Law Review), No. 28.

Shoup Mission (1949) *Report on Japanese Taxation*. General Headquarters, Supreme Commander for the Allied Powers (SCAP). Tokyo: Japan.

Sims, C. A. (1980) Macroeconomics and Reality. *Econometrica*, 48: 1–48.

Shoda, K. (1932) *Chusho Daisugaku* (Abstract Algebra). Tokyo: Iwanami Shoten.

Skidelsky, R. (1992) *John Maynard Keynes: The Economist as Saviour 1920–1937*. London: Macmillan.

Slutsky, E. (1915) Sulla teoria del bilancio del consumatore (On the theory of the budget of the consumer) *Giornale degli Economisti e Rivista di Statistica*, 51: 1–26. In *Readings in Price Theory*, edited by K. E. Boulding and G. J. Stigler, selected by the American Economic Association. Chicago: R. D. Irwin, 1952. London: Allen & Unwin, 1953.

Smethurst, J. Richard (2007) *From Foot Soldier to Finance Minister: Takahashi Korekiyo, Japan's Keynes*. Cambridge, Mass.: Harvard University Asia Center, distributed by Harvard University Press. Trans. as Korekiyo Takahasi: Nihon no keinzu sono shogai to shiso by Masato Shizume, Daisuke Hayakawa and Mari Ounki, Tokyo: Toyo Keizai Shinposha.

Smith, Thomas C. (1959) *The Agrarian Origins of Modern Japan*. Stanford, Calif.: Stanford University Press.

Smith, Thomas C. (1988) *Native Sources of Japanese Industrialization, 1750–1920*. Berkeley and Los Angeles: University of California Press.

Solow, Robert (1956) Book review: Elements of Pure Economics. *Econometrica*, 24: 87–9.

Sono, Masazo (1943) Kakaku hendo ni tomonau bunrikanouzai no jukyu hendo. *Kokumin Keizai Zasshi*, 74: 1–51. English version published as Sono (1961).

Sono, M. (1944) Shijo kinko no antei joken (Stability conditions for market equilibrium). *Keizai Ronso*, 58: 17–51.

Sono, M. (1955) Positive and negative relations and stability conditions. *Osaka Economic Papers*, 3: 15–28.

Sono, M. (1961) The effect of price changes in the demand and supply of separable goods. *International Economic Review*, 2: 239–71. English version of Sono (1943) made available by K. Sato.

Soong, T. V. (1937) Lessons of Chinese monetary policy. In Gayer (ed.) (1937) *The Lessons of Monetary Experience: Essays in Honor of Irving Fisher*. New York: Rinehart and Company, pp. 347–62.

Sprague, O. M. W. (1910) *History of Crises under the National Banking System* (National Monetary Commission). Washington, DC: Government Printing Office. Reprint, Fairfield, NJ: Augustus M. Kelley, 1977.

Stackelberg, H. v. (1933) Zwei kritische Bemerkungen zur Preitheorie Gustav Cassel (Two comments on Gustav Cassel's theory of price). *Zeitschrift für Nationalökonomie*, 4: 456–72.

Streissler, E. W. (1992) Comment on A. Ikeo "When economics harmonized mathematics in Japan", at the tenth world congress of the International Economic Association in Moscow on August 24.

Sugihara, Shiro (1987a) Kei Shibata. In J. Eatwell, M. Milgate and P. Newman (eds) (1987) *The New Palgrave: A Dictionary of Economics*. London and Tokyo: Macmillan and Maruzen, vol. 4, p. 325.

Sugihara, S. (1987b) *Nihon no Keizaizasshi* (Japanese Economic Magazines). Tokyo: Nihonkeizaihyoronsha.

Sugihara, Shiro (1988) Economists in journalism: Liberalism, nationalism and their variants. In Sugiyama and Mizuta (eds) (1988) *Enlightenment and Beyond: Political Economy Comes to Japan*. Tokyo: University of Tokyo Press, pp. 237–53.

Sugihara, S. (1990) *Nihon no Keizaishisokatachi* (Japanese Economic Thinkers). Tokyo: Nihonkeizaihyoronsha.

Sugihara, S. and T. Tanaka (eds) (1998) *Economic Thought and Modernization in Japan*. Cheltenham, UK: Edward Elgar.

Sugimoto, Eiichi [1935] (1937) *Beikoku Juyo-hosoku no Kenkyu* (A Study on the Law of Demand for Rice). Tokyo: Japan Society for the Promotion of Science.

Sugimoto, E. (1942). Moore no keiryo-keizaigakuteki kenkyu to sono hikaku-seitaironteki seikaku (Moore on econometric study and its comparative-static nature). *Keizaigaku Kenkyu*, 7: 59–163.

Sugiyama, Chuhei and Hiroshi Mizuta (eds) (1988) *Enlightenment and Beyond: Political Economy Comes to Japan*. Tokyo: University of Tokyo Press.

Sugiyama, C., Ikuo Omori and H. Takemoto (1993) Adam Smith in Japan. In *Adam Smith: International Perspectives*, edited by H. Mizuta and C. Sugiyama. Basingstoke and London: Macmillan, Chapter 16.

Suzumura, Kotaro (1999) Report on the Far Eastern Activities of the Econometric Society. *Econometrica*, 67: 221–33.

Takagi, Senjiro (1913a) Fisha-shi no bukkachousetsusaku ni taisuru Kanbe-Yamazaki ryohakushi no hihyo ni tsukite (On Dr. Kanbe and Yamazaki's comments on Mr.

Fisher's plan of compensating the level of prices). *Kokka Gakkai Zasshi*, 27(7): 981–1007, July.

Takagi, S. (1913b) Kaheikachi ni tsukite Kanbe-hakushi ni kotau (Answers to Dr. Kanbe on the value of money). *Kokka Gakkai Zasshi*, 27(9): 1377–97, September.

Takagi, S. (1913c) Bukkachosetsu ni kanshite futatabi Yamazaki-hakushi no oshie wo kou (Questions to Dr. Yamazaki on the compensation of money, II). *Kokka Gakkai Zasshi*, 27(10): 1457–90, October.

Takagi, S. (1914) Kaheikachi ni tsukite Kanbe-Yamazaki ryohakushi no hanmon ni kotau (Answers to Dr. Kanbe and Yamazaki on the value of money). *Kokka Gakkai Zasshi*, 28(4): 537–62, April.

Takagi, Teiji (1920) Über eine Theorie des relative Abel'schen Zahlkörpers (On a relative Abelian number field). *Journal of the College of Science, Imperial University of Tokyo*, 41: 1–133.

Takagi, T. (1935a) [1930] *Daisugaku Kogi* (Lectures on Algebra), third edn. Tokyo: Kyoritsushuppan.

Takagi, T. (1935b) Nihon no sugaku to Fujisawa Hakase (Japanese mathematics and Dr. Fujisawa). *Kyoiku*, 3: 1342–6.

Takahashi, Korekiyo (1936a) *Takahashi Korekiyo Jiden* (Autobiography of Korekiyo Takahashi). Reprint, Tokyo: Chuokoronsha, 1976.

Takahashi, K. (1936b) *Zuisoroku* (Memories). Tokyo: Chikura Shobo.

Takashima, Saichiro (1915) *Kahei to Bukka no Genri* (Principles of Money and Prices). Tokyo: Saibunkan.

Takata, Yasuma (1929–32) *Keizaigaku Shinko* (New Lectures on Economics). Tokyo: Iwanami Shoten.

Takata, Y. (1937) Unemployment and wages: A critical review of Mr. Keynes' theory of employment. *Kyoto University Economic Review*, 12(1): 1–18.

Takata Yasuma Memorial Committee (ed.) (1981) *Takata Yasuma Sensei no Shogai to Gakusetsu* (Yasuma Takata: His Life and Theory). Tokyo: Sobunsha.

Takemura, Eiji (1997) *The Perception of Work in Tokugawa Japan: A Study of Ishida Baigan and Ninomiya Sontoku*. Lanham, MD., New York and Oxford: University Press of America.

Taketani, M., R. Kubo, E. Sugimoto, Z. Takashima and S. Tsuru (1949) *Shizen Kagaku to Shakai Kagaku no Gendaiteki Koryu* (Contemporary Communication between Natural and Social Scientists). Tokyo: Rironsha.

Takizawa, S. (1991) Toporoji (Topology) In *Gendai Surikagaku Jiten* (1991) (Encyclopedia of Modern Mathematical Science), edited by H. Hironaka and the Editorial Committee. Osaka: Osaka Shoseki and Maruzen, pp. 1067–82.

Tamaki, N. (1995) *Japanese Banking: A History, 1859–1959*. Cambridge: Cambridge University Press.

Tanaka, Ikuo (1985) [1980] *Nihon Ginko Kin'yu Seisakushi* (A History of Financial Policies by the Bank of Japan). Student edn. Tokyo: Yuhikaku.

Tanaka, I. (1989) *Showa Zenki Tsukashi Dansho* (Toward a Monetary History during the First Half of the Showa Era). Tokyo: Yuhikaku.

Tanese, Shigeru (1953) Sugimoto Eiichi kyoju nenpu (The chronological record of Professor Eiichi Sugimoto). *Hitotsubashi Ronso*, 29: 93–112.

Tedzuka, Sumio (1920) *Gossen Kenkyu* (A Study of Gossen). Tokyo: Dobunkan.

Thünen, J. H. v. (1842) *Der isolierte Staat in Beziehung auf Landswirtschaft und Nationalökonomie* (Isolated State with respect to Agriculture and Political Economy).

Rostock: Leopold. Reprint, Jena, Germany: G. Fischer, 1921. Trans. by Y. Kondo as *Koritsukoku*, Tokyo: Seibido Shoten, 1929.

Tinbergen, J. (1930) Bestimmung und Duetung von Angebotskurven Ein Beispiel. *Zeitschrift für Nationalökonomie*, 1: 667–79.

Tobata, S. and K. Ohkawa (1938) *Beikoku no Jichiteki Hanbai Tosei* (Autonomous Sales Organ of Rice). Tokyo: Japan Society for the Promotion of Science.

Tobin, J. (1958) Estimation of Relationships for Limited Dependent Variables. *Econometrica*, 6: 24–36.

Tohoku University (1960) *Tohoku Daigaku Gojunenshi* (A Fifty-year History of Tohoku University). Two volumes. Sendai: Tohoku Daigaku.

Tomita, Kokei (1883) *Hotokuki* (A Peasant Sage of Japan). Tokyo: Department of Imperial Household. Dainokai, 1890. *Hochu Hotokuki* (A Peasant Sage of Japan with Notes), translated into contemporary Japanese and annotated by Norihiko Sasai, 1954. Revised version, Ichienyugokai, 1976.

Tomita, Kokei (2012) [1912] *A Peasant Sage of Japan: The Life and Work of Sontoku Ninomiya*, translated by Tadasu Yoshimoto from Tomita (1883). London, New York, Bombay and Calcutta: Longmans, Green and Co., 1912. Reprint, General Books LLCTM, 2012.

Tomonaga, Sin-itiro (1949) *Ryoshi Rikigaku* (Quantum Mechanics). Revised edn., 1951. Tokyo: Misuzu Shobo.

Touffut, Jean-Philippe (ed.) (2007) *Augustin Cournot: Modelling Economics*. Cheltenham. UK: Edward Elgar.

Toyo Keizai Shinposha, Committee for Publishing A Hundred Year History (1996) *Toyo Keizai Shinposha Hyakunenshi* (A Hundred Year History of Toyo Keizai Shinposha). Tokyo: Toyo Keizai Shinposha.

Trepp, G. (1993) *Bankgeschäfte mit dem Feind* (Banking with the Enemy). Zürich: Rotpunktverlag. Trans. by Y. Komagome and Y. Sato as *Kokusai Kessai Ginko no Senso Sekinin*, Tokyo: Nihonkeizaihyoronsha, 2000.

Tsuru, S. (1964a) *Kindai Keizaigaku no Gunzo* (Modern Economists). Tokyo: Nihon Keizai Shimbunsha.

Tsuru, S. (1964b) Survey of economic research in postwar Japan. *American Economic Review*, 54(4), Part Two, Supplement, pp. 79–101.

Tsuru, S. (1984) A survey of economic research in Japan, 1960–1983. *Economic Review* (Hitotsubashi University), 35: 289–306.

Tsuru, S. (1992) Scientific humanism as an ideal. In *Eminent Economists: Their Life Philosophies*, edited by M. Szenberg. New York: Cambridge University Press. Trans. by S. Tsuru (and his former students) as *Gendai Keizaigaku no Kyosei*, Tokyo: Iwanami Shoten, 1994.

Tsurumi, S. (1983) Ryotaisenkan no Nihon Ginko (The Bank of Japan in the interwar period). In Kato (ed.) (1983) *Nihon Kin'yuron no Shitekikenkyu* (Historical Development of Monetary Economics in Japan). Tokyo: Tokyo Daigaku Shuppankai, pp. 52–100.

Tucker, A. W. (1950) A two person dilemma. Mimeo. Stanford University. (Brander 1985).

University of Tokyo, Department of Economics (1976) *Tokyo Daigaku Keizaigakubu Gojunenshi* (A Fifty-year History of the Economics Department, the University of Tokyo). Tokyo: Tokyo Daigaku Shuppankai.

Uyeda, Teijiro (ed.) (1938) *The Small Industries of Japan: Their Growth and Development*. London: Oxford University Press.

Uzawa, H. (1962) Walras's existence theorem and Brouwer's fixed-point theorem. *Kikan*

Riron Keizaigaku (Economic Studies Quarterly), 13: 59–62. Also in Uzawa's *Preference, Production and Capital: Selected Papers of Hirofumi Uzawa*. Cambridge: Cambridge University Press, 1988, pp. 175–8.

Uzawa, H. (1999) Born in the shadow of the mountains. In A. Heertje (ed.) (1999) *The Makers of Modern Economics*, vol. 4. Cheltenham, UK: Edward Elgar.

Valk, W. L. (1928) *The Principles of Wages*. London: P. S. King & Son.

van der Waerden, B. L. (1930–1) *Moderne Algebra* (Unter benutzung von vorlesungen von E. Artin und E. Noether), two vols. Berlin: Springer Verlag. Zweite Verbesserte Auflage (Second enlarged edition), 1937. Trans. by F. Blum and J. R. Schulenberger as *Modern Algebra*, New York: Ungar, 1953.

Vickrey, William (1947) *Agenda for Progressive Taxation*. New York: McGraw-Hill.

Volpe, G. La (1936) *Studi Sulla Teoria Dell' Equilibrio Economico Dinamico Generale*. Naples: Jovene. Trans. by H. Ampt (with foreword by M. Morishima and M. Di Matteo) as *Studies on the Theory of General Dynamic Economic Equilibrium*. London: Macmillan, 1993.

Wakita, Shigeru (2001) Efficiency of the Dojima rice futures market in Tokugawa-period Japan. *Journal of Banking & Finance*, 25: 535–54.

Wald, A. (1935) Über die eindeutige positive Lösbarkeit der neuen Produktionsgleichungen (I). In K. Menger (ed.) (1931–7) *Ergebnisse eines Mathematischen Kolloquiums*. Leipzig and Vienna: Franz Deuticke. Trans. by W. Baumol as On the unique non-negative solvability of the new production equations, part I, in Baumol and Goldfeld (ed.) (1968), pp. 281–88.

Wald, A. (1936a) Über die Produktionsgleichungen der ökonomischen Wertlehre (II). In K. Menger (ed.) *Ergebnisse eines Mathematischen Kolloquiums*. Leipzig and Vienna: Franz Deuticke. Trans by W. Baumol as On the production equations of economic value theory II, in Baumol and Goldfeld (1968) *Precursors in Mathematical Economics*. London: London School of Economics, pp. 289–93.

Wald, A. (1936b) Über einige Gleichungssysteme der mathematischen Ökonomie. *Zeitschrift für Nationalökonomie*, 7: 637–70. Trans. by O. Eckstein as On some systems of equations of mathematical economics, in *Econometrica*, 19: 368–403.

Walras, Léon (1874–7) *Eléments d'économie politique pure, ou, Théorie de la richesse sociale*. Lausanne: Corbaz. Fourth edn., Lauanne: Rouge, 1900. New edn., 1926. Trans. by S. Tedzuka as *Junsui Keizaigaku Yoron*, Tokyo: Moriyama Shoten. Trans. by W. Jaffe as *Elements of Pure Economics: or, The Theory of Social Wealth*, Homewood. Ill.: Irwin, 1954. *Oeuvres economiques completes: Auguste et Léon Walras*, Volume 10, Paris: Economica, 1992.

Walras, L. (1896) *Études d'économie sociale*. Lausanne: F. Rouge et cie, s. a. Paris: R. Pichon et R. Durand-Auzias.

Walras, L. (1898) *Études d'économie politique appliquée*. Lausanne: F. Rouge.

Waseda University History Center (ed.) (1982) *Miyako no Seihoku* (The Northeast of the Metropolis). Waseda University.

Watanabe, Kan (1932) Juyo oyobi kyokyu no danryokusei yori doshutsuseru keikijunkan no ichiriron (A theory of the business cycle derived from the elasticity of supply and demand). In *Nosei to Keizai* (Agricultural Policy and the Economy), pp. 238–50, edited by Hokkaido Imperial University.

Watanabe, M. (1924) W. E. Johnson no "The pure theory of utility curves" to A. W. Zotoff no "Notes on the mathematical theory of production" nitsuite (On W. E. Johnson's "The pure theory of utility curves" and A. W. Zotoff's "Notes on the mathematical theory of production"). *Shogaku Kenkyu*, 3: 1001–46.

Watanabe, M. and M. Hisatake (1933) *Keizai heno Sugaku no Oyo* (Application of Mathematics to Economics). Tokyo: Iwanami Shoten.

Weintraub, E. R. (1983) The existence of a competitive equilibrium: 1930–1954. *Journal of Economic Literature*, 21: 1–39.

Weintraub, E. R. (1985) *General Equilibrium Analysis: Studies in Appraisal*. New York: Cambridge University Press.

Weintraub, E. R. (1987a) Abraham Wald. In Eatwell *et al.* (eds) (1987), vol. 4, p. 849.

Weintraub, E. R. (1987b) Stability theory via Liapunov's method: a note on the contribution of Takuma Yasui. *History of Political Economy*, 19: 615–20.

Weintraub, E. R. (1991a) *Stabilizing Dynamics: Constructing Economic Knowledge*. New York: Cambridge University Press. Trans. by T. Kojima as *Keizai Dogaku no Keifu*, Tokyo: Bunka Shobo Hakubunsha, 1993.

Weintraub, E. R. (1991b) Allais, Stability, and Liapunov Theory. *History of Political Economy*, 23: 615–20.

Weintraub, E. R. (2002) *How Economics Became a Mathematical Science*. Durham, NC: Duke University Press.

Weintraub, E. R. and T. Gayer (2000) Negotiating at the Boundary: Patinkin v. Phipps. *History of Political Economy*, 32(3): 441–71. In Weintraub (2002) *How Economics Became a Mathematical Science*. Durham, NC: Duke University Press.

Weintraub, E. R. and T. Gayer (2001) Equilibrium proofmaking. *Journal of the History of Economic Thought*. In Weintraub (2002) *How Economics Became a Mathematical Science*. Durham, NC: Duke University Press.

Weintraub, E. R., S. J. Meardon, T. Gayer and H. S. Banzhaf (1998) Archiving the History of Economics. *Journal of Economic Literature*, 36: 1496–1501.

Weintraub, E. R. and P. Mirowski (1994) The pure and applied: Bourbakism comes to mathematical economics. *Science in Context*, 7(2): 245–72.

Whitehead, A. N. and B. Russell (1925–7) *Principia Mathematica*. Cambridge: Cambridge University Press.

Wicksell, K. (1934–5) *Lectures on Political Economy*. Trans from Swedish by E. Classen and edited with an introduction by L. Robbins. London: Routledge & Kegan Paul.

World Bank (1993) *The East Asian Miracle: Economic Growth and Public Policy*. Oxford: Oxford University Press. Trans. by M. Shiratori as *Higashiajia no Kiseki*, Tokyo: Toyo Keizai Shinposha, 1994.

Yagi, Kichiro (1997) Keinzu paper nimiru nihonjin honyakushatachi (Japanese translators found in the Keynes paper). In *Keinzu no Sogoteki Kenkyu*, edited by S. Sechiyama. Kyoto: private.

Yagi, Yoshinosuke (1932). *Beika oyobi Beika Toshei Mondai* (A Study on the Prices of Rice and Their Control). Tokyo: Yuhikaku.

Yago, Kazuhiko (2013) *The Financial History of the Bank for International Settlements*. London: Routledge.

Yajima, Michifumi (1991) Sato Nobuhiro no "jushoshugi" shiso saiko (Nobuhiro Sato on "mercantilism," reconsidered). In *Kindaika no Kokusai Hikaku* (Modernization in International Comparison). Tokyo: Sekai Shoin.

Yajima, M. (2003) *Kinsei Nihon no jushoshugi shiso kenkyu* (A Study of Early Modern Japanese Mercantilism). Tokyo: Ochanomizushobo.

Yamada, Isamu (1934) Kojinteki juyo kansu no sugakuteki riron (On the mathematical theory of individual demand function) [The translation of Hicks and Allen (1934)]. *Shogyo Keizai Ronso*, 12: 255–86.

Yamada, I. (1940) Bukka shisuron niokeru R. Frisch no danryokusei nitsuite (R. Frisch on Elasticity in Price Index Theory). *Annual Report of Japan Statistical Society*, 8: 23–33.

Yamada, I. (1961) *Theory and Application of Interindustry Analysis*. Economic Research, No. 4. Institute of Economic Research, Hitotsubashi University. Tokyo: Kinokuniya.

Yamada, Yuzo (1934) *Chunen Bunpairon no Kenkyu* (A Study on Thünen's Theory of Distribution). Tokyo: Moriyama Shoten.

Yamada, Y. (1951) *Nihon Kokumin Shotoku Suikei Shiryo* (Toward the Estimation of Japanese National Income). Tokyo: Toyo Keizai Shinposha.

Yamada, Y. (1959) *Kokumin Shotoku Ron* (National Income). Tokyo: Iwanami shoten.

Yamaguchi, Seiichi (2000) *Earnest Francisco Fenollosa: Published Writings in English*, three volumes. Tokyo: Edition Synapse.

Yamane, Taro (1962) *Mathematics for Economists; An Elementary Survey*. Englewood Cliffs, NJ: Prentice Hall. Revised edn., 1968.

Yamane, T. (1967) *Statistics: An Introductory Analysis*. New York: Harper & Row.

Yamazaki, Kakujiro (1911) Kinka no ryutsusezaru kinhon'ikoku (On the countries with the gold standard without gold currencies). *Hogaku Kyokai Zasshi*, 29(5): 669–82.

Yamazaki, K. (1912) *Kahei Ginko Mondai Ippan* (A Consideration of the Problems in Money and Banking). Tokyo: Yuhikaku Shobo. Fourth edn., 1920.

Yamazaki, K. (1913a) Kahei no kachi wo choseisentosuru Fisha kyoju no koan ni tsukite (On Professor Fisher's Plan for compensating the Value of Money). *Kokka Gakkai Zasshi*, 27(6): 817–38, June.

Yamazaki, K. (1913b) Fisher kyoju no koan ni taisuru hihyo ni tsukite Takagi Senjiro-shi ni kotau (Answers to Mr. Senjiro Takagi's comments on Professor Fisher's Plan). *Kokka Gakkai Zasshi*, 27(8): 1205–17, August.

Yamazaki, K. (1914a) Kahei no kachi ni kanshite futatabi Takagi kyoju ni kotau (Answers to Professor Takagi on the value of money, II). *Kokka Gakkai Zasshi*, 28(1): 55–76, January.

Yamazaki, K. (1914b) Futatabi kinka no ryutsusezaru kinhon'ikoku ni tsuite (On the countries with the gold standard without gold currencies, reconsidered). *Hogaku Kyokai Zasshi*, 32:4, 553–74.

Yasui, Takuma (1933) Junsui keizaigaku to kakaku riron (Pure economics and the price theory). *Keizaigaku Ronshu*, 3(9). Reprinted in Yasui (1970a) *Yasui Takuma Chosakushu*, vol. 1 (The Selected Papers of Takuma Yasui: I: On Walras). Tokyo: Sobunsha.

Yasui, T. (1934) Kizoku riron to genkai seisanryoku setsu (Imputation theory and marginal productivity). *Keizaigaku Ronshu*, 4(4). Reprinted in Yasui (1970a) *Yasui Takuma Chosakushu*, vol. 1 (The Selected Papers of Takuma Yasui: I: On Walras). Tokyo: Sobunsha.

Yasui, T. (1936) Jikanyoso to shihonrishi (The time element and capital interest: the concept of "natural interest" in Walras. *Keizaigaku Ronshu* (University of Tokyo), 6. Also in Yasui (1970a) *Yasui Takuma Chosakushu*, vol. 1 (The Selected Papers of Takuma Yasui: I: On Walras). Tokyo: Sobunsha.

Yasui, T. (1940a) Kinko bunseki to katei bunseki (Equilibrium analysis and process analysis). *Keizaigaku Ronshu*, 10(1)(2)(3)(7). In Yasui (1970a) *Yasui Takuma Chosakushu*, vol. 1 (The Selected Papers of Takuma Yasui: I: On Walras). Tokyo: Sobunsha.

Yasui, T. (1940b) Juyo no hosoku nitsuite (On the law of demand). *Keizaigaku Ronshu*, 10(6). Reprinted in Yasui (1970b) *Yasui Takuma Chosakushu*, vol. 2 (The Selected Papers of Takuma Yasui: II: The Problems of Economic Statics). Tokyo: Sobunsha.

Yasui, T. (1944) Surutsuki riron niokeru bunrisei no shiso to dojisei no katei (Slutsky on the idea of separability and homogeneity postulate). *Keizai oyobi Keizaigaku no Saishuppatsu* (The Fresh Start of the Economy and Economics), edited by The Newspaper Club of Kobe University of Commerce. Tokyo: Nihon Keizai Hyorohsha, 1944. Reprinted in Yasui (1970b) *Yasui Takuma Chosakushu*, vol. 2 (The Selected Papers of Takuma Yasui: II: The Problems of Economic Statics). Tokyo: Sobunsha.

Yasui, T. (1948a) Shurensei no kojun to dogakuteki antei joken (The convergency postulate and dynamic stability conditions). *Shakaikagaku Hyoron* (1/2), July. In Yasui (1971) *Yasui Takuma Chosakushu*, vol. 3 (The Selected Papers of Takuma Yasui: III: The Problems of Economic Dynamics). Tokyo: Sobunsha.

Yasui, T. (1948b) Keizaiteki kinko no dogakuteki antei joken (Dynamic stability conditions for the economic equilibrium). *Keizai Shicho* (9), September. In Yasui (1971) *Yasui Takuma Chosakushu*, vol. 3 (The Selected Papers of Takuma Yasui: III: The Problems of Economic Dynamics). Tokyo: Sobunsha.

Yasui, T. (1950) Antei no ippan riron (A general theory of stability). *Economic Studies Quarterly*, 1(1): 13–32. In Yasui (1971) *Yasui Takuma Chosakushu*, vol. 3 (The Selected Papers of Takuma Yasui: III: The Problems of Economic Dynamics). Tokyo: Sobunsha.

Yasui, T. (1970a) *Yasui Takuma Chosakushu*, vol. 1 (The Selected Papers of Takuma Yasui: I: On Walras). Tokyo: Sobunsha.

Yasui, T. (1970b) *Yasui Takuma Chosakushu*, vol. 2 (The Selected Papers of Takuma Yasui: II: The Problems of Economic Statics). Tokyo: Sobunsha.

Yasui, T. (1971) *Yasui Takuma Chosakushu*, vol. 3 (The Selected Papers of Takuma Yasui: III: The Problems of Economic Dynamics). Tokyo: Sobunsha.

Yasui, T. (1980) *Kindai Keizaigaku to Watashi* (Modern Economics and My Experiences). Tokyo: Bokutakusha.

Yasui, T. (1988) *Watashi no Ayunda Keizaigaku no Michi* (Recollections: My economic path), Tokyo: Soka Daigaku Keizaigakkai.

Yasukawa, M. (1996) J. M. Keinzu kyo to Fukuda Tokuzo hakushi (Lord J. M. Keynes and Dr. Tokuzo Fukuda). *Mita Hyoron*, 977: 90–3 and photographs.

Ye, T. (1997) An analysis of the historical study of Chinese economic thought in the 1920s and 1930s. In A. Ikeo (ed.) (1997) *Economic Development in Twentieth Century East Asia: The International Context*. London: Routledge, pp. 35–54.

Yoshie, T. (ed.) (1946) [1937] *Shoto Jobibun Hoteisiki* (An Introduction to Ordinary Differential Equations), seventh edn. Tokyo: Shoka Bo.

Yoshikawa, H. (1995) *Keinzu* (Keynes). Tokyo: Chikuma Shobo.

Young, Warren (2008) Negishi's contributions to the development of economic analysis: Research programs and outcomes. *International Journal of Economic Theory*, 4: 151–65.

Yuasa, M. (1980) *Nihon no Kagaku Gijutsu Hyakunenshi* (A Hundred-year History of Science and Technology in Japan), vol. 1. Tokyo: Chuo Koronsha.

Zeuthen, F. (1932) Das Prinzip der Knappheit, technische Kombination, und ökonomishe Qualität (The principle of supply shortage, technical combination, and economic quality). *Zeitschrift für Nationalökonomie*, 4: 1–24.

Zotoff, A. W. (1923) Notes on the mathematical theory of production. *Economic Journal*, 33: 115–21.

Index

Page numbers in *italics* denote tables, those in **bold** denote figures.